Finding Myth and History in the Bible

Finding Myth and History in the Bible

Scholarship, Scholars and Errors

Essays in Honor of Giovanni Garbini

Edited by

Łukasz Niesiołowski-Spanò, Chiara Peri and Jim West

Equinox Publishing Ltd

SHEFFIELD UK   BRISTOL CT

Published by

Equinox Publishing Ltd
Office 415, The Workstation, 15 Paternoster Row, Sheffield, South Yorkshire S1 2BX, UK
SD, 70 Enterprise Drive, Bristol, CT 06010, USA

www.equinoxpub.com

First published 2016

© Łukasz Niesiołowski-Spanò, Chiara Peri, Jim West and contributors 2016
Photo of Giovanni Garbini © Chiara Peri

All rights reserved. No part of this publication may be reproduced or transmitted in any form or by any means, electronic or mechanical, including photocopying, recording or any information storage or retrieval system, without prior permission in writing from the publishers.

British Library Cataloguing-in-Publication Data
A catalogue record for this book is available from the British Library.

    ISBN   978-1-78179-126-4 (hardback)
                978-1-78179-127-1 (paperback)

Library of Congress Cataloging-in-Publication Data
Finding myth and history in the Bible : scholarship, scholars and errors / edited by Łukasz Niesiołowski-Spanò, Chiara Peri and Jim West.
     pages cm
  Includes bibliographical references and index.
    ISBN 978-1-78179-126-4 (hb) -- ISBN 978-1-78179-127-1 (pb) 1. Bible. Old Testament--History of Biblical events. 2. Bible. Old Testament--Historiography. 3 Bible. Old Testament--Criticism, interpretation. etc. 4. Myth in the Old Testament
I. Niesiołowski-Spanò, Lukasz, editor. II. Peri, Chiara, editor. III. West, Jim, 1960– editor .
  BS635.3. 56 2015
  221.6'7--dc23
                         2014044377

Typeset by Forthcoming Publications Ltd (www.forthpub.com)
Printed and bound by Lightning Source

Professor Giovanni Garbini

Contents

Abbreviations	ix
Editorial Preface	xi

GIOVANNI GARBINI AND MINIMALISM
Thomas L. Thompson   1

GIOVANNI GARBINI AND THE POETRY OF LEAH GOLDBERG
Francesco Bianchi   5

"TO EACH HIS OWN JOB": ON JOB 42:1–6
Thomas M. Bolin   18

THE SILOAM TUNNEL REVISITED
Philip R. Davies   30

HOSEA 2:2 AND THE DATING OF THE BOOK OF HOSEA
Giovanni Deiana   51

BEYOND GARBINI'S ANTI-MOSAIC PENTATEUCH:
NEHUSHTAN AS LITERARY TIE BETWEEN THE TORAH
AND THE HISTORICAL BOOKS
Philippe Guillaume   61

"WHEN DREAMS COME TRUE":
JERUSALEM/HIEROSOLYMA AND JEWISH NATIONALISM
IN THE HELLENISTIC AND ROMAN PERIODS
Ingrid Hjelm   72

THE SAME OLD STORY
Niels Peter Lemche   85

TOPONYMY RIDDLES
Mario Liverani   96

DIVIDING THE IMAGE OF GOD:
THE CREATION OF MAN AND WOMAN IN GENESIS
   Caterina Moro   103

FAREWELL TO THE "BLIND AND LAME" (2 SAMUEL 5:6–10)
   Łukasz Niesiołowski-Spanò   116

FROM MOSES TO THE ESSENES
   Étienne Nodet, O.P.   123

A VIEW FROM THE WEST:
THE RELATIONSHIP BETWEEN PHOENICIA AND
"COLONIAL" WORLD IN THE PERSIAN PERIOD
   Ida Oggiano   147

A COUPLE OF STONE DISKS OR SIMPLY A PAIR OF DISKS?
ABOUT THE HEBREW WORD *OBNAYIM*
(EXODUS 1:16; JEREMIAH 18:3)
   Fabrizio A. Pennacchietti   181

JONAH AND THE TRIFFID:
A SUGGESTION FOR THE *QIQAYON*
   Chiara Peri   188

ON FINDING MYTH AND HISTORY IN THE BIBLE:
EPISTEMOLOGICAL AND METHODOLOGICAL OBSERVATIONS
   Emanuel Pfoh   196

"HISTORICAL" ISRAEL AND "BIBLICAL" ISRAEL,
OR ETHNICITY AS A SYMBOL
   Gian Luigi Prato   209

ETHNICITY AND THE BIBLE: MULTIPLE JUDAISMS
   Thomas L. Thompson   223

CORRESPONDENCE
   Jim West   233

Index of References   244
Index of Authors   251

ABBREVIATIONS

AAT	Ägypten und Altes Testament
AB	Anchor Bible
ABD	*Anchor Bible Dictionary*. Edited by D. N. Freedman. 6 vols. New York, 1992
ABRL	Anchor Bible Reference Library
AfO	*Archiv für Orientforschung*
ANET	*Ancient Near Eastern Texts Relating to the Old Testament*. Edited by J. B. Pritchard. Princeton, 3rd edn, 1969
ATANT	Abhandlungen zur Theologie des Alten und Neuen Testaments
BAR	*Biblical Archaeology Review*
BASOR	*Bulletin of the American Schools of Oriental Research*
BDB	Francis Brown, S. R. Driver and Charles A. Briggs (eds.), *A Hebrew and English Lexicon of the Old Testament*. Oxford: Clarendon Press, 1907
BETL	Bibliotheca ephemeridum theologicarum lovaniensium
BHS	*Biblia Hebraica Stuttgartensia*. Edited by K. Elliger and W. Rudolph. Stuttgart, 1983
BHT	Beiträge zur historischen Theologie
BN	*Biblische Notizen*
BZAW	Beihefte zur Zeitschrift für die alttestamentliche Wissenschaft
CAD	Ignace I. Gelb et al. (eds.), *The Assyrian Dictionary of the Oriental Institute of the University of Chicago*. Chicago: Oriental Institute, 1964
CBQ	*Catholic Biblical Quarterly*
CBOT	Coniectanea biblica. Old Testament series
CIS	Copenhagen International Series
CRB	*Cahiers de la Revue biblique*
CSCO	*Corpus scriptorum christianorum orientalium*. Edited by I. B. Chabot et al. Paris, 1903–
CWSSS	N. Avigad, *Corpus of West Semitic Stamp Seals*. Revised and completed by B. Sass. Jerusalem: The Hebrew University, 1997
DBAT	*Dielheimer Blätter zum Alten Testament und seiner Rezeption in der Alten Kirche*
DBS	*Dictionnaire de la Bible: Supplément*. Edited by L. Pirot and A. Robert. Paris, 1928–
DCH	*Dictionary of Classical Hebrew*. Edited by D. J. A. Clines. 9 vols. Sheffield, 1993–2014
DDD	K. van der Toorn, B. Becking and P. W. van der Horst (eds.), *Dictionary of Deities and Demons in the Bible*. Grand Rapids, MI: Eerdmans; Leiden: E.J. Brill, 2nd extensively rev. edn, 1990
DJD	Discoveries in the Judaean Desert
DWhG	Schriften der Deutschen Wasserhistorischen Gesellschaft

EB	M. D. Cassuto et al. (eds.), *Encyclopaedia Biblica*. Jerusalem: The Bialik Institute, 1950–88
ErIsr	*Eretz Israel*
HALOT	Ludwig Koehler and Walter Baumgartner (eds.), *The Hebrew and Aramaic Lexicon of the Old Testament*. Translated by M. E. J. Richardson. Rev. W. Baumgartner and J. J. Stamm. Leiden: E. J. Brill, 1994–99
HLS	*Holy Land Studies*
HSM	Harvard Semitic Monographs
HTR	*Harvard Theological Review*
HUCA	*Hebrew Union College Annual*
JAOS	*Journal of the American Oriental Society*
JBL	*Journal of Biblical Literature*
JBTh	Jahrbuch für Biblische Theologie
JHS	*Journal of Hellenic Studies*
JJS	*Journal of Jewish Studies*
JNSL	*Journal of Northwest Semitic Languages*
JQR	*Jewish Quarterly Review*
JSJ	*Journal for the Study of Judaism in the Persian, Hellenistic, and Roman Periods*
JSOT	*Journal for the Study of the Old Testament*
JSOTSup	Journal for the Study of the Old Testament: Supplement Series
JTS	*Journal of Theological Studies*
LAI	Library of Ancient Israel
LCL	Loeb Classical Library
LHBOTS	The Library of Hebrew Bible/Old Testament Studies
LXX	Septuagint
MT	Masoretic Text
NTOA	Novum Testamentum et Orbis Antiquus
OBO	Orbis biblicus et orientalis
RB	*Revue biblique*
REJ	*Revue des études juives*
RLA	Erich Ebeling and Bruno Meissner (eds.), *Reallexikon der Assyriologie und Vorderasiatischen Archäologie*. Berlin: de Gruyter, 1928–2012
RS	Ras Shamra (Ugarit)
RQ	*Revue de Qumran*
SBLDS	Society of Biblical Literature Dissertation Series
SBS	Stuttgarter Bibelstudien
SHANE	Studies in the History of the Ancient Near East
SJOT	*Scandinavian Journal of the Old Testament*
STDJ	Studies on the Texts of the Desert of Judah
TAVO	Tübinger Atlas des Vorderen Orients
TDOT	G. J. Botterweck, H. J. Fabry and H. Ringgren (eds.), *Theological Dictionary of the Old Testament*. Grand Rapids, MI: Eerdmans, 1974–2006
Vg	Vulgate
VT	*Vetus Testamentum*
VTSup	Supplements to Vetus Testamentum
ZAW	*Zeitschrift für die alttestamentliche Wissenschaft*
ZDMG	*Zeitschrift der deutschen morgenländischen Gesellschaft*

Editorial Preface

Giovanni Garbini has been one of the most influential Semitists and historians of the ancient Near East for decades. His works have proved provocative, productive, and profound. His gift for noticing the remarkable and his ability to remark sagaciously on ancient texts have propelled him to the pinnacle of academic respectability.

Unfortunately, in spite of the fact that he has proven so influential, many of his works remain untranslated. Most of his contributions (on Semitic languages, history and religion of the Phoenicians and the biblical studies) were published in Italian, and – therefore – are not available to wider audience unfamiliar with this language. This is, we believe, a shame. Ideally, all of his works will one day find their way into the wider (English-dominated) world of biblical and historical studies. Until then, it was our hope and is our hope to bring to the broader academic community some of the fruits of his labors as manifested in the works of his students, colleagues, and friends.

Accordingly, we offer this *Festschrift* to Giovanni Garbini in celebration of his contributions to our scholarship and to the scholarship of many other scholars. The essays on the following pages all share in common marks of the influence of Garbini's work.

Thomas Thompson begins the collection by offering his own take on the development of the study of Israel's history: a field to which Garbini has contributed massively and influentially. Francesco Bianchi's engaging piece, "Giovanni Garbini and the Poetry of Leah Goldberg," offers readers a window on the importance of extra-historical disciplines for historical and biblical work. Thomas Bolin's "'To Each His Own Job': On Job 42:1–6" gives a fresh reading of a complex text and provides a solution to an old problem. Philip Davies' "The Siloam Tunnel Revisited" opens up new questions on an old archaeological debate. Giovanni Deiana provides, in his "Hosea 2:2 and the Dating of the Book of Hosea," fresh and engaging insights into the question of the compositional history of Hosea. Philippe Guillaume's "Beyond Garbini's Anti-Mosaic Pentateuch: Nehushtan as Literary Tie Between the Torah and the Historical Books" is an interesting look into the Greek underpinning of a key biblical text.

Ingrid Hjelm does contemporary scholarship a huge service by showing the interconnectivity between ancient texts and modern ideology in her "'When Dreams Come True': Jerusalem/Hierosolyma and Jewish Nationalism in the Hellenistic and Roman Periods." Niels Peter Lemche, as only he can, shows how slow scholarship has been to catch up to the cutting edge exemplified in Garbini's work and the work of the so-called "Copenhagen School" in a delightful essay titled "The Same Old Story." Mario Liverani's brief "Toponymy Riddles" guides readers into a new appreciation of the ways in which the names of places carry political and ideological freight. Caterina Moro's "Dividing the Image of God: The Creation of Man and Woman in Genesis" is an exceptional piece of exegesis, opening new windows of understanding on the Creation Narrative.

Other essays include Łukasz Niesiołowski-Spanò's exegetical "Farewell to the 'Blind and Lame' (2 Samuel 5:6–10)," which is a fine example of linguistic study in the service of exegesis. Étienne Nodet's "From Moses to the Essenes" serves to show the importance of extra-biblical historical texts for a proper understanding of Israel's history.

Readers will also find Ida Oggiano's "A View from the West: The Relationship Between Phoenicia and 'Colonial' World in the Persian Period," Fabrizio Pennacchietti's "A Couple of Stone Disks or Simply a Pair of Disks? About the Hebrew Word *obnayim* (Exodus 1:16; Jeremiah 18:3)," and Chiara Peri's "Jonah and the Triffid: A Suggestion for the *Qiqayon*" to be immensely instructive.

Emanuel Pfoh's "On Finding Myth and History in the Bible," Gian Luigi Prato's "'Historical' Israel and 'Biblical' Israel, or Ethnicity as a Symbol," and Thomas L. Thompson's "Ethnicity and the Bible: Multiple Judaisms" round the collection off and show cleverly and convincingly how the Bible as an ideological/theological product has been utilized as political tool.

The last entry, by Jim West, is titled "Correspondence" and sheds a more personal light on Professor Garbini by featuring letters by him in response to various and sundry questions posed.

Our hope is that this collection of essays will spur interest in the work of the man who has influenced us all so energetically. If that goal is achieved, our purpose will have been fulfilled.

The Editors

GIOVANNI GARBINI AND MINIMALISM

Thomas L. Thompson

For international Old Testament studies, it was Giovanni Garbini, more than anyone else, who brought a "hermeneutics of suspicion" into everyday use as an analytical tool. This, for him, habitual mode of looking at a text brought him not only to question the historicity of Ezra 7–10 and Neh 8 and 12, but to interpret these texts as *origin stories* for the figure of Ezra as the Rabbinate's founding father. In the analysis of this development by Ingrid Hjelm, Garbini is understood not to deny the *existence* of Ezra so much as to reject the *historicity* of the book of Ezra as well as the recognition of any autonomous existence of such a person, until we come to sources that are later than Josephus; for Josephus is merely satisfied with a rational paraphrase of 1 Esdras![1] Garbini's minimalism here is centred on an analysis of precisely what is implied by the texts he reads. Garbini concluded that Ezra was a synonymous portrayal of the figure of Alcimus and his reform of around 159 BCE, as narrated in 1 Maccabees – a reform which he saw as fundamental to the establishment of the Qumran community as a Zadokite alternative to the temple. With an intertextual approach to commonly reiterated themes implied in texts by authors from different contexts, Garbini analyses their interrelationship. It is, indeed, the historicity of 1 Maccabees, rather than the narratives in the books of Ezra or Nehemiah, which should be of interest to the historian. It is on such a question regarding 1 Maccabees that Garbini's argument stands or falls. It is – again in Hjelm's analysis – not the response of our text's reader which is critical in decoding the sociological context of our reiterated narrative, but the methods used by the author to use the past created by the story "to hide both whatever history did not fit his perspective," as well as the message he did wish his story to bare.[2]

While one might well argue that Garbini's very original studies, *I Fenici* and *I Filistei*,[3] are his most important singular contributions to Palestine's history, filling such huge gaps in our knowledge of Palestine as they do. One might also say that his many, timely and invaluable critical observations on Iron Age inscriptions have created the solid foundation to his reputation in Semitic studies,[4] it is hardly to be doubted that it was rather the timely publication of a collection of his essays in 1986 and its translation to English in 1988 which enabled us to anchor the radical transformation and rapid deconstruction of biblical, historical and archaeological scholarship of the 1970s and 1980s, which formed his point of departure and clearly marked his abiding influence on so many different scholars, the world over.[5] Whether or not one chooses to apply to him the highly tendentious description, "minimalist," Garbini, much like John Van Seters, Axel Knauf and Nadav Na'aman (in regard to his "retrospective history"), has consistently understood the biblical tradition as a form of creative historiography, which expressed the ideologies, perspectives and distortions of its authors and reflected the historical and political worlds and conflicts of its origins and transmission. That is, he sees biblical narrative as a refraction of a specific – and potentially identifiable – real world.[6] Also like Van Seters, Knauf and Na'aman, Garbini has been a central contributor to that wave of scholarship, which has transformed both critical biblical analysis and the development of historical methodologies for writing Palestine's history.

Although in the early 1990s I strongly resisted his assertion of such "realism" and, not least, his understanding of biblical narrative as historiography,[7] which was so closely related to the ideological function Garbini attributed to biblical literature, his understanding did effectively carry the discussion of origins well beyond the arguments of Miller and Soggin.[8] Garbini's reappraisal of Israel's earliest history stands systemically apart from any theologically motivated defence of a biblically driven historiography. Any critical history of ancient Palestine, Israel and Judah included, needed to be independent of biblical perspectives. Garbini is also refreshingly consistent, already in the early 1980s, whenever he deals with biblical origin stories: there was no "patriarchal period," no conquest and no "period of the Judges." Indeed, no biblical tradition can be understood as historically reliable without confirmation from extra-biblical sources. He is also entirely consistent in focusing on the extreme fragility of any modern historiography of Palestine – even when addressing the construction of the Iron II patronage states of Israel and Judah, as can be seen in his treatments of such issues as the chronology for the invasion of Sheshonq, claimed distinctions between Hebrew and Phoenician or a so-called Josianic reform. He understands the whole of biblical history – including the "post-exilic" period, as an artificial construct: rooted in ideologically based fictions of much later periods. Indeed, for him, one cannot understand the exile as translatable within the construct of an historical period. The "exile" is rather an ideological concept: standing, not at the conclusion of a narrative, but at its beginning.[9] Critical history must begin apart from and independently of the perspective of the biblical narrative – even down to and including the Hellenistic period. Garbini's deconstructive work is both provocative and exciting.

I agree with Garbini that the biblical text created a past and that it is, indeed, this figment that is the primary referent from which it develops its ethos.[10] I emphatically agree with Garbini's assertion that the basis of our critical evaluation lies wholly apart from the biblical traditions and rather in the epigraphical, archaeological and regional history of Palestine. Therein lay the different histories of Israel we must write, culminating rather than beginning in the biblical tradition. I also agree with Garbini in understanding that perceptions of a coherent biblical tradition, arising out of the intellectual milieu of the late Persian and early Hellenistic periods, cause great difficulty in affirming the historicity of the Israel of tradition in any way at all; for we are here dealing with an entity which is an entirely new creation. With Garbini, we need to assert that only very few biblical narratives involve historiography at their primary level and that not a single historiographic assertion of consequence can be confirmed.[11] With Garbini, we need to assert that the critical judgments involved in biblical literature relate more to the genres of religious interpretation, ideology and propaganda than they do to historiography. This is clearly indicated by the idealistic and utopian orientation of every chronological trajectory in our texts. The prophetic books created their utopian future through their creation of a failed past as their paradigm. It was not a failed past which gave hope to the future. With Garbini, our Israel has not been any historical Israel at all. To speak of an historical Jezebel is as irrelevant as speaking so of Lady Macbeth! Ideologically motivated traditions and the drama of fiction dominate the whole of what we understand as biblical Israel.

It is a distinct privilege to offer this brief preface to a volume honouring the work of Professor Garbini. Certainly if ever there were a scholar who nearly single-handedly shifted the historical paradigm, it is he.

Notes

1. Ingrid Hjelm, *The Samaritans and Early Judaism: A Literary Analysis* (Sheffield: Sheffield Academic Press, 2000), pp. 273–76.
2. Hjelm, *The Samaritans and Early Judaism*, p. 274; Giovanni Garbini, *History and Ideology in Ancient Israel* (London: SCM Press, 1988), pp. 165–69.
3. Giovanni Garbini, *I Fenici: Storie e Religioni* (Naples: Istituto Universitario Orientale, 1980), idem, *I Filistei: Gli Antagonisti di Israele* (Milan: Rusconi, 1997).
4. G. Garbini, "Sull'afbetario di Isbet Sartah," *Oriens Antiquus* 17 (1978), pp. 287–95; idem, "L'iscrizione aramaica di Tel Dan," *Atti della Academia nazionale dei Lincei, Scienze morali, storiche e filologiche rendiconti* 9.5.3 (1994), pp. 461–71.
5. Garbini, *History and Ideology in Ancient Israel*.
6. Thomas L. Thompson, *The Early History of the Israelite People: From the Written and Archaeological Sources* (Leiden: Brill, 1992), p. 167.
7. T. L. Thompson, "Historiography: Israelite," in *ABD*, s.v.
8. J. M. Miller and J. H. Hayes, *A History of Ancient Israel and Judah* (Philadelphia: Westminster, 1986); J. A. Soggin, *Le Origini d'Israele Problema per lo Storiografico? Le Origini de Israele* (Rome: Accademia nazionale dei lincei, 1987).
9. See T. L. Thompson, "Reiterative Narratives of Exile and Return: Virtual Memories of Abraham in the Persian and Hellenistic Periods," in P. R. Davies and D. Edelman (eds.), *The Historian and the Bible: Essays in Honour of Lester L. Grabbe* (London: T&T Clark International, 2010), pp. 46–54; idem, "Memories of Return and the Historicity of the 'Post-Exilic' Period," in P. Carstens and N. P. Lemche (eds.), *The Receptions and Remembrance of Abraham* (Piscataway, NJ: Gorgias, 2011), pp. 119–46; idem, "Memories of Esau and Narrative Reiteration," *SJOT* 25/2 (2011), pp. 174–200; idem, "The Faithful Remnant and Religious Identity: The Literary Trope of Return – A Reply to Firas Sawah," in E. Pfoh and K. W. Whitelam (eds.), *The Politics of Israel's Past: The Bible, Archaeology and Nation-Building* (Sheffield: Sheffield Phoenix, 2013), pp. 77–88.
10. Garbini, *History and Ideology in Ancient Israel*, pp. 52–65; cf. Thompson, *The Early History of the Israelite People*, pp. 124–26.
11. Thompson, *The Early History of the Israelite People*, pp. 353–54.

GIOVANNI GARBINI AND THE POETRY OF LEAH GOLDBERG

Francesco Bianchi

> *To G. Garbini, who taught me to search also where there was apparently nothing to find.*

In over six decades of fruitful and challenging scholarship, Giovanni Garbini has explored almost every corner of the Near East, as the bibliography personally collected by him with the help of Chiara Peri[1] has aptly shown. In such a long and prolific career, one that mirrors so closely that of the *Altmeister* of the nineteenth century, there has also been room, though ephemeral, for the Modern Hebrew literature. Just 50 years ago, at the request of S. Moscati,[2] Garbini[3] penned a short note on the poetry of Leah Goldberg and especially on the poem "On the Hills of Jerusalem." These few pages hold many insightful remarks, yet they have gone largely unnoticed. I want to use them in order to present here a fresh analysis of Leah Goldberg's poetry and her links with the Song of Songs, of which Garbini has been a ground-breaking interpreter.

When Garbini's short note saw the light of day, L. Goldberg (b. Königsberg, May 29, 1910–d. Jerusalem, January 10, 1970) already had behind her a remarkable career:[4] since her arrival in the Mandatory Palestine in 1935 from Lithuania, she had worked tirelessly[5] as poet,[6] as translator of many European literary masterpieces into Hebrew[7] and eventually as Lecturer of Comparative Literature at the Hebrew University of Jerusalem.[8] As far as poetry is concerned, the critics pointed out that her poems shifted from the longing for an unaccomplished love and for the Lithuanian landscape[9] to a deeper reflection on life, death, art and to an integration of Israel's nature and landscape into her poetic soul. This shift is clearer especially in the four short poems which comprise the cycle "On the Hills of Jerusalem," which were written in a simple and lucid Hebrew[10] reminiscent of the Hebrew used in the biblical period and the Middle Ages[11] and following the example of modernistic poetry. These poems were published for the first time in the collection *Al ha-Periḥah* (*Of Blossoming*, 1948), a work which became increasingly well known in the 1950s. The poems helped to generate a lively debate on the essence of Goldberg's poetry: was it "intellectualistic poetry," as some critics assumed, or was it rather a "learned poetry" that expresses strong feelings and emotions?

To answer these questions, let us analyze the four poems themselves. The first opens with a impressive, almost autobiographical, description of the poet's life:[12]

> I lie like a stone on the hill
> Indifferent and silent
> In the withered sun-seared grass.
> Pale skies touch rock
> Where does the yellow-winged butterfly come from?
> A stone among stones, I do not know
> the ancientness of my life
> or who will yet come
> and with a kick

Garbini[13] noted in these words a feeling of bereavement, dismay and loneliness before nature. The poet sketches – perhaps during one of her lonely trips around Jerusalem – a dry and hostile nature, one that contrasts markedly with the green woods and majestic rivers left behind in Lithuania. Such a kind of *straniamento* led the poet to compare herself to one of the many stones that make up this landscape. As we shall see, the image of the stone – well known in biblical imagery[14] – appears time and again in Goldberg's poetry. For instance, the late poem "The Stone which the Builders Refused" (the title is drawn from Ps 118:22), ends with the following lines: "The time is come to scatter stones, though I have not found any treasure." The first part surely refers to Eccl 3:5, where Qohelet pairs the time of scattering stones with the time of gathering them. Scholars have fiercely debated the interpretation of these words:[15] do they describe normal human activities or do they have an erotic undertone, as suggested by the late Jewish interpreters who saw the scattering of stones as a fairly unambiguous reference to sexual intercourse? The absence of any treasure could refer to a lack of satisfaction or to the lack of children,[16] turning upside down the great generative power of the stone in Lithuanian and Baltic folklore.[17] Henceforth, the stone underlines the idea of motionlessness, the lack of consciousness and, ultimately, death (e.g. 1 Sam 25:37 describes Nabal's death as if he became like a stone). Some years later, in the collection

Last Words (1959), "The Quarry" will describe the poet's feelings accordingly: "Stubborn, deaf, mute/this stone in its refusal. Still, still, still, the secret of its heart."[18] Only the quarrying hand of the lover will communicate to the wounded and broken stone a measure of happiness and love. All these images could perfectly be rooted in the Western representation of the Near East as a static society, where the poet came to share its antiquity[19] and whence, as her ancestors, she could be driven out just because of a "whim." The verb נדה, "to banish" – used as the future and with a first person plural suffix – confirms the menace of an impending exile. In such a dismal picture, the sudden presence of a butterfly[20] introduces a sign of grace and beauty. Five lines, all introduced by the conjunction אולי, "perhaps," follow that description. They strengthen time and again the idea of immobility and eternity through a strange oxymoron that speaks about "a beauty frozen forever." One can wonder about an image that evokes the Lithuanian winter and the following ones about a dream split between death and love.

The final stanza comes back to the image of the stone along with thorns and thistles. These shrubs intimately belong to the biblical landscape; according to Gen 3:16, because of Adam's sin, "the land will bring forth thorns and thistles" and will make all human work harder. In another poem Goldberg will compare her two homelands, the one having snow, the other thorns. Back to our poem, we note that it simply assumes a human presence (note the images of a road sliding towards a near city), yet without any sign of human activity. At this juncture falls the three last verses:

> Soon the wind which blesses all things
> Will come to caress the pine crests
> And the dumb stones.

The wind seems to function as a sign of life – as a lot of biblical passages show – and it awakens a motionless world, just as in the theophany of Elijah. It is worth noticing how the wind brushes the pine's crest and the dumb stones. As for the pines, it is notable that these trees are another favourite subject of Goldberg's poetry. For instance, in the cycle "Trees," Goldberg addresses the pine in the following way: "Like you I was transplanted twice, like you, pine trees, I grew with roots in two different landscapes." As Chelly Abraham-Eitan[21] has pointed out, tree imagery explains quite well that idea of "dual-rootedness," also called "the heartache of two homelands" or "the sorrow of severed roots" which embrace the ego, the landscape, the homeland, and the language and culture. Goldberg's poem makes clear to the reader that the pine is simply a metaphor for the dual-rootedness of the speaker. By means of that metaphor, which has otherwise become a symbol for Jewish poets coming from the Arab world, L. Goldberg describes her longing for the snowy landscapes of Europe and for the culture of her childhood. And yet, the stones continue to be mute and dumb. The last words reveal the awakening of the poetic "I" – as Garbini noted[22] – and the powerful burst of passion for life of the second poem. At first an infinite stream of things except love stand before the poet: that image clearly alludes to Gen 2:10, where God brought all the beasts before the man in order for him to name them. Whereas we see the powerful poetic word at work, an old language becoming new, the poet reports the request of the landscape:

> The landscape with its old man's understanding
> Begging to live
> One more year, one more year.
> One generation, two, three generations,
> one more eternity.

In my opinion, the landscape's request presupposes Job 12:12, where understanding and old age are paired. But what is amazing is the following triplet of words: year, generation (one, two, three) and eternity. They encompass the time of men and the time of the world, as the word "eternity" assumes.[23] However, begging for more life will bring only more thorns. The last action is expressed though the verb שתק which describes in Jonah 1:11–12 and Ps 107:30 the calming of a stormy sea. The poet does not say whether these memories belong to the history of this landscape, with whom her poems betray a conflicting relationship,[24] or from her past life. The last stanza ends with the word תשקה: this word too stands in Gen 3:16, where it expresses the woman's longing for the man, and in Song 7:11, where it has the same sense. The adjective רקח underlines again the vanity of the effort of being. All told, the second poem stops in mid-air: caught between life and death, the longing cannot be true.

After having described these two realities, the third poem finally introduces the image of the bird. Birds too are a favourite image in Goldberg's poetry: they are suspended between earth and sky just as the poet is suspended between her two homelands. In the poet's words, "birds make the sky sprout wings and breath," and during their wanderings westward they ask for a safe return home, just because they like singing there. Their dangerous flight mirrors the painful labours of love that the poet lives and their wings trace the same despairing circle as Jerusalem's inhabitants. Nevertheless, the birds descend upon the poet described as a tree in the desert and fill her with songs of joy. The third poem presents birds as a symbol of lightness, as compared to a static, heavy landscape. The first stanza runs as follows:

> How could a blythe bird
> Lose itself in these hills?
> With a love song in her throat,
> her little heart throbbing with gladness,
> the promise of young ones soon in the next
> her wings hymning love.
> But suddenly,
> from the blue height
> unrolls before her
> a wasteland stoned to death.

Garbini[25] pointed out that the bird as a symbol of a poet's feeling is widespread throughout world literature and was able to list Petrarch, Keats and Shelley among the poets who used it, not to mention the Jewish poets from Medieval Spain. Garbini stressed especially the similarity to P. B. Shelley's "To a Skylark," since, in his opinion, the Hebrew words אלצה ספור were akin to the "blythe spirit" as well as the general description of its love pouring from the heart and of a flight higher than the sky. As far as Shelley's poem is concerned, Shelley grasps the bird's flight only thanks to its lovely song. It fills the earth and sky in a way that exceeds the earthly reality, because its power comes from Heaven and is free from all that gives pain and fear. Accordingly, Shelley made of the skylark a symbol of pure, unalloyed and unrestricted happiness, although it knew about death – "things more true and deep" than human beings.

As this short summary shows, L. Goldberg's joyful bird surely shares with the Shelleian one some features. Nevertheless, I believe that the image of the bird could open an unsought path of research. It is universally known that at the beginning of Modern Hebrew literature stands H. N. Bialik's *El-Hassipor*.[26] In this poem, whose originality did not lie in the biblical imagery but in the rhythm and in the claim of speaking for all Jewish people, Bialik asks the beautiful bird to tell him, "about the land in which my fathers found life and death!" He also makes inquiries on a series of biblical places paired with their botanic features and he compares them to his tearful longing for Zion. Bialik's poem voiced the hopes and the wishes of the Hibbat Zion movement, which, from the 1880s onwards, advocated the revival of Jewish life and created agricultural settlements in Palestine. His "I," just like a prophet, speaks already on behalf of all the Jewish nation.[27]

In comparison to this vision, L. Goldberg's poem depicts a quite different reality, one made of stones and destruction. Is it so blatant to see in it a conscious subversion of Bialik's poem? Furthermore, Bialik asks whether God had mercy on Zion, "though she is yet left with her graves?," whereas L. Goldberg speaks only of individual graves of love. Here too there is at work a poetics centred upon self rather than on a collective perspective, far from Rachel Bluwstein's enthusiasm for the Zionistic return to the agriculture and land of the fathers. The bird eventually stands in strong opposition to the landscape, as its flight reverses the biblical image of Ps 84:4, where it is said: "Also the bird finds its house." Here, on the contrary, the *sippor* does not find a home. Its singing, lovingly and joyfully preparing its nest, could be a symbol of the poet's *alyiah*. It was full with expectations nurtured since her childhood study of Hebrew as well as her attendance of Zionist meetings, but a waste and desolate land was awaiting her. An impressive series of words stresses the peculiarities of the land, as a quick examination of the vocabulary shows. First, the land is called שממה. This word mainly describes, in the prophetical books of the Hebrew Bible, the desolation caused by a foreign invasion; no less amazing is the astounding construct state רגם. אבנים רגומת usually means the stoning to death of criminals in the fields outside the city. The land has seemingly suffered such a penalty, without the executor being exactly known. Could he be God? L. Goldberg did not have a religious education and was close to holding an atheistic vision, although some poems are dressed as prayers.[28] Strange to say, the same desolation and the same violence also marks the Lithuanian landscape.[29] Before that desolation, the poet asks to save the innocence of the blythe bird, so that it does not see "the corpses of every love" and "the grave of every joy."[30] That oxymoron seems to communicate that happiness and love border death, the major source of impurity in Judaism. After that, the poem comes to its end:

> In her blue
> Heights
> Singing
> She is suspended
> And she does not grasp
> That death
> In front of her.

That last image points to two different sources: the first – as Garbini[31] already noted – is surely an echo from Shelley's work; yet Leah Goldberg introduces another destructive image by two rare biblical words: אחבים could mean "caresses" in Prov 5:10,[32] whereas גלמוד ranges from Biblical Hebrew "sterile, barren," to Mishnaic Hebrew "solitary" and lastly to Aramaic "rock or stony." Worth noticing is Job 3:7, where Job asks the night in which he was born to be barren and grievous. The last adjective seems to portray the poet as one of the famous Chagall's characters hanging between earth and sky; the love song puts the bird both outside of human reach and beyond the grasp of death. The opposition between the frail bird and the hostile world sets the tone for the last poem. This starts with the particle איכה, which directly evokes the distressing *overture* of the biblical book of Lamentations:

> How can one lone bird
> carry the entire sky
> on fragile
> wings
> above the desolation?
> The sky is vast and blue
> resting on her wings
> upheld by the power of her song.

The image of a lonely bird carrying the sky on her frail wings plays off another biblical image – Exod 19:4, where God carries Israel out of Egypt on eagle's wings towards their new homeland. Whereas the eagle (גשר) betokens strength and force, here a humble bird, a common *sippor*, carries in the sky her song of thanks alone.[33]

The same is true as far as the heart of the poet is concerned. Her love shares the characteristics of the sky – it is vast and blue, but gazes at the desolation and at a heap of ruins. Once again the poet moulds two unusual chains of words: the first joins אי and מפלת, while the image of the depth of despair is more puzzling. תחומות obviously means "abysses," but its association with *yagon* is strange: as תחומות probably alludes in Ps 71:20 to Sheol, could the phrase recall Jacob's statement in Joseph's history about going to Sheol with despair? At this juncture it is useful to observe that in the Song of Sea, the Egyptians fell as stones in the abyss as well as the poet's heart losing strength and becoming silent. And so the end runs:

> My mute, wounded love
> How can one bird alone
> Carry the entire sky?

The fourth and last poem ends with a repetition, the so-called "anaphora" that Goldberg often used as if it were a refrain in a song[34] and which can also be found in Ps 8:1–10. Although that device serves to close a perfect circle and to restate the situation described in the opening verse, worthy of noting is the first sentence: "My mute, wounded love." It seems to create a parallelism between this bird alone and not the reciprocated love that the poet faced in her lifetime. In spite of these disappointments and failures, that love is able to carry all the sky.

At this juncture we can attempt to answer the question set at the beginning concerning the nature of Leah Goldberg's poetry. As we have seen, her poetry is built upon a refined lexical choice, but it does not share the rhetoric of its predecessors and the bombastic force of some of its contemporaries. E. Spicehandler[35] noted that Goldberg was the least ideological of all the poets of the Palestinian period; she disregarded nationalist and Jewish subjects in favour of mainstream consensus of the modern world poetry and chose a conversational style, a symbolic vocabulary confined to the familiar everyday words and to such universal matters as childhood, nature, love, aging and death.[36] As Garbini observed, these images and phrases were connected with her personal readings and moulded into a new poetic context. Accordingly, Goldberg's poetry is surely learned, but not intellectual.[37]

This last statement must be compared now with the polemical attacks that since 1960 some Israeli critics have levelled against L. Goldberg's poetry. To begin with, D. Miron labelled Goldberg's poetry as a sort of "minor poetry." The prominence of the "poetic I," the limited experience, the bare symbolism, and the regular patterns made her unable to draw from and seek inspiration from her personal picture album.[38] Some years later, the same critic[39] ascribed that poetical choice to Goldberg's impossibility, insofar as she was a woman, to write on more "important" intellectual and national themes. Such a choice would have denied the hidden demand of women's poetry to be simple and understandable. The poet Nathan Zach later sharpened that evaluation: in his opinion, Goldberg's poetry does not present any development, since from the beginning to the end it deals with just one topic alone – the pain of love seen from a subjective point of view. Against this narrow horizon, her expression is too brusque, her images too blatant and her ideas too overstated, meaning that nothing is left to the reader's imagination. Furthermore, she lacks associative power as well as a true musical dimension.

Against these evaluations we can observe how the absence of Zionistic topics in Goldberg's poetry was a deliberate choice, born out of her personal disinterest. She focused instead upon the so-called "realms of the wounded soul" experienced by so many of her readers,[40] Goldberg recalled for her readers, as A. Hirschfeld[41] wrote, the severance from childhood memories, the doom of European Jewry[42] and last but not least the animosity that Judaism felt towards Nature. In that sense, her poetry also shows the shaping of the Israeli Culture through the encounter and the clash of different trends.[43] The first was the culture of the *shtetl* – the Jewish village of Eastern Europe in which the works of S. Aleichem or I. B. Singer took root; the other was modern urban Eastern European

Jewish culture, influenced by Russian revolutionary Socialist movements and by several linguistic (Yiddish, German, Russian, Hebrew) or literary influences (symbolism, modernism, etc.). The last one was the hot, arid, sandy space of Eretz Israel, where no rivers and no woods are to be found. At the end of this troublesome process, it was only the sandy and rocky space, which survived both the biblical text which usually summoned the Jewish people to remember their religious history and their archaeological or biblical meaning. This is quite evident in Goldberg's poems: feelings and memories are set against the background of the landscape and there is no room for history or sacrifice for the nation, as in N. Alterman's or H. Goury's poems. The same is true as far as her books for children are concerned. As O. Amichai[44] has pointed out, these well-crafted compositions written in the late 1930s and early '40s always avoided "crude indoctrination through association with holy days" and sought to give the feasts, especially Hanukah, more of a humanistic and universal meaning than a nationalistic one (see the silence on the heroism of Judah Maccabee). By the way, the same appeal to tolerance and to kindness surfaces in her short or long stories for children too, as the famous "A Flat for Rent."[45]

In some way, L. Goldberg adhered to Berdyczewsky's assumption that Hebrew literature had to focus on individual themes in order to become a developed cultural entity. In her opinion, literature needed to express an emotional need and the love of nature and human beings – all of this in spite of war, as she outspokenly wrote in the weekly bulletin of the *Ha-Shomer ha-Tsa'ir* movement, soon after the outbreak of World War II. These observations not only strengthen Garbini's assumption about the intimate and personal tone of Goldberg's poems, but they allow one to dare to make a comparison with the poetics of the Song of Songs such as G. Garbini[46] offered in his ground-breaking analysis. A score of direct or indirect quotations from Song of Songs surface in Goldberg's poems and becomes prevalent in the poetical cycle "Three Days,"[47] which is to be found in the collection *Last Words* (1959). As R. T. Back wrote, "this entire section seems to be in dialogue with Song of Songs – in particular lines 3, 9, 15 which echo Song of Songs 5:2" ("the voice of my beloved knocks saying, Open to me..."). After having described herself as being in the heart of the desert and facing absolute loneliness, L. Goldberg used thrice that phrase "I cried out: 'Answer me!' No one answered. I knocked: 'Open!'. No one opened."[48] The female speaker goes on knocking from gate to gate until the morning comes and eventually the city watchman finds her. The episode is clearly built upon the fifth chapter of the Song of Song and dwells upon the situation of the *paraklausithyron* – that is to say, the lover knocking at the door of the loved one. Interestingly enough, a fragment of the *Palatine Anthology*, a collection of erotic epigrams and poems written in Alexandria, has a *paraklausithyron* whose main character is a lovesick girl, searching for her beloved through the streets of the town.[49] Another interesting affinity between Goldberg's lyric "I" and the free woman of the Song in 5:2–8 is the search for love as something absolute, yet ultimately unattainable[50] and the anguish that this produces in their souls. A. Lieblich's biography has copiously described how the absence of actualized love marked the life and the poetry of Leah Goldberg.[51] The ending of "Three Days" illustrates quite well such an attempt: in the morning of the fourth day, when the memory of the lover is gone, the poet discovers from a window opposite the sea, "in the salty gust of wind – the scent of the sea, nor the taste of my tears."[52] We are left with a statement that tries to remove the pain of a lost love and that, notwithstanding the deeply sentimental nature of Leah Goldberg's poetry pointed out by G. Garbini, still hides longing for the lost world far across the sea.[53]

Notes

1. Cf. *L'opera di Giovanni Garbini. Bibliografia degli scritti 1956–2006* (Brescia: Paideia Editrice, 2007).

2. For an assessment of S. Moscati's life, see F. Bianchi, "Sabatino Moscati," in *Al primo posto le Scritture. Biblisti italiani del Novecento* (Palermo: Salvatore Sciascia, 2014), pp. 208–14.

3. G. Garbini, "Una nota su Leah Goldberg," *Annali dell'Istituto Orientale di Napoli* 12 (1962), pp. 195–98. A year earlier, G. Garbini published a paper on a similar topic; see G. Garbini, "La canzone del deserto di T. Carmi," *Annali dell'Istituto Orientale di Napoli* 12 (1962), pp. 21–25, where he presented a full grammatical and lexical analysis of the text and of its links with biblical poetry,

4. Leah Goldberg attended the Hebrew Gymnasium of Kovno, before studying Semitics and German at the Universities of Kovno, Berlin and Bonn. Here she earned a doctorate in Semitic Studies under P. Kahle on the Samaritan Targum of the Pentateuch. The thesis, *Das Samaritanische Pentateuch Targum. Eine Untersuchung seiner handschriftlichen Quellen* (Stuttgart Bonner Orientalische Studien; Stuttgart: Kohlhammer, 1935), was reviewed by S. Krauss, *AfO* 11 (1935/1936), pp. 384–86. On this period of Goldberg's life, see Y. Weiss, "A Small Town in Germany: Leah Goldberg and German Orientalism in 1932," *Jewish Quarterly Review* 99/2 (2009), pp. 200–229.

5. The only female member of the *bohemian* circle of modernist poets which met at nighttime in the cafés of Tel Aviv, Goldberg worked as a teacher, an advertiser, and as a writer for the newspapers *Davar* and *Al Ha-Mishmar*; she was also editor for the publishing house *Sifriyat Po'alim*, and author of several children's books.

6. For all her poetic work see Leah Goldberg, *Collected Poems* (3 vols.; Tel Aviv: Sifriat Poalim, 1979).

7. Worth noticing are the translations of Petrarca's sonnets and Dante's *Comedy* from Italian (Goldberg learned and spoke Italian with great proficiency), Tolstoy's *War and Peace* from Russian, Ibsen's dramas from Norwegian, and many others.

8. Goldberg taught there from 1952 until her death in 1970. On her strained relationship with the academic world, see A. Lieblich, *Learning about Lea* (London: Athena Press, 2003), pp. 98–100.

9. The river, the snow, the trees are among the most common symbols; they voiced, in her very words, "the headache of both homelands."

10. The Hebrew language was the light, of which "*And this is the Light,*" the largest prose work by Goldberg, spoke. Since her youth, she read all that was written in Modern Hebrew and tried to find in it her roots. As she wrote in that unique piece of narrative, "From early childhood on we are learning *three, if not four languages. And we have root in none.*" On "*And this is the Light,*" see the remarks of Lieblich, *Learning about Lea*, pp. 54–55, and the critiques by N. Scharf Gold and R. P. Scheindlin, "Rereading *It Is the Light,* Lea Goldberg's Only Novel," *Prooftexts* 17 (1997), pp. 245–65.

11. A. Hirschfeld, "Modern Hebrew Poetry 1960–1990," in S. Burnshaw et al. (eds.), *The Modern Hebrew Poem Itself: A New and Updated Edition* (Detroit: Wayne State University Press, 2003), p. 338, observed that Hebrew was rather an idealized language, whereas the presence of Modern Hebrew arose only towards the end of her creative period.

12. R. Friend, *Found in Translation: Modern Hebrew Poets: A Bilingual Edition* (New Milford, CT/London: The Toby Press, 2nd rev. edn, 2006), pp. 102–103 provides the Hebrew text and an English translation not always faithful to the original text. Henceforth, we use R. T. Back's translation, to be found in *Lea Goldberg: Selected Poetry and Drama* (Poetry selected, translated and with an introduction by Rachel Tzvia Back; New Milford, CT/London: The Toby Press, 2005), pp. 78–81.

13. Garbini, "Una nota," p. 196. That is to say that a first Italian translation of the poems was already published by P. Luisada, "Sui Monti di Gerusalemme," *La Rassegna Mensile di Israel* 19 (1953), pp. 556–58, but Garbini seemingly was not aware of it.

14. See P. Lamarche, "Pierre," in X. Leon-Dufour et al., *Vocabulaire de Theologie Biblique* (Paris: Cerf, 1974), pp. 1000–1001.

15. For a summary of the various interpretations, see J. Crenshaw, *Ecclesiastes: A Commentary* (Old Testament Library; London: SCM, 1988), pp. 94–95.

16. Thus Lieblich, *Learning about Lea*, p. 124, explains the image as that of a woman "left alone by her children, who scatter like stones."

17. M. Gimbutas, *I Baltici* (Milan: Il Saggiatore, 1967), p. 191 (Italian translation of *The Balts* [Ancient Peoples and Places 33; London: Thames & Hudson, 1963).

18. See the translation of Back (ed.), *Lea Goldberg*, p. 113.

19. In my opinion, the Hophal passive of the verb נטל implies a sort of unwilling exile whence such a surprise is born.

20. The Hebrew root פרפר means "never-ending movement" and suggests an attempt of escape through the presence of beauty.

21. See Ch. Abraham-Eitan, "The Landscape of Israel in the Poems of the Generation of Transition," *Hebrew Studies* 51 (2010), pp. 287–302. In this regard

the first poem is highly meaningful, "From the Songs of My Beloved Land" (1955). Here the two beautiful yet poor motherlands are compared: the one has "seven days of spring a year rain and chill all the rest," whereas the other has "seven holydays a year, work and hunger all the rest" (see Back [ed.], *Lea Goldberg*, p. 108).

22. Garbini, "Una nota," p. 196. It is important to stress the use of the first person singular when the first person plural was the rule.

23. נסח is used here as an absolute noun, whereas in the Bible it always preceded by the preposition *lamed* to indicate duration or permanence in relation to a divine punishment or to faith in divine reliability. It is worth noticing that נסח, that is to say "eternity," is the name of the fourth *sefirot* in the Kabbala.

24. Goldberg's last poems let this sort of incommunicability with the surrounding world to increase: "Even the landscape does not want to hear the beautiful words I made for it." The same is true for the tree. See Y. Milman, "Screaming Words into the White: The Poetics of Fragmentation in Leah Goldberg's End of Life Poetry," *Hebrew Studies* 45 (2004), pp. 79–97, for an evaluation of these poems.

25. Garbini, "Una nota," p. 197.

26. As the poem is strangely absent from A. Hadari (ed.), *Songs from Bialik: Selected Poems of Hayim Nahman Bialik* (Syracuse New York: Syracuse University Press, 2000). The text is to be found in H. N. Bialik, *El-Hasippor*, available online at www.benyehuda.org/bialik. The poem written around 1891 while Bialik lived between Vorozhin and Odessa, was published in 1892 in the journal *Hapardes*.

27. D. Miron, *H. N. Bialik and the Prophetic Mode in Modern Hebrew Poetry* (The B. G. Rudolph Lectures in Judaic Studies New Series Lecture Two; Syracuse, NY: Syracuse University Press, 2000).

28. Lieblich, *Learning about Lea*, p. 236.

29. A poem to be found in the collection "*The Remnants of Life*," published in 1978, eight years after Goldberg's death, runs as follows: "Snow fell and in a foreign land there was a war and they died in the snow (as they do here in the spring) in a foreign land" (Back [ed.], *Lea Goldberg*, p. 21).

30. The joy is expressed through the word חודה. This is a late Aramaism, which in Neh 8:10 describes joy coming from God.

31. Garbini, "Una nota," p. 197.

32. Appearing in Hos 8:9 only in the plural and with the meaning of occasional, hired love.

33. מזמור stands at the beginning of many Psalms along with the name of the supposed author.

34. R. Tzvia Back, "Introduction: On Forms and Motifs," in Back (ed.), *Lea Goldberg*, p. 19, speaks of "a captivating litany-like lyricism of her work."

35. E. Spicehandler, "An Outline History of Modern Hebrew Poetry 1880–1965," in Burnshaw et al. (eds.), *The Modern Hebrew Poem Itself*, pp. 317–18.

36. Spicehandler, "Lea Goldberg," in Burnshaw et al. (eds.), *The Modern Hebrew Poem Itself*, p. 125.

37. Garbini, "Una nota," p. 197.

38. Lieblich, *Learning about Lea*, pp. 154–55.

39. D. Miron, *Imahot meyasdot, ahayot horgot: al shtey hathalot ba-shirah ha-Eretsysreelit ha-modernit* (Tel Aviv: Hakibbutz Hame'uchad, 1993), pp. 169–76.

40. See N. Stahl, "We left Yeshu': On Three Twentieth Century Hebrew Poets' Longing for Jesus," in N. Stahl (ed.), *Jesus among the Jews* (London/New York: Routledge, 2012), pp. 187–202, 188–89.

41. A. Hirschfeld, "'Al mishmar ha-naʾiviyut: ʿal tafidah ha-tarbuti shel shirat Lea Goldberg," in R. Kartun-Blum and A. Weisman (eds.), *Pegishot ʿim meshoreret: Masot u-meḥkarim ʿal yetsiratah shel Leʾah Goldberg* (Jerusalem/Tel Aviv: Sifriyat Poalim, 2000), pp. 136–38.

42. The play "The Lady in the Castle," produced in 1956 by the Cameri Theatre at Tel Aviv, is Goldberg's attempt to reflect on that event. The play tells the story of Lena, a Jewish girl, whom Count Zabrodsky hid during the War in his castle somewhere in Central Europe. After the War, some Israeli visitors found the girl and revealed to her that the War had ended. Lena eventually chooses to leave the dead, European world, filled with artistic and historical memories, for the fresh air of Palestine (an English translation by T. Carmi is available in Back [ed.], *Lea Goldberg*, pp. 243–314). See R. Feldhay Brenner, "Discourses of Mourning and Rebirth in Post-Holocaust Israeli literature: Leah Goldberg's 'Lady of the Castle' and Shulamith Hareven's 'The Witness,'" *Hebrew Studies* 31 (1990), pp. 71–85.

43. I owe that observation to D. Miron, "In the Matter of Israeli Culture," in A. Barzel (ed.), *Israele. Arte e Vita, 1906–2006* (Milan: Proedi, 2006), p. 282.

44. O. Amichai, "A Candle of Freedom, a Candle of Labor, or the Candle of Judah," *Prooftexts* 28 (2008), pp. 28–52. Pages 37–38 underline how "the fact that her works were published in *Davar li-yeladim*, which was an ideological and party-affiliated magazine, only intensified the subversive nature of her work."

45. In this fairy-tale four animals – the fat hen, the tidy black cat, the busy cuckoo bird, and the voracious squirrel – own an apartment and want to rent it out after the mouse suddenly deserted it. Many potential tenants – the ant, the rabbit, the nightingale – come to look at the apartment, but each one of them despises one of the neighbours. At the end it is the peaceful and tolerant dove that appreciates the new neighbours and decides to live along with them.

46. G. Garbini, *Cantico dei Cantici* (Brescia: Paideia, 1992). Garbini sometimes thought the author was a woman from the Hasmonean court.

47. See the comment by Back, "Notes on the Poems," in Back (ed.), *Lea Goldberg*, p. 218.

48. Back (ed.), *Lea Goldberg*, p. 129.

49. See M. H. Pope, *Song of Songs* (Anchor Bible 7C; New York: Doubleday, 1977), pp. 523–24.

50. Garbini, *Cantico dei cantici*, pp. 314–15. According to Garbini, the girl searching for love has some similarity to the Platonic idea of Love, as she embodied the idea of the soul searching for Love. The author of the Song of Songs would have moved further from the Platonic idea, as in the Hebrew thought Ahavah generates love and eventually coincides with God.

51. Lieblich, *Learning about Lea*, pp. 299–301.

52. Back (ed.), *Lea Goldberg*, p. 130. This last image seems to evoke the bohemian years at Tel Aviv, to which also the presence of city watchmen refer.

53. See, for instance, the poem "Tel Aviv 1935," in Burnshaw et al. (eds.), *The Modern Hebrew Poem Itself*, pp. 135–36, with E. Spicehandlers' commentary.

"TO EACH HIS OWN JOB":
ON JOB 42:1–6

Thomas M. Bolin

In a 1942 work entitled "La Guida" ("The Guide"), the Italian poet Trilussa[1] describes being lost in the woods at night and encountering an old blind woman who offers to guide him out. When Trilussa voices his concern that a sightless person would be able to steer him rightly in the dark, the blind woman replies by grabbing his hand and ordering him to walk ("La Ceca, allora, me pijò la mano e sospirò: – Cammina!"). Only in the poem's last line is the old woman identified as the personified virtue of faith ("era la Fede"). The poem is thus revealed only at its very end to be an allegory of the life of a believer, for whom faith is a paradox that challenges him to deny his senses and reason. Ingeniously, the poem urges the dethronement of the senses as the criterion for faith while at the same time showing their inadequacy even in the visible world. After all, the poet relies on his senses to pass judgment on the woman's abilities, and so fails to realize that she is not who she first seems to be. Trilussa is clearly alluding to the opening scene of Dante's *Inferno*,[2] but goes beyond that great expression of medieval religious faith and the fount of Italian poetry. He replaces Dante's beautiful guide, Beatrice, with an old blind woman, and the Florentine dialect of *The Divine Comedy* with that of Trilussa's native Rome.

I begin this essay in honor of Professor Giovanni Garbini with Trilussa's poem for two reasons. First, like Trilussa, Professor Garbini lives in Rome and has been immersed in the *romanesco* in which Trilussa wrote his poetry. Second, the blind faith extolled in "La Guida" is similar to the all too trusting attitude of many biblical scholars toward the historical veracity of the Hebrew Bible, which Garbini has long criticized.[3] That being said, the text I will examine in this essay is not one whose fictional nature has been in question. Nevertheless, interpretation of Job has been influenced by the religious attitudes of readers since antiquity.[4] This is due both to the book of Job's difficult and often enigmatic language, and its treatment of the highly charged question of divine justice. Consequently, readers over the centuries have struggled to make sense of obscure passages, and have also construed differently the meaning of clear passages. Among exegetes, the result has been scores of studies with an array of scholarly positions. In the course of his prolific career, Garbini published just two short philological studies on Job.[5] One, a study of the description of Job's wealth in the prologue, displays the qualities that have marked Garbini's scholarship throughout his career: he notes overlooked philological connections, pays careful attention to the versions, is not hesitant to diverge from the "assured results" of earlier scholarship, and even includes a nod to Wellhausen's work as an Arabist. In the spirit of that study, this essay examines Job's final words to God in 42:1–6, hopefully without getting lost in the book's interpretive weeds, but instead arriving at some conclusions about Job's composition and meaning.

Some Preliminary Thoughts on Reading Job

At the outset, I want to distinguish between reading the book of Job and attempting to determine how the book came together. While this is necessary when studying any biblical book, it is especially so for Job, whose ability to captivate readers cannot be underestimated. The poignancy of the issue of human suffering, and the expressive poetry used to describe it can work as much on readers' emotions as their intellects. David J. A. Clines rightfully points out that, despite the myriad readings of Job, almost every reader adopts a charitable or sympathetic stance toward the book.[6] That is to say, our emotional response to the story of Job colors our critical reaction to it. In his article on Job's wealth discussed above, Garbini observes how the difficulty of reading Job leads to a kind of exegetical solipsism, and he describes this phenomenon by means of the gnomic phrase (used also as the title for this essay), "A ciascuno il suo Giobbe – To each his own Job."[7] However, the book's ability to spur thought is also considerable. Careful readers not only pick up on the irony of the friends' erroneous explanations for God's punishment of Job, but also recognize those arguments as the very same still used by believers – perhaps even themselves – in analogous situations. One is reminded of Horace's well-known, biting line: *Quid rides? Mutato nomine de te fabula narratur.*[8] However, unlike Horace, the author of Job remains unseen in his narrative, and we readers are left on our own to spot the mirror held up before us.

The interpretive stakes in Job are high because Job's theological opponent is God. As is true of any debate over theodicy, the dispute in Job participates in a zero-sum game in which one is forced to choose between human dignity (and is hence outraged by undeserved suffering) and divine justice (which admits no error in God's judgment). The history of interpretation of Job is nothing more or less than the choices of readers between these two alternatives.[9] This is evident from Job's earliest interpreters, the translators of the LXX and Targum, both of whom emphasized God's righteousness while at the same time either toning down Job's rhetoric or amplifying his sinfulness or remorse. In the modern era, some readers have chosen to take Job's side in the debate, and seen in the figure of Job not a role model of faith in God and submission to the divine will, but rather an example of revolt against an authoritarian, capricious deity or an otherwise meaningless cosmos.

This is all well and good, for what readers do is create meaning from texts by means of a dialectical encounter with them. But this is quite different from the academic exercise of ascertaining when the book of Job was written, whether it draws upon other texts or traditions, how it came to be in its present form, and what its words mean. Too often exegetes are captivated by Job's aesthetic or theological force and import their intellectual or emotional reactions as readers into the historical and cultural contexts of a piece of ancient Israelite literature. Below, I hope to examine Job's final speech in 42:1–6, specifically his final words in v. 6, with an eye to those ancient contexts, in the hope that they may act as boundaries delineating plausible exegetical results.

Trying to Read Job 42:6

Much scholarly attention has been devoted to Job's final speech, resulting in a number of plausible readings, which makes it a fitting microcosm for the book of Job as a whole. The speech contains a number of philological and grammatical ambiguities, remarkable even for a book as linguistically difficult as Job.[10] In addition to the commentaries and monographs on Job, there have been a number of articles devoted specifically to all or part of 42:1–6.[11] Scholars have by far most puzzled over v. 6, which reads as follows in both the MT and the two oldest versions:[12]

MT:	עַל־כֵּן אֶמְאַס וְנִחַמְתִּי עַל־עָפָר וָאֵפֶר
LXX:	διὸ ἐφαύλισα ἐμαυτὸν καὶ ἐτάκην, ἥγημαι δὲ ἐμαυτὸν γῆν καὶ σποδόν
11QTgJob:	על כן אתנסך ואתמהא ואהוא לעפר וקטם

The MT gives us a seven-word sentence containing two verbs followed by two nouns, creating a line of two perfectly balanced halves – a fact noticed by the Masoretes, who placed an *athnach* under the second verb. The verbs are introduced by an adverbial construction and a conjunction, respectively, and the nouns are joined by a conjunction and governed by a preposition,

Both verbs in v. 6 pose exegetical problems. Regarding אמאס, scholars disagree whether it comes from מאס I ("despise, reject")[13] or מאס II < מסס ("melt"). The translators of the ancient versions were equally as puzzled. The LXX and 11QTgJob translated the single verb in the Hebrew with two separate verbs covering the meanings of both מאס I and מאס II, the LXX using φαυλίζω ("disparage") and τήκω ("melt"). It then added a third verb to the verse to govern the phrase "dust and ashes." 11QTgJob translated אמאס with נסך ("pour out") and מהא ("dissolve").[14] The dictionaries are also unsure how to classify אמאס in 42:6. *HALOT* lists a distinctive meaning for Job 42:6 ("to reject what one has said previously, to revoke"). *DCH* lists the occurrence of מאס in Job 42:6 three times: under מאס I as either Qal ("feel loathing, contempt, revulsion)" or Piel ("accept, prefer") and under מאס II as Qal ("waste away").

The problem with reading אמאס in 42:6 as the Qal of מאס I, is that it normally requires an object, which v. 6 does not supply. Both versions understood Job himself to be the implied object, and accordingly rendered אמאס as reflexive, the LXX by means of the pronoun, ἐμαυτόν, (followed by BDB) and 11QTgJob by use of the Ithpael for both verbs. Other proposed implied objects include: the reference to Job's words in 42:3–4, everything Job has said in chs. 3–31, God, or the prepositional phrase על עפר ואפר, despite the fact that it is governed by the second verb in the verse. Of the seventy occurrences of מאס in the Qal throughout the Hebrew Bible, only four lack an object, and all four are in Job (7:16; 34:33; 36:5; 42:6).[15] The verb in the Qal also occurs with an object another seven times in Job (5:17; 8:20; 9:21; 10:3; 19:18; 30:1; 31:13).[16] Quite a lot is at stake here. The verb's object determines the meaning of Job's speech, and it is no exaggeration to say that the meaning of Job's final words affect the interpretation of the entire book. If he is rejecting his prior speeches, then Job has surrendered to God. If he is rejecting God, then his experience of undeserved suffering has led to his abandonment of his loyalty to Yahweh. Given the ambiguous nature of the evidence, scholars are divided over whether אמאס in 42:6 is an expression of Job's surrender to or rejection of Yahweh's explanation of his treatment of Job.[17]

Taking the second option, and translating אמאס in 42:6 as a form of מאס II ("melt," or perhaps, "waste away"), gives Job's utterance a metaphorical quality that is difficult to understand, but that most exegetes view as connoting repentance or self-abasement.[18] The verb is thus an expression of Job's humiliation before Yahweh, the god of the cosmos who has revealed his power in the preceding speeches to Job. While there is no certain evidence to help decide the root of אמאס in 42:6, it merits mention that a form of מאס II occurs in Job 7:5 in a clause with the noun עפר, just as in 42:6 (לבש בשרי רמה וגיש עפר עורי רגע ויאמס). This could serve as support for reading the same root in Job's final words.

The second verb in 42:6, נחמתי, can be read as either a Qal ("repent") or Niphal ("am comforted"). If it is understood as the Qal, then the prepositional phrase, על עפר ואפר, is taken as an evocative expression of repentance.[19] If the verb is read as a Niphal, then the prepositional phrase is read to connote mourning (perhaps alluding to the ashes on which Job sits in 2:8) and the phrase is interpreted to mean that Job has been convinced by Yahweh's speeches and will henceforth cease to lament his sorry lot.[20] Whether the verb is read as a Qal or Niphal, על עפר ואפר can also be read as hendiadys for humankind, a usage found in Gen 18:27, and one that stresses the insignificance of human beings.[21] This is the reading closest to the versions. The LXX uses the verb ἡγέομαι ("consider") and the reflexive pronoun ἐμαυτὸν, thus making the phrase a self-expression of Job's worthlessness.[22] 11QTgJob is more economical, simply writing אהוא ("I am") but achieving the same result as LXX.

This is quite the exegetical thicket to traverse,[23] but it is important to remember that the interpretive difference between reading אמאס in Job 42:6 as a form of either מאס I or II only matters if one *both* sees the verb as a form of מאס I *and* maintains that the verb's implied object is God. Otherwise, the phrase can only be understood to say that Job has repented, or acknowledged his faults, limitations, or smallness before God.[24] Consequently, there are two essential questions to be asked in the translation of אמאס in Job 42:6. First, is the verb from מאס I or II? Second, if the verb is from מאס I, what is its object? Regarding the second question, I do not find it plausible to view Job as rejecting God in 42:6, and I think we commit an anachronism when we see the author of Job as an iconoclast attacking religious belief. The roots of this view lie, paradoxically, in the much older Christian reading of Job which viewed him as a Christ-like figure. This focus on Job as a representative of virtue worthy of emulation opened up an interpretive path that has been well-traveled ever since. Since the beginning of the modern period, Job has also been viewed as the embodiment of the interpreter's preferred theological or philosophical position. Kant saw Job as the perfect example of a person living according to the categorical imperative, while for Voltaire, Job was an ideal deist.[25] Among biblical scholars, the realization that Job is a fictional character required that any such praise be transferred to the book's author. Consequently, it has long been a commonplace in scholarly studies of Job to find reference to the author's literary skill, theological daring, or simply, genius.[26] This is a manifestation of what the literary critic Hans Robert Jauss calls "the aesthetics of negativity," a hermeneutical position in which authors and their works are assumed to be challenging and ironic vis-à-vis the dominant cultural values of their day.[27] We must determine, and not assume, that the author of Job was a radical, counter-cultural, or otherwise advanced theological voice in Israelite religion. To answer this, we are thrust back upon the question of the social location of biblical authors. For Garbini, the Hebrew Bible represents "the ideology of the Jerusalem priesthood of the Hellenistic age."[28] Given what we know of ancient literacy, which admittedly is not very much, it can safely be assumed that the author of Job is an elite with access to a high degree of literary education. The quality of the Hebrew in Job, specifically its rare vocabulary and vivid imagery, attests to this. But he need not necessarily be a priest, nor certainly a theological radical. Great poetry is not the exclusive province of countercultural misfits, or loners. The author of Job is no more "radical" than the authors of the *Babylonian Theodicy* or the *Debate Between the Man and His Ka*. Consequently, I would argue that Job's final speech in 42:1–6 was intended to be read as a capitulation to Yahweh, rather than a revolt against the divine.

Job's Final Speech and the Composition of the Book of Job

In addition to the interpretive weight borne by Job's final speech, its placement in the final chapter of the book raises other exegetical questions, because Job 32–42 show signs of editorial activity. Among the most obvious is the awkward role played by the Elihu speeches, which have long been regarded as an insertion.[29] There are also oddities in Yahweh's speeches, and not a few commentators have excised Yahweh's second speech in chs. 40–41 and combined Job's remarks in 42:1–6 with his earlier speech to Yahweh in 40:3–5. This results in both Yahweh and Job each having one speech in chs. 38–42.[30] This excision does not withstand scrutiny, however. Job's first speech to Yahweh ends with his unequivocal statement that he will cease speaking, and to have him continue for five more verses makes little sense of the text. I think a more significant trace of editorial activity in the text that has been virtually overlooked by exegetes is the awkward transition between 42:6 and 42:7. As Kember Fullerton noted ninety years ago, v. 6 marks the end of Job's final speech, while 42:7 begins as if *Yahweh* had just finished speaking (ויהי אחד דבר יהוה את הדברים האלה אל איוב).[31] This underscores the already noticed oddity in the epilogue, namely that Yahweh never really acknowledges Job's final words or even Job himself, a silence that has given rise to much speculation concerning the exact referent of God's claim in 42:7 that Job has spoken rightly about him.

It is likely that Job's final speech in 42:1–6 is an addition to the book, which already shows evidence of significant redactional activity in its final ten chapters. David Carr notes that in ancient Near Eastern literature, reworked texts are more likely to be expanded than reduced, and that this expansion is more likely to occur at the beginning and end of a text.[32] This would apply to the evidence of significant textual activity in the last ten chapters of Job. Moreover, Carr demonstrates that biblical scribes, quoting texts from memory based on their training in an oral-literate culture, would not always quote verbatim.[33] This makes sense of a couple of curious features in Job 42:4. First, Job repeats Yahweh's words from the divine speeches back to him, but not verbatim. Job 42:4 reads מי זה מעלים עצה בלי דעת, while Yahweh's original remark in 38:2 is מי זה מחשיך עצה במלין בלי דעת. The apparatus in *BHS* notes that some mss. have amended these citations to make them exact quotations. Second, the phrase, שמע־נא ואנכי אדבר, echoes Eliphaz's statement to Job in 33:31, and not anything that Yahweh has said to Job.[34] These features support the view that Job's speech has been appended to the end of Yahweh's second speech, with the scribe quoting earlier portions of Job from memory. If the poems in Job ended with Yahweh's second speech, a copyist might well have found the absence of a reply from Job troublesome and added one of his own. The same thing happened in the book of Jonah, where Yahweh's final words to Jonah in 4:10–11 were supplemented in the midrashic tradition by an added reply from Jonah acknowledging Yahweh's sovereignty.[35] Similarly, scholars have long recognized the final verses of Qohelet as an editorial addition seeking to mitigate the book's more heterodox content. Job's earlier speech in 40:3–5 does not make clear that Job has abandoned his case against Yahweh. At best, Job has made clear in that first speech that he will no longer attempt to engage Yahweh in a discussion about what has happened (אחת דברתי ולא אענה ושתים ולא אוסיף, v. 5). It stands to reason that Job's final speech in 42:1–6 would have been added in order to make clear Job's surrender to God.[36] My reading of 42:6 above also supports this claim.

By Way of Conclusion: Revisiting an Old Idea

That Job's speech in 42:1-6 is an addition, therefore, can be explained both by its use of other texts in Job, by the plausible rationale that it was inserted into the book to make clear Job's surrender to Yahweh, and by the rough transition between vv. 6-7. I think it appropriate here to revive the position of Richard Simon, articulated in 1685, that the prose prologue and epilogue postdate the poems, and are themselves secondary additions to the book of Job.[37] The majority viewpoint since the early nineteenth century has argued the opposite, that the author of Job appropriated an old folktale and subsequently inserted the poetic dialogue.[38] Those earlier exegetes who agreed with Simon were more inclined to give priority to the poems because of romantic notions of the relatively primitive nature of poetry vis-à-vis prose. But there are now better reasons to support this claim. As mentioned above, textual expansion in the ancient Near East is more likely to occur at the beginnings and ends of texts. More significantly, Job's name occurs in the poetic portion of the book only in introductory formulae, and never in the body of a dialogue's poems. Otherwise, Job's name appears only in the prologue, the epilogue, and the Elihu speeches, which are acknowledged by many exegetes as a later addition. The speeches of Job, the three friends, and Yahweh correspond to psalms of lament, comfort, and praise, respectively, and it is likely that the poems in chs. 3-31, 38-41 originated among highly trained scribes connected with priestly circles. Originally unattributed, these poems were later collected, arranged, and assigned to Job and his three friends *before* the prologue and epilogue were added. These were then added to frame this collection of poems, with Job's final speech in 42:1-6 being added sometime later to make explicit his capitulation.[39] The attribution of these speeches to Job, and the addition of the prologue and epilogue must be post-exilic, for the reference to Job in Ezek 14 clearly predates the story of Job (as the book of Daniel is later than the reference to Danʾel in that same chapter of Ezekiel).[40] The importance of sacrifice in both the prologue and the epilogue betray a writer who is most likely a priest. Even more curiously, the power of intercessory prayer stressed in both the prologue and epilogue directly contradicts the viewpoint of Ezek 14's mention of Job. In its final form the book of Job is the product of priestly elites concerned not to attack divine sovereignty but rather to affirm it and the ongoing efficacy of sacrifice.

Notes

1. The pen name of Carlo Alberto Salustri (1873–1950); the text of "La Guida" can be found in C. A. Salustri, *Tales of Trilussa* (trans. J. Duval; Fayetteville, AR: University of Arkansas Press, 1990), pp. 132–33.
2. Compare the opening of both poems: "Nel mezzo del cammin di nostra vita, mi ritrovai per una selva oscura, ché la diritta via era smarrita" (*Inferno* 1.1–3); "Quella Vecchietta ceca, che incontrai, la notte che me spersi in mezzo ar bosco, me disse: Se la strada nu' la sai, te ci accompagno io, chè la conosco" ("La Guida," 1–4).
3. E.g. *History and Ideology in Ancient Israel* (New York: Crossroad, 1988), pp. 1–20.
4. Surveyed and analyzed in S. J. Vicchio, *The Image of the Biblical Job: A History* (3 vols.; Eugene, OR: Wipf & Stock, 2006).
5. Giovanni Garbini, "Le ricchezze di Giobbe," in M. Weippert and S. Timm (eds.), *Meilenstein: Festgabe für Herbert Donner* (AAT 30; Wiesbaden: Harrassowitz, 1995), pp. 27–32, and "La meteorologia di Giobbe," *Rivista Biblica* 41 (1995), pp. 85–91. See R. Contini, *L'Opera di Giovanni Garbini: Bibliografia degli scritti 1956–2006* (Brescia: Paideia, 2007), p. 108.
6. D. J. A. Clines, "Why Is There a Book of Job and What Does It Do to You if You Read It?," in W. A. M. Beuken (ed.), *The Book of Job* (BETL 114; Leuven: Peeters, 1994), pp. 1–20. Clines states: "Readers of the book of Job, in other words, have almost always agreed with it. It is hard to find a reader who says, I believe I understand what the book of Job is saying, and I don't agree with it" (pp. 19–20).
7. Garbini, "Le ricchezze di Giobbe," p. 32.
8. "Are you laughing? Change the name, and the story is told about you" (*Satires* 1.69–70).
9. A good discussion of this is to be found in T. Tilley, "God and the Silencing of Job," *Modern Theology* 5 (1989), pp. 257–70.
10. For example: the *ketiv/qere* of ידעת in v. 2; the referent of the phrase הגדתי ולא אבין in v. 3; the connotation of נפלאות in v. 3; whether the *waw* in v. 5 is disjunctive or conjunctive; see E. van Wolde, "Job 42,6: The Reversal of Job," in Beuken (ed.), *The Book of Job*, pp. 223–50 (242) and E. Ho, "Job's Anticipation of Death in Job 42:6," *Eastern Great Lakes and Midwest Biblical Societies: Proceedings* 27 (2007), pp. 31–45. Philippe Guillaume and Michael Schunck wryly observe that, "[i]n Job, the problem of suffering applies first and foremost to the translators" ("Job's Intercession: Antidote to Divine Folly," *Biblica* 88 [2007], pp. 457–72 [462]).
11. K. Fullerton, "The Original Conclusion to the Book of Job," *ZAW* 42 (1924), pp. 116–36; L. J. Kuyper, "The Repentance of Job," *VT* 9 (1959), pp. 91–94. D. Patrick, "The Translation of Job XLII 6," *VT* 26 (1976), pp. 369–71; J. B. Curtis, "On Job's Response to Yahweh," *JBL* 98 (1979), pp. 497–511; B. Lynne Newell, "Job: Repentant or Rebellious?," *Westminster Theological Journal* 46 (1984), pp. 298–316; W. Morrow, "Consolation, Rejection, and Repentance in Job 42:6," *JBL* 105 (1986), pp. 211–25; C. Muenchow, ""Dust and Dirt in Job 42 6," *JBL* 108 (1989), pp. 597–611; A. Wolters, "'A Child of Dust and Ashes' (Job 42,6b)," *ZAW* 102 (1990), pp. 116–19; T. F. Dailey, "And Yet He Repents – On Job 42,6," *ZAW* 105 (1993), pp. 205–9; van Wolde, "Job 42,6"; Ho, "Job's Anticipation of Death in Job 42:6"; T. Krüger, "Did Job Repent?," in T. Krüger, M. Oeming, K. Schmid and

C. Uehlinger (eds.), *Das Buch Hiob und Seine Interpretationen* (ATANT 88; Zurich: Theologische Verlag, 2007), pp. 217–29. The best discussion in print is D. J. A. Clines, *Job 38–42* (WBC 18B; Nashville, TN: Thomas Nelson, 2011), pp. 1204–24.

12. The Targum will not be considered, given that it has heavily edited its *Vorlage* along theological lines. It rendered 42:6 as מטול היכנא מאסית עותרי ואתניחמית על בני דהנון עפר וקטם.

13. *HALOT* notes that מאס I appears to be related to Akkadian, *mêšu*, "to despise, to have contempt for, to disregard" (*CAD*, vol. 10, pp. 41–42)

14. J. P. M. van der Ploeg and A. S. van der Woude, *Le Targum de Job de la Grotte XI de Qumràn* (Leiden: Brill, 1971), pp. 84–85; M. Pope, *Job* (AB 15; New York: Doubleday, 1965), pp. 349–50; D. Shepherd, *Targum and Translation: A Reconsideration of the Qumran Aramaic Version of Job* (Studia Semitica Neerlandica 45; Assen: Van Gorcum, 2004), p. 232.

15. Ezekiel 21:18 may be another instance of מאס in the Qal without an object, but the text is suspect.

16. Discussion in Patrick, "The Translation of Job XLII 6"; Curtis, "On Job's Response to Yahweh"; and Morrow, "Consolation, Rejection, and Repentance."

17. By way of example, van Wolde understands אמאס to indicate Job's turning away from his old attitudes of anger and distrust in God ("Job 42,6," p. 250). In contrast, Curtis maintains that in all but one of the passages in Job that use מאס without an object, Job feels loathing and revulsion toward God. Consequently, "there can be little doubt that the unexpressed object of the loathing is God" ("On Job's Response to Yahweh," p. 504); cf. the different explanations of this evidence in Kuyper ("The Repentance of Job," p. 94) and Morrow ("Consolation, Rejection, and Repentance in Job 42:6," p. 214).

18. E. Dhorme, *Commentary on the Book of Job* (trans. H. Knight; London: Thomas Nelson, 1967), pp. 107–108; Morrow, "Consolation, Rejection, and Repentance," pp. 214–15; and Muenchow, "Dust and Dirt in Job 42:6," p. 611.

19. So Dhorme, *A Commentary on Job*, p. 646; Pope, *Job*, pp. 347–50; R. Gordis, Gordis, *The Book of God and Man: A Study of Job* (Chicago: University of Chicago Press, 1965), pp. 304–305; and Newell, "Job: Repentant or Rebellious?," p. 315.

20. So N. Habel, *The Book of Job* (Cambridge: Cambridge University Press, 1975), pp. 575–80; E. M. Good, *In Turns of Tempest: A Reading of Job* (Stanford, CA: Stanford University Press, 1990), pp. 376–78; Patrick, "The Translation of Job XLII 6," p. 370; van Wolde, "Job 42:6," p. 249; and Clines, *Job 38–42*, p. 1222.

21. So Curtis, "On Job's Response to Yahweh," pp. 500–501; Wolters, "'A Child of Dust and Ashes'"; and Ho, "Job's Anticipation of Death," pp. 38–39.

22. This is similar to the reading of Muenchow, for whom the phrase עפר ואפר in 42:6 indicates Job's submission to Yahweh and his physically sinking down to the earth. "There is thus a distinctly affirmative tone in the scene of Job's shaming. On his knees in the dust and dirt, Job nonetheless has been acknowledged and affirmed by his lord. In Yahweh's very acknowledgment of Job's lowliness, Job finds his derivative worthiness" ("Dust and Dirt in Job 42:6," p. 611).

23. Morrow argues that the author of 42:6 is deliberately ambiguous: "[N]o translation of 42:6 is without difficulty or free from ambiguity... Job 42:6 is a polysemous construction, which even its original readers would have heard

differently, depending on their evaluation of the meaning of Yahweh's address to Job" ("Consolation, Rejection, and Repentance in Job 42:6," p. 223). However, Morrow overstates the ancient author's capacity for ambiguity. While some biblical texts are phrased to elicit more than one meaning, such as the meaning of נהפכת in Jonah 3:3, or the use of תם in Job, it is not clear that an ancient author would deliberately write a text so that it would support a multiplicity of meanings.

24. So C. A. Newsome, who notes that Job "either retracts his words or abases himself" (*The Book of Job: A Contest of Moral Imaginations* [Oxford/New York: Oxford University Press, 2003], p. 29).

25. See the discussion in S. J. Vicchio, "Job in the Modern World," in *The Image of Job: A History*, vol. 3 (Eugene, OR: Wipf & Stock, 2006), pp. 60–78.

26. One finds this in older studies, such as Fullerton's, which describes Job's author as "a shining example of that rare phenomenon in the history of literature, a great humanist with a profound religious insight" ("The Original Conclusion to the Book of Job," p. 135). But this is also present in recent scholarship. Even Clines, who has noted how Job can captivate its readers, describes Yahweh's speeches as evidence of the author (whom Clines calls a "poet," itself a positive value-laden term) as shifting the theological debate in the book "from the didactic to the lyrical" ("Coming to a Theological Conclusion: The Case of the Book of Job," in J. Middlemas, D. J. A. Clines, and E. K. Holt [eds.], *The Centre and the Periphery: A European Tribute to Walter Brueggemann* [Sheffield: Sheffield Phoenix, 2010], pp. 209–23 [216]).

27. T. M. Bolin, *Freedom Beyond Forgiveness: The Book of Jonah Re-Examined* (JSOTSup 236; Sheffield: Sheffield Academic, 1997), pp. 54–55.

28. G. Garbini, *Myth and History in the Bible* (London: Sheffield Academic, 2003), p. 100. On the Hasmonean editing of the biblical text, see D. Carr, *The Formation of the Hebrew Bible: A New Reconstruction* (Oxford/New York: Oxford University Press, 2011), pp. 166–78.

29. C. Westermann, *The Structure of the Book of Job* (trans. C. A. Muenchow; Philadelphia: Fortress, 2nd edn, 1981).

30. See the summary and rebuttal of this position in Gordis, *Book of God and Man*, pp. 121–23; see also Westermann, *Structure of the Book of Job*, pp. 124–25. Gordis does not excise chs. 40–41 but sees Job's two utterances in 40:3–5 and 42:1–6 as one speech. Similarly, Charles Muenchow sees Job's two responses as parts of a whole and evidence of the agonistic nature of an honor–shame culture ("Dust and Dirt in Job 42:6").

31. Fullerton, "Original Conclusion," p. 127. Van Wolde observes that 42:7 reads, "as if verses 1–6 have not taken place" ("Job 42,6," p. 238). She is following Édouard Dhorme, who notes that "[t]he natural sequel to 41:26 would be 42:7. But the poet wished to bring on to the scene for the last time the hero of his story" (*A Commentary on the Book of Job* [trans. H. Knight; London: Thomas Nelson, 1967], p. 645).

32. Carr, *The Formation of the Hebrew Bible*, pp. 37–56.

33. On the variation to be expected in quotations made from memory, see Carr, *The Formation of the Hebrew Bible*, pp. 13–36.

34. Good, *In Turns of Tempest*, pp. 371–72; Clines, *Job 38–42*, p. 1215. Gordis notes that Job also quotes his opponents' words at the end of the first and second cycles of speeches (*Book of God and Man*, pp. 185–88).

35. In the *Yalkut Shimoni*, Jonah responds to Yahweh's final speech by falling on his face and quoting Dan 9:9; see the discussion in Bolin, *Freedom Beyond Forgiveness*, p. 178.

36. Fullerton, "Original Conclusion," pp. 125–26.

37. Richard Simon, *Histoire Critique du Vieux Testament* (repr., Frankfurt: Minerva, 1967), Book 1, Chapter 1, p. 30.

38. E.g. B. Duhm, *Das Buch Hiob* (Freiburg: Mohr-Siebeck, 1897); K. Budde, *Das Buch Hiob Übersetzt und Erklärt* (Göttingen: Vandenhoeck & Ruprecht, 2nd edn, 1913). See the discussion and overview in Newsom, *The Book of Job*, pp. 3–31; K. N. Ngwa, *The Hermeneutics of the 'Happy' Ending in Job 42:7–17* (BZAW 354; Berlin/New York: de Gruyter, 2005), pp. 71–75. See also G. Fohrer, "Zur Vorgeschichte und Komposition des Buches Hiob," *VT* 6 (1956), pp 249–67.

39. Compare Fohrer's reasoning for believing the prologue and epilogue to have been earlier than the poetry: "Ein Redaktor wäre schwerlich auf den Gedanken fallen, eine Rahmenerzählung zu verwenden, in der von den Verwandten und Bekannten Hiobs die Rede war, und deren Erwähnung an ihrer Stelle nicht einfach beizubehalten, sondern durch die im Gedicht genannten Freunde zu ersetzen und ausserdem noch die stilistischen Feinheiten der verschiedenartigen Verwendung von Prosa Poesie und der Gottesbezeichnungen zu beachten. Der Dichter hat die übernommene Erzählung so ausführlich und genau wie möglich beibehalten. Von da aus erklären sich die stilistischen Unebenheiten an den Stellen, wo er sich zu Eingriffen oder Änderungen genötigt sah. Sie beruhen auf der Spannung zwischen der Treue zur Tradition, die möglichst kein überliefertes Wort missen wollte, und dem Erfordernis der Anpassung an die neue Situation, die mit der Einführung der drei Freunde gegeben war" ("Zur Vorgeschichte und Komposition des Buches Hiob," p. 265).

40. Cf. Carr (*The Formation of the Hebrew Bible*, p. 210) who notes the possibility of Job's dependence on Jeremiah.

The Siloam Tunnel Revisited

Philip R. Davies

Pseudo-facts

In every discipline there exist conclusions that are accepted everywhere as facts, even when they are not. Because they are accepted as facts, it is unusual for them to be questioned; to challenge them will not occur as a matter of course, because it is not in the nature of most scholarly work to aim at overturning facts. But now and then a challenge to established facts will arise, for whatever reason, and such challenges face various difficulties in being accepted. One is inertia: the force of the consensus, the reluctance to rethink or review a reigning paradigm that makes us comfortable and frames our research agendas. Another is the participation of specialized expertise. A scholarly consensus is usually maintained through the mutual trust that exists between practitioners of different specialties. Attempts to challenge such bodies of knowledge from outside the circle often encounter a certain disdain for the "outsider" whose opinions may be dismissed as "amateur" and whose conclusions dubbed as "pseudo-scholarship."

In a volume dedicated to Giovanni Garbini, a scholar with little or no respect for the habitual consensus, it seems appropriate to address the issue of "known facts" that are in fact not known at all, and for this purpose I choose the case of the so-called "Siloam Tunnel," better known as "Hezekiah's Tunnel," and its curious inscription. The "fact" in question is that the Siloam Tunnel was built by Hezekiah to secure Jerusalem's water supply just before the arrival of Sennacherib in 701 BCE. This "fact" is based on other "facts," archaeological, historical, exegetical and paleographic. The congruence of these respective bodies of knowledge seemed until fairly recently more than capable of protecting the "fact" from any challenge, because even when in each of these there exists a degree of doubt or approximation, the possibility or probability in each case cumulates into a certainty when they are combined. The certainty of the overall conclusion protects each of these from individual investigation. This is how scholarly argumentation works, understandably and perhaps necessarily. But the last 40 years or so of biblical scholarship have reminded us how many "facts" of history have needed to be undone: indeed, whole tranches of historical "knowledge" have been devastated. In the wake of this destruction it is not a bad idea to revisit some of the surviving certainties. I do so, however, not to establish a new fact, nor to replace discarded knowledge with new knowledge. Rather I wish to champion the cause that believes in challenging the most established facts, because these are the facts that most often escape scrutiny.

In 1996 my colleague John Rogerson and I published an article in *Biblical Archaeologist*[1] which considered all of the bodies of knowledge that comprised the "fact" of "Hezekiah's Tunnel," and demonstrated that none of them individually pointed to Hezekiah as the builder of the tunnel. Instead, we suggested that one of the Hasmonean kings of the second century BCE was responsible. It is fair to point out, however, that this was not the real beginning of the story. A partial challenge to the archaeological consensus had already been issued by David Ussishkin,[2] who had suggested that the famous tunnel did not end at the Siloam Pool, but continued eastward to the Kidron Valley, and that the inscription marked not its lower point but the midway point. He therefore connected the Siloam Pool with the "King's Garden" mentioned in Neh 3:15 and suggested that the tunnel was constructed to supply water to it. Yet while Ussishkin denied its strategic motive, he did not challenge the view that Hezekiah was responsible. Yet without associating the tunnel with the impending arrival of Sennacherib, why was it plausible to ascribe this work to Hezekiah at all?

We did not (as perhaps we should have) include Ussishkin's proposal in our article, but we built a more comprehensive reassessment, suggesting that the tunnel and inscription had nothing to do with Hezekiah, or even the Iron Age. This was received by a majority of those who responded as outrageous. To us, this was neither surprising nor unintentional, for we concluded that something fairly dramatic was needed to shake a widespread conviction. We nevertheless regretted that the editor of *Biblical Archaeologist* himself drew criticism for allowing it even to be published (the readers who bypassed it remaining presumably unknown) and subsequently had to leave his post. There was a sober response to the paleographical arguments in the same journal,[3] but the editor of the downmarket rival *Biblical Archaeology Review* (*BAR* 1996) gleefully assembled a feature entitled "Defusing Pseudo-Scholarship: The Siloam Inscription Ain't Hasmonean," with contributions from Jo Ann Hackett, Frank Moore Cross and P. Kyle McCarter (all connected with Harvard University), Ada Yardeni, André Lemaire, Esther and

Hanan Eshel and Avi Hurvitz. Like Hendel (though sometime less politely), these contributors addressed almost exclusively the paleographical arguments, as if these alone settled the matter. And these arguments were, according to them all, unassailable. To quote Hendel: "the script of the Siloam inscription fits uniformly into the eighth–seventh century sequence...right around the time of Hezekiah."[4] Likewise, Hanan Eshel affirmed "...paleography alone can only tell us that the Siloam Inscription may have been written at the end of the eighth century or in the seventh century B.C.E..." The paleographical "facts" were reargued and reaffirmed, and the implication of the response was that the ascription to Hezekiah could be sustained purely on the basis of paleography (though one contributor reasserted that the Bible referred to Hezekiah's building of the tunnel, as if we had not argued otherwise).[5] One response that did review the archaeological arguments found them cogent,[6] but rejected the other arguments.

From Villains to Heroes?

This paleographical conclusion has, nevertheless, now to be somewhat reconsidered, at least in the light of recent research (to be discussed below). In a *BAR* response to some of this work, entitled "Will King Hezekiah be Dislodged from His Tunnel?," the editor, Hershel Shanks, now bestows upon us the accolade of "respected scholars" (not even "respected *pseudo*-scholars") in conceding the possibility that we may have been at least correct in dissociating the tunnel from Hezekiah.[7] But he states that our argument was based "largely" on the inscription, which is incorrect: we also anticipated some of the archaeological reasoning against Hezekiah, and showed that the biblical texts claimed to connect Hezekiah with the tunnel did not necessarily do so at all. Shanks was, however, right to remark that we never responded to the initial attack on "pseudo-scholarship." Had we decided to, however, we would certainly not have chosen *Biblical Archaeology Review*. This was not entirely because of the flavour and editorial agenda of that particular periodical, but also because our case did not rest purely on paleography, and because the "star-studded"[8] array of experts also made some questionable assertions, such as that of Jo Ann Hackett that had the inscription been Hasmonean, the spelling would have been *plene*, in apparent ignorance of the fact that the contemporary Qumran manuscripts show variation between *plene* and non-*plene* spelling, as does the Masoretic text, which, as far as we can tell, was being fixed at about the same time (for other errors in the paleographical arguments see below). At any rate, in his review of the new archaeological finds and reasoning, Shanks did not consider that both the biblical "evidence" and the paleography were being challenged by these new findings. Not surprisingly, Shanks expresses doubts about these findings and indeed he is right to point out that the reasoning is not (as it might be put) watertight.

The article Rogerson and I had written did, I feel, a service in showing that the various lines of evidence did not add up; but it was unfortunate that our proposal for a Hasmonean dating permitted many scholars to focus on that new dating, and, in rejecting it, to overlook the arguments against Hezekiah, which stood, and stand, independently of our arguments about the inscription. But these wider arguments have now been buttressed by the excavations in the Gihon water system, which coincidentally commenced in 1995 and have been prolonged to the present. During this process, several reassessments of the date and purpose of various parts of the water system have been generated. Our conclusions about a Hasmonean date have not been supported, but our critique of the archaeological and historical reasoning has been endorsed, and our case that the biblical "evidence" does at least not *necessarily* point to Hezekiah stands. It is for us a satisfactory outcome, so far.

Archaeology

The Siloam Tunnel was virtually unknown[9] until discovered in 1838 by Edward Robinson and Eli Smith, and the legend of Hezekiah's construction dates (like that of Solomon's mines[10]) to the nineteenth century: there is no earlier allusion to it. The inscription on the tunnel wall near the Siloam Pool was noticed much later (1880), when paper squeezes and a casting were made (the cast is now at the Palestine Exploration Fund in London), and in 1881 Archibald Sayce published a translation. In 1890 the inscription was illegally chiseled out of the rock wall, and when recovered was sent to Istanbul, where it is now housed in the Archaeological Museum. The pool at the lower end of the tunnel had been excavated by Guthe in 1881 and Bliss in 1894–97, and the tunnel itself cleared in 1909–11 by a group that included L. H. Vincent and the notorious Montague Parker, who was searching for treasure rather than historical knowledge. It is from Vincent's magnificent account of the exploration and excavation that we derive the numbering of the tunnels and channels.

In 1923–24 Weill[11] excavated the southern end of the Ophel hill, and discovered a channel, partly tunneled, carrying water from the Gihon eastwards from the Siloam Pool into the Kidron Valley. As noted earlier, Ussishkin was the first to argue that this was part of the same waterway and not a later extension.[12] Most investigators have not followed his lead, and attention has recently tended to focus rather on the Gihon end than the Siloam. The water system was more recently examined as part of Kenyon's Jerusalem dig of 1961–67 and in more detail by Y. Shiloh in 1978–85. From 1995 Ronny Reich and Eli Shukron have been concentrating their attention on the Gihon Spring area as part of the development of the "City of David" as an archaeological park. Their sequence of reports[13] helpfully charts the progress of their work and the evolution of their conclusions, on which I shall concentrate.

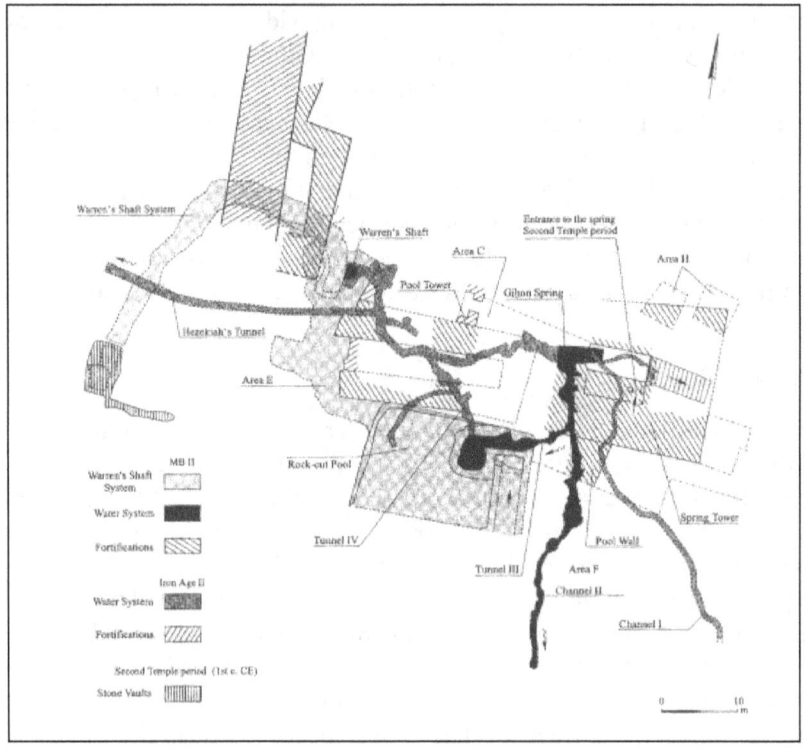

Figure 1. The Gihon water system.[14]

The complicated water systems connected in antiquity to the Gihon spring on the northeastern side of the Ophel hill consist of several interconnected channels or tunnels, whose history is difficult to unravel (Fig. 1). The earliest water system within this complex may be what is referred to as Channel II, which ran from the spring southwards and continued mostly outside the city wall, along the slope, partly under and partly over ground: vents in the side suggest it was used for irrigation. Its final destination is assumed to be the *Birket el-Hamra* in the Kidron

Valley.[15] For reasons that will shortly emerge, it is important to note that this tunnel runs at a higher level than the "Siloam Tunnel" (Channel VIII). Channel II also fed, by means of the short passage known as Tunnel III, part of a rock-cut space, which was discovered in 1909 by the famous/infamous Parker expedition and documented by Vincent, who dubbed it the "Round Chamber." Further excavation by Reich and Shukron has revealed that this is actually the lower level of a larger chamber which they term the "Rock-Cut Pool." The use of a pool to provide water inside the walls of the city was necessary because the Gihon spring gushes only intermittently.

Access to this chamber was gained by a stepped tunnel inside the ancient city wall, leading to a gently sloping curved tunnel, about 30 metres long. A 14-metre deep shaft, the so-called "Warren's Shaft" lay on or near this conduit. The system just described was assigned to the Iron Age by the Shiloh excavators but Reich and Shukron have uncovered evidence that it was originally of Middle Bronze construction, though renovated in the Iron Age, when the strong fortifications, protecting the entire watercourse, were also strengthened, rendering the water supply even more secure in the event of an attack.

Warren's Shaft was, until recently, thought to have been part of the earliest water system from the Middle Bronze period, but Reich and Shukron believe it to have been discovered only during the Iron Age renovation. It was at this time, they conclude, that a tunnel (Tunnel IV) was cut to connect the Shaft with the "Rock-Cut Pool." But then another tunnel (VI) was cut between the spring and Tunnel IV, bypassing the Rock-Cut Pool, and rendering the newly built Tunnel IV, and in fact the entire Middle Bronze system, unnecessary. It is these two tunnels that are central to the reconstruction offered by Reich and Shukron.

The change of mind implied by first cutting off Tunnel IV and then rendering it redundant betrays, in the view of Reich and Shukron, a (we may presume, fairly sudden) decision to construct the "Siloam Tunnel" (Tunnel VIII), which they initially assigned to Hezekiah, along with the other reconstruction work in the area. But further excavations in the Rock-Cut Pool have convinced them otherwise. For when Tunnel VI was opened, the pool ceased to be used, and indeed, since Tunnel VI was at a lower level than Tunnel II, the pool actually dried up. Later, a house was built over the site of the pool, raised on a fill, the pottery from which has been dated to the ninth or early eighth century.[16] At this date Tunnel VI must already have been open, and since Tunnel VIII, the Siloam Tunnel, when finished ran from Tunnel VI and not from the pool via Tunnel IV, then Hezekiah can be ruled out as the builder of the tunnel ascribed to him. It must have been one of his predecessors.

Reich and Shukron's conclusion relies partly on their reconstruction of the process of cutting the Siloam Tunnel. They argue that it could not have been dug directly from the Spring, since the water would have flooded the workers as they hewed. Hence, it was dug from the Gihon end from Tunnel IV and at the same time from the southern end, and only when the two sections were joined was Tunnel VI then cut to bring the water directly from the Gihon spring into the new tunnel. A panel at the junction of Tunnels IV and VIII, possibly for an inscription matching the one at the Siloam end, may support this reconstruction. This argumentation is plausible, but not conclusive. The evidence of the panel seems powerful, but the panel near the Siloam Pool is not precisely at the point where the tunnel enters, but some way further up, and so it does not follow that the panel at the top end also marks the place where it commenced. The problem of the panels is, in any case, more complicated if there were more than two, one at each end, as may well be the case. The extant inscription near the Siloam Pool was, moreover, cut on the lower part of a larger panel that was left blank. If these panels were intended for inscriptions, why were they not written – a question that is more acute if the tunnel was not cut in an emergency (and if it was, how and why was the existing inscription made?). It is also not very plausible that Tunnel IV, apparently intended to link the pool with Warren's Shaft, was built just before Tunnel VIII was cut. How certain can we be that Tunnels IV and VI (which are quite similar in construction, but unlike the Siloam Tunnel) were in fact constructed in the Iron Age and not earlier, and that Warren's Shaft was unknown until this time. Might not the system that allowed access to water from Warren's Shaft belong to an earlier phase? Again, could not the water flow from the Gihon have been controlled otherwise (e.g. dammed at the head of the tunnel itself, allowing water still to flow in Tunnel IV and/or VI?) so that the Siloam Tunnel workers were not flooded?[17] Guil[18] has recently reviewed Reich and Shukron's proposal and suggested that "the whole 9th century BCE administrative center was cleared off and dumped into the Rock Cut Pool. Consequently, the fill is just a fill and cannot give any indication as to the exact date of the dumping of the fill into the Rock Cut Pool nor of the construction of Tunnel VIII (The Siloam Tunnel)." In fact, he argues, as Rogerson and I did, for a Hasmonean date. There remain, in any case, many unanswered questions about the dates we have and their interpretation. But one conclusion, which Reich and Shukron arrived at early in their work, is reliable: that the Siloam Tunnel was not strategically necessary, and this constitutes a powerful objection to the theory that it dates from around 701 – which is in fact the chief reason for its ascription to Hezekiah in the first place.

The puzzle does not end with the Gihon end, either, which, as mentioned earlier, might provide further evidence that the Siloam Tunnel did not serve to protect Jerusalem's water supply in the event of attack. Since 2004, Reich and Shukron have directed their attention to the Siloam Pool area, including the relationship between it and the *Birket el-Hamra*[19] to which Ussishkin and Faust also drew attention (and in fact had been noted already by Vincent, as these authors recognize). It is therefore likely that there will soon be further data on the history of the connection between these two pools. At this point, where the problem of the tunnel's purpose is in view, it is convenient to turn to the historical issues surrounding its construction.

History

Historical considerations have, as just pointed out, played an important role in identifying Hezekiah as the builder of the Siloam Tunnel. Reich and Shukron's proposed dating to the late ninth or early eighth century for the Siloam Tunnel, based on both the pottery dates from Tunnel IV and the strong fortifications of the Gihon water system, offer a context that is nevertheless not very plausible. Whether Judah (and/or Jerusalem) enjoyed sufficient political independence from a powerful Israel (and Aram) to allow such a project at this time, or if, alternatively, the work was carried out by the rulers of Israel, to whom the rulers of Jerusalem were no doubt clients, such a technologically daring and difficult project seems an odd enterprise. The need to supply water to another part of the city hardly applies, and the alternative possibility of provision of water to a "royal garden" does not suggest itself as a priority. But even if they are not correct, their serious challenge to the traditional Hezekian context threatens the collapse of a great deal of reconstructed history.

One element of this reconstructed history is the building of a new city wall. Such a wall has been conjectured from a small section of masonry on the Western hill, a so-called "broad wall" discovered by Nahman Avigad in the 1970s, which runs for 65 metres and is 7 metres thick and in places 3.3 metres high[20] (Fig. 6). The only physical remains display a curve in the wrong direction, and to date there is no physical evidence of any of the rest of this hypothetical wall elsewhere, though it appears as a fact in most modern discussions of the history of the period that I have consulted.

The wall is a plausible outcome of a sudden expansion of the city's population somewhere in the late eighth century or early seventh, which is admittedly a well-established datum. But when it was built and what its extent was are unknown, and no other traces of it have yet been identified. Its ascription to Hezekiah, and the deduction that it did not encircle merely the Western hill, but joined the western side of the existing city wall, is a supposition necessitated by the fact that the Siloam Pool lies outside the line of that previous wall, rendering the tunnel strategically useless. On the assumption that such a wall was built, various conjectures have been offered as to its course (Fig. 2). Kenyon's is the most northerly, and while her proposal is odd in accepting the idea that the wall existed, but ran *inside* the Siloam Pool, it both represents the strategically preferable course and also reflects the fact that her own excavations yielded no Iron II remains in the vicinity of the pool. While Shiloh[21] objected that Kenyon's conclusions were based on too limited evidence, his own excavations found no Iron Age relics here either,[22] and he dated the remains of the pool and its associated fortifications to the Second Temple period.[23]

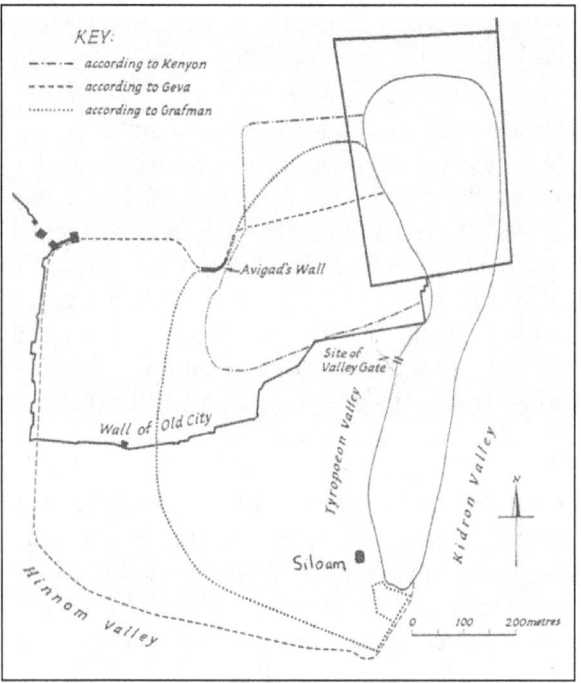

Figure 2. Proposals for the line of "Hezekiah's wall."

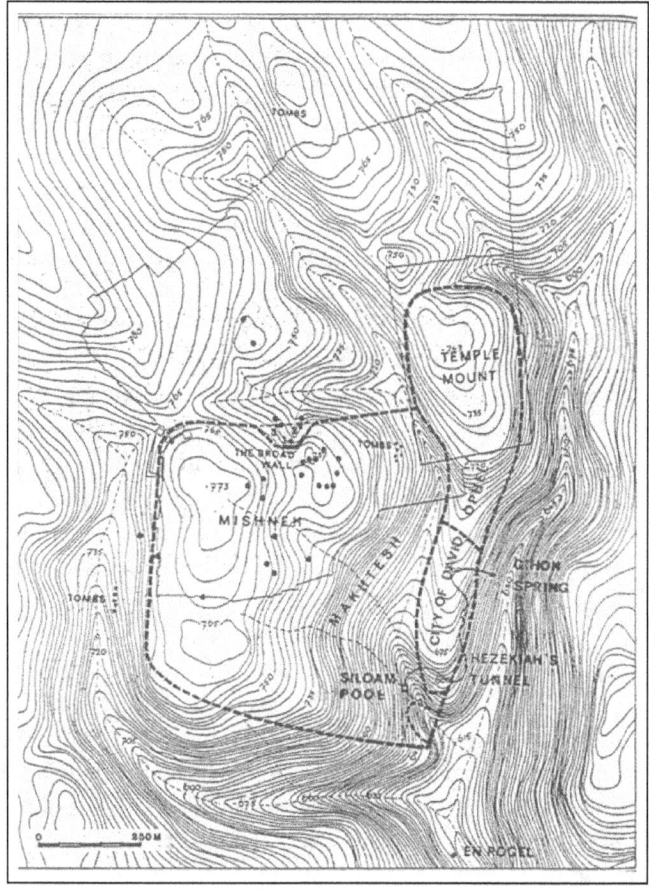

Figure 3. A contoured map of "Hezekiah's Wall" showing
(at "The Broad Wall") the site of the only physical remains.

The contoured map (Fig. 3) shows the location of the pool and Avigad's maximally conjectured line, including a small kink to make the actual remains of extant masonry fit in with the conjectured shape. This map also shows that since the pool lies close to the bottom of a wadi, it had probably always existed there, collecting rainwater. It also shows how the southern line of the wall crosses the very steep valley slope at an improbably low point almost at its floor. Avigad expresses the common but mistaken view that this is where "it must have been, according to the Bible, as well as according to logic."[24]

The "logic" to which Avigad referred is based on the premise of Hezekiah's construction of the tunnel, for which strategic purpose was the supply of water, securely, to the new population on the Western hill which therefore must have issued inside the city walls. But this logic leads further. This population expansion (which seems to have been quite swift) can, on the proposed date of the tunnel, only be explained by the arrival of refugees from Samaria after 722 BCE.[25] Whether such a flight is really plausible, however, may be doubted. For what reasons would farmers from Samaria have to flee, and if they did abandon their land, why flee to a city, why to the capital of an Assyrian client, and how would their presence be sustained beyond a few years? A more plausible explanation is that the new population was either the result of a flight to the city from the Judean cities devastated by Sennacherib or as a result of the increased economic role of the city under Manasseh due to its incorporation into the Assyrian empire's economic system (or a combination of both). Under these circumstances we can still explain the construction of a wall and even tunnel, both built with Assyrian approval, to protect the city from Egyptian attack and to improve water access from the western hill or even supply a royal garden. But we are still not obliged to accept that either a wall or the tunnel was in fact built at this time or for these reasons.

A Biblical Tradition?

Space does not permit the repetition of the case that Rogerson and I assembled against any clear biblical reference to a Hezekian Tunnel. Here I observe only that a link between Hezekiah and Jerusalem's water supply apparently circulated in the Late Persian–Early Hellenistic period, as reflected in both 2 Chr 32 and Ben Sira.[26] Neither of these can offer reliable historical information, and there is no trace of such a tradition in any later period – notably in either Josephus, or Eusebius: to them both the tunnels even seem to have been unknown. We cannot, in the manner of "biblical archaeologists," mine texts directly for historical nuggets but consider when the texts might have been written, the likely extent of their authors' knowledge and evaluate their image of the past in terms of "memory" and not hard data.[27] A study of the growth of the legend of Hezekiah would be a very useful contribution to our understanding of Judean cultural memory and perhaps throw light on the origin of his perceived connection to the city's water supply.[28] That the water system in Jerusalem known to later writers was attributed to a noteworthy monarch of the past, who famously withstood a siege of the city, would not be unexpected.

Geology

Geology has also provided controversial contributions to the puzzle of the Siloam Tunnel. A central issue has been, and remains, to what extent the work exploited existing karstic fissures. This is not the place to review that long discussion,[29] which mostly does not have a bearing on its date or purpose. But recently an intriguing article appeared in the *Journal of Archaeological Science*.[30] Frumkin, Shimron and Rosenbaum provided the results of their survey of the tunnel, noting the innovative nature of such a long excavation, well in advance of previous Assyrian techniques. They dismiss earlier notions that the tunnel was enabled by a natural (karstic) cleft or clefts, thus making the construction even more remarkable (and the time needed for its construction even longer). They noted five karst shafts, only two open to the surface, but all allowing rainwater into the cleft. The deviations in the tunnel close to these shafts were interpreted to mean that the tunnelers used them to communicate with a surface team. Also detected was evidence of many false starts before the meeting of the two teams, while the floor level had to be revised to ensure an even slope. Frumkin and his colleagues offer a fairly complicated explanation of the winding course, but basically suggest that the route kept close to surface level, where communication with the surface would be easier.

On the question of dating, the survey arrived at some surprising conclusions. Secondary materials were encountered in the tunnel which allowed C14 analysis, and stalactites formed by water dripping into the tunnel offered the possibility of some kind of calculation, based on the rate of growth. The researchers furthermore distinguished four different kinds of plaster, interpreted as successive, and therefore showing that the tunnel was maintained over time. Some plaster between the spring and Warren's Shaft was dated to the Mamluk period (thirteenth–fifteenth century). Analysing wood fragments in the most ancient plaster, the authors calculate from C14 a date of 822–796 for the wood and two ranges of 790–760 and 690–540 for a short-lived plant (unspecified). Thorium and Uranium isotope (Th-U) tests on some stalactites were conducted at the Open University in the UK and gave dates of c. 2500 BP. The authors conclude with the calculation of a date of "c. 700 BCE or slightly earlier" for the tunnel, which coincides very precisely (suspiciously so?) with the date of Sennacherib's siege of Jerusalem. The range and precision of this analysis seems impressive and unassailable, and few historians are competent to evaluate the data or the reasoning.

The non-specialist can nevertheless produce a number of qualifications. First: C14 dates are not as precisely reliable as the authors suggest, and also C14 dates furnish a *terminus a quo* and do not give a close range for the construction itself: materials in plaster may have existed elsewhere before being mixed into the plaster. Second: the results of the thorium analysis have been "recalibrated" to two centuries earlier. The crude date is actually 500 BCE for the beginning of their formation. Third: the stalactite analysis also assumes a steady rate of accumulation, and of course also depends on the accuracy of the calculation of the baseline average. Fourth: it is now standard practice to use more than one laboratory for testing: results from a single source are usually not acceptable. Fifth: the tunnel between Warren's Shaft and the Gihon Spring is probably not part of Tunnel VIII and its evidence is not relevant. The conclusions regarding the use of karstic shafts and the explanation of the course of the tunnel are of course hypothetical. Finally, it may be observed that the margin of error, which the researchers have somewhat minimized to the required date, does not rule out the reign of Manasseh, and so the conclusion that the tunnel is Hezekiah's does not actually follow from the analysis.[31]

The reign of Manasseh is, in fact, the time proposed by the authors of another study,[32] who revert to the theory that the tunnel follows existing karstic cavities and runs close to the groundwater table. Their analysis of the time required to construct the tunnel (even using existing cavities) also leads them to reject the notion that Hezekiah could have completed it in time for the expected arrival of Sennacherib, and consequently they prefer the reign of Manasseh. Shimron and Frumkin have duly responded,[33] reasserting their arguments. As we have pointed out, the reign of Manasseh would fit in either case. But can other periods be definitively ruled out?

Paleography

Can the inscription deliver a certainty that other methods cannot? The only picture of it *in situ* was taken by Clermont-Ganneau in 1888, which also shows an area above it prepared apparently for further inscription. The writing begins only halfway down the panel. And even when it stood above the waterline, was it not more conspicuously displayed, if the contents were for public information: or were they for more private consumption?[34]

That the text of the inscription itself is intrinsically odd has often been remarked. Altmann's recent survey of possible genres[35] makes it clear that it does not conform to the epigraphic style of any other Iron Age document. No author is given, no king named, no deity thanked, no date provided. Several interpreters have noted that the style reflects biblical prose; and the beginning of the text is an odd commencement, without any kind of preamble. In addition, the first discoverers of the inscription actually found what they described as a "graffito" consisting of 27 large letters inscribed above the Hebrew text, apparently in Greek.[36] This was, apparently, impossible to read, but was assumed to be the names of recent visitors to the tunnel on account of the date 1843 which was also thought to be carved there (which would have been five years after the discovery of the tunnel but well before the discovery of the inscription). The evidence was removed when the inscription was cut out.

But it is the script that provides the crucial element. Nearly every opinion now dates it to the eighth or seventh century BCE, a dating which has long served as a basis for the dating of other inscriptions. First impressions, as we related earlier, were very different. Rogerson and I have been criticized for citing the opinions of earlier paleographers[37] but the scripts have not differed and the existence of many more Iron Age inscriptions does not really affect the comparison to a high degree. More importantly, apart from the non-lapidary forms of the Qumran paleo-Hebrew manuscripts, hardly anything of this alphabet from the Hasmonean era is extant. The best comparison is with coins, despite the limited range of letter forms.

In any case, the argument is not about an Iron Age script versus a second-century script, as if there were an evolution from one to the other. The Hasmonean script seems to have been based on the revival of older forms. Hanan Eshel was wrong when he stated[38] that "paleography can tell us with certainty that the inscription was not written in the second century BCE, as Rogerson and Davies strongly suggest." Such an assertion depends on knowledge, not of Iron Age forms, but of Hasmonean forms. In the same article, Cross commented that while we cited the study of Hasmonean and Roman Paleo-Hebrew scripts by McLean,[39] we did not take into account his conclusions. He then speaks of the "evolution" of the characters, presumably meaning during this period. But this is not the issue: the issue is whether or not it evolved between being generally replaced with the square script from the sixth century onwards, and its reuse under the Hasmoneans. For this to occur an occasional limited use is not sufficient: what is needed is regular practice.

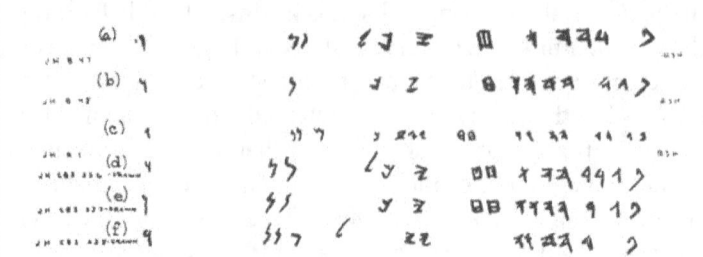

Figure 4. Coin scripts of Hyrcanus I.[40]

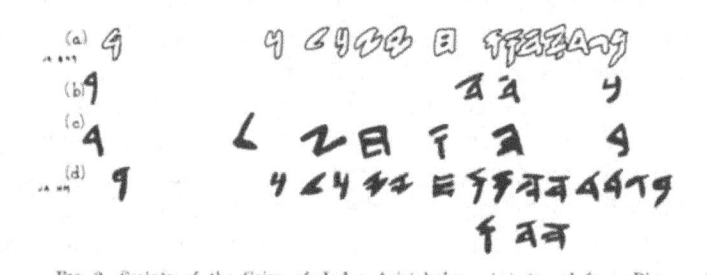

Figure 5. Coin scripts of Aristobulus.[41]

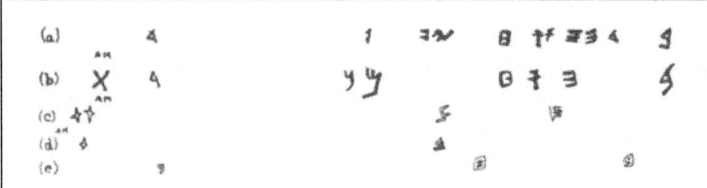

Figure 6. Coin scripts of Antigonus Mattathias.[42]

Given the lack of sufficient evidence to prove the case either way, the study by Hanson of Hasmonean coins[43] showed that on the coinage of John Hyrcanus (Fig. 4) the majority of letters closely resemble seventh- and sixth-century forms, but with *bet*, *he*, *waw*, *yod* and *kaph* showing some differences. On the coins of Aristobulus, however (Fig. 5), there is actually a closer resemblance to even earlier forms, while the Mattathias coins (Fig. 6) look almost like *imitations* of earlier forms still, from the seventh- and six-century forms. The Qumran Paleo-Hebrew manuscripts are, according to Hanson, derived largely from Hasmonean coin scripts, though it can be observed that in some cases they are closer even than the coin scripts to Late Iron Age forms. For example, the *kaph*, unlike the coins, has the three-pronged head; the *bet* has the closed loop and leg; the *waw* is not simplified and shortened, and the *yod* is less distinctive.[44]

Hanson's conclusions throughout, however, are that not only is there an evolution within the Hasmonean/Qumran scripts, there is also evolution between the seventh-/sixth-century scripts, from which he infers a continued use of the alphabet. But it seems to me, without at all challenging Hanson's analysis of the letter forms, that a sequence is not an evolution, and that the number of instances where later coins have letter forms that more closely resemble Iron Age forms than earlier coins may suggest that "sequence" is sometimes a more accurate word than "evolution." In cases where every instance of a letter form differs from any Iron Age exemplar (very few), it does not follow that there has been any lengthy evolution of several centuries, nor a continued use of the script (indeed, the differences in that case might have been greater). Another evaluation of the letter forms from a different perspective than Hanson's (which seems to have been influenced by Cross) might not deliver such a confident verdict.

Thus, we remain convinced that it is not always possible to prove on the basis of paleographic analysis alone whether a text in Paleo-Hebrew dates from, say, the eighth–seventh centuries, or is Hasmonean or later.[45] To assert that a script is clearly Iron Age (whether ninth, eighth or seventh century) is not, in our view, to assert that it may not appear in the second century. We may now also ask: Can paleographers, as Eshel claimed, really date these scripts to within 50 years? If so, then they must all reject the dates proposed by Reich and Shukron.[46] It will be interesting to see if any other paleographers now feel that their precise sequence can be shifted by a century (or more).

Lessons

The aim of this essay is not to argue again for Hasmonean dating, which, given the intensity of research on the tunnel, may indeed prove to be impossible. It is rather a modest foray into the sociology of knowledge, of the way overconfidence in one's methods and conclusion can lead to error, and to the way in which hypotheses are sometimes supported by introducing more hypotheses. The only substantive conclusion that I can offer regarding the origin of the tunnel is that we actually do not know who had it built, or when, or why, but that Hezekiah is a poor candidate. We have just discovered something most of us thought we knew but did not. On paleography, which may not be at all decisive for the final verdict (if there is one), I have perhaps been unduly influenced by an equally incorrect reliance upon Cross's famous typology of Qumran scripts, which created a precise (25-year span) chronology. But that depended on the manuscripts emanating from a single school, and also ignored the mechanisms by which the writing of scripts was learned. The chronology is nevertheless still routinely observed. I therefore remain sceptical of the way in which typology is applied (the typology itself is secure enough: anyone can compare shapes), and I suspect that "pseudo-scholarship" may more justly be applied to it.[47] There are also grounds, which I have given, for doubting that either geology or archaeology can be relied on uniquely to determine the facts, at least as of now. Yet, I entertain a nagging doubt whether Hezekiah will be, as Shanks says, "dislodged" from the tunnel that is very probably not his. Where the biblical past is concerned, scholarship does not often win out, and we make it worse for ourselves when we begin with assumed facts rather than prioritizing data and keeping an open mind.

Notes

1. J. W. Rogerson and P. R. Davies, "Was the Siloam Tunnel Built by Hezekiah?," *Biblical Archaeologist* 59 (1996), pp. 138–49.

2. D. Ussishkin, "The Original Length of the Siloam Tunnel," *Levant* 8 (1976), pp. 82–95.

3. R. S. Hendel, "The Date of the Siloam Inscription: A Rejoinder to Rogerson and Davies," *Biblical Archaeologist* 59 (1996), pp. 233–37.

4. Hendel, "The Date of the Siloam Inscription," pp. 236–36.

5. To illustrate the depth of commitment to the old consensus, despite recent modifications in the archaeological data, Rochell Altmann could write as recently as 2007: "most questions with regard to the Siloam Tunnel have been resolved" (R. I. Altmann, "Some Notes on Inscriptional Genres and the Siloam Tunnel Inscription," *Antiguo Oriente* 5 [2007], p. 35).

6. S. Norin, "The Age of Siloam Inscription and Hezekiah's Tunnel," *VT* 48 (1998), pp. 37–48.

7. H. Shanks, "Will King Hezekiah Be Dislodged from His Tunnel?," *BAR* 39 (2013), pp. 52–61 (53).

8. Shanks, "Will King Hezekiah Be Dislodged?," p. 53.

9. E. Robinson, *Biblical Researches in Palestine*, I (Boston: Crocker & Brewster, 1838), pp. 337–38, commented that the "subterranean passage" is first mentioned in about 1625, with a possible earlier reference to the tunnel in 1509. He notes that careful observers such as Monconys (1677), Doubdan, le Brun and Maundrell (1757) described "fountains" but said nothing about the tunnel.

10. See P. R. Davies, "King Solomon's Mines: Birth of a Legend," *Palestine Exploration Quarterly* 145 (2013), pp. 87–88.

11. See R. Weill, *La Cité de David: Compte-rendu des fouilles executes, a Jérusalem, sur le site de la ville primitive: Campagne de 1923–1924* (2 vols.; Paris: Geuthner, 1947).

12. An argument elaborated by A. Faust, "A Note on Hezekiah's Tunnel and the Siloam Inscription," *JSOT* 90 (2000), pp. 3–11.

13. R. Reich and E. Shukron, "The System of Rock-cut Tunnels Near Gihon in Jerusalem, Reconsidered," *RB* 107 (2000), pp. 5–17; "The Excavations at the Gihon Spring and Warren's Shaft System in the City of David," in H. Geva (ed.), *Ancient Jerusalem Revealed, Reprinted and Expanded Edition* (Jerusalem: Israel Exploration Society, 2000), pp. 327–39; "Reconsidering the Karstic Theory as an Explanation for the Cutting of Hezekiah's Tunnel in Jerusalem," *BASOR* 325 (2002), pp. 75–80; "Channel II in the City of David, Jerusalem: Some of Its Technical Features and Their Chronology," in C. Ohlig, Y. Peleg, and T. Tsuk (eds.), *Cura Aquarum in Israel, Proceedings of the 11th International Conference on the History of Water Management and Hydraulic Engineering in the Mediterranean Region, Israel, May 2001* (DWhG 1; Siegburg: Deutschen Wasserhistorischen Gesellschaft, 2002), pp. 1–6; "The History of the Gihon Spring in Jerusalem," *Levant* 36 (2004), pp. 211–23; "The Siloam Pool in the Wake of Recent Discoveries," *New Jerusalem Studies* 11 (2005), pp. 137–40 (Hebrew); "On the Original Length of Hezekiah's Tunnel: Some Critical Notes on David Ussishkin's Suggestions," in A. Maeir and P. Miroschedji (eds.), *"I Will Speak the Riddle of Ancient Times": Archaeological and Historical Studies in Honor of Amihai Mazar on the Occasion of His Sixtieth Birthday* (Winona Lake: Eisenbrauns, 2006), pp. 795–800; "Some New Insights and Notes on the Cutting of the Siloam Tunnel, in City of David," *Studies of Ancient Jerusalem* 2 (2007), pp. 133–61 (Hebrew); "A New Segment of the Middle Bronze Fortification in the City of David," *Tel Aviv* 37 (2010), pp. 141–53; "The Date of the Siloam Tunnel Reconsidered," *Tel Aviv* 38 (2011), pp. 147–57.

14. Reich and Shukron, "The History of the Gihon Spring in Jerusalem."

15. According to E. W. Cohn, *New Ideas About Jerusalem's Topography* (Jerusalem: Franciscan Printing Press, 1987), p. 11, E. G. Masterman had followed the course for 54 metres before traces disappeared.

16. A. De Groot and A. Fadida, "The Pottery Assemblage from the Rock-Cut Pool Near the Gihon Spring," *Tel Aviv* 38 (2011), pp. 158–66.

17. This is more or less Shanks's own suggestion: H. Shanks, "Will King Hezekiah Be Dislodged from His Tunnel?," *BAR* 39 (2013), pp. 52–61, 73.

18. Sh. Guil, "Description and Proposed New Dating of the Various Components of the Siloam Water System," online: http://www.academia.edu/3008768/A_New_Perspective_on_the_Various_Components_of_the_Siloam_Water_System_in_Jerusalem (2012).

19. Sh. Guil has challenged the common opinion of the late eighth-century *aleph* and in fact supports our proposal of a Hasmonean date: 'Identifying the Form of the Formal Hebrew Aleph Prevalent During the Times of King Hezekiah', online: http://www.academia.edu/3838604/Identifying_the_Form_of_the_Formal_Hebrew_Aleph_Prevalent_During_the_Times_of_King_Hezekiah.

20. N. Avigad, *Discovering Jerusalem* (Nashville, TN: Nelson, 1983), pp. 55–56.

21. Y. Shiloh, *Excavations at the City of David*. I. *1978–1982: Interim Report of the First Five Seasons* (Qedem 19; Jerusalem: Hebrew University, 1984), pp. 25 and 35 n. 16.

22. H. Geva, *Ancient Jerusalem Revealed* (Jerusalem: Israel Exploration Society, 1994), p. 6.

23. Shiloh, *Excavations ai the City of David*, p. 23.

24. Avigad, *Discovering Jerusalem*, p. 60.

25. This thesis has been most vigorously advanced by I. Finkelstein. See especially his "Temple and Dynasty: Hezekiah, the Remaking of Judah and the Rise of the Pan-Israelite Ideology," *JSOT* 30 (2006), pp. 259–85, based on the population decline in southern Ephraim at this time.

26. 2 Chronicles 32:3–4: "He planned with his officers and his mighty men to stop the water of the springs that were outside the city; and they helped him. A great many people were gathered, and they stopped all the springs and the brook that flowed through the land, saying, 'Why should the kings of Assyria come and find much water?'" 2 Chronicles 32:30: "This same Hezekiah closed the upper outlet of the waters of Gihon and directed them down and west to the city of David. And Hezekiah prospered in all his works." Ben Sira 48:17 describes Hezekiah as "piercing the rock with iron" and "enclosing the pool with (or 'in') mountains."

27. One obvious example of this procedure is in 2 Sam 5:8, the story of the capture of Jerusalem, usually a possible reference to part of the Gihon water system (Warren's Shaft, for example), though from a text we cannot date. The episode cannot be taken as direct historical evidence of the existence of any structure at the time the text describes.

28. Note, for example, the exemplary encounters of the prophet Isaiah with Ahaz and the Assyrian commander in Isa 7:3 and 36:2 at the "upper pool" (Siloam?) and the reference in Isa 22:8.

29. For earlier work, see D. Gill, "How They Met: Geology Solves Mystery of Hezekiah's Tunnelers," *BAR* 20/4 (1994), pp. 20–33, 64.

30. A. Frumkin, A. Shimron and J. Rosenbaum, "Tunnel Engineering in the Iron Age: Geoarchaeology of the Siloam Tunnel, Jerusalem," *Journal of Archaeological Science* 33 (2005), pp. 227–37. See also the authors' letter in *Nature* 425/11 (2003), pp. 169–71.

31. Guil, "Description," pp. 48–49, has commented more fully, as follows: "1. It should be verified that the 'fine plant fragments that are extraordinarily well preserved' are not water plants which are known to give results of older dating when analysed by carbon dating process, given that we are relating to an area of the Gihon

spring. Research is done in this field by E. Boaretto of the Weizmann Institute, Israel. 2. The two carbon datings are 2620 ± 35 yr BP (do we need to supply '=Before Present'?) and 2505 ± 35 yr BP, obviously not identical. The thorium age 2,317 ± 18 yr, is terminus post quem. These dates do not lead to a neat conclusion that the 'Siloam Tunnel was most probably constructed in about 700 BC.' 3. Was the quantity of the organic material used sufficient for an effective carbon dating, having been extracted from plaster lining the tunnel? 4. Reich and Shukron claim ('The Date of the Siloam Tunnel Reconsidered,' *Tel Aviv* 38 [2011], pp. 147–57) that the northern section of the Siloam Tunnel was dug in the following sequence: Tunnel IV, Tunnel VI and Tunnel VIII. This would imply that carbon dating of the plaster in these tunnels should give similar results. 5. Frumkin et al. state that 'The ancient plaster is a very fine hydraulic lime plaster, composed of recarbonated lime (CaO) binder with a filler of soil, chips of marl, organic materials and bone fragments, as well as rare charcoal and ash.' Marl is lime-rich mud which contains variable amounts of clays and aragonite ($CaCO_3$). It is obvious that filler of soil, dug randomly from the ground, may contain organic material which is not contemporary to the manufacturing of the plaster. Such organic material may be of much earlier periods and may therefore give rise to wrong dating of the plaster."

32. A. Sneh, E. Shalev, and R. Weinberger, "The Why, How, and When of the Siloam Tunnel Reevaluated," *BASOR* 359 (2010), pp. 57–65.

33. A. E. Shimron and A. Frumki, "The Why, How, and When of the Siloam Tunnel Reevaluated: A Reply to Sneh, Weinberger, and Shalev," *BASOR* 364 (2011), pp. 53–60.

34. See K. D. Smelik, "A Literary Analysis of the Shiloah (Siloam) Inscription," in J. Aitken, K. J. Dell, and B. A. S. Mastin (eds.), *On Stone and Scroll: Essays in Honour of Graham Ivor Davies* (Berlin: de Gruyter, 2011), pp. 101–10.

35. R. I. Altmann, "Some Notes on Inscriptional Genres and the Siloam Tunnel Inscription," *Antiguo Orient* 5 (2007), pp. 35–88.

36. For information about the graffito, see A. H. Sayce in *The Athenaeum*, 7 February 1881: "Whether this is in any intelligible system of writing I cannot say; some of the letters look like cursive Greek, but at the beginning of two lines the Arabic ciphers 1843 seem to occur." See also H. Guthe, "Die Siloahinschrift," *ZDMG* 35 (1882), p. 729, who says that there are 27 large letters in Greek which, however, could not be read or understood by Antonin the Russian Archimandrate or Photius, Head of the Greek Seminary of the Monastery of the Cross.

37. Such as E. J. Pilcher, "The Date of the Siloam Inscription," *Proceedings of the SBA* (1897), pp.165–82.

38. *BAR* 1996.

39. D. M. McLean, "The Age of the Siloam Tunnel and Hezekiah's Tunnel," *VT* 48 (1998), pp. 37–48.

40. R. S. Hanson, "Paleo-Hebrew Script in the Hasmonean Age," *BASOR* 175 (1964), pp. 26–42 (27).

41. From Hanson, "Paleo-Hebrew Script in the Hasmonean Age," p. 30.

42. From Hanson, "Paleo-Hebrew Script in the Hasmonean Age," p. 32.

43. Hanson, "Paleo-Hebrew Script in the Hasmonean Age," cited by us, but not by the *BAR* contributors.

44. If the script of the Qumran manuscript 4QpaleoExod^m is compared with that of the Siloam Inscription, the similarities are impressive. With the exception of *tet* and *samekh*, which are not attested in the Siloam text, the only letters that are not very similar are *waw*, *yod* (where the 4Q *yod* has a hook on the tail, a feature which is, however, missing from the addition to the Qumran manuscript at Exod 11:8–12:2 and whose *yod* is very similar to that in the Siloam script), *kaph* (which, in any case, is quite singular), and *quph*. When Renz's typologies and parallels are studied (unfortunately, they omit seals and weights) there is not one single text that has as many similarities with the Siloam script as 4QpaleoExod^m.

45. This is illustrated, for example, by the white marble stone found in 1968 on Mount Ophel, whose fragmentary inscription was dated to the end of the eighth century by Mazar but in the Herodian period by Yadin, on the grounds of its similarities with Jewish coins. Renz's own view is that a definitive decision is difficult, *because all the letters also have pre-exilic parallels* [emphasis added]: J. Renz, "Die althebräische Inschriften," Part 1 of J. Renz and W. Röllig, *Handbuch der althebräischen Epigraphik* (Berlin: Wissenschaftliche Buchgesellschaft, 1995), I, p. 190.

46. In a private communication to me, Christopher Rollston has stated: "I have been wanting to write an article about their proposal. Suffice it to say that I do not consider their redating to be cogent. Based on the script, it's just too difficult to date the Siloam Tunnel that high. The script of Siloam fits nicely in the script typology of the late 8th or early 7th century…but not earlier."

47. Guil, "Identifying the Form," has challenged the common opinion of the late eighth-century aleph and in fact supports our proposal of a Hasmonean date.

HOSEA 2:2 AND THE DATING OF THE BOOK OF HOSEA*

Giovanni Deiana

It is generally believed that the book of Hosea preserved the prophet's original message thanks to his disciples, who are said to have sought refuge in the kingdom of the South after Assyria's capture of Samaria,[1] taking with them not only the manuscripts of Hosea's prophetic oracles but also a good part of his memoirs, which were later to be included both in the Pentateuch and in Deuteronomistic History.[2]

Of course, none failed to observe that the current text of Hosea provides a Judeo-centric vision of the prophecy, but this was seen as the result of a long-lasting philo-Judaic editing of the text to adapt the prophet's original message to the demands of the Judaic community of Jerusalem, for whom the book was ultimately intended.[3] For example, the promise to restore the Davidic dynasty (Hos 3:5) cannot have been well received by the public in the kingdom of Samaria, as it was precisely the conflict with the heirs of David that had led to the schism (1 Kgs 12:16–17). It is possible that Judas appropriated the religious heritage of the kingdom of the North, but this would probably have taken a certain length of time.[4]

Scholars believed that these changes and additions nevertheless would not have significantly altered the original content of the book, as it had already taken a form approaching its definitive one in the pre-exilic period.[5]

This reconstruction of the textual history of the book of Hosea was undermined in the 1990s by studies on the composition of the so-called "Book of the Twelve."[6] These studies' increasing influence led to a change in approaches to the texts of individual prophets. While traditionally, studies on minor prophets focused on individual books (formation, historical context, structure, and theological message), over the last years scholars have striven to look at the work of the twelve prophets as a whole.[7] By studying individual prophets comparatively, we realized that the Book of the Twelve is not a mere collation of texts, but the result of a long and complex editing that managed to weave a single final message into the traditional material making up the book. This message is spelled out in some of the themes in the Book of the Twelve.[8]

In other words, the attention of scholars has shifted from individual prophets to the work as a whole. Undoubtedly, the discovery at Qumran[9] of proof that the texts of the twelve prophets were written on a single scroll has forced scholars to look more closely into biblical and extra-biblical testimonies about the Book of the Twelve. In this regard, Sir 49:10, which mentions the bones of the twelve prophets, provides a fundamental chronological anchor: in the time of Sirach, around 180 BCE, the Twelve thus formed a single entity.[10] This is confirmed by Rabbinic tradition, which ascribes the composition of the Book of the Twelve to the members of the Great Assembly.[11] This new approach to the Book of the Twelve has also shed light on the editing process that led to the current literary complex of the so-called "Minor Prophets." This is presumed to have formed gradually. Initially, it is argued, Hosea's text was joined with that of Amos, and this material was subsequently merged with the writings traditionally ascribed to Micah and Zephaniah.[12] This editing work is believed to carry the unmistakable stamp of the *deuteronomistic*[13] school, which flourished in the exilic period.[14]

Of course, not all scholars have found this reconstruction convincing.[15] One of the most sceptical is undoubtedly Ben Zvi.[16] It is his opinion that the material traditionally ascribed to individual prophets was actually continually revised, and that this is true not only of the minor prophets but also of Isaiah, Jeremiah and Ezekiel. The existence of this editing practice – broadly applied to the Old Testament – however, does not in itself lend credibility to the hypothesis that the Minor Prophets were a self-standing unit. In other terms, textual tradition suggests that the collection of the *Nebi'im* was composed, not of four literary blocks – Isaiah, Jeremiah, Ezekiel and the Book of the Twelve – but rather of a group of fifteen prophetic books regarded as "authoritative" in the Judaic religious milieu.[17] Although Ben Zvi[18] admits that Nogalski's hypothesis is stimulating, he thinks it implausible that the Twelve Prophets formed a single unit.[19] As to the composition of Hosea, Ben Zvi argues that it was written by men of letters for other men of letters, certainly at a time when the monarchy was a thing of the past.[20] According to this eminent scholar, the strongest argument for a composition of the Hosean text in the post-exilic period is the theme of exile itself, which is prominent throughout the text. This makes the Persian period the most likely historical background for this work.[21] In fact, the Qumran testimonies relative to the prophetic texts have suggested to some scholars that these texts were still in a fluid state not only during the Persian period, but even as late as the Hellenistic period.[22]

In the light of these data, it appears unlikely that the text of the Minor Prophets as a whole did not itself undergo in-depth revision, which may also have eventually taken the form of homogenizing editing work. Unfortunately, comparative analysis across the whole Book of the Twelve is still at an early stage. We consequently lack objective data allowing us to state with absolute certitude that the individual prophetic texts were actually modified to produce a final unified *version*. However, considering the frequent revisions undergone by the other books of the Old Testament, we can presume that the Book of the Twelve was not spared this thorough editing.

As to Hosea's text, it is generally believed to have been constantly updated until the version handed down by the Hebrew Bible, where one can easily detect traces of editing by the sapiential school (Hos 14:10).[23]

My aim of course is not to solve the dilemma of whether the Book of the Twelve was simply collated by juxtaposing the individual booklets or was the result of an editing work whereby the original message of each prophet was radically reinterpreted. More modestly, also in consideration of space limits, I will try to draw from my examination of Hos 2:2 some elements that may contribute to shed light on the historical context of the composition of the verse and the pericope in which it is included.

The verse appears in a block of text containing a consistent message, whose aim is in essence to communicate to the reader the hope that the punishments announced in Hos 1:2–9 will be cancelled.

Here is the translation of the text:

> (Hos. 2:1) And the number of the children of Israel will be like the sand of the sea, which will not be measured or counted, and it will come to pass that instead of it being said to them "You (are) not my people" one shall call them "Sons of the living God."
>
> (2:2) And the children of Judah and the children of Israel will be gathered [or "will gather"][24] together and will appoint for themselves a single leader and go up from the land,[25] for great will be the day of Jezreel.
>
> (2:3) Say [pl.] to your brothers "my people" and to your sisters "*ruḥāmāh*."

So Hos 2:2 is part of the pericope composed of vv. 1–3, which most scholars view as an interpolation that interferes with the literary continuity of the text;[26] this is why the Greek version of the LXX places the pericope in the first chapter, while MT places it in the second.

Since the passage has already been painstakingly analysed, it is not necessary to go over exegetical data that are already well established.[27] I will dwell, instead, on elements providing some clues about the historical milieu in which the text was composed.

The first of these elements is the phrase "*the number of the children of Israel*" in v. 1. Here the word "Israel" does not designate the kingdom of the North ruled by Jeroboam, as in 1:1, but a political entity resulting from the merging of the two kingdoms, as will be mentioned in Hos 2:2. This new kingdom is to witness a phenomenal demographic growth fulfilling the promise God made to the patriarchs: the exact same phrase "like the sand of the sea" occurs indeed in Gen 41:49 and Isa 10:22. Elsewhere it occurs in different, slightly longer phrasing, "like the sand of the *shore* of the sea" (Gen 22:17; 1 Sam 13:5; 1 Kgs 5:9) or "like the sand that is along the sea" (2 Sam 17:11; 1 Kgs 4:20).[28]

Since biblical texts usually reflect the historical period of their writing,[29] is it possible to single out a period when such a prodigious demographic growth actually occurred? Possibly, although with all the uncertainties arising from the subjectivity of the methods adopted by individual scholars understood. We owe it to archaeology that today we have some hope of reconstructing the demography of Palestine for its whole historical period. Here we are concerned with the post-exilic period, since the prevalent opinion among scholars is that our pericope is from that period. Carter[30] was the first to study the demographic situation of Jerusalem in the Persian period. This scholar has calculated that its population remained stable at around 1250–1500 individuals throughout the period of Achaemenid rule, and that at that time the whole province of Judah had a population of about 20,000. Lipschits[31] estimates the population of Jerusalem at no more than 3,000, and that of Judah as a whole at 30,000. As we can see, these figures diverge, but we can nevertheless confidently state that during the Persian period there was no increase in the population either of Jerusalem or of the Judean province.[32] Finkelstein,[33] for his part, hypothesizes that Jerusalem had a population of 400–500, which would mean only 100 adult individuals! This scholar concludes that it is very doubtful that the historical and social context of the Persian and early Hellenistic periods could have spawned the elaborate literary works that literary critics usually ascribe to them.[34] The situation changed remarkably during the Hellenistic period. On the evidence of archaeological excavations,[35] it appears that economic conditions changed dramatically during this period compared to the previous Persian period. A consequence of the general improvement in economic prosperity was demographic expansion. It is around this time that Jerusalem reached the peak of its growth. The population grew from at most 1500[36] in the Persian period to 12,000 in the late Hellenistic period, and more precisely around 140 BCE, and in Judah as a whole from 20,000 to over 100,000.[37] In the religious centre of Mount

Gerizim, too, archaeological excavations have revealed extraordinary population growth, estimated at 10,000. If we are looking for a historical match to the promise of an Israel as numerous "as the sand of the sea," as announced in Hos 2:1, the middle Hellenistic period – that is, the first half of the second century BCE – would seem to be the most likely candidate.

In Hos 2:2 we find the promise that Judah and Israel will be united and that there will be a single leader (ושמו להם ראש אחד). This prophecy, too, may not be a mere wish but may actually reflect specific historical circumstances. There was indeed a period when the two peoples, the Samaritans and the Jews, adopted the same name of Israel. Evidence in this regard is offered by two inscriptions from Delos mentioning "Israelites giving a contribution for the sanctuary of Argarizein."[38] Since the temple of Mount Gerizim had a well-established cultic tradition going as far back as the mid-fifth century BCE, scholars agree in identifying the donors as members of a colony of Samaritans residing in Delos[39] who periodically contributed to the cult with offerings. It is important that they consider themselves to be Israelites, that is, the cultural heirs of the kingdom of Israel. But it is also important that the inhabitants of Judah, too, call themselves Israelites. 1 Maccabees 3:15, 41; 7:9, 13, 23 are eloquent testimonies in this regard. But it is 2 Macc 5:22–23 that states without a shadow of a doubt that Samaritans and Judeans regarded themselves as a single people: "He left overseers to oppress the lineage (*to genos*): in Jerusalem, Philip, a Phrygian by origin, but more barbaric in his ways than those who had appointed him to his office, and Andrónicus on the Gerizím; and besides them Menelaus, who was haughty more than the others with his fellow citizens, as he nourished a declared hostility against the Judeans."

The text of 2 Macc 5:22, after describing the predatory politics of Antiochus IV (see v. 21), designates both the inhabitants of Jerusalem and those of Mount Gerizim as *to genos*, "the lineage." Thus, in this period there is no separation between those who were later to be called Samaritans and Judeans. They are of the same stock. The excavations of Mount Gerizim confirm this.[40] It is well known that Antiochus III, after his victory at Panion in 200 BCE, with the decisive aid of the Judeans, granted tax privileges to the city of Jerusalem and also financed the restoration of the temple of Jerusalem (*Ant.* 12.138–144). Excavations by Magen revealed that the temple on Mount Gerizim was significantly renovated at the same time as the temple of Jerusalem, and that this is when the settlement reached the peak of its growth. According to Dušek, the archaeological evidence "indicates that the edict of Jerusalem was also applied to Samaria."[41] This somehow suggests two possibilities: that the Samaritans participated in the assistance offered by Antiochus III, and hence that Samaria, too, benefited from Antiochus' gratitude; or that the Seleucids did not regard Samaria and Jerusalem as two distinct ethnic entities, but as a single *ethnos*, since both worshiped the same deity and had the same Torah.[42] Dušek deems this second hypothesis "more probable."[43] The fact that the inhabitants of Samaria and Jerusalem both worshipped Yhwh led the Seleucid administration to regard these two religious groups as parts of a single "Israel."[44]

The rift between the Samaritans and the Judeans certainly came about only with the destruction of the temple on Mount Gerizim by John Hyrcanus (111–110 BCE).[45] Before that event, all the evidence indicates that there was a distinction between the two groups, but no conflict.[46] Recent studies on the composition of the Samaritan Pentateuch point in the same direction. According to Pummer,[47] this was the period when the Judeans and Samaritans shared the Pentateuch. This was allegedly composed by the literary elite of the two communities, merging a textual tradition that had long been handed down in the religious centers of the two groups, Bethel and Jerusalem. In the light of studies on the Qumran texts, the argument that the Samaritans received the Pentateuch from Jerusalem does not hold water. "Everything suggests that the inhabitants of the kingdom of the north did not passively and suddenly accept the Pentateuch of the Judeans, but actively contributed to its composition."[48] Today it is generally believed that the Samaritan Pentateuch was derived from a text that circulated in Palestine and was shared by all the worshipers of Yhwh, whether from Gerizim or Jerusalem. This obviously implies that the Yahwist communities had long shared the same religious heritage that was later codified in the Pentateuch.[49]

The papyri of Elephantine, from the fifth century BCE, also bear witness to certainly not conflictive relations between Jerusalem and Samaria. As is well known, the Egyptian Judaic community was the victim of a violent attack by the local population, which resulted, among other things, in the destruction of the temple dedicated to Yahô. The community turned both to the governor of Judea (Bagôhî) and to Dalayah and Šelemiah, the sons of Sin'uballit, governor of Samaria, to obtain permission to rebuild the temple.[50] The answer of both Bagôhî and Dalayah is preserved in a letter authorizing the community to rebuild the temple "as it had been previously" so that traditional worship could be resumed in it.[51] Although the details are not totally clear, it is evident that at the end of the fifth century BCE there was no conflict between Samaria and Jerusalem.

On the other hand, the existence of two distinct authorities for Samaria and Jerusalem, respectively, clearly indicates that there was a separation between the two groups, at least in political terms, and an agreement on religious matters whose details are not known to us.

Conclusion

Recent studies on the book of Hosea, especially as part of the Book of the Twelve, suggest that its final version was put together not during the pre-exilic period, but sometime within the first half of the second century BCE. This is the period when the Samaritans and the Jews formed a single *genos* or "lineage" (2 Macc 5:21). Within this lineage, the conditions arose for the composition of a shared religious text, the Pentateuch, which was to become the synthesis of the shared religious heritage of the Samaritans and the Jews even after the destruction of the temple of Mount Gerizim by John Hyrcanus.

Notes

* I am pleased to dedicate this investigation to Professor G. Garbini, who made the dating of biblical texts a recurrent theme in his research.

1. L. L. Grabbe, *Ancient Israel: What Do We Know and How Do We Know It?* (New York: T&T Clark International, 2007), pp. 149–50. There are several doubts regarding the capture of Samaria, including that of the identity of the Assyrian king responsible for it (Sargon II or Shalmaneser V) and whether the town was actually destroyed and its population deported.

2. J. Jeremias, *Der Prophet Hosea* (Göttingen: Vandenhoeck & Ruprecht, 1983), p. 18; H. W. Wolff, *Hosea* (Hermeneia; Philadelphia: Fortress, 1974), pp. 19–32.

3. Jeremias, *Der Prophet Hosea*, p. 13; Wolff, *Hosea*, p. 11; R. E. Wolfe, "The Editing of the Book of Twelve," *ZAW* 53 (1935), pp. 91–92.

4. N. P. Lemche, "Shechem Revisited: The Formation of Biblical Collective Memory," in J. L. Berquist and A. Hunt (eds.), *Focusing Biblical Studies: The Crucial Nature of the Persian and Hellenistic Periods: Essays in Honor of Douglas A. Knight* (London: T&T Clark International, 2012), pp. 46–47.

5. Jeremias, *Der Prophet Hosea*, p. 18.

6. Although this thesis was put forward after 1990, as early as 1935 Wolfe (*Hosea*, pp. 90–128) pointed out that the current corpus of the twelve prophets was obtained by merging individual prophecies collected in a single scroll. To my knowledge, in more recent times the first to draw attention to the unity of the Twelve Prophets was P. R. House, *The Unity of the Twelve* (JSOTSup 97; Sheffield: Sheffield Academic, 1990).

7. J. Nogalski, *Literary Precursors to the Book of the Twelve* (BZAW 217; Berlin: de Gruyter, 1993); *Redactional Processes in the Book of the Twelve* (BZAW 218; Berlin: de Gruyter, 1993); "Un et douze livres: la nature du processus rédactionnel et les implications de la présence de matériau cultuel dans le Livre des XII

Petits Prophètes," in J.-D. Macchi at al. (eds.), *Les recueils prophétiques de la Bible: Origines, milieux, et contexte proche-oriental* (Genève: Labor et Fides, 2012), pp. 361–86.

8. See J. Wöhrle, "So Many Cross-References! Methodological Reflections on the Problem of Intertextual Relationships and Their Significance for Redaction Critical Analysis," in J. D. R. Albertz, J. D. Nogalski, and J. Wöhrle (eds.), *Perspectives on the Formation of the Book of the Twelve: Methodological Foundations – Redactional Processes – Historical Insights* (Berlin: de Gruyter, 2012), pp. 3–20.

9. R. E. Fuller, "Hebrew & Greek Biblical Manuscripts: Their Interpretations & Their Interpreters," in A. Lange et al. (eds.), *The Dead Sea Scrolls in Context: Integrating the Dead Sea Scrolls in the Study of Ancient Texts, Languages, and Cultures*, I (Leiden: Brill, 2010–11), pp. 101–10.

10. See R. E. Garton, "Rattling the Bones of the Twelve: Wilderness Reflections in the Formation of the Book of the Twelve," in Albertz, Nogalski, and Wöhrle (eds.), *Perspectives*, pp. 237–52 (237).

11. *Baba Bathra* 14b: "The Men of Great Assembly wrote…the Twelve (אנשי שנים עשר...כתבו הגדולה כנסת); on this text, see I. Epstein (ed.), *Baba Bathra*, I (London: Soncino, 1976), *ad. loc.*; on the Great Assembly, see M. Leuchter, "The Book of the Twelve and 'The Great Assembly' in History and Tradition," in Albertz, Nogalski, and Wöhrle (eds.), *Perspectives*, pp. 336–52: since Ezekiel and Daniel are also ascribed to the Great Assembly, in addition to the twelve prophets (p. 338), we should presumably place the editorial activity of the Great Assembly in the late Persian period and the Hellenistic period (pp. 348–49).

12. J. Nogalski, *Redactional Processes in the Book of the Twelve* (BZAW 218; Berlin: de Gruyter, 1993), p. 274.

13. Nogalski, "Un et douze livres," p. 363; Wöhrle, "So Many Cross-References!," p. 4.

14. Nogalski, "Un et douze livres," p. 363; Wöhrle, "So Many Cross-References!," p. 3.

15. On this subject, see the position of J. Day, "Hosea and the Baal Cult," in J. Day (ed.), *Prophecy and the Prophets in Ancient Israel* (London: T&T Clark International, 2010), p. 222.

16. E. Ben Zvi, "L'hypothèse d'un Livre des Douze est-elle possible du point de vue des lecteurs anciens?," in Macchi et al. (eds.), *Les recueils prophétiques*, pp. 387–423.

17. Ben Zvi, "L'hypothèse d'un Livre des Douze," p. 391.

18. E. Ben Zvi, *Hosea* (The Forms of the Old Testament Literature; Grand Rapids: Eerdmans, 2005), pp. 13–14.

19. Ben Zvi, "L'hypothèse d'un Livre des Douze," p. 391.

20. Ben Zvi, *Hosea*, p. 13.

21. Ben Zvi, *Hosea*, pp. 14–15.

22. J. D. Macchi and T. Römer, "La formation des livres prophétiques: enjeux et débats," in Macchi et al. (eds.), *Les recueils prophétiques*, pp. 21–25.

23. A. A. Macintosh, *A Critical and Exegetical Commentary on Hosea* (Edinburgh: T. & T. Clark, 1997), pp. 582–83.

24. This is a Niphal perfect of *qābaṣ*, "gather," preceded by an inversive *waw*. It could be literally translated either with a reflexive form ("they will gather") or a passive one ("they will be gathered"). The LXX *synachthēsontai*, passive future third person plural, opts for the passive voice in spite of the fact that *agō* has the middle voice (*axomai*). See also the Vg (*congregabuntur*).

25. The expression is a *crux interpretum* that has still not found a generally accepted solution. It can be regarded as an allusion to the exodus, or, if ארץ actually means "netherworld," an allusion to a possible resurrection. The latter possibility is especially intriguing, considering the close relationship between Hos 2:2 and Ezek 37:22, which both announce the merging of the two peoples and their rule by a single king. The scene of the dry bones pictured in Ezek 37 casts the revival of Israel as a resurrection. On this subject, see Macintosh, *Hosea*, pp. 31–32.

26. D. Stuart, *Hosea – Jonah* (Waco: Word Books, 1987), pp. 36–37.

27. Macintosh, *A Critical and Exegetical Commentary*, pp. 30–38.

28. For a longer list, see Stuart, *Hosea – Jonah*, p. 38.

29. Ch. Levin, *The Old Testament: A Brief Introduction* (Princeton: University Press, 2005), pp. 129–33, who proposes the post-exilic polemic between the Judeans and the Samaritans as the historical background of the book of Hosea.

30. C. E. Carter, *The Emergence of Yehud in the Persian Period: A Social and Demographic Study* (JSOTSup 294; Sheffield: Sheffield Academic, 1999), pp. 200–201.

31. O. Lipschits, "Changes in Judah Between the Seventh and the Fifth Centuries B.C.E.," in O. Lipschits and J. Blenkinsopp, *Judah and Judeans in the New Babylonian Period* (Winona Lake: Eisenbrauns, 2003), pp. 323–76.

32. Lipschits, "Changes in Judah," pp. 332–33.

33. I. Finkelstein, "Jerusalem in the Persian (and Early Hellenistic) Period and the Wall of Nehemiah," *JSOT* 32 (2008), pp. 501–520, especially p. 507.

34. Finkelstein, "Jerusalem in the Persian (and Early Hellenistic) Period," p. 514.

35. I. Finkelstein, "The Territorial Extent and Demography of Yehud/Judea in the Persian and Early Hellenistic Periods," *RB* 117 (2010), pp. 49–50: while in the Persian period Judea had 88 towns with an urbanized surface of 47 hectares, corresponding to a population of about 10,000, in the Hellenistic period it had 203 towns, an urbanized surface of 232 hectares, and a population of 47,000.

36. Finkelstein, "The Territorial Extent and Demography," p. 44, speaks of a few hundred people, while Carter, *The Emergence of Yehud*, p. 288, proposes a figure of 1500.

37. I. Finkelstein, "The Territorial Extent and Demography," pp. 39–54, especially p. 54. This scholar argues that the inhabited surface of Jerusalem expanded from 2–2.5 to 60 hectares. Assuming a density of 200 people per hectare, this would yield a population of 12,000. Finkelstein argues that the population of Judea underwent extraordinary growth, from 12,000–20,000 to over 100,000 (p. 52).

38. These inscriptions have been thoroughly studied and, small divergences in interpretation aside, their content is not in doubt. See P. Bruneau, "Les Israélites de Délos et la Juiverie Délienne," *Bulletin de correspondance hellénique* 106 (1982), p. 469; M. White, "The Delos Synagogue Revisited: Recent Fieldwork in the Graeco-Roman Diaspora," *HTR* 80 (1987), p. 141; J. Dušek, *Aramaic and Hebrew*

Inscriptions from Mt. Gerizim and Samaria Between Antiochus III and Antiochus IV Epiphanes (Culture and History of the Ancient Near East 54; Leiden: Brill, 2012), pp. 75–79.

39. P. Bruneau, "Les Israélites de Délos et la Juiverie Délienne," *Bulletin de correspondance hellénique* 106 (1982), pp. 465–504 (469); M. White, "The Delos Synagogue Revisited," p. 141; Dušek, *Aramaic and Hebrew Inscriptions*, pp. 75–79; A. K. de Hemmer Gudme, *Before the God in This Place for Good Remembrance: A Comparative Analysis of the Aramaic Votive Inscriptions from Mount Gerizim* (BZAW 441; Berlin: de Gruyter, 2013), p. 63.

40. Y. Magen, *Mount Gerizim Excavations.* II. *A Temple City* (Jerusalem: Staff Officer of Archaeology, 2008).

41. Dušek, *Aramaic and Hebrew Inscriptions*, p. 73.

42. Dušek, *Aramaic and Hebrew Inscriptions*, p. 73.

43. Dušek, *Aramaic and Hebrew Inscriptions*, p. 73.

44. Dušek, *Aramaic and Hebrew Inscriptions*, p. 73.

45. Magen, *Mount Gerizim Excavations*, p. 178.

46. The Samaritan papyri of Wadi Daliyeh have allowed the succession of governors of Samaria to be reconstructed with a good degree of accuracy. See J. Dušek, *Les manuscrits araméens du Wadi Daliyeh et la Samarie vers 450–332 av. J. C.* (Culture and History of the Ancient Near East 30; Leiden: Brill, 2007), pp. 516–49, especially pp. 548–49.

47. R. Pummer, "The Samaritans and Their Pentateuch," in G. N. Knoppers and B. M. Levinson (eds.), *The Pentateuch as Torah: New Models for Understanding Its Promulgation and Acceptance* (Winona Lake: Eisenbrauns, 2007), pp. 237–69 (263).

48. Pummer, "The Samaritans and Their Pentateuch," p. 264.

49. De Hemmer Gudme, *Before the God in This Place for Good Remembrance*, p. 62.

50. For the text, see B. Porten and A. Yardeni, *Textbook of Aramaic Documents from Ancient Egypt: Newly Copied, Edited and Translated into Hebrew and English*, I (Jerusalem: Hebrew University, 1986), A 4.8 (ll. 1.28)

51. Porten and Yardeni, *Textbook of Aramaic documents*, A 4.9.

BEYOND GARBINI'S ANTI-MOSAIC PENTATEUCH: NEHUSHTAN AS LITERARY TIE BETWEEN THE TORAH AND THE HISTORICAL BOOKS

Philippe Guillaume

As stated in the introduction of the English translation of Giovanni Garbini's *Storia e Ideologia nell'Israele Antico*, "in Italy it is possible to be a semitic scholar without being primarily a biblical scholar."[1] Freer than theologians in his approach to the Hebrew Scriptures, Garbini elaborated hypotheses that went against the current of Old Testament scholarship. For instance, Garbini concluded that the Pentateuch had been deeply remodeled centuries later than is commonly thought. Instead of a Hexateuch turned into a Pentateuch by shifting the conclusion from the settlement of Israel in Canaan to Moses' death, Garbini posited the replacement of an original Pentateuch into the present one through the amputation of the book of Joshua and its replacement by the book of Genesis. Even more striking, Garbini dated this process not long before the Pentateuch was translated into Greek. He was well aware that his view of "a whole Mosaic Pentateuch replaced by the end of the second century by the current one" was "sensational."[2] While many scholars would still consider sensational Garbini's claim that "the final redaction of the Pentateuch and the Septuagint almost coincide on a chronological level,"[3] the role of the Ptolemaic court and of Alexandrian scholars in the canonization of the Hebrew Bible is now getting greater attention.[4]

Decades before the scholarly mainstream, Garbini also opined that the Joshua–Judges–Samuel sequence in the historical books arose in the wake of the formation of the New Pentateuch, three centuries later than was postulated by Martin Noth. Garbini gave due weight to the books of Nehemiah's library listed in 2 Macc 2:13. Besides the books about kings, the prophets' books, David's books and letters of the kings about the offerings there is no mention of writings corresponding to the Pentateuch and to the book of Joshua.[5] As a "history of Moses, which extended to the conquest of Palestine and to its partition between the tribes would include all the contents of the Book of Joshua and would make superfluous a part of the Book of Judges," Garbini logically concluded that "the library of Nehemiah contained historiographical books only about kings, including perhaps also Abimelech and Gideon."[6]

The Chronology of the Hexateuch

Garbini's view of the very late insertion of the book of Genesis in front of the current Pentateuch as a replacement for the amputated book of Joshua produces problems of its own. For instance, it implies that the chronological framework that runs through the Torah was produced at the end of the process, after the insertion of Genesis since the chronology begins in Gen 1. But since the same chronology extends at least as far as Josh 5, it preserves the logical conclusion of the Exodus narrative with the settlement of Israel in the land, which belies the notion that the insertion of Genesis was meant to sever Joshua from the narrative of Israel's origins. Hence, I view the chronology as a strong indicator of the existence of a narrative which started in Genesis and closed with the settlement in Canaan, whether or not this represented a "Hexateuch." Yet, it would be possible to argue that the chronology is late by evoking the work of the Alexandrian chronographers. Jewish translators would have emulated their colleagues by anchoring their origins right back into the creation of the world. In this case, however, the fact that the Torah's chronology is based on the 364-day calendar rather than upon a calendar in use at Alexandria supports an earlier date for the chronological framework, in the Persian rather than in the Ptolemaic era.[7] Moreover, the presence of the story of Joseph at the end of the Torah hardly supports Garbini's characterization of Genesis as anti-Egyptian and the current Pentateuch as anti-Mosaic.[8]

Jerusalem or Rome?

A further difficulty is the silence over Jerusalem, not only in Genesis, but also in the entire Torah, which hardly matches the view of the current Pentateuch as the work of a Jerusalem hierocracy. Before Pss 76:3 and 110:2–4 equate Melchizedek's Salem (Gen 14:18) with Zion, there is no explicit relation between Abraham and Jerusalem in the Torah itself. The silence over Jerusalem does not support Garbini's understanding of the current Pentateuch as an anti-Egyptian work of the Jerusalem priesthood. Garbini draws a sharp contrast between "an economically prosperous, intellectually capricious" Egyptian Judaism and a Jerusalem hierocracy "shut up in a city which seemed to have lost all political authority... preoccupied with the internal quarrels which divided it...turned in on itself and within its own walls...thinking back on the tradition from which it was born, in Babylon."[9] The description of the Jerusalem priesthood of the time as "Pious priests, preoccupied with their modest economic privileges and their liturgical prerogatives" and who "no longer managed to think about the great problems of evil...evaded in an ambiguous sexual sphere"[10] may reflect more the Roman context in which Garbini worked than the Jerusalem hierocracy of the last centuries before the turn of the era.

Garbini's portrayal of Moses as "just anyone, the mere instrument of God, incapable even of speaking fluently...[someone who] was thought unworthy even to set foot in the Promised Land because he was Egyptian by birth"[11] is hard to reconcile with the place held by the figure of Moses in the minds of readers of the Hebrew Bible, a position second only to YHWH's.[12] While it seems likely that one of the functions of the motif of Moses' stutter is to prepare the introduction of Aaron and of the priesthood as official interpreters of the Mosaic corpus (Exod 4:14), this does little to set Jerusalem against Egypt. Moses still does most of the talking in the Exodus story, and preaches the entire book of Deuteronomy with no help from Aaron. As Aaron bears the same punishment as Moses, for the same unclear sin, and as the death of each brother is followed by the same forty days of mourning, the new ideal reflected in the current Pentateuch maintains the parity between Moses and Aaron, having the older Aaron (Exod 6:7) die before his younger brother (Deut 33:5). The stutter motif is soon forgotten and Moses remains the towering figure throughout the Torah. That Aaron as much as Moses is prevented from entering Canaan is hardly in favor of any priesthood.

Garbini's very late date for the formation of the Pentateuch as a recent version produced by the priestly class of Jerusalem in the second century BCE and soon translated into Greek remains very contentious and many would still find this date implausibly late.[13] Nevertheless, the role of Alexandria in the formation of the Bible is, I believe, one of Garbini's main contributions, especially if it applies to the Historical Books. For the formation of the historical collection as the sequel of Alexandria's Septuagint, the second century BCE is not such an implausible date. An argument can be built on Garbini's comments on the episode of Hezekiah's destruction of Moses' Nehushtan.

Nehushtan and the Social Memory of Moses

In 2 Kgs 18:4b Hezekiah destroys the *bamot* and *maṣṣebot*, the Asherah, and the brazen serpent which Moses had made:

וכתת נחש הנחשת אשר עשה משה כי עד הימים ההמה היו בני ישראל
מקטרים לו ויקרא לו נחשתן

> He crushed the serpentine serpent[14] which Moses had made because until these days they, the sons of Israel, were incensing it. He called it / it was called Nehushtan. (2 Kgs 18:4b)

Given Moses' standing in the Hebrew Bible, ascribing the making of the snake to Moses is highly significant, but it has stirred up scarce interest among biblical scholars. Chronicles ignores the Nehushtan entirely, as do some recent studies of Hezekiah.[15] A recent essay on the function of the report of Hezekiah's destructions rather than on the date of the reform or whether the serpent was an Egyptian or an Assyrian cultic object makes nothing out of this unique mention of Moses' serpent outside the Torah. Garbini is clearly an exception. In an article devoted to Moses' snake, Garbini had noted the similarity between Hezekiah's destruction of the fertility symbol and the disappearance of the uraeus in the Judaean glyptic of the eighth century BCE.[16] To the question of why Hezekiah destroyed the serpent, Garbini evokes iconoclasm motivated by a gradual change in the significance of the serpent. From the apotropaic symbol used on a specific occasion, Moses' serpent was assimilated to the widespread Canaanite fertility symbol. Later on, Garbini considered the solution he suggested in his article as no longer adequate.[17] As the historicity of Hezekiah's reform became increasingly dubious,[18] the focus shifted towards the significance of the crushing of the serpent. For Garbini, "an act like Hezekiah's would have been inconceivable in the Jerusalem of the second century BCE and it is not by chance that the Chronicler avoided mentioning it."[19]

Since consideration for Moses made it difficult to think that he made an object which pious Hezekiah would later treat in the same way as the abhorrent high places, the standing stones and the Asherah,[20] Garbini concludes that if "Hezekiah could break into pieces a liturgical vessel made by Moses himself, this means that Moses was far from having the assumed authority and charisma he has in later texts."[21]

The episode is a key element in Garbini's reconstruction of the formation of the Pentateuch, in particular in his characterization of the current Pentateuch as anti-Mosaic and anti-Egyptian. Since Chronicles stems clearly from Jerusalem, Garbini presumably assumes that the anti-Mosaic bias of the Jerusalem priesthood expressed in the Pentateuch had minimal effect on the Chronicler. If I understand him correctly, Garbini also seems to imply that the episode of Hezekiah's destruction of Moses' snake was produced *earlier* than the current Pentateuch, at a time when the figure of Moses bore even *less* charisma. While the notion of an anti-Mosaic Pentateuch is debatable, the report that Hezekiah had no consideration for a cultic object made by Moses deserves serious consideration. Such a statement is not innocent. There was no need to add Moses' serpent to the standard list of idolatrous cultic objects to display Hezekiah's piety and present him as Josiah's forerunner. Whoever added or retained Moses' serpent in the list had a good reason to do so. We shall never be in a position to read the writer's mind, but a few suggestions can be made as to what motivated such a statement.

First, the justification of Hezekiah's action argues against Garbini's inference that for the writer Moses did not bear the authority and charisma he has in other texts. The destruction of Moses' serpent is carefully justified by the offering of incense to the snake. The designation 'serpentine serpent' (נחש הנחשת) evokes the bronze out of which the snake was made as well as certain divinatory practices (נחש [Piel], 2 Kgs 17:17). These practices are banned by Lev 19:26; Deut 18:10.[22] The unease that may arise from the lack of consideration for Moses' craftsmanship is further countered by the attribution of the idolatrous offering of incense to the *bene Israel*. Hence, Hezekiah's destruction is carefully framed, so that it cannot be taken as inimical towards the memory of Moses. Rather, it demonstrates Hezekiah's thoroughness in extirpating every idolatrous manifestation even when it involved the annihilation of a precious relic such as the one handed down by the very writer of the Torah, the prototypical prophet, teacher and wonder-maker. Hence, the crushing of Nehushtan enhances Hezekiah's stature while making no dent in Moses'.

Second, that the blame for the destruction falls upon Israelites rather than on Judeans conveniently suggests that, before the punishment for the sin of Jeroboam fell upon them and they were deported by the Assyrians, some Israelites did travel to Jerusalem. To be sure, they went there for idolatrous practices, but at least they recognized the temple of Jerusalem as the only dwelling chosen by YHWH for his name.

Third, as Hezekiah does not grind (טחן) the snake as Moses did the Golden Calf (Exod 32:20), but crushes (כתת) it as Moses did in his own retelling of his destruction of the Calf in Deut 9:21,[23] it is not quite true that the destruction of the brazen snake is the only element in that episode that does not reflect 'stereotypical Deuteronomistic phraseology and concerns'.[24] The concern is the eradication of idolatry, while the phraseology comes from Deuteronomy, even though it is the only mention of Moses' snake outside the Torah. By naming the snake Nehushtan, the writer displays his intimate knowledge of the entire Torah by drawing upon a range of associations with the figure of Moses, the healing saraf of Num 21:9 and his answer to his father-in-law in Exod 18:14 in which he explains that through him the Israelites practised divination (דרש). The skillful scribe also hinted at the snake trick in Exod 4:3–4 where, instead of seizing (אחז) his staff turned snake as YHWH ordered, Moses gets hold (חזק) of it or hardens it, thus anticipating the name of the king who would crush Moses' serpent, Hezekiah (חזקיה).

Fourth, the crushing of Nehushtan turns Hezekiah into a second Moses. When Moses saw the Golden Calf, he did not hesitate to smash the tables of the law made by God himself (Exod 24:12; 31:18; 32:16). When he saw the Israelites venerate the brazen snake, Hezekiah did not hesitate to crush it although it had been made by Moses himself.

Fifth, the mention of Nehushtan presupposes that Moses' serpent had reached the temple and thus forges the missing link between Jerusalem and the Exodus. While Num 21 offers no hint that the bronze snake became a cultic object, 2 Kings bridges the gap between the wilderness and Hezekiah's reign. Stating that Nehushtan eventually reached the temple of Jerusalem made up for its absence from the list of desert relics stored in the ark, the facsimile of the tables of the law (Deut 10:5; 1 Kgs 8:9; 2 Chr 5:10) and the relics associated with Aaron: the omer of manna and the inscribed rod (Exod 16:33; Num 17:10). Somewhat paradoxically, the destruction of the snake results in its presence in the temple.

Finally, the destruction of Moses' serpent may constitute another trace of the notion of Moses' entry into the land. Garbini reads it as a reflection of traditions transmitted outside the Pentateuch, traditions that belonged to a "corpus" of normative writings ascribed to Moses: the "books of the law" and "books of the Covenant" (1 Macc 1:16–57), the "book of the Covenant" and the "Law of Moses" (Ben Sira 24:23).[25] As the mention of Hobab as Moses' father-in-law in Judg 1:16 and 4:11 is another echo of the tradition that presented "Moses as constructor of a prodigious metal talisman, since the Kenites were blacksmiths,"[26] Hezekiah's destruction of the talisman could well betray the writer's acquaintance with the notion reported by Hecataeus that Moses founded the Jerusalem cult (Diodorus Siculus XL.3).[27]

This writer ignored, willfully or not, the version of the death of Moses on Mount Nebo in Deut 34, a version that was made official by the Septuagint. The other versions never obtained similar status because they were not translated into Greek and thus did not enter the thriving intellectual scene of Hellenism. While I agree with Garbini that Genesis anchored the Moses–Exodus cycle in world history with a starting point at Creation, this does not mean that Genesis was placed as the introduction of the Pentateuch as late as the Ptolemaic period. The translation of the Pentateuch enabled the synchronization of Noah's flood with the flood narratives of Utnapishtim and Xisuthrus. In the process, the Hebrew date of the biblical flood was adjusted to fit other floods and some antediluvian lifespans were lengthened to connect Methuselah with the giants who survived the flood.[28] These alterations are duly transmitted in the Septuagint, but they entail minor changes compared with those Garbini postulates for the formation of the current Pentateuch. As I see it, the reshuffling of entire books occurred after rather than within the Pentateuch.

Before the Alexandrian chronographers could correlate the Pentateuch with Egyptian, Babylonian, Athenian and Argive material for the production of comprehensive world chronicles, they also needed chronological data to fill the gap between the death of Moses at the end of the Torah and biblical figures that could be synchronized with Assyrian and Egyptian chronologies. Hence the Jewish documents which, according to Demetrius of Phalerum, were missing to complete the Library of Alexandria (ἑτέροις ὀλίγοις, *Let. Aris.* §30) had to be supplied and translated. To prepare them for translation, the books were organized into a chronological sequence. The collection which the Hebrew Bible terms "Former Prophets" in reaction to the Greek historical books was formed in the wake of the translation of the Law.

The Alexandrian Historiography

The existence of the periodization of Israel's past as we know it cannot be proven before 200 BCE. It is only ca. 170 BCE that Ben Sira's Praise of the fathers (Ben Sira 44–49) names the title of each book of the *Nebi?im* in the canonical order. The transition between Torah and *Nebi?im* is marked by a hortatory blessing (45:26). The verses dedicated to Joshua (Sira 46:1–8, twice as long as for Moses) refer more to the book than to the figure of Joshua. Ben Sira upholds the Torah as the sum of Wisdom (Sira 24:23) while affirming that the Torah is not self-sufficient but should be studied in light of wisdom and prophets (Sira 39:1–3).[29] Ben Sira devotes much more space to the Former Prophets (Sira 46:1–49:7) than to the Latter Prophets (Sira 48:20–23; 49:6–10) because he is struggling to prove the value of the historical collection by presenting it as part of a Prophetic corpus. Joshua is thus cast as prophet, David is presented in the wake of Nathan's prophetic activities, and Hezekiah is led by Isaiah (Sira 48:22–23). For Ben Sira, the books of Kings tell the story of prophets, much more so than do Chronicles. Ben Sira is the first witness to the prophetization of the Joshua–Kings chronography, and a clear support for the notion that the "Former Prophets" did not result from some original unity of conception but achieved a relative degree of homogeneity only inasmuch as a process of editing can achieve.[30] Instead of starting as a comprehensive Deuteronomistic Historiography in the sixth century BCE, Joshua, Judges and Samuel–Kings developed independently until minor editorial notes such as 1 Sam 12:9–11 and 2 Kgs 23:22 presented the judges as a distinctive era before Samuel. The *inclusio* that connects Isa 49:10, Mal 3:23–24 and Elijah (Sira 48:10) suggests that the juxtaposition of the prophetic and the "historical" books into one collection was recent and needed justification. Therefore, the burden of Ben Sira consists as much in securing the connection between former and latter prophets as the connection between the Torah and the historical books read as prophetic. As Ben Sira presupposes the existence of the chronographic sequence Joshua–Judges–Kings, this threefold periodization must have been crafted some time before he wrote his Wisdom. The most likely cradle for the biblical historical books is Alexandria,[31] despite the enduring influence of Martin Noth's Deuteronomistic History which is due mostly to modern historical factors.[32]

Besides the book of kings that gave the lie to Hecataeus' report that the Jews never had kings, a pre-monarchic period of the Judges consisting of the books of Judges and Ruth was inserted between the days of Joshua and the time of the monarchy.[33] While it is impossible to prove that the placement of the book of Ruth after Judges in the Greek canon is earlier than its placement among the Writings in the Hebrew, the absence of mentions of pre-monarchic judges in Ezek 20:27–29, and the lateness of the reference to the saviours (judges) in Neh 9:27–28 are clues of the late formation of the periodization of Israel's past, including a pre-monarchic period. The historiography with its period of the judges was not widely recognized and Eupolemus mentions Samuel immediately after Joshua (Frag. 2:1–2).[34]

As for the reference to Moses' snake in 2 Kgs 18:4, it consolidates the ties between the historical books and the Torah. For the scribe who wrote it, the historicity of the fabrication of the snake by Moses and of Hezekiah's destruction of it was moot. He took these narratives at face value. Upon reaching the end of the list of cultic images destroyed by good king Hezekiah, he added the bronze snake he knew Moses once cast to heal his people.

Conclusion

In conclusion, Hezekiah's destruction of Moses' Nehushtan can hardly be taken as a denigration of Moses. Against Garbini, I do not believe that "an act like Hezekiah's would have been inconceivable in the Jerusalem of the second century BCE."[35] If Hezekiah could be depicted as breaking into pieces the snake made by Moses himself, this does not mean that Moses lacked the authority and charisma he enjoyed in the rest of the Hebrew Bible. Telling such a story echoes the memory of Moses' role in the foundation of Jerusalem, despite the claim to the contrary in Deuteronomy.

Attributing the destruction of Nehushtan to Hezekiah in by-gone days, and claiming that it was done in response to the deviant practices of Israelite worshippers produced a safe distance while insisting that the Jerusalem temple was the only acceptable place for the lawful worship of YHWH. Alexandria's role in the diffusion of the Hebrew Bible continued after the production of the Septuagint, which spurred Jerusalem to add a collection of historical writings that would allow chronographers to introduce the Jews into the thriving Hellenistic *oecumene*. Besides their foundational myths of origins recorded in the Torah, Jews could also boast of their great heroes and mighty kings, thus refuting Hecataeus' conclusion that the Jews never had kings. In this sense, Garbini is right in viewing the Jerusalem priesthood as being in opposition to Egyptian Jews whose social memory Hecataeus transmitted.

Notes

1. G. Garbini, *History and Ideology in Ancient Israel* (London: SCM Reprints, 1997, first published 1988), p. ix.
2. G. Garbini, *Myth and History* (JSOTSup, 362; Sheffield: Sheffield Academic, 2003), p. 70.
3. Garbini, *Ideology and History*, p. 146.
4. See Nodet in this volume, as well as in A. Fantalkin and O. Tal, "The Canonization of the Pentateuch When and Why?," *ZAW* 124 (2012), pp. 1–18, 201–12.
5. Garbini, *Myth and History*, p. 59.
6. Garbini, *Myth and History*, p. 70.
7. I argue that the seven-day week was a biblical innovation derived from the pseudo-weeks of the Zoroastrian calendar and thus reflects the Persian era in P. Guillaume, "Non-violent Re-readings of Israel's Foundational Traditions in the Persian Period (the Calendar System in P)," in D. V. Edelman and A. Fitzpatrick-McKinley and P. Guillaume (eds.), *Religion in the Achaemenid Persian Empire. Emerging Judaisms and Trends* (Tübingen: Mohr Siebeck, 2015), pp. 57-71.

8. Garbini, *Myth and History*, p. 63.
9. Garbini, *Ideology and History*, pp. 149–50.
10. Garbini, *Ideology and History*, p. 150.
11. Garbini, *Ideology and History*, p. 140.
12. E. Ben Zvi, "Exploring the Memory of Moses the Prophet in Late Persian/Early Hellenistic Yehud/Judah," in D. V. Edelman and E. Ben Zvi (eds.), *Remembering Biblical Figures in the Late Persian and Early Hellenistic Periods* (Oxford: Oxford University Press, 2013), pp. 335–64 (363).
13. Garbini, *Myth and History*, p. 63.
14. The same formulation appears in Num 21:9, which shows that the two texts echo one another. See S. Beyerle, "Die 'Eherne Schlange' Num 21,4-9: synchron und diachron gelesen," *ZAW* 111 (1999), pp. 23–44 (32).
15. For instance, E. van den Berg, "Fact and Imagination in the History of Hezekiah in 2 Kings 18–20," in J. W. Dyk et al. (eds.), *Unless Some One Guide… Festschrift for Karel A. Deurloo* (Amsterdamse Cahiers voor Exegese van de Bijbel en zijn Tradities, Supplement series 2; Maastricht: Shaker, 2001), pp. 129–36; B. Becking, "Between *Realpolitiker* and Hero of Faith: Memories of Hezekiah in Biblical Traditions and Beyond," in Edelman and Ben Zvi (eds.), *Remembering Biblical Figures*, pp. 182–98 (188).
16. G. Garbini, "Le serpent d'airain et Moïse," *ZAW* 100 (1988), pp. 264–67.
17. Garbini, *Myth and History*, p. 58.
18. See S. Schroer, *In Israel gab es Bilder* (OBO 74; Fribourg: University Press; Göttingen: Vandenhoeck & Ruprecht, 1987), pp. 107–9; N. Na'aman, "The Debated Historicity of Hezekiah's Reform in the Light of Historical and Archaeological Research," *ZAW* 107 (1995), pp. 179–95. Nevertheless, there is artifactual evidence for the snake. See R. D. Barnett, "Layard's Nimrud Bronzes and Their Inscriptions," *ErIsr* 8 (1967), pp. 1–7; Y. Yadin, "A Note on the Nimrud Bronze Bowls," *ErIsr* 8 (1967), p. 6; K. R. Joines, "The Bronze Serpent in the Israelite Cult," *JBL* 87 (1968), pp. 245–56; J. J. M. Roberts and K. L. Roberts, "Yahweh's Significant Other," in L. Day and C. Pressler (eds.), *Engaging the Bible in a Gendered World* (Louisville: John Knox, 2006), pp. 176–82 (183–84); K. A. Swanson, "A Reassessment of Hezekiah's Reform in Light of Jar Handles and Iconographic Evidence," *CBQ* 64 (2002), pp. 460–69; H. Shanks, "The Mystery of the Nechushtan: Why Did King Hezekiah of Judah Destroy the Bronze Serpent That Moses Had Fashioned to Protect the Israelites?," *BAR* 33/2 (2007), pp. 58–63.
19. Garbini, *Myth and History*, p. 57.
20. R. A. Young, *Hezekiah in History and Tradition* (VTSup, 155; Leiden: Brill, 2012), p. 237.
21. Garbini, *Myth and History*, p. 57.
22. I. Hjelm, *Jerusalem's Rise to Sovereignty* (JSOTSup 404; London: T&T Clark International, 2004), p. 79.
23. Hjelm, *Jerusalem's Rise to Sovereignty*, p. 80.
24. D. Edelman, "Hezekiah's Alleged Cultic Centralization," *JSOT* 32 (2008), pp. 395–434 (425).
25. Garbini, *Myth and History*, p. 56.
26. Garbini, *Myth and History*, p. 60.

27. Diodorus of Sicily, *Historical Library* (trans. F. R. Walton; LCL; London: Heinemann, 1967), p. 283. C. Zamagni, "La tradition sur Moïse d'Hécatée d'Abdère d'après Diodore et Photius," in P. Borgeaud, T. Römer and Y. Volokhine (eds.), *Interprétations de Moïse. Egypte, Judée, Grèce et Rome* (Jerusalem Studies in Religion and Culture 10; Leiden: Brill, 2010), pp. 133–69, demonstrates that parts of the text may also be attributed to Hecataeus of Miletus (end of sixth century BCE), rather than to Hecataeus of Abdera (end of fourth century BCE).

28. See P. Guillaume, "Sifting the Debris: Calendars and Chronologies of the Flood Narrative," in J. M. Silverman (ed.), *Opening Heaven's Floodgates* (Piscataway; Gorgias, 2013), pp. 57–83 (78).

29. A. Goshen-Gottstein, "Ben Sira's Praise of the Fathers: A Canon-conscious Reading," in R. Egger-Wenzel (ed.), *Ben Sira's God* (Berlin: de Gruyter, 2002), pp. 235–67 (253–54).

30. P. R. Davies, "The Hebrew Canon and the Origins of Judaism," in P. R. Davies and D. V. Edelman (eds.), *The Historian and the Bible* (New York: T&T Clark International, 2010), pp. 194–206 (202).

31. See P. Guillaume, "Alexandria as Cradle of Biblical Historiography," in P. McKechnie and P. Guillaume (eds.), *Ptolemy II Philadelphus and His World* (Leiden: Brill, 2008), pp. 247–55.

32. In response to Alfred Rosenberg's (1893–1946) *Der Mythus des 20. Jahrhunderts*, the most influential Nazi text after Hitler's *Mein Kampf*, Albrecht Alt, Gerhard von Rad, Martin Noth and other colleagues responded with the history catchword and developed a confrontation between the twentieth-century myth and the biblical understanding of history. In this context, it made sense to attribute to Jerusalem the invention of history a good century before Herodotus, thus "proving" that the Israelite genius lay in its deep faith in a god that works in history. See K. Balzer, "Comments on McKenzie's and Knoppers Commentaries on Chronicles," in M. D. Knowles (ed.), "New Studies in Chronicles: A Discussion of Two Recently Published Commentaries," *JHS* 5 (2005), pp. 10–21 (11–12).

33. P. Guillaume, "From a Post-monarchical to the Pre-monarchical Period of the Judges," *BN* 113 (2002), pp. 12–17.

34. J. H. Charlesworth, *The Old Testament Pseudepigrapha* (Garden City, NY: Doubleday, 1983), II, p. 866 and note e. B. Z. Wacholder, *Eupolemus* (Cincinnati: Hebrew Union College, 1974), links Eupolemus and Demetrius the Chronographer with a biblical chronographical school which flourished during the reign of Ptolemy IV Philopater (221–204 BCE).

35. Garbini, *Myth and History*, p. 57.

"WHEN DREAMS COME TRUE":
JERUSALEM/HIEROSOLYMA AND JEWISH NATIONALISM IN THE HELLENISTIC AND ROMAN PERIODS

Ingrid Hjelm

I

The Babylonian conquest of the Kingdom of Judah at the beginning of the sixth century BCE left the country and the royal capital almost totally depopulated.[1] Both were thoroughly razed by the Babylonian armies, whose leaders quickly lost interest in Palestine. The Persian takeover in 539 did not alter circumstances much. They did not take care to improve infrastructure or create subsistence for whatever minor population had remained in the country or recently returned from exile, unless in the service of exploitation.[2] Although Judaea had much in common with its northern neighbour Samaria,[3] these regions did not form a political unity. The Babylonian conquest had not affected Samaria as much as it had Judaea. Its population remained rather intact and it did not suffer the impoverishment that had become the fate of Judaea. Any attempt at political cooperation between the two groups, however, was prohibited by the Persian administration. Such cooperation as well as attempts at developing common literary and cultic traditions seem not to have occurred before the Hellenistic period.[4] From archaeology it is now confirmed that the reign of Antiochus III in the third–second century BCE supported an enlargement of the Yahwist temple on Samaria's Mount Gerizim and the further development of a large temple city around it.[5] The temple was in existence already in the early Persian period (450 BCE or earlier) and served as a regional cult site in Samaria.[6] The Persian-period structure resembles the layout in Ezek 40–48 and the Temple Scroll. Both phases of the holy precinct on Mount Gerizim corroborate a "Pentateuchal" Yahwist offertory cult without any traces of syncretism.[7] Flavius Josephus told several stories about the Samaritans, none of which, however, have been confirmed by the archaeological finds.[8] He did not mention the Persian-period temple or its enlargement in the Hellenistic period. He wrongly dated its destruction to the beginning of John Hyrcanus' reign rather than towards its end; more precisely around 110 BCE as testified by the archaeology.

In *Ant.* 12.132–53, Josephus tells stories about Antiochus III's support for an enlargement of Jerusalem's temple. The authenticity of Antiochus' decree, the so-called "Seleucid charter"[9] is an unresolved matter of dispute.[10] Backing up his account with reference to Polybius of Megalopolis, Josephus addresses all of Antiochus' "documents" to the restoration of the temple and temple cult in Jerusalem (*Ant.* 12.133–46). In spite of Bickerman's analysis which established its authenticity for the majority of scholars,[11] Josephus' quotation of Polybius preceding Antiochus' letter to Ptolemy does not give any reason to believe the letter is in fact authentic or has anything to do with circumstances in Jerusalem. The letter does not name the place and it is only 12.141's remark that the timber is to be brought from "Judaea itself and from other nations" that provides a likely reference to Jerusalem. It is not necessary, however, to claim that the letter is a Samaritan forgery of Herodian times, which ascribed to Antiochus III certain grants given to the Samaritan temple on Mount Gerizim, such as Büchler did in his analysis.[12] The letter's resemblance to other decrees given by Persian, Hellenistic and Roman rulers can be used either to support or reject its authenticity. Josephus' quotation of Polybius that "those Jews who live near the temple of Jerusalem, as it is called," came over to him (Antiochus III), together with his remark in *Ant.* 12.156 that the "Samaritans (*Samareis*), who were flourishing, did much mischief to the Jews by laying waste their land and carrying off slaves," seems to point to a period of hard conditions for the Judaean Jews (218–198 BCE). Whether a forgery or not, the archaeology of the temple city on Gerizim evidences a very prosperous period for the Samaritans in the third–second century BCE.[13] The entire discussion must be taken up afresh in light of this new evidence from Samaria and Gerizim, but for now we must state that Antiochus III might have favored Jerusalem as well. The growth of Judaean territories and Jerusalem from that of a minor temple city to a capital in the Hasmonaean state, however, was a slow process that had only begun in the early second century BCE.[14]

II

From the time of the Seleucid takeover, Jewish authors fostered ideas of independence and dreams of "the twelve tribes," and "the Promised land given to the fathers." Literature of the second century BCE elaborated on utopian visions of nationalism and greatness in prophetic writings, and Jerusalem and its temple were made the most important symbols of national political independence. Influenced by Hellenistic history writing, Jewish authors retold the past with similar interest in national, territorial, cultural and religious matters as did their Hellenistic colleagues.[15] Such also implied ideas of cult centralization, which, during the expansion of Jewish borders, became disastrous for other Yahwist cult places.[16]

Giving voice to the wish for a development of a single religious centre in Jerusalem, the literature became idealistically descriptive of what was not yet created. The literature both argued defensively for the re-establishment of an idealized past which once had one temple, one priest-king and a united people in Jerusalem, and denigrated other cult places that had a strong connection to the most beloved strands of the tradition. This, however, was not entirely different from the biblical tradition's denigration of past institutions, which in the Deuteronomistic History's elaboration of the Shechem and Bethel traditions rejects these prior to the establishment of the cult in Jerusalem.[17] That Jerusalem itself is rejected in the closure of that story forms part of a theological discourse on sin and punishment that governs the entire narrative in the books of Kings.

The second-century BCE book of *Jubilees*' retells the Patriarchal and Exodus narratives and conveys the message that none of the cult places visited by Abraham, Isaac and Jacob is the proper place for future worship. These were only temporary and awaited the building of the Davidic–Solomonic temple in Jerusalem, which *Jubilees* also called Zion and "the navel of the earth" (*Jub*. 8:19; cf. Exod 15:13; Judg 9:37; Ezek 38:12). Also *Jubilees*' addition to Gen 22:14's "mountain where Yahweh shows himself" becomes identified as Mount Zion in *Jub*. 18:13. Yahweh's prohibition of Jacob's plans of building a temple and a wall in Bethel and of making the place holy for himself and his children (*Jub*. 32:16–24), both implies that Jacob becomes Israel here (v. 18) and that this Israel does not belong to Bethel (v. 23): "Do not build this place and do not make an eternal sanctuary, and do not dwell here because this is not the place. Go to the house of Abraham, your father." The text implies that the houses of Jacob and Abraham become united and one might suspect that this is an allusion to Samaritan–Judaean controversies over the proper place for Yahweh's sanctuary.[18] That Jacob becomes Israel (32:18), which is not Bethel, and returns to his father's house in Beersheba (44:1) symbolizes a unification of the houses of Abraham, Isaac and Jacob prior to their descent to Egypt (32:24). Upon their return, the Tabernacle shall be set up temporarily in the midst of the land until the building of the House of the Name of Yahweh (49:18). Although *Jubilees* does not mention Jerusalem, the book implicitly answers Deut 12's unresolved problem – explicitly asked by the late Medieval Samaritan Chronicler Abu'l Fath,[19] about where Yahweh had been worshipped before the building of the Temple. The answer given is that the worship took place in the Tabernacle, which *Jubilees'* audience will know has been replaced by Jerusalem's temple (*Jub.* 49:21). A similar answer is given in Sir 24:7–12 regarding Wisdom's unsuccessful search for a resting place for her tent, which made the "Fashioner of all" (i.e. God) choose a place; namely the holy tent (i.e. the Tabernacle), given rest in Zion-Jerusalem.[20] The Babylonian Talmud's enumeration of the Tabernacle's stay in Gilgal (14 years), Shiloh (369 years), Nob and Gibeon (57 years) (*b. Zeb.* 118b) adds up nicely to a 440-year period matching the Egyptian bondage and the Exodus (cf. Gen 15:13; Deut 1:3).

The second-century BCE Jewish writer Eupolemus wrote a work entitled *On the Kings in Judea*.[21] Here he wrote elaborate narratives about Saul, David and Solomon, whom he set in the context of second-century BCE geopolitical and ethnographic circumstances[22] that focused on the antiquity, exclusivity and superior legitimacy of Jerusalem's temple.[23] Without mentioning David's census, Eupolemus relates that David requested God to show him a place for the altar: "Then an angel appeared to him standing above the place where the altar is set up in Jerusalem" (*Praep. ev.* 9.30.5). In Eupolemus' description of the temple, he uses a mixture of elements, virtually creating a new Temple, in a synthesis of "the Tabernacle, the Solomonic temple and the Second temple," in order to create "structural" continuity, however, surpassing the "poor condition" of the temple of his own time.[24] Having built the temple, Solomon "encircled Jerusalem as a city with walls and towers and trenches and he built a palace for himself" (*Praep. ev.* 9.34.10). The trenches are wholly unscriptural, and they reflect rather the "elevated" temple of the Maccabaeans mentioned by Josephus (*Ant.* 13.217). Having completed the temple and the city walls, Solomon went to Shiloh to bring offerings and carry the tent, the altar of sacrifice and the vessels, which Moses had made, to Jerusalem to be placed in the House. Implicitly confirming that Solomon actually built the temple, Eupolemus relates that "the shrine was first called the 'Temple of Solomon' (*hieron*

Solomōnos)," which later gave its name to the city (*hierusalēm*); and "by the Greeks it is correspondingly called 'Hierosolyma'" (*Praep. ev.* 9.34.11). Josephus offers variant traditions that connect the name of the city with Abraham's encounter with Melchizedek in Salem (Gen 14:17–24; Josephus, *War* 6.438; *Ant.* 7.68).[25]

The "poor condition" of the present temple (that is, the post-exilic temple, is a theme found in many third- and second-century writings which connect the first (that is, the Solomonic) temple with a coming temple. In *1 Enoch* both the first and the coming temple are viewed as places of purity in contrast to the second temple, in which impure food is served (*1 En.* 89:73).[26] As the first temple had been entirely destroyed (by the Babylonians or the Edomites as 1 Esd. 4:45 has it) – "they burned that tower and plowed that house" (*1 En.* 89:67; 90:29)[27] – the building of the third temple on its foundations (*1 En.* 90:29) will be initiated by a removal of the second temple, its pillars, columns and ornaments (*1 En.* 90:28). Likewise, various Dead Sea Scrolls, 4Q174 (= 4QFlor); 5Q15 and *The Temple Scroll*, envision a future temple.

Such discussions went on for centuries and we find the first-century CE Jewish author Flavius Josephus' revision of the past even more striking in his denigration of patriarchal cult places for the sake of Shiloh as the place that preceded the transfer of the temple cult to Jerusalem.[28] Here he actually agrees with Eupolemus[29] and Samaritan Eli traditions.[30]

1 Maccabees is a quasi-historical work from the first century BCE about the Maccabaean wars and fight for independence. Its main goal is to recount the story of the Hasmonaean[31] family from the outbreak of the revolt against the Seleucids (ca. 167 BCE) until the end of the reign of Simon (141–134 BCE) and the ascension of his son John Hyrcanus I (134–104 BCE).

Structurally, 1 Maccabees' story of three brothers resembles Eupolemus' story of Judaea's (three) kings, Saul, David and Solomon. As in Eupolemus, but unlike the biblical story, no genealogical or ideological opposition appears between Saul and David.[32] 1 Maccabees' "brothers" (1 Macc 2:2) succeed each other, albeit Judas Maccabaeus might not have originally been from that family.[33] In successive waves of conquests, these brothers free Israel of its Seleucid occupants, though at the expense of part of its population, which is accused of siding with the foreigners. They cleanse and rebuild the temple more than once, restore the cult and bring home scattered inhabitants. In their newly won independence they establish amicable contacts with mighty Rome and Sparta.

The historicity of 1 Maccabees is basically assumed, however much it is also known that the book's presentation is literarily and theologically motivated. Not only are Judaean heroes presented in images of their glorious biblical ancestors, but their adversaries, the Seleucid rulers, are imitations of Assyrian kings from the eighth–seventh centuries BCE. The composition of the book so much reflects the composition of the Deuteronomistic History that it jeopardizes the historicity of both.[34] The parallels are structural and thematic and relate to a great number of details, such as the reiterative use of the Hezekiah narrative in 1 Maccabees' sevenfold threats against Jerusalem;[35] the introduction of the Zion motif in the liberation of the temple with its parallel in 2 Sam 5 and the number of heroes and their fight for supremacy, leaving the corpses of their relatives along the road as in the David–Solomon transition.[36] The continuation that we find in Josephus (*Ant.* 13.299) has the 31 years of John Hyrcanus' reign paralleling the 31 years of Josiah's (2 Kgs 22:1; 2 Chr 34:1), whose acts he "imitates." Both kings are ascribed a cult centralization, which leads to a destruction of Samarian/Samaritan cult places in Bethel and on Gerizim. It is, in fact, impossible to know whether the biblical "Bethel" is a euphemism for Gerizim or the Northern cult as such.[37] The introduction of kingship during Alexander Janneus, like the biblical narratives, is initiated by a discussion of kingship versus high priesthood/prophet. The fight over that kingship finally leads to Pompey's division of the kingdom between the grandsons of John Hyrcanus, Aristobolus II and Hyrcanus II (Josephus, *Ant.* 13.301).[38]

In the book's reuse of familiar traditions, we find that in their father Mattathias' testimony to his sons (1 Macc 2:49–68), he reminds them of their obligation to fight zealously for the Law and follow in the paths of biblical heroes like Abraham, Joseph, Phinehas, Joshua, Caleb, David, Elijah, Hananiah, Azariah, Mishael and Daniel. As each is rewarded for his conduct, the implication is that by imitating and "emulating"[39] these heroes the sons will share similar rewards. Like Abraham, God will regard them as righteous; like Joseph, God will raise them to be master over Egypt; like Phinehas, God will assign them an everlasting priesthood; like Joshua, they will become judges in Israel; like Caleb, they will have the land as their inheritance; like David, they will inherit an everlasting kingship; like Elijah, they will be taken up to heaven; like Hananiah, Azariah and Mishael, they will be rescued from the flames; like Daniel, they will be saved from the mouth of the lions. The list functions programmatically to create the image of the Hasmonaeans as righteous leaders, priests, judges, kings and prophets, whose reward is land and eternity. Compositionally, David, the only king mentioned, is placed in the centre of the list of eleven "generations," the future of which depends on the initiative and faithfulness of the twelfth generation – the Hasmonaeans. Similar to the David narratives (1 Sam 22:1–2), 1 Maccabees begins in disunity, as small armies of warriors (1 Macc 2:42–44) fight against the much larger armies of their enemies.[40] After several setbacks, which give each hero warrior something to do, the story ends in "the whole" people's recognition of Simon as high priest, commander and ethnarch of Judah (1 Macc 13:8; 14:25–46). The initial goal of their fight is the liberation of Jerusalem, the restoration of its temple and cult and a return of the people scattered. The thematic structure of 1 Maccabees' narrative about Jerusalem's rise to sovereignty suggests that a proper title for the book might be *Jerusalem-Zion versus Antioch: Fighting the Seven-Headed Monster*.[41] At the advent of Antiochus IV, the western capital of the Seleucid Empire was Antioch on the Orontes, which at that time had become the third greatest city after Rome and Alexandria. The name of the city occurs seven times in 1 Maccabees[42] and seven plus two times in 2 Maccabees,[43] but rarely if at all in the apocryphal literature. As a symbol of power, the city's impotence in these writings is significant.[44]

Judaism's concentration on Jerusalem reflects well our knowledge of political circumstances, which in the establishment of a partly independent Jewish state in the middle of the second century BCE created the basis for a literary delimitation of Judaism's geographical boundaries. Presented as a fight against foreigners, the opposition to the Maccabaean revolt is as internal[45] as it is external, and "civil war" is an equally appropriate term for the narrative reality, most of which revolves around the sons of Antiochus III (223–187 BCE): Seleucus and Antiochus and their descendants' struggle for the throne.[46] Navigating between the demands of loyalty towards these kings and their governors in order to maintain their own interests, the second-century Jews of 1 Maccabees were as exposed to the wills and whims of the occupation powers as their biblical ancestors had been. In addition to the Seleucids, the Jews also had Egypt, Rome and Sparta as their interlocutors. The establishment of the state also implied an establishment of a more politically oriented high priestly office in a combined role of leadership (*stratego*) and high priest. The elevation of Simon and his sons also implied an elevation of Zion-Jerusalem's temple.

The semi-independent Jewish state that arose from the ashes of the Maccabaean wars in 141 BCE lasted until the Roman takeover in 63 BCE. Conquered peoples in, for example, the Galilee, Perea and Idumea chose or were forced to adopt Judaism and competing cult places were destroyed. Although the Bible reports a cult centralization from as early as the eighth–seventh century BCE, history only testifies to its execution in the second–first century BCE, when regional borders were removed as a result of Hasmonaean expansion. In all other periods of the first millennium BCE, the cult of Yahweh was disseminated from a number of centers known to us,[47] such as Haran, Babylonia, Elephantine,[48] Lachish, Hebron, Samaria, Gerizim, Tabor, Carmel, Mamre, Deir ʿAlla, Tell es-Saʾidiyeh, Araq el-Emir and Leontopolis. To this list we must add inscriptional and onomastic evidence from Kuntillet ʿAjrud,[49] Khirbet el-Qom/Maqqedah[50] and Hamath,[51] as well as the many cult places/synagogues in Jewish and Samaritan diaspora from the third century BCE onwards, such as Alexandria, Delos,[52] and Antioch.

After the Roman conquest, the Idumean magnate Antipater made himself useful to the Romans and his family held power for about a century under Roman control. Antipater's son Herod the great (40/37–34 BCE) rebuilt the Jewish temple and magnificently expanded it. In yet another reiteration of what was seen as a glorious past, he consciously presented himself in the image of the biblical David and Solomon.[53] In 70 CE, the Romans sacked Jerusalem and burned down its Jewish temple, allegedly because of insurrection. The failed Bar Kokhba revolt in 135 BCE put an effective end to Jewish aspirations of independence. Jews were banned from the city, though not from the land – the *Provincia Judea*, which from then on was named *Provincia Syria Palaestina*.[54]

The visions for a glorious Jerusalem – also called "Zion" and "the holy city" (Isa 48:2; 52:1; Dan 9:24; Neh 11:1, 18) and built on the holy mountain (Pss 48:2; 87:1; Zech 8:13) – which the biblical prophets and psalmists preached, however, was never the mundane city, but a place made holy by Yahweh's presence.[55] Its role as "navel of the earth," *axis mundi*, was intended for all people of the world.

Notes

1. O. Lipschits, "Demographic Changes in Judah between the Seventh and the Fifth Centuries B.C.E.," in O. Lipschits and J. Blenkinsopp (eds.), *Judah and Judaeans in the Neo-Babylonian Period* (Winona Lake, IN: Eisenbrauns, 2003), pp. 323–76; E. Stern, "The Babylonian Gap," *BAR* 26 (2000), pp. 45–51; idem, *Archaeology of the Land of the Bible*. II. *The Assyrian, Babylonian and Persian Periods (732–332 B.C.E.)* (ABRL; New York: Doubleday, 2001), pp. 14–57; idem, "The Babylonian Gap: The Archaeological Reality," *JSOT* 28 (2004), pp. 273–77; C. E. Carter, *The Emergence of Yehud in the Persian Period: A Social and Demographic Study* (Sheffield: Sheffield Academic, 1999); idem, "Ideology and Archaeology in the Neo-Babylonian Period: Excavating Text and Tell," in Lipschits and Blenkinsopp (eds.), *Judah and Judaeans in the Neo-Babylonian Period*, pp. 301–22. For a different opinion, see H. M. Barstad, "After the 'Myth of the Empty Land': Major Challenges in the Study of Neo-Babylonian Judah," in Lipschits and

Blenkinsopp (eds.), *Judah and Judaeans in the Neo-Babylonian Period*, pp. 3–20. Further references can be found in I. Hjelm, "Changing Paradigms: Judaean and Samarian Histories in Light of Recent Research," in M. Müller and T. L. Thompson (eds.), *Historie og Konstruktion. Festskrift til Niels Peter Lemche i anledning af 60 års fødselsdagen den 6. september 2005* (Forum for Bibelsk Eksegese 14; Copenhagen: Museum Tusculanums Forlag, 2005), pp. 161–79 (165–66).

2. L. Fried, *The Priest and the Great King: Temple–Palace Relations in the Persian Empire* (Winona Lake, IN: Eisenbrauns, 2004), pp. 208–12; A. Kuhrt, *The Persian Empire: A Corpus of Sources from the Achaemenid Period* (2 vols.; London/ New York: Routledge, 2007), II/4, p. 672: "The system of taxation drew the empire's subjects together into a web of obligations to the central power. It made its presence manifest through settlement, call-up duties, crown officials managing local resources and tax collectors. It allowed the government to reach into the very heart of local systems, with manpower, production and enterprise all focused on, and profiting from, meeting supra-provincial requirements." For an in-depth discussion, see P. Briant, *From Cyrus to Alexander: A History of the Persian Empire* (Winona Lake, IN: Eisenbrauns, 2002), Chapters 10–11.

3. G. N. Knoppers, "In Search of Postexilic Israel after the Fall of the Northern Kingdom," in J. Day (ed.), *In Search of Pre-exilic Israel* (JSOTSup 406; London/New York: T. & T. Clark/Continuum, 2004), pp. 150–80; idem, "Revisiting the Samaritan Question in the Persian Period," in O. Lipschits and M. Oeming (eds.), *Judah and the Judeans in the Persian Period* (Winona Lake, IN: Eisenbrauns, 2006), pp. 265–89; idem, *Jews and Samaritans: The Origins and History of Their Early Relations* (Oxford: Oxford University Press, 2013), esp. pp. 109–25.

4. E. Nodet, *A Search for the Origins of Judaism: From Joshua to the Mishnah* (JSOTSup 248; Sheffield: Sheffield Academic, 1997; rev. Eng. translation [by E. Crowley] of idem, *Essai sur les origines du Judaïsme: de Josué aux Pharisiens* [Paris: Cerf, 1992], p. 191); Knoppers, *Jews and Samaritans*, p. 192.

5. Y. Magen, *Mount Gerizim Excavations II: A Temple City* (trans. E. Levin and C. Ebert; Judea and Samaria Publications 8; Jerusalem: Staff Officer of Archaeology, Civil Administration of Judea and Samaria, 2008), p. 176.

6. Y. Magen, H. Misgav, and L. Tsefania, *Mount Gerizim Excavations I: The Aramaic, Hebrew and Samaritan Inscriptions* (Eng. trans. by E. Levin and M. Guggenheimer; Judea and Samaria Publications, 2; Jerusalem: Staff Officer of Archaeology, Civil Administration of Judea and Samaria, 2004 [English and Hebrew]); Magen, *Mount Gerizim Excavations II*; Hjelm, "Changing Paradigms," pp. 167–71.

7. Magen, *Mount Gerizim Excavations II*, pp. 140–60; idem, "The Dating of the First Phase of the Samaritan Temple on Mount Gerizim in Light of the Archaeological Evidence," in O. Lipschits, G. N. Knoppers, and R. Albertz (eds.), *Judah and the Judaeans in the Fourth Century BCE* (Winona Lake, IN: Eisenbrauns, 2007), pp. 157–211; I. Hjelm, "Lost and Found? A Non-Jewish Israel from the Merneptah Stele to the Byzantine Period," in I. Hjelm and T. L. Thompson (eds.), *History, Archaeology and the Bible Forty Years After "Historicity"* (London: Routledge, 2016), pp. 112–28.

8. For detailed analyses of Josephus' Samaritan material, see R. Pummer, *The Samaritans in Flavius Josephus* (Texts and Studies in Ancient Judaism 129; Tübingen: Mohr Siebeck, 2009); I. Hjelm, *The Samaritans and Early Judaism:*

A Literary Analysis (JSOTSup 303; CIS 7; Sheffield: Sheffield Academic, 2000), Chapter 5; F. Dexinger, "Der Ursprung der Samaritaner im Spiegel der frühen Quellen," in F. Dexinger and R. Pummer (eds.), *Die Samaritaner* (Wege der Forschung 604; Darmstadt: Wissenschaftliche Buchgesellschaft, 1992), pp. 67–140; R. Egger, *Josephus Flavius und die Samaritaner. Eine terminologische Untersuchung zur Identitätsklärung der Samaritaner* (NTOA 4; Göttingen: Vandenhoeck & Ruprecht, 1986).

9. E. Bickerman, "La charte séleucide de Jérusalem," *REJ* 100 (1935), pp. 4–35, repr. as "The Seleucid Charter," in E. Bickerman, *Studies in Jewish and Christian History* (2 vols.; Leiden: E.J. Brill, 2007 [1980]), II, pp. 315–56.

10. Hjelm, *The Samaritans and Early Judaism*, pp. 234–35.

11. See the discussion by Ralph Marcus in LCL 365, Appendix D; Bickerman, "La charte séleucide de Jérusalem"; Nodet, *A Search for the Origins of Judaism*, pp. 216–25.

12. A. Büchler, *Die Tobiaden und die Oniaden im II. Makkabäerbuche und in der verwandten Jüdisch-hellenistischen Litteratur. Untersuchungen zur Geschichte der Juden von 220–160 und zur jüdisch-hellenistischen Litteratur* (Vienna: Alfred Hölder, 1899), pp. 143–71.

13. Magen, *Mount Gerizim Excavations II*, pp. 175–78.

14. I. Finkelstein, "The Territorial Extent and Demography of Yehud/Judea in the Persian and Early Hellenistic Periods," *Revue Biblique* 117 (2010), pp. 39–54.

15. D. Mendels, *The Land of Israel as a Political Concept in the Hasmonaean Literature* (Tübingen: J. C. B. Mohr, 1987); idem, *The Rise and Fall of Jewish Nationalism* (New York: Doubleday, 1992).

16. I. Hjelm, *Jerusalem's Rise to Sovereignty: Zion and Gerizim in Competition* (JSOTSup 404; CIS 14; London/New York: T&T Clark International, 2004), p. 209

17. Hjelm, *Jerusalem's Rise*, pp. 195–210.

18. Hjelm, *The Samaritans and Early Judaism*, pp. 276–78; eadem, *Jerusalem's Rise*, pp. 259–60.

19. See P. Stenhouse, *The Kitāb al Tarīkh of Abu ʾl-Fatḥ: Translated into English with Notes* (Sydney: The Mandelbaum Trust, University of Sydney, 1985), Chapter 19, p. 76; Arabic editions: P. Stenhouse, "The Kitāb al Tarīkh of Abu ʾl-Fatḥ: New Edition" (unpublished Ph.D. dissertation, University of Sydney, 1980); E. Vilmar, *Abulfathi Annales Samaritani* (Gothae: F.A. Perthes, 1865).

20. Hjelm, *Jerusalem's Rise*, p. 260.

21. The title appears in Clement of Alexandria, *Stromata* 1.153.4. Eupolemus' work has survived in fragments only, transmitted through Alexander Polyhistor, Clement of Alexandria and Eusebius of Caesarea. Of these, Eusebius is considered to be closest to the original; cf. B. Z. Wacholder, *Eupolemus: A Study of Judaeo-Greek Literature* (Cincinnati: Hebrew Union College Press, 1974), pp. 46–49; F. Fallon, "Eupolemus," in J. H. Charlesworth (ed.), *The Old Testament Pseudepigrapha* (2 vols.; London: Darton, Longman & Todd, 1983–85), II, pp. 861–72; Hjelm, *Jerusalem's Rise*, pp. 260–63.

22. Mendels, *Land of Israel*, pp. 35–40.

23. Mendels, *Land of Israel*, p. 32; idem, *Jewish Nationalism*, p. 144.

24. Mendels, *Land of Israel*, p. 44.

25. See further Hjelm, *Jerusalem's Rise*, p. 262.

26. Hjelm, *Jerusalem's Rise*, pp. 263–66; G. W. E. Nickelsburg, *Jewish Literature between the Bible and the Mishnah: A Historical and Literary Introduction* (Oxford: Clarendon, 1986), p. 94; P. A. Tiller, *A Commentary on the Animal Apocalypse of 1 Enoch* (Early Judaism and Its Literature 4; Atlanta: Scholars Press, 1993), p. 47 n. 65: "The negative evaluation of the Second Temple can be paralleled in a number of texts, e.g. *T. Mos.* 4.8; 5.3–4; *T. Levi* 14.7–16.5; *Jub.* 23.21." See also Tob 14:5. See, further, J. A. Goldstein, "How the Authors of 1 and 2 Maccabees Treated the "Messianic Promises,"" in J. Neusner, W. S. Green, and E. S. Frerichs (eds.), *Judaism and Their Messiahs at the Turn of the Christian Era* (Cambridge: Cambridge University Press, 1987), pp. 69–96 (70).

27. Cf. Jer 26:18; Mic 3:12: "because of you, Zion shall become plowed as a field and Jerusalem a heap of ruins."

28. Hjelm, *Jerusalem's Rise*, pp. 197–201.

29. Wacholder, *Eupolemus*, p. 211, notes: "He [Eupolemus] seems to maintain that Shiloh remained the only shrine of Yahweh until, by God's command and the angel's guidance, the site of Solomon's temple was chosen. Just as Joshua, Moses' assistant in the desert, formed a link between the sanctuary of the desert and that of Shiloh, so Eli, the chief priest of Shiloh, according to Eupolemus, was present at Solomon's coronation." Cf. also Jeremiah's replacement of Shiloh with Jerusalem and his narratives about Judah's last kings mirrored against David.

30. B. Tsedaka, "Special Samaritan Traditions in non-Samaritan Sources," in A. Tal and M. Florentin (eds.), *Proceedings of the First International Congress of the Société d'Études Samaritaines Tel-Aviv, April 11–13, 1988* (Tel-Aviv: Chaim Rosenberg School for Jewish Studies, Tel-Aviv University), pp. 189–201; idem, "The Origin of the Samaritans From the Children of Israel: The Quarrel Between the High Priest Azzi and the Priest Eli," *A.B.- The Samaritan News* 801–803 (2001), pp. 23–33 (Hebrew); Hjelm, *Jerusalem's Rise*, p. 203; eadem, *Samaritans and Early Judaism*, pp. 244–45.

31. The name, otherwise unknown, occurs for the first time in Josephus, *War* 1.36, who calls Matthatias "son of Asamonaios."

32. On this see also Giovanni Garbini, "Eupolemo storico guideo," in *Rendiconti dell'Accademia Nazionale dei Lincei*, ser. IX, 9 (1998), pp. 613–34; idem, "Eupolemo e Flavio Giuseppe," in *Rendiconti dell'Accademia Nazionale dei Lincei* ser. IX, 11 (2000), pp. 367–82; idem, *Myth and History in the Bible* (JSOTSup; London/New York: T&T Clark International, 2005), p. 84.

33. Nodet, *A Search for the Origins of Judaism*, pp. 215–16, 237–48.

34. For a literary analysis of the book, see Hjelm, *Jerusalem's Rise*, pp. 266–88; eadem, "1 Makkabæerbogs helte mellem fortælling og virkelighed," in T. L. Thompson and H. Tronier (eds.), *Frelsens biografisering* (Forum for Bibelsk Eksegese 13; Copenhagen: Museum Tusculanum, 2004), pp. 63–78; eadem, "Whose Bible Is It Anyway? Ancient Authors, Medieval Manuscripts and Modern Perceptions," *SJOT* 18 (2004), pp. 108–34; Arabic version: "Whose Bible Is It Anyway? 1st Millennium BCE Iron Age History of Palestine based on 1st Millennium CE Manuscripts," in K. Whitelam, T. L. Thompson, N. P. Lemche, I. Hjelm and Z. Muna, *Al ğadīd fī tārīkh filasṭīn alqadīm* (New Information about the History of Ancient Palestine; Damaskus and Beirut: Cadmus, 2004), pp. 141–61.

35. Hjelm, *Jerusalem's Rise*, pp. 272–84.

36. Hjelm, *Jerusalem's Rise*, p. 287.
37. Hjelm, *Jerusalem's Rise*, pp. 164–65
38. Hjelm, *Jerusalem's Rise*, p. 288.
39. Goldstein, "Authors," p. 79; Hjelm, *Jerusalem's Rise*, p. 269.
40. E.g. 1 Macc 3.10, 15; 4.30; 5.6, 38; 6.6, 41; 7.10, 27; 9.43, 60; 10.69, 73; 11.63; 12.24; 13.1, 12; 16.5.
41. Hjelm, *Jerusalem's Rise*, p. 272.
42. 1 Macc 3.37; 4.35; 6.63; 10.68; 11.13, 44, 56.
43. 2 Macc 4.33; 5.21; 8.35; 11.36; 13.23, 26; 14.27; plus 4.9, 19: the "Antiochenes of Jerusalem."
44. Hjelm, *Jerusalem's Rise*, pp. 272–74.
45. 1 Macc 2.44–48; 7.5–25; 9.23–27; cf. Dan 11:31–35. E. J. Bickerman, *Der Gott der Makkabäer. Untersuchung über Sinn und Ursprung der makkabäischen Erhebung* (Berlin: Schocken, 1937), pp. 168–69; V. Tcherikover, *Hellenistic Civilization and the Jews* (New York: Atheneum, 1975), pp. 190–92; J. Sievers, *The Hasmoneans and Their Supporters: From Mattathias to the Death of John Hyrcanus I* (Studies in the History of Judaism 6; Atlanta: Scholars Press, 1990), pp. 15–16.
46. Seleucus' line held power: Seleucus IV (187–175); Demetrius I (162–150); Demetrius II (145–140 + 129–126); Antiochus VII, brother to Demetrius II (138–129). Antiochus' line held power: Antiochus IV (175–164); Antiochus V (+ Lysias; 164–162); Alexander Balas (150–145). Alexander's son Antiochus VI (145–142) was killed by Trypho, who claims himself "king" of the Seleucid Empire (142–138). See L. L. Grabbe, *Judaism from Cyrus to Hadrian* (2 vols.; Minneapolis: Fortress Press, 1992), II, pp. 624–26.
47. M. S. Smith, *Palestinian Parties and Politics That Shaped the Old Testament* (New York: Columbia University Press, 1971), pp. 82–98 (93); H. Niehr, *Der Höchste Gott: Alttestamentlicher JHWH-Glaube in Kontext syrisch-kanaanäischer Religion des 1. Jahrtausend v. Chr* (BZAW 190; Berlin: de Gruyter, 1990); idem, "The Rise of YHWH in Judahite and Israelite Religion," in D. V. Edelman (ed.), *The Triumph of Elohim: From Yahwisms to Judaisms* (Kampen: Kok Pharos, 1995), pp. 45–72.
48. A. Vincent, *La Religion des Judéo-Araméens d'Éléphantine* (Paris: Geuthner, 1937); T. Bolin, "The Temple of Yahu at Elephantine and Persian Religious Policy," in Edelman (ed.), *The Triumph of Elohim*, pp. 127–42; B. Porten (ed.), *The Elephantine Papyri in English: Three Millennia of Cross-Cultural Continuity and Change* (Leiden: Brill, 1996); R. Kratz, "The Temple of Jeb and of Jerusalem," in Lipschits and Oeming (eds.), *Judah and the Judeans in the Persian Period*, pp. 247–64.
49. M. Weinfeld, "Kuntillet ʿAjrud Inscriptions and Their Significance," *Studi Epigrafici e Linguistici* 1 (1984), pp. 121–30; K. van der Toorn, "Yahweh," in K. van der Toorn, B. Becking and P. W. van der Horst (eds.), *Dictionary of Deities and Demons in the Bible* (Leiden: E. J. Brill, 1995), pp. 1712–30.
50. A. Lemaire, "New Aramaic Ostraca from Idumea and Their Historical Interpretation," in Lipschits and Oeming (eds.), *Judah and the Judeans in the Persian Period*, pp. 413–56.

51. J. H. Tigay, *You Shall Have No Other Gods: Israelite Religion in the Light of Hebrew Inscriptions* (HSM 31; Atlanta: Scholars Press, 1986); S. Dalley, "Yahweh in Hamath in the Eighth Century BC," *VT* 40 (1990), pp. 21–32; K. van der Toorn, "Anat-Yahu, Some Other Deities, and the Jews of Elephantine," *Numen* 39 (1992), pp. 80–101; T. L. Thompson, *The Bible in History: How Writers Create a Past* (London: Jonathan Cape, 1999), pp. 168–78.

52. P. Bruneau, "Les israelites de Délos et la juiverie delienne," *Bulletin de Correspondance Hellenique* 106 (1982), pp. 465–504; M. Kartveit, *The Origin of the Samaritans* (Leiden: Brill, 2009), pp. 216–25.

53. For a recent analysis, see A. K. Marshak, "Glorifying the Present Through the Past: Herod the Great and His Jewish Royal Predecessors," in S. E. Porter and A. W. Pitts (eds.), *Christian Origins and Hellenistic Judaism: Social and Literary Contexts for the New Testament* (Leiden: Brill, 2013), pp. 51–82.

54. S. Sand, *The Invention of the Jewish People* (London/New York: Verso, 2009), p. 133.

55. Hjelm, *Jerusalem's Rise*, pp. 248–58.

THE SAME OLD STORY

Niels Peter Lemche

It is an honour to contribute to this collection of essays celebrating the 80th anniversary of Giovanni Garbini, who has since his first book relating to biblical studies been in opposition to the strange ways of biblical scholarship.[1] Garbini was also one of the few scholars who, from the beginning, questioned the status of the Tel Dan inscription as a genuine contribution to the history of Israel in ancient times.[2] This position earned him few friends and accusations of the sort usually directed against the minimalists; he was accused of being a dilettante and not knowing what he is talking about, in spite of Giovanni Garbini's merits within Northwest Semitic philology and epigraphy exemplified by at least two books and several articles.[3]

Being what it is, mainstream biblical scholarship has never been willing to incorporate new ideas that may mean a breakdown of its traditional paradigms. As Jack Sasson described the situation in a recent lecture at a conference at the University of Copenhagen titled *Changing Perspectives* in October 2013, biblical scholarship is a juggernaut just going on without regard for changes around it and impossible to stop.[4] It is therefore hardly a surprise when methodologies in biblical studies continue to appear without regard and definitely without understanding the reasons for any change that may have happened. The following discussion is based on some reflections on the study of the Bible and its historicity by the leading Israeli archaeologist Amihai Mazar, not because he stands out among his colleagues in Israeli archaeology but because he has formulated what could be called the traditional historical-critical view of the Bible and history shared by, probably, a majority of biblical scholars and definitely by many archaeologists working in Israel.

Maximalist, the Middle, and the Minimalists

Among the contributions to the discussion between him and Israel Finkelstein, edited by Brian Schmidt, Amihai Mazar presents an overview of his idea about how to proceed with the study of Israelite history.[5] The problem for biblical archaeology has, for some generations, been related to the question of how to relate archaeological discoveries "on the ground" to textual facts from the Old Testament. Several well-known biblical scholars have addressed this issue in a critical fashion, among them, as long ago as 50 years, no less than Martin Noth.[6] In general, such a debate should be seen in the light of previous optimism such as that represented by William Foxwell Albright and Yigal Yadin, who represented a kind of "bible and spade" archaeology which is no longer in vogue among archaeologists, not even among present-day exponents of biblical archaeology,[7] or this is at least what we are led to believe.[8]

In his discussion in the previously mentioned book of maximalism versus minimalism, Amihai Mazar places himself in the middle, just like his colleague Israel Finkelstein, his collocutor in this volume. This centre seems to be somewhat overcrowded as Finkelstein and Mazar do not agree on much except that they belong to the middle. It is also a strange position that will only cause trouble to persons inhabiting it, as they will be fired at from both sides. But in Mazar's case it is a desperate case of wanting to keep up rather conservative positions (such as the historicity of the Israelite kingdom in the tenth century BCE) and still be respected as a scholar of importance except among scholars to the far left.

For this reason, Mazar opens the discussion of maximalism and minimalism by introducing Kenneth A. Kitchen as a maximalist, and as his opponents representing the scholars who belong to the minimalist side, Philip R. Davies and Niels Peter Lemche.[9] In this way it is easy to belong to the middle. However, Mazar is using a strategy which was many years ago denounced by Mario Liverani in his extended review of Roland de Vaux's *Histoire ancienne d'Israël*.[10] Roland de Vaux wanted to place himself between, on one side Albright as represented by John Bright in the first edition of his *A History of Israel*,[11] and on the other Martin Noth in his *Geschichte Israels*.[12] Liverani makes it clear that this is false positioning: Noth was not to the left when de Vaux published his *Histoire*. At the progressive side at that time we find George E. Mendenhall, who already in 1962 had published his "The Hebrew Conquest of Palestine."[13] By 1970 Noth truly belonged to the middle. By introducing Kenneth Kitchen, Mazar is not referring to a scholar who belongs to the maximalist position. As is evident from Kitchen's works relating to the history of Israel, Kitchen is far to the right of the maximalists; he is in James Barr's words definitely a fundamentalist, having absolutely no respect whatsoever for critical biblical scholarship of any kind.[14]

It is clear that by his placing Kitchen among the maximalists, Mazar is definitely positioning himself in the centre. But, as has already been said, Kitchen is not a maximalist. To people belonging to Kitchen's clan of evangelical scholars those who are normally reckoned maximalists, such as William G. Dever, are minimalists indeed, simply because they use at least a modicum of critical analysis when referring to the Bible and archaeology. This is made clear in a note by Mark W. Chavalas and Murray R. Adamthwaite: "...also the conversation, 'Face to Face...' where N. P. Lemche, T. L. Thompson, W. Dever, and P. Kyle McCarter Jr. expound their minimalist views."[15] No minimalist would include William G. Dever among their number, and he would probably not like to be part of their company.[16] Mazar definitely belongs to the same kind of thinking as Dever. He is definitely not in the middle; he is a maximalist. Evidently he links critical study to people in the middle position, and most likely also includes those to the left of his own position. He does not understand that people to the right of his position, people like Kenneth Kitchen, are simply not interested in a critical exchange with scholars not belonging to their congregation. Is this way, the discussion taking place among critically minded scholars will not include non-critical scholars who represent a monologue of their own. They have little in common with, on the one hand, scholars like Amihai Mazar, Gary Rendsburg, William G. Dever, and more, and on the other hand true minimalists (leftists would be a more appropriate term) like Philip R. Davies, Niels Peter Lemche, and Thomas Thompson. In contrast to evangelical scholars, maximalists as well as minimalists accept a common ground of methods and attempt to engage in dialogue with the other party – or that is at least what we are induced to believe.

The Maximalist's Idea of Scholarship

In the article by Amihai Mazar discussed here, he argues that biblical stories really include information from the past. Mazar will not object to a date of the beginning of biblical historiography as early as the eighth to sixth century BCE and accepts the presence of later redactions of this historiography to exilic and post-exilic periods, although he will not engage in any technical discussion of biblical historiography. This is a fair positioning by an archaeologist who accepts the limitations of his trade which does not allow for extended textual criticism but relies on conclusions made by textual specialists. However, when it comes to playing the role of a historian, the archaeologist again displays his fundamental lack of understanding of how historians work.

For more than two hundred years historians have been instructed, before anything else, to apply source criticism to their material. Within general history it began with Barthold Georg Niebuhr (the son of the explorer Carsten Niebuhr), who applied source criticism in 1810 in a series of lectures at the University of Berlin on Livy's history of Rome,[17] and it is still the basic tool of modern historians. The idea is to sift sources and divide them into primary and secondary evidence. Later reworking of the system of source criticism had shown that this division is far from sufficient. Working with ancient sources means that the problem sharpens because even a primary source may be a secondary source if it is removed by any considerable time from the period which it is describing. In that situation it becomes a primary source of the time that produced this source.[18] Applied to biblical historiography, the primary source for, for example, the period of the Judges is the biblical book of Judges. Because even to the most conservative estimates this book must have been written a considerable time later than the period described in the book, it is also a secondary source, but a primary source to the time when it was put into writing.

This does not mean that a primary source is an objective source. Such a thing hardly exists. Assyrian annals and annalistic reports are not objective descriptions of events that took place at the time when they were composed. But in general, the events described in texts such as the annals of Sennacherib actually took place, like Sennacherib's campaign to Palestine in 701 BCE.[19] The biblical description of this event in 2 Kgs 18–19 is easily divided into a primary source, 1 Kgs 18:13–16, and a secondary source, 1 Kgs 18:17–19, 37, including all sorts of elaborations on the short annalistic note that marks the primary source. The primary source in this instance is not a neutral description of what happened, neither is the Assyrian version. Something is left out or added in the two versions. In the biblical version the note in Sennacherib's text that the daughters of Hezekiah were handed over to the Assyrian king cannot be found. As far as the Assyrian annalistic text goes, the number of people deported from Hezekiah's kingdom far exceeds the number of people living there at the end of the seventh century BCE. Still, there is no doubt that Sennacherib attacked Hezekiah's kingdom at this time, and destroyed it. Sennacherib's acts in Palestine are well-documented also from archaeology, and this is one of those instances where archaeology and historical interpretation really goes hand-in-hand.[20] And of course there are other examples, most notably the Babylonian conquest of Jerusalem in 597 BCE recorded in the Old Testament (2 Kgs 24:10–17) *and* in a Babylonian Chronicle.[21] There is no external evidence of the second conquest of Jerusalem normally dated to 587 BCE which included the destruction of the city. Neither the Babylonian Chronicle nor 2 Kings says anything about destruction in 597 BCE, which makes the second conquest likely, especially because the city was really destroyed at this time.

However, returning to the criteria for early sources included in a historiography dated by Mazar to ca. 800–600 BCE, he lists the following points:[22]

1. The archives of the Jerusalem Temple library.
2. Palace archives.
3. Public commemorative inscriptions, perhaps centuries old.
4. The oral transmission of ancient poetry.
5. Folk stories and aetiological stories rooted in a remote historical past.
6. Earlier historiographic writings.

When we look at what we really have, the following has to be said:

Point 1: The Temple Archive. Such a thing has never been found or heard of. It might have been there but there is not a scrap of evidence speaking in favour of such an archive. The argument is not an argument at all; it is an assertion, as no falsification is possible.

Point 2: Palace archives. First we have to find the palaces where such archives were stored. Second, we have to date such palaces. The sad reality is that we have until now not found any evidence of the existence of palace archives in Iron Age Jerusalem. Furthermore, there is an ongoing discussion among Israeli archaeologists whether or not an Iron Age palace has really been found, with dates running between the tenth century and the Hellenistic Period (stones are difficult to date if no artefacts are discovered at the same time that can be related to a certain structure that may date it).[23] Furthermore, it is a subject of discussion whether there was a state in the southern part of the central highlands with Jerusalem as its centre before the eighth century BCE.[24] The evidence of the expansion of Jerusalem towards the end of the eighth century and at the beginning of the seventh century BCE – whether or not it was caused by refugees from Samaria after 722 BCE as was Albrecht Alt's old idea,[25] or by refugees from the parts of Hezekiah's kingdom destroyed by Sennacherib in 701[26] – is in this connection immaterial and testifies only to the existence of a small state normally described as

Judah. This means that from ca. 700 BCE there *might* have been a palace archive in Jerusalem, but until we have found evidence of its existence, it is no more than an assertion that it really was there.

Point 3: Public commemorative inscriptions. Mazar adds that so far not a single example has been found. The Siloam inscription – and it is of no consequence when it was written – is no public commemorative inscription, as it was never intended for public display, being situated in the middle of a long underground tunnel. The sad fact is that no royal inscriptions have been found dating to the time of the kingdoms of Israel and Judah. This might be a coincidence – we only have to find them. At least this is the normal argument on this subject. It is, on the other hand, very peculiar since no stretch of land has been excavated so extensively as the territories of the Iron Age states of Israel and Judah. Based on what we know it would be safer to say that such inscriptions probably never existed. This would be in accordance with the archaeological evidence, and then the speculation should be about why we don't have royal inscriptions from these two states in central Palestine. The discovery of the royal inscription from Ekron does not change anything, except that it tells us that royal inscriptions were known from other parts of Palestine in the Iron Age.[27] It might have to do with the character of kingship,[28] or it might reflect the status of the state, although relative poverty can hardly be the reason when we think about Ahab's state and his presence among the allies that fought the Assyrians at Qarqar in 853 BCE.[29] To argue that ancient historiographers used royal commemorative inscriptions from Judah and Israel is, however, one more assertion beyond falsification.

Point 4: Oral transmission of ancient poetry. Amihai Mazar is referring to such texts as evidence as the Song of Deborah, the Blessing of Jacob, and other ancient poetic texts. The problem with all of this is that such texts only exist in a written form; moreover, that they are hard to date.[30] The issue of oral tradition is most complicated and the idea that such traditions should include valuable historical information about the past is contested. In spite of Robert D. Miller II's recent sympathetic study on oral tradition,[31] which seeks to reclaim a sense of historical importance for oral sources, he is up against a prevailing scepticism expressed by some well-known scholars, including Walter J. Ong and Jack Goody. Goody's point of view is actually that oral societies remember nothing which squares well with the old observation that oral traditions are new formulations every time they are being performed, until the moment when they are reduced to writing.[32] We have no oral transmission in the Old Testament, only a few examples of literature that may rely on oral tradition. We know nothing about the sources, not even the age of such traditions, and it is really not an argument worthy of discussion, except in the sense already mentioned regarding secondary historical sources: they are testimonies about the time when they are performed, although the examples of oral tradition often referred to, such as the Song of Deborah, are no longer oral tradition but written tradition, and should be seen as a secondary source to, for instance, the battle against Sisera. While it is possible, even likely that oral tradition was around in central Palestine in the Iron Age, we have no access to it and it is therefore impossible to evaluate its value as a historical source.

Point 5: Folk stories and aetiological stories. Very much the same can be said about such stories as about oral tradition – we have no control of their origins seen as historical sources. However, the folktale as a phenomenon has been studied for more than two hundred years, ever since the Brothers Grimm published their collections of *Kinder- und Hausmärchen* between 1812 and 1815.[33] Few would accept such stories as historical sources except as testimonies of popular culture in the period in which they were collected. It should also be remembered that such collections as the one by the Grimm brothers represent the transfer of popular tales orally transmitted to a written media with all the changes that go along with the change of medium. Then we have the aetiological legends which were in the past sometimes seen as sources of information about, mostly, the origins of holy places. That these are not historical sources in the usual sense of the word has been made very clear in a recent study of aetiological narratives by Łukasz Niesiołowski-Spanò,[34] who in an almost Wellhausenian style writes: "Attempts at dating the myths about the origins of holy places necessitate the establishment of the time when these sanctuaries functioned…"[35] Łukasz Niesiołowski-Spanò defines these legends as myth and therefore not historical in any sense of the word.

Point 6: Earlier historiographic works. Mazar is referring to such texts as 2 Kgs 22:39, calling upon the reader to consult "the Chronicles of the Kings of Israel." We also find reference to other similar sources, but as we have no idea of what such sources may have included, it is hardly a useful source of any kind. And again – not a scrap has been preserved.

Summing Up

Reviewing the six points discussed here, we may characterize the first three as no more than assertions, simply because it is not possible to falsify them in any sensible way. They cannot be proven or disproven; they are simply of no value in a scholarly discussion. This is serious because it tells us that nothing has changed in the "methodology" of traditional historical-critical scholarship. To a large degree, traditional historical-critical scholars of the old school never bothered to invest time in proper historical methodology, that is, such methods that were currently in use among their colleagues within the discipline of general history. It is, as a matter of fact, a surprising discovery that until fairly recently no histories of Israel included much in the way of methodological reflection. Seen in this light it is hardly surprising that even the most elementary logical mistakes were made, such as relying on circular argumentation and in this case on blanket assertions.[36] Such elementary mistakes mark out the scholarship in question as worthless. There is really no reason to continue a discussion based on these kinds of "arguments," or rather non-arguments, and it is of no consequence that so many biblical scholars believed in such arguments, and quite a number still do. The breakdown in recent times of traditional historical-critical scholarship was simply caused by scholars who would not subscribe to the bad habits of previous scholarship.

Mazar's two references to oral tradition and folktales and aetiologies may not be considered in the same class as the first three parts of his argumentation. There is no reason to doubt the presence of orally transmitted stories in ancient Palestine. Definitely any basically illiterate society will tell stories of this kind. Writing was hardly an option outside of a narrow circle of administrators, whether religious or secular (if such a division makes any sense). Our problem is that this oral literature is absolutely useless to historians. There is no way of reconstructing the history of oral traditions except in the few cases – like Sennacherib *ante muros* – where all parts of this story, except the annalistic type (e.g. in 2 Kgs 18:13–16), are obviously inventions by the historiographer. Neither is it possible to evaluate the historical content of sources orally handed down and therefore not in existence anymore, and basing any argument on non-existent sources would be the end of any kind of historical study of the Old Testament.

Notes

1. G. Garbini, *Storia e Ideologia nell'Israele Antico* (Brescia: Paideia Editrice, 1986; ET *History and Ideology in Ancient Israel* [London: SCM, 1988]). This part of Garbini's work has been followed up in his *Myth and History in the Bible* (JSOTSup 362; Sheffield: Sheffield Academic Press, 2003), and *Letteratura e politica nell'Israele antico* (Brescia: Paideia, 2010).

2. G. Garbini, "L'iscrizione aramaica di Tel Dan," *Atti della Academia Nazionale dei Lincei* 391 (1994), pp. 461–71.

3. Cf. G. Garbini, *Il Semitico di Nord-ovest* (Naples: Istituto Universitario Orientale di Napoli, 1960), and *Il Semitico Nordoccidentale: Studi di storia linguistica* (Studi Semitici N.S. 5; Rome: Università degli studi "La Sapienza," 1988). Of course, both works are in Italian, making it possible for his critics to ignore them. In contrast to their colleagues within Oriental Studies, many biblical scholars (mainly Anglo-Saxon) seem unable to move freely within other modern languages than English. I am constantly urging my students to acquire knowledge of both French and German, as well as – if possible – also Italian and Spanish. Thus the enormous important area of Mari studies will be closed to them if they do not know French (and/or Akkadian).

4. J. Sasson, "Ins and Outs of Bible Research: The Case of the Mari Archives," October 9, 2013. The proceedings of the conference will be published. An abstract of this lecture can be found online: http://www.teol.ku.dk/abe/arrangementer/changing-perspectives/AbstractsFinal23092013.pdf/.

5. B. B. Schmidt (ed.), *The Quest for the Historical Israel: Debating Archaeology and the History of Early Israel* (Atlanta: Society of Biblical Literature, 2007), pp. 21–33. Amihai Mazar's lecture at the IOSOT meeting in Munich in August 2013, "Archaeology and the Bible: Reflections of Historical Memory in the Deuteronomistic History," which was subsequently published in *Congress Volume: Munich, 2013* (VTSup 163; Leiden: E. J. Brill, 2015), pp. 347–69, shows that he has not changed his mind since the publication of Schmidt's volume.

6. M. Noth, "Der Beitrag der Archäologie zur Geschichte Israels," in *Congress Volume: Oxford, 1959* (VTSup 7; Leiden: E. J. Brill, 1960), pp. 262–82; cf. already his "Grundsätzlicher zur Geschichtlichen Deutung archäologischer Befunde auf dem Boden Palästinas," *Palästinajahrbuch* 34 (1938), pp. 7–22. His articles on the subject are reprinted in M. Noth, *Aufsätze zur biblischen Landes- und Altertumskunde* I (ed. H. W. Wolff; Neukirchen–Vluyn: Neukirchener, 1971), pp. 1–51.

7. Cf. among other works W. F. Albright, *The Archaeology of Palestine: From the Stone Age to Christianity* (Harmondsworth: Penguin, 1940; rev. edn, 1960). As to Y. Yadin (and biblical scholarship in Israel after independence), his contributions to *Views of the Biblical World* (Jerusalem: Jordan Publications, 1st Intl. edn, 1959) should be enough.

8. That the procedure of digging with the Bible in one hand and a spade in the other is still in force can see in a reference to E. Mazar (more about her excavations below), who readily admits that she uses this "method," according to an interview in the *Moment Magazine*: "I work with the Bible in one hand and the tools of excavation in the other. That's what biblical archaeologists do. The Bible is the most important historical source and therefore deserves special attention."

9. Mazar, *The Quest for the Historical Israel*, pp. 28–29.

10. R. de Vaux's *Histoire ancienne* was, because of the author's death in 1971, never finished. It appeared between 1971 and 1973 (Paris: J. Gabalda). Liverani's review was published in *Oriens Antiquus* 15 (1976), pp. 145–59.

11. J. Bright, *A History of Israel* (London: SCM, 1960 [US edition 1959]).

12. M. Noth, *Geschichte Israels* (London: SCM, 1960 [US edition 1959]).

13. *The Biblical Archaeologist* 25 (1962), pp. 65–87 (reprint: *The Biblical Archaeologist Reader 3* [New York: Doubleday, 1970], pp. 100–20).

14. Cf. J. Barr, *Fundamentalism* (London: SCM, 1977), pp. 130–32. Barr has the following characterization of Kitchen's *Ancient Orient and Old Testament* (London: Tyndale, 1966): "there is perhaps not a single book among the conservative evangelical works read in the research for this study that so fully breathes the spirit of total fundamentalism as does Kitchen's work." The same can without qualification be said about Kitchen's second major contribution to biblical studies, *On the Reliability of the Old Testament* (Grand Rapids: Eerdmans, 2006). Cf. also my review of this work of Kitchen's recent book in the *JAOS* 124 (2004), pp. 375–77.

15. M. W. Chavalas and M. R. Adamthwaite, "Archaeological Light on the Old Testament," in D. W. Baker and B. T. Arnold (eds.), *The Face of Old Testament Studies: A Survey of Contemporary Approaches* (Grand Rapids: Baker Books, 1999), pp. 59–96 (80 n. 97).

16. If we can believe his characterization of minimalists, e.g., in his *What Did the Biblical Writers Know and When Did They Know It? What Archaeology Can Tell Us about the Reality of Ancient Israel* (Grand Rapids: Eerdmans, 2001), pp. 23–52.

17. Cf. Also his *Römische Geschichte*, I–II (Berlin: In der Realschulbuchhandlung, 1811–12; repr. in 3 vols. with a register; Boston: Adamant Media Corporation, 2001).

18. This has been clear at least to Danish historians since the days of the "father" of Danish historians Kristian Erslev (1852–1930), who published his methodology *Historisk Teknik. Den historiske Undersøgelse fremstillet i sine Grundlinjer* (*Historical Technique: The Main Lines of Historical Research*) in 1911 (Copenhagen, 1911). Alas none of Erslev's technical publications have ever been translated.

19. See D. D. Luckenbill, *The Annals of Sennacherib* (Oriental Institute Publications, II; Chicago: Chicago University Press, 1924), for a transcription and translation.

20. As also illustrated on the walls of Sennacherib's palace, where reliefs could be found describing the conquest of Lachish as the major event of this campaign. See also D. Ussishkin's marvelous edition of these reliefs, *The Conquest of Lachish by Sennacherib* (Tel Aviv: The Institute of Archaeology, 1982).

21. D. J. Wiseman, *Chronicles of Chaldean Kings (626–556 B.C.) in the British Museum* (London: The Trustees of the British Museum, 1956). A revised edition was published by A. K. Grayson, *Assyrian and Babylonian Chronicles* (Locust Valley/Glückstadt: J. J. Augustin; repr. Winona Lake, IN: Eisenbrauns, 2000), pp. 87–104.

22. Mazar, *The Quest for the Historical Israel*, pp. 29–30.

23. This is not the place to go into the recent debate about Eilat Mazar's discovery of monumental architecture on the Ophel in Jerusalem, triumphantly published as the palace of David. Cf. E. Mazar, "Did I Find King David's Palace?," *Biblical Archaeology Review* Jan./Feb. 2006; digital version: http://www.biblicalarchaeology.org/daily/biblical-sites-places/jerusalem/did-i-find-king-davids-palace/. A critique was published by I. Finkelstein, Z. Herzog, L. Singer-Avitz and D. Ussishkin, "Has King David's Palace in Jerusalem Been Found?," *Tel Aviv: Journal of the Institute of Archaeology of Tel Aviv University* 34 (2007), pp. 142–64, online: http://isfn.skytech.co.il/articles/King%20David%20palace,%20Tel%20Aviv%202007.pdf). Cf. also I. Finkelstein, "The 'Large Stone Structure' in

Jerusalem: Reality versus Yearning," *Zeitschrift des Deutschen Palästina-Vereins* 127 (2011), pp. 1–10.

24. On Jerusalem's expansion, see I. Finkelstein, "The Settlement History of Jerusalem in the Eight and Seventh Centuries BC," *Revue Biblique* 115 (1008), pp. 499–515.

25. Cf. on this N. P. Lemche, "The Deuteronomistic History: Historical Reconsiderations," in K. L. Noll and B. Schramm (eds.), *"Raising Up a Faithful Exegete: Essays in Honor of Richard D. Nelson"* (Winona Lake, IN: Eisenbrauns, 2010), pp. 41–50. Alt's article "Die Heimat des Deuteronomiums" was published in his *Kleine Schriften zur Geschichte Israels*, II (Munich: Beck, 1953), pp. 250–75.

26. On Sennacherib's destruction, cf. Sennacherib's own words in Luckenbill, *The Annals of Sennacherib*, pp. 32–33, III: 18–35.

27. For the Ekron inscription, see S. Gitin, T. Dothan, and J. Naveh, "A Royal Dedicatory Inscription from Ekron," *Israel Exploration Journal* 47 (1997), pp. 9–16.

28. Cf. Also A. Faust, "Decoration versus Simplicity: Pottery and Ethnic Negotiation in Early Israel," *Ars Judaica* 9 (2013), pp. 7–18 (17). Abraham Faust kindly provided me with a copy of his article. Professor Faust also indicated (personal communication) that he does not think that there were no such inscriptions at all, which would indeed have been an absolutistic argument that might easily be corrected.

29. Ahab at Qarqar, cf. *ANET* p. 279.

30. Cf. thus G. Garbini, "Il Cantico di Debora," *La Parola del Passato* 1978, pp. 5–31; reprinted in *Letteratura e politica nell'Israele antico*, pp. 32–60.

31. R. D. Miller II, *Oral Tradition in Ancient Israel* (Eugene: Cascade, 2011).

32. W. J. Ong, *Orality and Literacy: The Technologizing of the World: 30th Anniversary Edition with Additional Chapters by John Hartley* (London: Routledge, 2012); Jack Goody, *Myth, Ritual and the Oral* (Cambridge: Cambridge University Press, 2010). See also the review by R. F. Person Jr., http://www.bookreviews.org/pdf/8361_9144.pdf.

33. G. Grimm, *Kinder- und Haus-Märchen. Gesammelt durch die Brüder Grimm* (Berlin: Realschulbuchhandlung, 1812/1815).

34. Ł. Niesiołowski-Spanò, *Origin Myths and Holy Places in the Old Testament: A Study of Aetiological Narratives* (CIS; London: Equinox, 2011).

35. Niesiołowski-Spanò, *Origin Myths and Holy Places*, p. 246, reminding us of Wellhausen's old saying that it is not possible to write the history of a nation before there is a nation.

36. For more on circular argumentation, see N. P. Lemche, *The Old Testament Between Theology and History: A Critical Survey* (Louisville: Westminster John Knox, 2008), pp. 110–12.

TOPONYMY RIDDLES

Mario Liverani

1. Akhetaten

When Rib-Adda, king of Byblos, at the end of his reign, was ousted from his city (following a joint coup-d'état by his brother and the city assembly), he found refuge in Beirut, wherefrom he addressed to Pharaoh a long and sad letter (EA 138). Among the several complaints, there is the fact that one of his sons, sent as a messenger to inform the Pharaoh of the situation and to ask for his intervention, had not even been granted an audience. Here is the pertinent passage: "Ten seconds after my arrival in Beirut, I sent my son to the royal Palace, but after four months he has not yet seen the king's face! My man says: 'I reached him in Tahda'."[1]

The city of Tahda (URU *ta-aḥ-da*^{ki}), the seat of a royal palace, the residence of the king himself, and presumably located southwards of Lower Egypt, cannot but be Amarna itself, the usual residence of Amenophis IV. This identification, however obvious it appears to me, has never been taken into account. In the commentary to Knudtzon's edition of the Amarna letters, reference is made to the identification with a small town called Ṭaḥta in Middle Egypt, but with no ancient remains to substantiate it.[2] Afterwards, nobody seems to have pursued any investigation on the problem, until my own hint at a possible identification with Amarna,[3] a hint that I intend to develop here.

The name Amenophis IV gave to his residence and new capital city was "Horizon of (god) Aten," *ȝḫt ʾitn* (cf. Cannuyer 1985 on writings and implications). In order to consider *ta-aḥ-da* as a cuneiform rendering of *ȝḫt ʾitn*, we have to maintain that the toponym was preceded by the determinative article (*tȝ*), which is unusual[4] but not impossible, and that the element *ʾitn* had been omitted or at least compressed. In the first case (i.e. "the Horizon" instead of "Horizon of Aten"), we would have an abbreviated and somewhat colloquial form of the toponym. In the second case (which I would prefer) we would have the unification of redoubled consonants and the elimination of the ending *-n*:[5] from *tȝ-ȝḫt-ȝtn* through *tȝḫt-ȝt* to *tȝḫt*. The cuneiform rendering comes out rather approximate – something not unexpected, however, considering the poor knowledge of Egyptian by the Byblos or Beirut scribes.

2. Pi-ṣidqi

In the funerary inscription of Ahmes son of Abana, in the narrative of the war led by Pharaoh Ahmosis I against the Hyksos, and culminating in their defeat and expulsion, a military clash is mentioned that took place "on the water in the canal *pȝ-ḏdkw* of Avaris" (Urk. IV, 3, 10; ARE II 9). Although the older dictionaries of Egyptian considered dubitatively *ḏdkw* as a possible common term (but a *hapax*!) for "canal,"[6] most common is its interpretation as a proper name of a canal (as shown by the final determinative), preceded by the article *pȝ*. The name, however, has no possible Egyptian meaning or etymology, and its "hyksos" context can suggest a Semitic reading.

The appropriate parallel is provided by the personal name Pī-ṣidqi belonging to a queen of Ugarit, the wife of Ammistamru II and queen-mother under Niqmadu II (ca. 1250–1220 BCE) (SAL *pí-ṣi-id-qi* in PRU III, p. 50: RS 16.277: 2; p. 51: RS 15.86: 4), whose meaning as "Mouth of justice" in the sense of "just utterance/order" is further confirmed by the similar name Pī-zibli "Mouth of lordship."[7] The identification presents no problems: Semitic ṣ is currently rendered by signs for ḏ in Egyptian, especially in the called "syllabic" writing of Asiatic toponyms like Ṣarepta, Ṣumura, Ḥaṣor, Ṣidon etc.[8]

Presumably, a canal with a name worthy of being mentioned should have been a major one: either the moat surrounding the citadel of Avaris (the siege of that city is mentioned in the preceding line of the same text) or a major canal derived from the Pelusium branch of the Nile, on whose bank the Hyksos capital city was located.[9] The North-West Semitic language of the Hyksos is no longer a matter of debate, but I think that our occurrence has a special relevance, because personal names often are transmitted through generations and can even be no longer understood in their original meaning; but a name (and one of ideological/political significance) given to a canal, probably a newly built one, was certainly a purposeful choice by the king of Avaris.

3. Atlantis

It is always embarrassing to deal with Atlantis, since 99.9% of the literature belongs to "historical fiction." Yet the problem of the choice of the name by Plato is a "normal" historical and philological problem, and

I will venture to address it. To do a thorough job of research, it would be necessary to enlarge the inquiry to the entire topic of "Atlantis before (and besides) Plato," and deal with the titan Atlas, with the mythical heroine Atalante, and so on, i.e., with the entire geographical imagery of Greek mythology. I have to limit myself here to the properly toponymic problem.

The only recent attempt, properly philological in nature, to provide an etymology for Atlantis, has been provided by the Egyptologist Wolfgang Schenkel[10] who suggested that the name derives from Egyptian ʾiw.tt rn-s, "(island) whose name does not exist," well fitting to an island that had disappeared – yet rather strange if applied to the island when still existing. An alternative hypothesis has been advanced by J. G. Griffiths[11] as ʿ3t rn.s, "'Great One' is its name." However, if the myth had been created by Plato himself, as most serious scholars agree, an Egyptian etymology creates a problem which can be gotten around only by assuming an Egyptian origin of the myth itself – but with no sound evidence for that (Griffiths' attempt in this direction is based on a series of vague and non-specific similarities).

I think we should start with Herodotus' passage (IV 181–85) listing and describing the inner Libyan peoples, following a sort of itinerary that starts from Siwa and ends on the middle Niger, with stages separating each other by distances of ten-day marches. The itinerary goes back to ca. 500 BCE and was possibly transmitted to Herodotus through Hecataeus. The three stages, i.e., the three peoples, located in the central Sahara, are the Garamantes, the Atarantes, and the Atlantes. In a previous study[12] I sought to demonstrate that the Garamantes are to be located around Jarma (Latin Garama), the great oasis in the Wadi Ajjal, as already commonly accepted; the Atarantes are to be located around Ghat, in the Wadi Tanezzuft; and the Atlantes are to be located in the Hoggar, near modern Ideles. The distance of ten days between one stage and the next, a current pace for Saharan caravans, makes these identifications quite reasonable, and the itinerary, beginning from the Siwa oasis, points directly towards the Middle Niger (towards Timbuctu, to use the medieval reference point). The direction taken by the caravaneers is "westwards," but more precisely in the direction WSW, using as a reference point the direction of the setting sun.

Now, the three peoples mentioned by Herodotus bear names of evident Berber etymology. The Garamantes are "those of the city" (it would be *Kel Aghram in modern Berber[13]), the Atarantes are "those of the mountain" (*Kel Tadrart,[14] but toponyms include also Tadrart), and the Atlantes are "those of the West" (*Kel Atarem[15]). The former proposal by Wilhelm Brandenstein[16] to explain Atlantis by Berber *adrar*, "mountain," did not take into account Herodotus' sequence, and ended with an identification with the Jebel Chelia (in the Aurès Massif), that looks devoid of any specific reason.

The three names in my own proposal are perfectly appropriate. The site called "The Town" (Aghram, Latin Garama, then in Arabic Jarma) was the major settlement of the area, the capital city of the Garamantes, who took their name therefrom. The "Mountaineers" (Atarantes) inhabited the area in between the mountain ranges of the (Tadrart) Akakus and the Tassili. And the "Westerners" (Atlantes) inhabited the westernmost part of the settled central-Saharan (later unified by the Garamantian expansion) area: note that Herodotus hints at a couple of more stages from the Atlantes to the Niger, but without giving them a name.

Later, when the proper direction of the itinerary (from ENE to WSW) had been forgotten, the idea remained that a region called Atlantis was located around a high mountain, so high that its top reached the cloudy sky, to the extreme west of the Sahara. In Greek mythology and mythical "mental map" the high mountain was identified with the Moroccan Atlas (which obviously received its name therefrom), and with the "columns" or better gigantic steles that Heracles erected at Gibraltar to mark the world's end. The process was already well advanced in Herodotus' times, when the "Atlantic Ocean" is known (I 203). Eventually, Plato will give the name of "Atlantis" to his imaginary island (or better continent) located on the extreme west of the known world.

4. Minoa

The connection between the name and the origin of a settlement was viewed differently in the past than it is in modern scholarship. In past times, especially in classical times, there was a strict correspondence between the name of a settlement and the name of his founder. History and myth interacted: no doubt dozens of Alexandriae had been founded by Alexander (or on his order), dozens of Seleuciae had been founded by a Seleucus, and Antiochiae by an Antiochus, and so on – not differently from older Mesopotamian usage, with Dur-Sharrukin founded by Sargon II, or Kar-Shalmaneser founded by Shalmaneser III. But when the toponym had no meaning in the inhabitants' language, and its foundation was not the work of a specific person, or went back to times before the personal memory of the inhabitants, they imagined that the site had been founded by a person whose name was similar. In other words, the name of a (pseudo-)historical founder-hero was deduced from the name of the settlement (Romulus from Rome, just to give a paradigmatic example).

Today we still accept – of course! – that historical foundations by a specific king could receive their names from the king's name. But we no longer accept the reverse trajectory, of explaining unknown toponyms with recourse to a mythical hero. The name of Rome was not derived from Romulus, but the name of Romulus derived from Rome, and his very historical existence was the result of the procedure that we can call "mythical etymology." Yet modern scholarship has not been prompt to admit that the existence of a Minos was the result of "mythical etymology" applied to the name of the several sites called Minoa spread through the Aegean area (one in the Argolic Gulf, two on the NE and the NW coasts of Crete, one in a small island facing Megara, plus the additional case of Heraclea Minoa in Sicily).

Now, a non-Greek toponym in the Aegean area, specifically applied to coastal sites, i.e., harbours, and presumably going back to the very early phase of the first millennium – being later on misunderstood by the Greek-speaking local population – could be a Phoenician name. The obvious candidate is a term derived from the root *nwḥ*, "to rest," meaning "resting place" or the like, as in Biblical Hebrew *mānôaḥ* and *měnûḥāh* which have such a meaning. Greek Minoa suggests a vocalization of the assumed Phoenician toponym as *minoaḥ, and a function of the sites that bear such a name as "stopping places" (certainly not true "colonies"!) regularly used by ships crossing the area. By the way, Sicilian Heraklea Minoa should be a *Minoaḥ Melqart.

The term is not attested in Phoenician inscriptions (for lack of contexts in which we would expect to find it). But one of the Amarna letters,[17] by Addu-dani (or Baʿlu-shipti) king of Gezer, contains a passage that seems fully pertinent to our proposal: "I had built a house, Manhate by name, in order to prepare in sight of (the arrival) of the (Egyptian) troops of the king my lord. But Maya requisitioned it, and put a commissioner of his own inside it. Entrust Rianap, my commissioner, with (the charge of) returning the town to me, and I will prepare in sight of (the arrival) of the (Egyptian) troops of the king my lord" (ll. 29–40).

In order to appreciate better the content of the letter, we have to bear in mind the standard procedure of the Egyptian administration, to send a letter asking the local kings to "listen" (*šemû*) to Pharaoh's word, to "protect" (*naṣāru*) the city entrusted to them, and to "prepare" (*šūšuru*) everything necessary for the arrival of an Egyptian military contingent, expecting a reply confirming that these orders will be obeyed.[18] And we have also to bear in mind the specific political juncture with a new commissioner Rianappa replacing the old one Maya.[19] But here what matters is that this site, Manhate, is called a "house" (*bītu*) or a "city/town" (*ālu*), being something in between the two. Moreover, the form Manhāte looks like a plural (from a singular *Manahtu), and the meaning could hint more properly at a set of buildings as resting places or lodgements for the travelling merchants or soldiers.

Since the mythical Minos is already attested in the eighth century (he is quoted in Odyssey XI 568–71), our proposal could be a proxy for the existence of a presence (or at least regular passages) of Phoenician merchants in/through the Aegean in the previous centuries, in the so-called "pre-colonial phase of the Mediterranean trade." But this topic should require additional time and competences that exceed my own.

Notes

1. On the idiom "ten seconds after" (i.e. "immediately after"), cf. W. L. Moran, *The Amarna Letters* (Baltimore/London: The Johns Hopkins University Press, 1992), p. 224 n. 17.

2. O. Weber, in J. A. Knudtzon, *Die El-Amarna-Tafeln* (Leipzig: Hinrichs, 1915), pp. 1240–41.

3. M. Liverani, *Le lettere di El Amarna* (Brescia: Paideia, 1998–99), II, p. 469; quoted but not accepted by J. A. Belmonte Marín, *Die Orts- und Gewässernamen der Texte aus Syrien im 2. Jt. v. Chr.* (TAVO Beihefte B 7, 12.2; Wiesbaden: L. Reichert, 2001), p. 283.

4. See H. Gauthier, *Dictionnaire des noms géographiques contenus dans les textes hiéroglyphiques* (Paris: Institut Français d'Archéologie Orientale), I, pp. 8–9, always without the article.

5. I thank Alessandro Roccati for confirming that in the Amarna age the ending -*n* was no longer pronounced.

6. A. Erman and H. Grapow, *Wörterbuch der aegyptischen Sprache* (Leipzig: Hinrichs, 1931), V, p. 635; R. O. Faulkner, *A Concise Dictionary of Middle Egyptian* (Oxford: Griffith Institute, 1962), p. 326.

7. See F. Gröndahl, *Die Personennamen der Texte aus Ugarit* (Studia Pohl 1; Rome: Pontificium Institutum Biblicum, 1967), pp. 170, 187, 347.

8. Since M. Burchardt, *Die altkanaanäischen Fremdworte und Eigennamen in Aegyptischen* (Leipzig: Hinrichs, 1909), I, §§ 149–53; W. F. Albright, *The Vocalization of the Egyptian Syllabic Orthography* (American Oriental Series 5; New Haven: American Oriental Society, 1934), pp. 66–67.

9. Cf. L. Habachi, *Tell el-Dabʿa, I. Tell el-Dabʿa and Qantir. The Site and Its Connection with Avaris and Piramesse* (Österreichische Akademie der Wissenschaften, Denkschriften XXIII; Vienna: Verlag der Österreichische Akademie der Wissenschaften, 2001), passim, and p. 105 for our passage.

10. W. Schenkel, "Atlantis: die 'namenlose' Insel," *Göttinger Miszellen* 36 (1979), pp. 57–60, followed with some qualification by M. Görg, *Aegyptiaca-Biblica. Notizen und Beiträge zu den Beziehungen zwischen Ägypten und Israel* (Ägypten und Altes Testament 11; Wiesbaden: Harrassowitz, 1991), p. 23.

11. J. G. Griffiths, "Atlantis and Egypt," in *Atlantis and Egypt, with Other Essays* (Cardiff: University of Wales Press, 1991), p. 22.

12. M. Liverani, "The Libyan Caravan Road in Herodotus IV.181–185," *Journal of the Economic and Social History of the Orient* 43 (2000), pp. 497–520.

13. See K.-G. Prasse, *Lexique Touareg – Français, deuxième édition revue et augmentée* (Carsten Niebuhr Publications 24; Copenhagen: Museum Tusculanum Press, 1998), p. 121 sub *aǧrĕm*, "ville"

14. See Prasse, *Lexique*, p. 42 sub *adrar*, "montagne."

15. See Prasse, *Lexique*, p. 334 sub *atăram*, "ouest, occident.'"

16. 1951, p. 72; see also earlier suggestions in Pauly-Wissowa Realencycl., II p. 2119.

17. EA 292 in Knudtzon, *Die El-Amarna-Tafeln*, and Moran, *The Amarna Letters* = LA 49 in Liverani, *Le lettere di El Amarna*, I.

18. M. Liverani, "A Seasonal Pattern for the Amarna Letters.," in Tz. Abusch, J. Huenergard and P. Steinkeller (eds.), *Lingering Over Words: Studies in Ancient Near Eastern Literature in Honor of W. L. Moran* (Atlanta: Scholars Press, 1990), pp. 337–48.

19. M. Liverani, "The Disgraced Commissioner: The Turnover in Amarna Officialdom," in P. Marrassini (ed.), *Semitic and Assyriological Studies Presented to P. Fronzaroli* (Wiesbaden: Harrassowitz, 2003), pp. 350–54.

DIVIDING THE IMAGE OF GOD:
THE CREATION OF MAN AND WOMAN IN GENESIS*

Caterina Moro

While researching for my Ph.D. on textual history of Hebrew *Proverbs*, under the tutelage of Giovanni Garbini, I began to study ancient exegesis of the Bible to investigate the attitude of the people who transmitted, copied and translated the biblical text. Exegesis was for me then a kind of screen between me and the "naked" text, a blindfold, something that had to be detected and removed, in order to reach for the real intentions of the ancient author.[1] Afterwards I learned that ancient interpreters sometimes preserve different versions of a story told in the Bible,[2] and sometimes can help us to shorten the distance between our mentality and the mentality of biblical authors.

The Creation of Humankind in P

In the so-called "Priestly" narrative, God creates humankind (אדם)[3] on the last day of creation; humans are to have dominion over all creatures (Gen 1:26–29). The most important prerogative of this *adam* is to be created, as the text repeats three times, in the image of God. The Hebrew word used, *ṣelem*, means "image," in most cases with the concrete meaning of "statue, representation."[4] The word *demut*, "likeness," used in parallel to *ṣelem* in v. 26,[5] has also the concrete meaning of "(resembling) representation," or "external aspect."[6] This physical meaning of the two terms is confirmed by linguistic comparison: in the Aramaic inscription of Tell-Feheriye *ṣalma* and *demuta* indicate the statue on which the text is inscribed.[7] According to an interpretation that has gained influence in the last century,[8] the author, saying that man is an image of God, a "living statue," invests him with a prerogative that in the ancient Near East was reserved to the king, as a representative of gods on earth. In Mesopotamia, for example, we find this concept expressed in the letters of the court official Adad-Shumu-Usur to his king Esarhaddon (seventh century BCE): "The father of the king, my lord, was the very image (*ṣalmu*) of Bel, and the king, my lord, is likewise the very image of Bel."[9] In Egypt we find some eight different terms for "image (of god)": six of them are used only for the king, especially from the end of the XVIIth Dynasty on, and four mean "statue."[10] The theology of image exalts the king's kinship with the sun-god Ra,[11] creator and preserver of the universe. The extension of royal prerogatives to humanity by the biblical author was not the consequence of a generic *democratization* of the concept, but of the conscious *rejection* of royal ideology after the fall of the kingdom of Judah (587 BCE) and, after the exile, the annihilation of the royal house of Judah with the death of Zerubbabel.[12] The institute of kingship is presented in the Hebrew Bible as something alien to Israel (Deut 17:14–20)[13] and dangerous (1 Sam 8:11–18), but in the historical books, besides the almost general condemnation of kings as idolaters and unfaithful, we can find some traces of the priestly role of the king: for example, in the narratives about the consecration of the Temple of Jerusalem by Solomon (1 Kgs 8), the covenant of King Josiah in 2 Kgs 23, or the institution of the temple in Bethel by Jeroboam in 1 Kgs 12 (see also Amos 7:13).[14] A trace of an ancient conception of king as the image of gods can be detected also in Ezek 28, where the king of Tyre is called (perhaps) "the seal of image" (v. 12).[15]

The idea that humanity as a whole is an image of God can be found also in Egypt, in the *Instructions for Merikara* (ca. 2060 BCE), where humankind is said to be the "herd of god" and "his likeness (*snn*) that came forth from his flesh."[16] But the time of composition of this work (First Intermediate Period) saw a deep crisis of the royal ideology, and a general appropriation of kings' prerogatives by commoners.[17]

Woman and the Image of God

Some commentators break v. 27 in two and say that the words "male and female he created them" are not related to the theme of the image of God, but with the blessing of fertility in v. 28.[18] In Christian tradition, the first who interpreted the two *cola* as parts of one sentence was Clement of Alexandria, followed by Augustine.[19] But besides the division of the traditional Hebrew text,[20] there are at least two considerations that make me think that the verse has to be considered a unit:

(1) Every kind of animal is created and blessed by God with the command "be fruitful and multiply," but only the *adam* is said to be created "male and female." So this piece of information, apparently obvious, must be somehow related to something that is only human, like being the image of God.

(2) The first sentence of v. 27 is in a narrative tense and follows the ordinary sequence verb–subject–object of Hebrew syntax, but the second and third sentences are of the type described by A. Niccacci as *X–qatal*, that is, have the finite verb in second position. This peculiar construction highlights the first element (adverbial, nominal or pronominal) of the sentence, that becomes its syntactical predicate, a new and significant bit of information. The second part of the sentence has the function of syntactical subject, as in the English construction called a "cleft sentence" ("It's George who came").[21] We can translate the second part of the verse with two cleft sentences in parallel.

(*narrative tense*)	ויברא אלהים את־האדם	So God created *adam*
	בצלמו	in his image
X	בצלם אלהים	it is as an image of God
QATAL	ברא אתו	that he created him;
X	זכר ונקבה	it is male and female
QATAL	ברא אתם	that he created them

"As an image of God" and "male and female" are two new pieces of information in parallel. The intention of the author was not to assert that man and woman are equal, or that God is asexual,[22] but the exact opposite: humankind (*adam*) as a whole was created to be an earthly image of God, *but* male and female, that is to say, the woman is a *sui generis* image of God.[23] In pre-exilic Israel God was the male part of a couple, as we know now from the inscription of Kuntillet 'Ajrud and Khirbet el-Qom. In these inscriptions YHWH was mentioned together with "his Asherah."[24] The memory of the goddess Asherah almost disappeared in the Hebrew Scripture, where this name seems to indicate (with important exceptions)[25] an object of the cult in the so-called "high places." The scanty notices from the few pre-exilic passages mentioning Asherah show that there was an image of that goddess in the Temple of Jerusalem, and that her cult was somehow linked with the royal family.[26] YHWH had a spouse, Anat, also in the Jewish temple of the military colony of Elephantine, in fifth-century Egypt.[27] Moreover, the metaphor of the marriage between God and Israel, so widespread in the Prophets, presupposes also a male God, and a hierarchical use of gender: Israel is subordinated to his God as a wife to his husband.[28]

Another limitation to the possibility for women to be an image of God is the relationship, in the author's mind, between kingship and the feminine. We know very little about queens in the pre-exilic kingdoms of Judah and Israel. It seems that queens can be very bad, as the examples of Jezebel and Athaliah show, or non-influential.[29] In every case, in the Old Testament there is no information on the queen's ideological role or her importance. In Egypt, where the ideology of the king as god's image is more developed, we have some examples of the application of this paradigm to women who called themselves *nsw-bity*, "king of Upper and Lower Egypt."[30] The most documented example of this application is Queen Hatshepsut, in the XVIIIth Dynasty. In her celebrative texts she takes the title "image of god," using the terms *ḥntj*, "statue," and *snnt*, "she-image" (of the male god Amon).[31] Her titulary and her representations fluctuate between male and female gender: she was *ḥrt*, "she-Horus," and *rȝt*, "she-Sun." According to E. Hornung, this shift could happen because the vital point of Egyptian theology about the image of god was "not the outward similarity between the king and a particular deity" but "a similarity of deeds" and "a comprehensive and fundamental kinship that links the king with all deities."[32] The position of Lana Troy on that matter is different: in her comprehensive study on queens in Egypt she maintains that "the kingship, with a function analogous to creator, combines the roles of male and female."[33] When the king is a man, royal women (mothers, wives and daughters of the king) are his feminine counterparts, symbolically related with the female deities of kingship, like the Two Ladies.[34] So, from royal woman to female monarch there was only "a short step."[35]

Creation of Man and Woman in Genesis 2[36]

In the second narrative of the creation of man and woman the hierarchy of sexes is more explicit: God created first a male individual called *adam*[37] and then animals and a woman as his helpers.[38] The *adam* is created not to be a representative of God but, apparently, to work in the garden of Eden.[39] Ancient Jewish interpreters, each one in his own way, tried to eliminate the contradiction between the two narratives: the most ancient witness to this tendency can be found in the book of *Jubilees*, written in Hebrew in the second century BCE:[40]

> After all this, [in the first week] he made mankind – as one man and a woman he made them. He made him rule everything on earth and in the seas and over flying creatures, animals, cattle, everything that moves about on the earth, and the entire earth… (*Jub.* 2:14)

Apparently, this first verse follows strictly Gen 1:26–28, even if it does not mention the image of God. The events of Gen 2 take place "in the sixth day of the second week", when only the woman is created.[41] The last verse of this narrative explains the sense of 2:14:

> In the first week Adam and his wife – the rib – were created, and in the second week he showed her to him. (*Jub.* 3:8)

What the text seems to say is that in Gen 1:27 God did not create two genders or two individuals, but a single (male) man including his wife as a part of his body.[42] In almost every ancient Jewish reading, the effort to compress two stories has the result of privileging the second one.[43] A similar proceeding can be found in the *Sibylline Oracles*[44] and in the *Greek Life of Adam and Eve*,[45] where the image of God is mentioned only when speaking about the man. It is this kind of exegesis that seems to lie behind the famous passage in 1 Cor 11:7–9:

> For a man ought not to have his head veiled, since he is the image and glory of God (εἰκὼν καὶ δόξα Θεοῦ ὑπάρχων); but woman is the glory of man. Indeed, man was not made from woman, but woman from man (ἀλλὰ γυνὴ ἐξ ἀνδρός). Neither was man created for the sake of the woman (διὰ τὴν γυναῖκα), but woman for the sake of the man (διὰ τὸν ἄνδρα).

The fifth-century CE midrash called *Bereshit Rabbah* (8:1) offers a quite different kind of harmonization:

> Rabbi Jeremiah b. Leazar said: When the Holy One, blessed be He, created Adam, He created him an androgyne, for it is said, *Male and female he created them and called their name Adam* (Genesis 5:2). Rabbi Samuel b. Nahman said: When the Lord created Adam He created him double-faced, then He split him and made him of two back, one back on this side and one back on the other side. To this is objected: But it is written, *And he took one of his ribs* etc. (Genesis 2:21) (מצלעתיו means one of his *sides*), replied he, as you read *And for the second side* (צלע) *of the tabernacle* etc. (Exodus 26:21).[46]

This tradition, clearly influenced by the speech of Aristophanes in Plato's *Symposium* (189E–190A),[47] could have been so ancient as to leave a trace in the Septuagint of Genesis, where צלע was translated πλευρά ("side"),[48] and is sometimes alluded to in the work of Philo of Alexandria.[49]

Is there a relationship between this exegesis and the Gnostic belief in an androgynous primordial being,[50] or with Egyptian beliefs about a creator that "combines the roles of male and female"?[51] The androgyne of *Bereshit Rabbah* does not seem to cooperate in any way with the creation process. But there is still another interesting piece of *midrash* on the creation of man and woman, quoted two times in *Bereshit Rabbah*, which appears, in a slightly different form, even in Paul (1 Corinthians):[52]

> They (the heretics) asked him (R. Simlai)[53] again: "What is meant by *And God said: Let us make man?*" "Read what follows," replied he "not 'And Gods created (*waybreʾu*) man' is written here, but 'And God created (*waybraʾ*)'."[54] When he went out his disciples said to him: "Them you have dismissed with a mere makeshift, but now will you answer to us?." Said he to them: "In the past Adam was created from dust and Eve was created from Adam: but henceforth it shall be *In our image, after our likeness* (Genesis 1:26); neither man without woman nor woman without man, and neither of them without the Divine Spirit (Shekina)." (*Bereshit Rabbah* 8.9)[55]

> Nevertheless, in the Lord there is no woman without man or man without woman, *for just as woman came from man* (ἐκ τοῦ ἀνδρός), *so man comes through woman* (διὰ τῆς γυναικός); but all things come from God. (1 Cor 11:11–12)

The words in italics in Paul are the part lacking in *Bereshit Rabbah*: as we can see, in Paul this *logion* is not yet related to Gen 1:26, and so it is not yet a *midrash*. In the latest form of the *logion* the creation "once and for all" ("in the past") is opposed to the daily generation of children by man and woman, cooperating with God (in his immanent aspect, the Shekinah), as an act of continuous creation.[56] What is at stake in this *logion*, especially when it becomes a *midrash*? In the first occurrence the answer is apparently the unity of God in face of the plural in v. 26. In my opinion, there is something more which began to appear as soon as the *logion* was related to 1:26.

It seems like there is no room for divine providence in the world of Gen 1: animals and plants can reproduce themselves and the creation of humankind, as a representative of God on earth, allows God to stay in his rest.[57] The second story of the creation presents the nature of humans more dramatically, but the conclusion is that humans are "like one of us" (the gods, or heavenly beings), two independent beings that can choose between good and evil and can live on their own, in the actual world – that is far from being an ideal place. The first and second narrative of creation of humanity, each one in his own way, seems to me to have some points of resemblance with the ideas that Josephus ascribes to the Sadducees.

> The Sadducees, the second of the orders, do away with Fate (Providence)[58] altogether, and remove God beyond, not merely the commission, but the very sight, of evil. They maintain that man has the free choice of good and evil, and that it rests with each one's will whether he follows the one or the other. (*War* 2.165)

The origins of the Sadducees and what they really thought are open to debate. The birth of the Saducean party is set by scholars in the third or second century BCE.[59] Can Gen 1–3 be so late? I would agree with such a late date, especially for the first (P) narrative. The second narrative can be somewhat older, but apparently it gained authority only at a late date.[60]

I would argue that there was a time when this way of depicting God was nothing more than a part of traditional Jewish thinking. But in the latest parts of the Old Testament, in parts of the wisdom literature and Psalms, thinking of YHWH as a transcendental deity what created the world and acted in the mythical past, but that is not directly involved with the present world (especially with the judgement and punishment of individuals),[61] began to be depicted as a form of atheism.

> The fool thinks: there is no God. (Pss 14:1; 53:2)

> And they say: how can God know? Is there knowledge in the Most High? (Ps 73:11)[62]

Saying that God cooperates in human reproduction, this midrash says that God *creates* man every day, every second of human history, with an explicit reversal of the spirit of "Saducean" creation. I do not know whether the interpreters quoted in *Bereshit Rabbah* were conscious of the "gender" implications of this reading of Genesis. Regardless, surely the idea of Providence taking care of the world is more "feminine," maternal, than creation once and for all. Perhaps the interpreters did not believe that women are images of God as well as men, but for them every individual is a threefold image of a God, a woman, and a man – and, in creating life, God, man, and woman can experience a moment of unity (the "us" of Gen 1:26) that does not belong to the mythical past, but to a perpetual present.

Notes

* This study is a revised version of the paper read in the VIIIth Congress of the European Association for Jewish Studies (Moscow, July 2006).

1. C. Moro, *"Ascolta la mia parola." Analisi testuale di* Proverbi *22,17–24,22* (Studi Semitici n.s. 17: Rome: Università degli Studi "La Sapienza," 2002), p. i.

2. See, for example, the analysis of the story of Moses in Hecateus of Abdera and other Hellenistic writers by G. Garbini, *History and Ideology in Ancient Israel* (trans. John Bowden; London: SCM, 1988), pp. 133–50, which was the starting point of all my following studies on this figure; see C. Moro, "L'historien Artapan et le passé multiethnique," in Ph. Borgeaud et al. (eds.), *Interprétations de Moïse. Égypte, Judée, Grèce et Rome* [Jerusalem Studies in Religion and Culture 10; Leiden/Boston: Brill, 2010], pp. 43–55, and *I sandali di Mosè* [Studi biblici 167; Brescia: Paideia, 2011]).

3. See Gen 5:2: "and He called *their* name *adam*."

4. F. Scagliarini, "ṢLM e altre parole per 'statua' nelle lingue semitiche," *Studi Epigrafici e Linguistici* 25 (2008), pp. 63–86, especially pp. 64–65.

5. The same parallel appears in Ezek 23:14, 15.

6. Scagliarini, "ṢLM e altre parole per 'statua'," p. 69. Ṣelem and *demut* have the same concrete meaning also in Rabbinic literature; see A. Goshen-Gottstein, "The Body as Image of God in Rabbinic Literature," *Harvard Theological Review* 87 (1994), pp. 171–95.

7. W. Randall Garr, "'Image' and 'Likeness' in the Inscription from Tell Fakhariye," *Israel Exploration Journal* 50 (2000), pp. 227–34; Scagliarini, "ṢLM e altre parole per 'statua'," pp. 66–68.

8. D. J. A. Clines, "The Image of God in Man," *Tyndale Bulletin* 19 (1968), pp. 53–103 (= "Humanity as the Image of God," in *On the Way of the Postmodern: Old Testament Essays, 1967–1998* [Sheffield: Sheffield Academic Press, 1998], II, pp. 447–97); J. A. Soggin, *Das Buch Genesis. Kommentar* (Darmstadt: Wissenschaftliche Buchgesellschaft, 1997), pp. 43–45, 50–53 (contra C. Westermann, *Genesis 1–11: A Commentary* [Minneapolis: Augsburg, 1984], p. 153); Garr, "Image and Likeness," p. 234 n. 37; idem, *In His Own Image: Humanity, Divinity and Monotheism* (Culture and History of Ancient Near East 15; Leiden: Brill, 2003), pp. 155–65.

9. For the text of the letters, see S. Parpola, *Letters from Assyrian Scribes and Scholars to the King Esarhaddon and Assurbanipal*. I. *Texts* (Neukirchen–Vluyn: Butzon & Bercker Kevelaer, 1970), n. 125.15; Clines, "The Image of God," p. 83. On the concept of king as image of god in ancient Near East, see also T. Römer, "La création des hommes et leur multiplication. Lecture comparée d'Atra-Hasis, de Gilgamesh XI et de Genèse 1; 6–9," *Semitica* 55 (2013), pp. 147–56, especially pp. 151–52.

10. E. Hornung, "Der Mensch als 'Bild Gottes' in Ägypten," in O. Loretz (ed.), *Die Gottebenbildlichkeit des Menschen* (Munich: Kösel-Verlag, 1967), pp. 123–56.

11. The title "Son of Ra" was used by three kings of the IVth Dynasty: in the Vth Dynasty it became a fixed part of the royal titulary; see A. H. Gardiner, *Egypt of the Pharaohs: An Introduction* [Oxford: Oxford University Press, 1961], p. 84).

12. P. Sacchi, "L'esilio e la fine della monarchia davidica," *Henoch* 11 (1989), pp. 131–48; G. Garbini, *Il ritorno dall'esilio babilonese* (Studi Biblici 129; Brescia: Paideia, 2001), pp. 145–72; idem, "La lancia del re. Indagini sull'ebraico šeleṭ," in P. G. Borbone et al. (eds.), *Loquentes linguis. Studi linguistici e orientali in onore di Fabrizio A. Pennacchietti* (Wiesbaden: Harrassowitz, 2006), pp. 301–305, especially pp. 304–305; idem, *Scrivere la storia d'Israele*, pp. 188–97.

13. On this passage, see G. Garbini, *Myth and History in the Bible* (JSOTSup 362; trans. C. Peri; Sheffield: Sheffield Academic, 2003), pp. 65–66; P. R. Davies, "The Place of Deuteronomy in the Development of Judean Society and Religion," in *Recenti tendenze nella ricostruzione della storia antica d'Israele* (Rome: Accademia Nazionale dei Lincei, 2005), pp. 139–55 (148).

14. On the covenant between God and kings in the Bible and its oriental parallels, see Garbini, *Myth and History*, pp. 65–66, 94–95.

15. Reading *ḥotam* (instead of *ḥetem*) *tabnit*. J. Van Seters thinks that this passage was one of the sources of the narrative of creation of man in Gen 2 (*Prologue to History: The Yahwist as Historian in Genesis* [Westminster: John Knox Press, 1992], pp. 119–22; see also T. Römer, "Le jardin d'Éden entre le ciel et la terre," *Journal Asiatique* 300 [2012], pp. 581–93, especially pp. 584–86)

16. E. Hornung, *Conceptions of God in Ancient Egypt: The One and the Many* (London: Routledge & Kegan Paul, 1983), p. 138 [English translation by J. Baines of *Der Eine und die Vielen* [Darmstadt: Wissenschaftliche Buchgesellschaft, 1971]).

17. Hornung, "Mensch als Bild Gottes," pp. 136, 146–47.

18. See, e.g., P. A. Bird, "'Male and Female He Created Them': Gen. 1,27b in the Context of the Priestly Account of Creation," *Harvard Theological Review* 74 (1981), pp. 129–59; eadem, "Sexual Differentiation and Divine Image in the Genesis Creation Texts," in K. E. Børresen (ed.), *Image of God and Gender Models in Judeo-Christian Tradition* (Oslo: Solum, 1991), pp. 11–53; D. J. A. Clines, "What Does Eve Do to Help? And Other Irredeemably Androcentric Orientations in Genesis 1–3," in idem, *What Does Eve Do to Help? And Other Readerly Questions to the Old Testament* (JSOTSup 90; Sheffield: Sheffield Academic, 1990), pp. 25–48, especially pp. 43–44.

19. K. E. Børresen, "Gender and Exegesis in the Latin Fathers," *Augustinianum* 40 (2000), pp. 65–76; eadem, "La Féminologie d'Augustin: création, chute et résurrection," in Børresen (ed.), *Christian and Islamic Gender Models* (Rome: Herder, 2004), pp. 67–83, esp. 70–71; on the position of Didymus, see, in the same volume, E. Prinzivalli, "Early Christian Anthropology: Gender Models in Creation of Resurrection," pp. 43–65, especially pp. 61–62.

20. The first division of the Hebrew text that appeared (in the Dead Sea Scrolls) was *per cola et commata* (e.g. in a part of 1QIsa); some later poetical manuscripts show a *colon* (half-verse) or a verse (*bicolon*) for each line (C. Moro, *"Ascolta la mia parola,"* pp. vii–viii and n. 16). The actual verse division of the entire Hebrew Bible is still later (around fifth century CE; see J. M. Oesch, *Petucha und Setuma* [Orbis Biblicus et orientalis 27; Freiburg/Göttingen: Vandenhoeck & Ruprecht, 1979], pp. 28–31), but nevertheless it is a feature of the text that has to be valued alongside other traditional data, like Tiberian vocalization.

21. A. Niccacci, *The Syntax of the Verb in Classical Hebrew Prose* (JSOTSup 86; Sheffield: Sheffield Academic, 1990), English translation by W. G. E. Watson of *Sintassi del verbo ebraico nella prosa classica* (Jerusalem: Franciscan Print Press, 1986), pp. 23–29 (definition of complex noun clause), pp. 166–67 (complex noun clause with adverbial predicate); idem, "Marked Syntactical Structures in Biblical Greek in Comparison with Biblical Hebrew," *Liber Annuus* 43 (1993), pp. 9–69, especially pp. 9, 13–15, 27, 32–34; idem, "Finite Verb in the Second Position of the Sentence: Coherence of the Hebrew Verbal System," *ZAW* 108 (1996), pp. 434–40, especially p. 434; idem, "Ebraico biblico e lingustica," *Henoch* 20 (1998), pp. 189–207; contra W. Gross, "Is There Really a Compound Nominal Clause in Biblical Hebrew?," in C. L. Miller (ed.), *The Verbless Clause in Biblical Hebrew: Linguistic Approaches* (Winona Lake, IN: Eisenbrauns, 1999), pp. 19–49, especially pp. 35–37.

22. Contra Bird, "Male and Female," p. 139 (= "Sexual Differentiation," pp. 16–17).

23. C. Moro, "Dividere e unire: la creazione dell'uomo e della donna nell'esegesi giudaica antica e nella critica moderna," *Studi e materiali di storia delle religioni* n.s. 28 (2004), pp. 123–43, especially pp. 131–32; P. Merlo, "L'immagine di Dio. Maschio e femmina in *Gn* 1,26–27 e nella figura di Dio," *Antropotes* 21 (2005), pp. 105–19.

24. On inscriptions, see P. Merlo, *La dea Ašratum – Atiratu – Ašera. Un contributo alla storia della religione semitica del Nord* (Rome: Mursia, 1998), pp. 197–209; J. M. Hadley, *The Cult of Asherah in Ancient Israel and Judah: Evidence for a Hebrew Goddess* (Cambridge: Cambridge University Press, 2000), pp. 84–155; W. G. Dever, *Did God Have a Wife? Archeology and Folk Religion in Ancient Israel* (Grand Rapids: Eerdmans, 2005), pp. 131–67; G. Garbini, *Introduzione all'epigrafia semitica* (Studi sul Vicino oriente antico 4; Brescia: Paideia, 2006), pp. 101–104; idem, *Dio della terra, Dio del cielo* (Biblioteca di cultura religiosa 70; Brescia: Paideia, 2011), pp. 53–55. In Eblaite documents there is a suffix pronoun in the name of the female member of a divine couple, for example, "the god X and his Y," see P. Xella, "Le dieu et 'sa' déesse: l'utilisation des suffixes pronominaux avec des théonymes d'Ebla à Ugarit et à Kuntillet 'Ajrud," *Ugaritische Forschungen* 27 (1995), pp. 599–610; Merlo, *La dea Ašratum*, pp. 196–97; Hadley, *The Cult of Ashera*, pp. 78, 104–105; for Asherah as YHWH's wife, see also Dever, *Did God Have a Wife?*, pp. 166–67. Of course, we know nothing about the hierarchical relationships in this divine couple.

25. E.g. 2 Kgs 21:7; 23:4; 1 Kgs 15:13.

26. Merlo, *La dea Ašratum*, pp. 193–94; Garbini, *Dio della terra, Dio del cielo*, pp. 199–200. In this study he also gave an interpretation of Gen 1:26 totally different from the one offered here: the *adam* is "male and female" according the image of the divine couple, with a female partner not revered any more but somehow alluded to under the name of Spirit/Wind (feminine in Hebrew) in Gen 1:2 and 3:8 (pp. 253–55). A similar opinion (without reference to the Spirit) is expressed also by Römer, "La création des hommes et leur multiplication," pp. 149–51.

27. We do not know if the "Queen of heaven" mentioned by Jeremiah (7:16–20; 44:15–19, 25), who was worshipped in Judah and then in Egypt, was Asherah or Anat.

28. For an early Christian formulation of this hierarchy, see 1 Cor 11:3.

29. In later Jewish traditions we find examples of glorified queens such as Esther and Bitya, the step-mother of Moses, but they were not queens of Israel or Judah.

30. Among the queens of Egypt are Sobekneferu (XIIth Dynasty), Hatshepsut (XVIIIth Dynasty), Tauseret (XIXth Dynasty)

31. Hornung, *Conceptions of God in Ancient Egypt*, p. 139; also *snn* means "statue," but not the cult statue that was carried out in processions. Along with *mity* it is the only word for "image" used also for non-royal persons (idem, "Der Mensch als Bild Gottes," p. 146).

32. Hornung, *Conceptions of God*, p. 139. See also idem, "Der Mensch als Bild Gottes," p. 151.

33. L. Troy, *Patterns of Queenship in Ancient Egyptian Myth and History* (Uppsala Studies in Ancient Mediterranean and Near Eastern Civilizations 14; Uppsala: Almqvist & Wiksell, 1986), p. 131.

34. *Nbty*, the vulture goddess of Upper Egypt and the cobra goddess of Lower Egypt. This king's title appeared as early as the first dynasty.

35. Troy, *Patterns of Queenship*, p. 132

36. For a history of research on Gen 2–3, see J.-L- Ska, "Genesis 2–3: Some Fundamental Questions," in K. Schmid and C. Riedweg (eds.), *Beyond Eden: The Biblical Story of Paradise (Genesis 2–3) and Its Reception History* (Forschungen zum Alten Testament 34; Tübingen: Mohr Siebeck, 2008), pp. 1–27.

37. *Adam* was interpreted by ancient versions as a proper noun (in Gen 2:23 calls himself *ʾiš*). The procedure of mixing clay with a divine element recalls Mesopotamian parallels such as the creation of man by Enki and Nintu in *Atrahasis* (English translation of the passage in S. Dalley, *Myths from Mesopotamia* [Oxford: Oxford University Press, 1989], pp. 15–16; for other Mesopotamian parallels, see Van Seters, *Prologue to History*, pp. 122–24).

38. The subordinate position of the woman emerges by her being created "for the sake of man," not by her being created "out of man" (that, at least, allows her to have a part of his "breath of life").

39. Gen 2:5; this theme too came to the biblical author from Mesopotamian epics (especially *Atrahasis*).

40. Some fragments of the original text have been found in Qumran; see J. C. VanderKam and J. T. Milik, "Jubilees," in H. Attridge et al., *Qumran Cave 4. VIII. Parabiblical Texts, Part 1* (Discoveries in the Judean Desert 13; Oxford: Clarendon, 1991), pp. 1–185. The complete text is preserved only in Ethiopic version; see J. C. VanderKam, *The Book of Jubilees* (CSCO 511; Scriptores Aethiopici 88; Lovanii: Peeters, 1989), pp. v–xxxviii; J. T. A. G. M. van Ruiten, "The Creation of Man and Woman in Early Jewish Literature," in J. P. Luttikhuizen (ed.), *The Creation of Man and Woman: Interpretations of Biblical Narrative in Jewish and Christian Traditions* (Themes in Biblical Narrative 3; Leiden: Brill, 2000), pp. 34–62, especially pp. 40–48; F. Corriente and A. Piñero, "Libro del los Jubileos. Traducción de la versión etiópica," in A. Díez Macho (ed.), *Apócrifos del Antiguo Testamento II* (Madrid: Ediciones Cristiandad, 1983), pp. 65–193.

41. There is no "second creation," neither for the man nor for the animals, which are simply "brought" to the man.

42. Van Ruiten, "The Creation of Man and Woman," pp. 46–47.

43. In his *Jewish Antiquities*, 1.32–36, Josephus explains the double creation in a way very similar to that of *Jubilees*, but without the chronological frame.

44. *Sibylline Oracles* 1:22–37; Van Ruiten, "The Creation of Man and Woman," pp. 48–54.

45. *Greek Life of Adam and Eve* 33:4–5: [Eve describing the death of Adam] "I myself saw golden censers and three bowls, and behold, all the angels with frankincense and censers and bowls came to the altar and breathed on him, and the fumes of frankincense hid the sky. And the angels fell down and worshiped God, crying out and saying, 'Holy Jael, forgive, for he is your image, and the work of your (holy) hands'"; see Natalio Fernández Marcos, "Vida de Adán y Eva (Apocalipsis de Moises)," in A. Díez Macho (ed.), *Apócrifos del Antiguo Testamento II* (Madrid: Ediciones Christiandad, 1983), pp. 317–52, especially pp. 334–35.

46. H. Freedman (trans.), *Midrash Rabba. I. Genesis* (London: Soncino, 1961), p. 54.

47. W. A. Meeks, "The Image of Androgyne: Some Uses of a Symbol in Early Christianity," *History of Religion* 13 (1974), pp. 165–208, especially pp. 185–86; see also G. Veltri, *Libraries, Translations, and "Canonic" Text: The Septuagint, Aquila and Ben Sira in the Jewish and Christian Traditions* (JSJSup 109; Leiden: Brill, 2006), pp. 112–14 (he supposes rather a Gnostic influence).

48. M. Harl, *La Bible d'Alexandrie*. I. *La Genése* (Paris: Cerf, 1986), p. 96.

49. *Opif.* 152; *Cher.* 59–60; *QG* 1.25; see J. Jervell, *Imago Dei. Gen. 1,26f. im Spätjudentum, in der Gnosis und in den paulinischen Briefe* (Göttingen: Vandenhoeck & Ruprecht, 1960), p. 68; Meeks, "The Image of Androgyne," p. 186 nn. 92–93.

50. Jervell, *Imago Dei*, pp. 161–65; Meeks, "The Image of Androgyne," pp. 188–97; M. R. D'Angelo, "Transcribing Sexual Politics: Images of Androgyne in Discourses of Antique Religion," in C. Locatelli and G. Covi (eds.), *Descrizioni e iscrizioni: politiche del discorso* (Labirinti 30; Trento: Università degli Studi, 1998), pp. 115–46, esp. 135–45.

51. While in Gnostic systems differentiation–division of the original unity is a bad thing, in Egypt it is the beginning of life. In CT 80 Atum, floating on the Nun, is weak and fat (pregnant?) until she gives birth to the twins Shu and Tefnut; see S. Bickel, "Un hymne à la vie. Essai d'analyse du Chapitre 80 des Textes des Sarcophages," in C. Berger, G. Clerc, and N. Grimal (eds.), *Hommages à Jean Leclant*. I. *Études pharaonique* (Bibliothèque d'Étude 106.1; Cairo: Institut français d'Archéologie Orientale, 1994), pp. 81–97.

52. On this parallel, see H. L. Strack and P. Billerbeck, *Kommentar zu neuen Testament aus Talmud und Midrash IV* (Munich: Beck 1926), p. 440; Jervell, *Imago Dei*, pp. 311–12; M. Boucher, "Some Unexplored Parallels to 1 Cor 11,11–12 and Gal 3,28: The NT on the Role of Woman," *CBQ* 31 (1969), pp. 50–58; M. R. D'Angelo, "The Garden: Once and Not Again," in G. A. Robbins (ed.), *Genesis 1–3 in the History of Exegesis: Intrigue in the Garden* (Studies in Women and Religion 27; Lewiston: Edwin Mellen, 1988), pp. 1–41.

53. Around 250 CE.

54. Cf. the same argumentation in *b. Sanh.* 38b (by R. Yohanan).

55. Freedman, *Midrash Rabba I*, p. 60. The same midrash (from "In the past…" on) is attributed to R. Akiba in 22,2 (Freedman, *Midrash Rabba I*, p. 181).

56. A. Goldberg, *Untersuchungen über die Vorstellung der Schekhina in der frühen rabbinischen Literatur* (Berlin: de Gruyter, 1969), pp. 352–53; according to Veltri (*Libraries, Translations*, pp. 111–12), the text means rather that "God first created Adam and Eve as prototypes, and with the help of these prototypes he created people as males and females." For other rabbinic witness to the theory of "three partners" in human reproduction, see R. Kiperwasser, "Three Partner in a Person: The Genesis and Development of Embryological Theory in Biblical and Rabbinic Judaism," *Lectio difficilior – European Electronic Journal for Feminist Exegesis* 9/2 (2009), pp. 1–37, especially pp. 1–13 (available online at http://www.lectio.unibe.ch/09_2/kiperwasser.html).

57. As Clines says, an image represents "one who is really or spiritually present, though physically absent… The god has his statue set up in the temple to signify his real presence there, though he may be in heaven, on the mountains of the gods" ("The Image of God," pp. 87–88); see also G. Garbini, "La cosmogonia fenicia e il primo capitolo della Genesi," in G. De Gennaro (ed.), *Il cosmo nella Bibbia* (Studio Biblico Teologico Aquilano; Naples: Dehoniane, 1982), pp. 127–48, esp. 146.

58. The word used by Josephus for Fate, *heimarmene*, is the word used for Providence by the Stoic school (see also Josephus, *Life* 2, "I began to govern my life by the rules of Pharisees, a sect having points of resemblance to that which the Greeks call the Stoic school").

59. According to Jewish tradition, all began with the dispute between two disciples of Antigonus of Soko (*Abot de R. Natan* A 5), a dispute that could take place by the end of the third or the second century BCE; see Günter Stemberger, *Pharisäer, Sadduzäer, Essener* (Stuttgarter Bibel-Studien 144; Stuttgart: Katholisches Bibelwerk, 1991), pp. 62–64. A third-century date is proposed also (with different motivations) by J. Lauterbach, "The Sadducees and Pharisees: A Study of their Respective Attitude Toward the Law," in idem, *Rabbinic Essays* (Cincinnati: Hebrew Union College Press, 1951), pp. 23–48, esp. 28–29 (originally in *Studies in Jewish Literature: Issued in Honour of K. Kohler* [Berlin: G. Reimer, 1913], pp. 176–98), and R. T. Beckwith, "The Prehistory and Relationships of the Pharisees, Sadducees and Essenes: A Tentative Reconstruction," *Revue de Qumran* 11 (1982), pp. 3–46. The first scholar who supposed a Epicurean influence on Sadducees was E. Baneth, "Ueber der Ursprung der Sadoqäer und Boëtosäer," *Magazin für die Wissenschaft des Judentums* 9 (1882), pp. 1–37, 61–95; see also G. Garbini, "La metereologia di Giobbe," *Rivista Biblica* 43 (1995), pp. 85–91; contra J. Le Moyne, *Les Sadducées* (Paris: Lecoffre, 1972), p. 34, 354–55, and Stemberger, *Pharisäer, Sadduzäer, Essener*, pp. 67–69.

60. For a late date of Genesis, see Garbini, *History and Ideology in Ancient Israel*, pp. 108–109, 139–40, 147–50; idem, *Myth and History*, pp. 62–63, 68–71; J. J. Collins, "Before the Fall: The Earliest Interpretations of Adam and Eve," in H. Najman and J. H. Newman (eds.), *The Idea of Biblical Interpretation: Essays in Honor of James L. Kugel* (Leiden: Brill, 2004), pp. 293–308 (see especially pp. 296–99 on Ben Sira 17, where humankind is said to be mortal and endowed of wisdom by God from the beginning, not as a consequence of a transgression). In particular, on a relative late date for chs. 2–3 and its reception as authoritative text, see Ska, "Genesis 2–3: Some Fundamental Questions," pp. 16–20; K. Schmid, "Loss of Immortality? Hermeneutical Aspects of Genesis 2–3 and Its Early Reception," in Schmid and Riedweg (eds.), *Beyond Eden*, pp. 58–78, especially p. 65.

61. On the punishment of Israel, see Lauterbach, "The Sadducees and Pharisees," pp. 35–38.

62. G. Garbini, "Letteratura e politica: consenso e dissenso nell'antico Israele," in *Cedant Arma. Letteratura, parole d'ordine e organizzazione del consenso nel mondo antico* (Como: New Press, 1991), pp. 15–22; Le Moyne, *Les Sadducées*, p. 39.

Farewell to the "Blind and Lame" (2 Samuel 5:6–10)

Łukasz Niesiołowski-Spanò

The biblical passage concerning the siege of Jerusalem by David (2 Sam 5:6–10) has drawn scholarly attention numerous times over the years. The formula of exclusion of the blind and lame from the Hebrew cult, which became popular in biblical literature, made this story particularly attractive. Despite the voluminous commentary devoted to this passage, there still remain alternative explanations and interpretations of the phrase that have not been sufficiently explored. To whit, it is possible that the passage contains words the original meaning of which have been forgotten. The present study aims to explore the possibility of re-interpreting the saying about blind and lame in Jerusalem and its role anew.

Leviticus 21:18–20 is linked to 2 Sam 5:8, which refers to exclusion from the faith-community and the prohibition from sacrificial offerings by the physically disabled: "For no one who has a blemish shall draw near, one who is blind or lame, or one who has a mutilated face or a limb too long, or one who has a broken foot or a broken hand, or a hunchback, or a dwarf, or a man with a blemish in his eyes or an itching disease or scabs or crushed testicles." Among the "physical blemishes" mentioned are those referred to in the story of David's conquest of Jerusalem: "blind" (עִוֵּר) and "lame" (פִּסֵּחַ).[1] Connecting these two physical disabilities is quite common in biblical texts; for example, it suffices to cite Job 29:15; Jer 31:8; Matt 11:5 and Luke 14:31. There is no doubt that the exclusion of "the disabled" from the temple service was well known, and very likely practiced in the world of the Ancient Hebrews. However, such a cultic restriction – regardless of its origin and the degree to which it was observed – in no way explains the reference to "blind and lame" at the walls of Jerusalem, during the attack of David's forces.

Recently, a fresh attempt to deal with the difficulties created by the passage in 2 Sam 5 was undertaken by Craig W. Tyson.[2] Tyson's argument focuses on the concept of insider/outsider opposition, and its role in exclusion, as seen in 2 Sam 5:8b. This study shows that with all our knowledge and previous studies, there are still biblical passages whose meanings remain obscure. Certainly this is the case with the passage in question.

2 Samuel 5:6–10 relates the story of David's conquest of Jebusite-inhabited Jerusalem. This well-known story includes the intriguing detail: "[The Jebusites] said to David, 'You will not come in here, even the blind and the lame will turn you back' – thinking, 'David cannot come in here'" (2 Sam 5:6). This phrase, often underlined in previous scholarship, expresses loathing and disdain towards David and his army ruling from Hebron, combined with confidence in the strength of Jerusalem's defences – which were presumably so strong that even the disabled would suffice to defend it.[3] However, in the next phrase the situation can no longer be interpreted in this manner: "David had said on that day, 'Whoever would strike down the Jebusites, let him get up the water shaft to attack the lame and the blind, those whom David hates.' Therefore it is said, 'The blind and the lame shall not come into the house'" (2 Sam 5:8). Despite the textual difficulties and lexical obstacles,[4] the sense of David's expression remains clear – the king put some sort of difficult task before his soldiers. This difficulty is openly stated in 1 Chronicles, where David's words are reported: "Whoever attacks the Jebusites first shall be chief and commander" (1 Chr 11:6). It would be rather nonsensical to interpret this task to have been a battle against the disabled.

There are widely different explanations proposed in scholarship for the presence of the blind and lame at Jerusalem's walls. Apart from the literal interpretations, accepting the text *prima facie*, commentators have sought a religious key to the scene. Religious rituals, during which soldiers took an oath in which they swore they should be blemished if they acted unfaithfully, have been suggested; the presence of disabled people would remind the soldiers of their oath.[5] Even if such an explanation is hard to disprove, though equally hard to prove, one might look for a simpler solution requiring fewer hypothetical constructs – for example, that there were in fact real soldiers at the Jerusalem wall, instead of disabled people. Posting a well-armed, high-quality force on the city walls during the siege would have been the most logical defence manoeuvre. Even should any religious ceremonies have taken place alongside the military action, their role and importance would have been secondary to fending off the attacking army. The presence of competent defenders would have been important to both sides; by providing hope to defenders, and real enemies, true obstacles to be surmounted, for the besiegers. The efficacy of a lame and blind military is questionable to say the least.

Perhaps the reason this passages has caused so many interpretative problems lies in our presuppositions concerning the very words used. As seen above, the lame and blind turned out to be proverbial, and yet the presence of the lame and blind themselves in the battle scene are not fundamentally questioned. In fact, these words may be key to understanding the passage. The possibility should not be excluded that the meaning of the words in 2 Sam 5:6–8 meant something else altogether at the time they were written, only acquiring their present meaning at a later date.

The blind mentioned above are referred to in the MT as העורים, from the root ʿwr. "The lame," הפסחים, derives from the root psḥ. The verb ʿwr is used very often in the Bible and its meaning is not disputed. Therefore, any challenges to the lexical consensus, supported by ancient versions, proposed emendations of the text or suggestions of alternate meaning should be based on a reinterpretation of the nouns used. The textual difficulties alone, without any support in ancient translations, make any emendation doubtful. However, one may look for different meanings of the words.

A hint may be found in the meaning of the root ʿwr, "to awake," "to rouse." This verb is used in the description of the heroic acts of David's soldiers, and its very meaning may shed light on our text. "Now Abishai son of Zeruiah, the brother of Joab, was chief of the Thirty. With his spear (חנית) he fought (עורר) against three hundred men and killed them, and won a name beside the Three" (2 Sam 23:18). Similar use of the verb is to be found in the description of the acts of another hero: "Jashobeam, son of Hachmoni, was chief of the Three; he wielded (עורר) his spear (חנית) against three hundred whom he killed at one time" (1 Chr 11:11).[6]

Abishai's and Jashobeam's act are described as הוא עורר את־חניתו, in 2 Sam 23:18 and 1 Chr 11:11, respectively. The verb ʿwr primarily means "to rouse oneself," "awake"; in Poel it has the meaning "to rouse" and "to incite to activity." This allows the phrase to be interpreted as: "He brandished the spear"[7] thus potentially lending the verb ʿwr a meaning linking it to military action. The verb is used in such a manner in Isa 10:26 where specifically a whip is wielded with God as the subject. Similarly, Zech 9:13 and 13:7, where the verb ʿwr refers to the sword (חרב), a military context is provided.[8] This usage of the verb in a military context, where ʿwr refers to a weapon and means "to brandish" or "to wave," links it with the noun העורים. If this is accepted, then the noun in 2 Sam 5:6–8 could be understood as "the brandishers" or "the wavers (of a weapon)." Such an interpretation of העורים suggests the existence of a certain category of military unit whose name reflected the fact that it was an armed unit, or of the particular kind of weapon with which it was equipped. This understanding would better suit the context of a siege and the need for the best soldiers to take part in the defence of the city. It stands to reason that if a term describing a specific unit or its arms was coined, their particular function, importance and skills could likewise be defined. The עורים may have been a highly prestigious military unit consisting of the best soldiers, armed with a particular weapon or using it in a particular way. Using this interpretation David was not fighting the blind but rather against specialized military units armed with spears or swords.

An alternate explanation of the meaning of עורים could be based on the Ugaritic verb ʿr/ʿrr, meaning "to guard"; in some instances, such as Deut 32:11; Job 8:6 and Mal 2:12, the verb ʿwr in the Bible have been interpreted as "to guard" or "to protect."[9] In Deuteronomy God's protection over Israel is compared to an eagle's care of its chicks and nest – כנשר יעיר קנו. The translation of this phrase as "like an eagle protecting its nest" seems most appropriate to the context. The phrase in Job 8:6 is more ambiguous, leaving it open to speculation whether the sense of protection should be rather than "to arouse." The interpretation of Mal 2:12 remains similarly inconclusive. In sum, the arguments for verb ʿwr's meaning "to protect," are rather weak. The strongest argument remains the Ugaritic verb, the influence of which on Hebrew remains possible though not incontrovertible. However, proving such a meaning would establish the link between the protection described by the verb ʿwr and the function of the military protectors mentioned in 2 Sam 5:6–8. Whatever the case may be, both these interpretations provide alternative ways of understanding the term in question and eliminate the unfortunate blind from the siege of Jerusalem.

Larger difficulties arise when interpreting the noun הפסחים. Usually this noun is linked to the root *psḥ*, and its primary meaning "to lame." Passover is supposedly linked to the same root, though no scholarly consensus has been reached regarding this etymology.[10] The link between Passover (the feast and the sacrifice) and the verb "to lame" is far from straightforward.[11] Even if dictionaries univocally claim the meaning of this verb as "to lame" or "to be lame," other Semitic languages hardly make use of such a verb in this way.[12] The primary meaning of the word derived from the root *psḥ*, and its understanding, is obviously conditioned by the name of Passover – the main Jewish feast. The connection between the verb and the name of the feast is explicitly stated: "It is the Passover sacrifice (זבח־פסח) to the Lord, for he passed over (פסח) the houses of the Israelites in Egypt, when he struck down the Egyptians but spared our houses" (Exod 12:27; cf. Exod 12:23).

The abovementioned sentence from Exodus mentions the act of God "passing over" the houses of the Hebrews. However, the meaning of passing over, is – in a way – derived from the primary meaning of the verb and within this context the expression could be understood as "protected" or "saved."[13] This was probably the original meaning of the sacrifice, which served as protection and guaranteed shelter under God's protection. This definition agrees with the LXX version of Exod 12:27, where the Hebrew verb *psḥ* is rendered in Greek as σκεπάσζω – "to protect, to cover, to hide, to shelter."[14] Setting aside the concept of the lame and concentrating on the Passover sacrifice as the price for God's protection and salvation, this particular element made Passover the most important feast for the Jews. This very meaning underlies the importance of this feast for the Jews, as well as the Christian understanding of Christian sacrifice, where Jesus – as the proper Passover sacrifice – protects (and saves) humankind.[15]

This is the sense in which the verb *psḥ* is used in the following passage from Isaiah: "Like birds hovering overhead, so the Lord of hosts will protect Jerusalem; He will protect and deliver it, He will spare (פסח) and rescue it" (Isa 31:5). In this verse the verb *psḥ* is used in conjunction with the verbs *gnn* ("to cover, surround, defend"), *nṣl* ("to snatch away, rescue, recover, deliver from") and *mlṭ* ("to slip away, escape, deliver"), to which it is probably semantically close. This interpretation of the phrase is supported by the Targum and the LXX. The Targumic version reads יגין וישיזיב יציל ויעדי. The verb *psḥ* from MT is here rendered as the Aramaic verb *ṭll* ("to cover"; cf. Hebrew and Aramaic *ṣl*, "shade," "protection"). The Greek version, however, may indicate a lack of understanding of this expression. Instead of four verbs in the MT, the Greek version uses only three: ἐξελεῖται ("to rescue"), περιποιέω ("to keep alive," "to preserve") and σώζω ("to save," "to keep alive," "to protect").

It would be appropriate to point out as well the existence of the proper name derived from the same root: Paseaḥ, mentioned in the Bible at Neh 3:6; Ezra 2:49 and 1 Chr 4:12, as well as in a seal dated to the seventh/sixth century BCE (*CWSSS*, 323). It is not impossible that someone would be named "lame"; however, consequently one is led to suppose that the name actually had a different meaning. This again points to the words deriving from *psḥ* having a broader meaning.

Accepting "to protect" as the meaning of the verb *psḥ*, instead of the commonly assumed meaning "to be lame," advances an alternate hypothesis concerning the usage of the term in 2 Sam 5:6–8. The פסחים used in the passage does not necessarily refer literally to the lame;

instead, it could refer to protectors or defenders of the city. In the light of the above, I am inclined to advance the hypothesis that there were neither blind nor lame people at the Jerusalem walls as referred to in 2 Sam 5:6–8, but rather a highly specialized military unit called "the brandishers" or "the protectors." Moreover, if the noun העורים ("the protectors, the guards") were preferred, both terms, העורים and הפסחים, would match close semantic parallelism. In either case, they have a similar meaning, referring to people devoted to protection in the strict military sense of the word. Another possible explanation of the term הפסחים takes into account the context of Passover. The people called פסחים may have been soldiers designated as Passover victims. This explanation, however, lacks any solid foundation even if the connection between Passover and the first-born can easily be established. I find this explanation unlikely. I would posit that the verb *psḥ* meant "to protect" and referred to a certain kind of soldier.

This proposal concerning the original meaning of the name of Passover is obviously not new. However, scholars still believe in the presence of the "lame" and "blind" at Jerusalem's walls. The suggested understanding of terms העורים and הפסחים in 2 Sam 5:6–8 as "brandishers" and "protectors," which may be technical terms for a kind of military unit, suits the context well. It may also adequately explain the phrase: "Therefore it is said, 'The blind and the lame shall not come into the house,'" which now may be well seen as the gloss, aiming to explain terms the meaning of which were already obscure to the editors.[16]

How should one explain the fact that these military terms were already unfamiliar to biblical editors and later ancient translators? Some hypothetical reconstruction is needed in order to answer. First, the addition of the gloss in 2 Sam 5:8b, containing the saying establishing the exclusion of the "lame and blind" from the temple service, and linking 2 Sam 5:8 to Lev 21:18–20 (and other cultic prohibition laws), may be both the result of the terms' obscurity as well as its reason. Second, the military terms were apparently not used in later times. One may even speculate whether such military terminology was part of the heritage of Jerusalem's pre-Judean society, whether it was Canaanite, Jebusite or Philistine. That would explain the presence of these terms in an old text and their subsequent obscurity. The other explanation would point to an intentional "hiding" of the original meaning, which is less likely, unless the reason for such manipulation can be found.

Notes

1. S. Olyan, "'Anyone Blind or Lame Shall Not Enter the House': On the Interpretation of 2 Samuel 5:8b," *CBQ* 60 (1988), pp. 218–27.

2. C. W. Tyson, "Who's In? Who's Out? II Sam 5,8b and Narrative Reversal," *ZAW* 122 (2010), pp. 546–57, with updated bibliography.

3. Samuel R. Driver, *Notes on the Hebrew Text and the Topography of the Books of Samuel* (Oxford: Clarendon, 2nd edn, 1913), p. 258; Baruch Halpern, *David's Secret Demons: Messiah, Murderer, Traitor, King* (Grand Rapids: Eerdmans, 2nd edn, 2004), pp. 319–20.

4. P. Kyle McCarter, *II Samuel* (Anchor Bible 9; Garden City: Doubleday, 1984), pp. 135–40.

5. Yigael Yadin, *The Art of Warfare in Biblical Lands: In the Light of Archaeological Study* (New York: McGraw-Hill, 1963), pp. 267–70; cf. the comments and further bibliography in McCarter, *II Samuel*, p. 138.

6. This verse allows scholars to change the text in 2 Sam 23:8: "Joshebbasshebeth a Tahchemonite; he was chief of the Three; he wielded (עדינו → עורר) his spear against eight hundred whom he killed at one time."

7. McCarter, *II Samuel*, pp. 488–90.

8. Cf. *TDOT*, vol. 10, p. 571.

9. *TDOT*, vol. 10, p. 569.

10. Cf. *TDOT*, vol. 12, pp. 1–29.

11. Giovanni Garbini, *Note di lessicografia ebraica* (Brescia: Paideia, 1998), pp. 105–11.

12. Cf. Garbini, *Note di lessicografia*, pp. 105–106.

13. W. H. Irwin, *Isaiah 28–33: translation with philological notes* (Biblica et Orientalia 30; Rome: Biblical Institute, 1977), p. 114; T. F. Glasson, "The 'Passover', a Misnomer: The Meaning of the Verb Pasach," *JTS* 10 (1959), pp. 79–84.

14. William H. C. Propp, *Exodus 1–18* (AB 2; Garden City: Doubleday, 1999), p. 401.

15. About the link between Passover and *molk* sacrifice, see Ł. Niesiołowski-Spanò, "Child Sacrifice in Seventh-Century Judah and the Origins of Passover," *Przegląd Humanistyczny* 437, no. 2 (2013), pp. 161–70.

16. *TDOT*, vol. 12, p. 27.

FROM MOSES TO THE ESSENES

Étienne Nodet, O.P.

Introduction

In a synthesis of many studies, Giovanni Garbini concludes that the biblical religion is the outcome of a syncretic activity during the Hellenistic period, and that true monotheism was not practiced before 70 CE, to wit Christianity and Rabbinic Judaism.[1] For many years he had aptly wondered at the lack of clear records for the Persian and early Greek periods, from Cyrus to the Maccabean crisis.[2] Indeed, Josephus himself is at a loss to fill in the Persian period, and between Alexander and the second century BCE his documentation is scant. The books of Ezra and Nehemiah are not easy to understand and seem to have been reworked in later times: Ben Sira, in his gallery of renowned ancestors, does not know Ezra, and only mentions Nehemiah as a builder (Sir 49:13); it is not a casual mistake, for Josephus, in his biblical paraphrase, only knows Nehemiah the same way, as a builder.

Canaan or Syria-Palestine stands between Syria and Egypt, or between Semitic Babylon and Greek Alexandria. The religion of Israel has been a blend of local features, reworked under the influence of the larger adjacent cultures. This study aims to deal with both ends: first, the Pentateuch has collected many traditions and components, but the final touch was given at the library of Alexandria, and Moses, with "all the wisdom of the Egyptians," is the character who provided a synthesis. From Babylon came other traditions, perhaps older, but no Scripture properly speaking; the cradle of the later Pharisees was there. At the other end we have the Essenes, and the great Emil Schürer almost renounced understanding them,[3] for they are in many respects very traditional and close to the Pharisees, but they display, too, specific features that have a Greek appearance.

So we will proceed in what follows in six steps: on the identity of the Egyptian Moses; on a definite Egyptian connection; on Babylon and the Pharisees; on the non-lunar calendar common to the Sadducees and Essenes; on the Essene components in Rabbinic traditions; and finally, on the Essenes as heirs of the Egyptian Therapeuts.

I. Moses as Lawgiver

There is a remarkable view surfacing in various places in the Bible that Moses' law had been forgotten for several centuries. According to 2 Kgs 22:8 the high priest Hilkiyah found the "Book of the Law" in the house of Yhwh. Then King Josiah proceeds to undertake a major reform, removing the idols, and orders a celebration of Passover as it is described in the "book of the Covenant," and it is said that nothing of this kind had been done since the days of the Judges and all the days of the kings of Israel and Judah (2 Kgs 23:22); the parallel verse of 2 Chr 35:18 has "since the days of Samuel the prophet." Incidentally, the traditional view that Josiah discovered Deuteronomy in the seventh century cannot stand, since the main places referred to in Canaan are Mounts Ebal and Gerizim, and – more importantly – the Samaritans of Shechem[4] must be held to be Israelites of old, and not as a second-rank Judeans.[5] Later, when Ezra proclaimed the Law of Moses to the returnees from exile, they began to learn it and celebrated the Feast of Booths and "the sons of Israel had indeed not done so from the days of Joshua the son of Nun to that day" (Neh 8:17–18).

These rediscoveries of Moses' Law entail a twofold statement: first, that it is very old; and second, that it only took effect late. For instance, *m. Para.* 3:5 states that the first high priest to perform the rite of the Red Heifer (Num 19:1) was Simon the Righteous, ca. 200 BCE. As for the kings of Israel, we may observe that King Solomon was a kind of Phoenician vassal: 1 Kgs 5:15 LXX says that when King Hiram of Tyre heard of David's death "he sent his servants to anoint Solomon king in place of his father." Later on, Solomon builds a beautiful temple, which has nothing to do with the tabernacle of the desert, and the dating is given in Phoenician months (1 Kgs 6:37). Before this, when David was anointed king over Israel and captured the stronghold of Zion, "then Hiram king of Tyre sent messengers to David with cedar trees and carpenters and stonemasons; and they built a house for David, and David knew that Yhwh had established him as king over Israel" (2 Sam 5:11–12).

We can add the testimony of the Elephantine Aramaic papyri. At the end of the fifth century BCE, the Judeans there had the same kind of relationship with Samaria and Jerusalem, for in 407 they wrote to Delayah and Shelemyah, sons of Governor Sanballat of Samaria, to ask for help, after a similar request to Jerusalem had elicited no results. Their religious tenets can be summarized from two documents. The first is the so-called "Passover papyrus"[6] (Cowley, n. 21; *TADAE*, I, A4.1), a letter written in Aramaic by one Hananyah, presumably from Jerusalem, to Yedonyah and his colleagues, in the fifth year of Darius II (419–418); he invokes the protection of the gods over them (אלהיא), then transmits some instructions of the king (the lines are lost), and eventually tells them to observe Passover and the days of Unleavened Bread, with a wording very close to Exod 12:6, 18 (in Aramaic). This means that Yedonyah, the head of the garrison, did not have an established written law. According to another papyrus (Cowley, n. 22), the same Yedonyah was in charge of an important religious collection, and shared it between Yaho, Ashim-Bethel, and Anat-Bethel, three gods. These two pieces do not portray pure monotheism, to say the least, though the proper names are definitely Yahwist. Moreover, among the many administrative and legal documents unearthed at Elephantine, the name of Moses never appears, and the same can be said of the Zenon papyri in the third century, which include documents signed by Jews or Israelites.[7]

It is currently assumed that the origin of Moses' name משה is the suffix -*mses*, which is used in compound names like *Ramses*, but this very name appears in Gen 47:11 and elsewhere as רעמסס, and משה cannot be easily reduced to the component מסס-. The name is explained in Exod 2:10: "Because I drew (משיתיהו) him out of the water." This is quite approximate, for משה may mean "drawing," but not "drawn" (משוי). In fact, the LXX has kept a form Μωϋσῆς, where the demotic *môu* "water" and *ousai* "draw, lift" can be recognized. The meaning is much better, all the more that the explanation is offered by an Egyptian woman.

A common view held by Jews, and later by early Christian writers,[8] was that the Greek philosophers, especially Plato, borrowed from Moses. The first witness is the priest Aristobulus, alluded to in 2 Macc 1:10 as an opponent of the Hasmonean dynasty. He wrote a book on the Hebrew laws for King Ptolemy VI of Egypt (181–146). It is lost, but Clement of Alexandria gives an excerpt in a section dealing with the openness of Plato to learn from everywhere (*Strom.* 1.15.1–3): according to Aristobulus, Plato and perhaps Pythagoras have followed "our code of laws," but the name of Moses does not appear in his account; he mentions the expulsion of the Hebrews (not "of the Jews") from Egypt, the arrival in the land, the fame of the people and its institutions.⁹ Eusebius, who knew the book and its date (176 BCE, *Chronikon*),¹⁰ adds that the main tenets of the Law "had been interpreted (διηρμήνευται) by others before Demetrius of Phalerus." He draws a lengthy comparison between Plato's *Laws* and various biblical precepts (*Praep. ev.* 12.0; 13.12.1–2). The cautious verb "interpreted" does not necessarily refer to a written translation, for Eusebius knew the *Letter of Aristeas*, which states that the Septuagint translation was performed at the behest of King Ptolemy II (283–246).

This dating is doubtful, but in spite of its legendary features, this *Letter* gives an interesting detail (§ 30): in his petition to king Ptolemy, the librarian Demetrius complains that he only has poor copies of the laws of the Jews "according to people in the know." This implies that there was a kind of rough draft of the Pentateuch before better copies as well as translators from the twelve tribes were sent along by the high priest Eleazar. In fact, there are at least two biblical hints at laws that were not given through Moses, and both are connected with Shechem or Bethel: before dying, Joshua acted as a lawgiver, for he gathered all the tribes and "made a covenant with the people that day, and made statutes and ordinances, and Joshua wrote there words in the book of the law of God" (Josh 24:25–26). Later, after the deportation of the Northern Kingdom and the resettling of Samaria, the local Israelites were supposed to "follow the statutes and the ordinances and the law and the commandment that Yhwh commanded the sons of Jacob, whom he named Israel" (2 Kgs 17:34 LXX).

The whole Pentateuch in its actual form was most probably published together at Alexandria in the third century BCE.¹¹ A clue to its authority as a corpus is provided by a Rabbinic saying (*b. Qid.* 30a) that indicates that the "center" of the Torah by word count is between two identical words דרש דרש (infinitive and perfect) of Lev 10:16, with the meaning "scrutinize intensely"; the center is the key. Such a clear "signature" can hardly have been accidental. In fact, there are so many inconsistencies that it is necessary to search and interpret beyond the plain meaning.

II. An Egyptian Connection

Demetrius' statement witnesses to the presence of learned Israelites in Alexandria in the third and second centuries BCE.¹² Now we turn to the book of Ben Sira. Written for believers ("God-Fearers") seeking wisdom, it includes wisdom precepts, a gallery of biblical characters, and a high reverence for the Jerusalem temple, especially with the prominent high priest Simon son of Onias. Some details are significant here: wisdom lies in Moses' law, termed "the book of the covenant of the most high God" (Sir 24:23); the Temple, offerings and sacrifices are of the utmost importance (Sir 7:31; 34:18–19 etc.), but neither Sabbath observance nor dietary laws are mentioned; purity is mainly taken in a moral sense. Some biographical allusions give us some material with which to sketch a portrait of the author, Jesus Ben Sira. He was in Jerusalem in his youth, and then he traveled abroad, looking for wisdom (Sir 51:13–14). From his experience, he knows that "because of unrighteous dealings, injuries, and riches obtained by deceit, the kingdom moves from one people to another" (10:8). He has been persecuted or accused (12:10; 25:7). There seems to be a paradox: besides his reverence for the high priest Simon, who restored the shrine and presided over impressive worship, he prays that God will restore Jerusalem with its Temple and gather together all the tribes of Jacob (and not only Judah, Sir 36:10–17). So he may have known the high priest Simon in his youth, but he is now facing a crisis looming in Jerusalem. The book, written in Hebrew, is usually dated around 180 BCE,[13] hence the paradox. But his grandson, who found it not in Jerusalem but in Egypt, and translated it there – say in Alexandria – gives in his prologue some clues for a better dating, for he says he came to Egypt in the thirty-eighth year of the late King Euergetes (Ptolemy VIII Physcon, 170–117). So he arrived in 132 BCE – his grandfather was probably dead – and completed his work after 117. This leaves room for a dating of the book after the beginning of the Hasmonean dynasty in 152 BCE, because Ben Sira's profile makes much more sense if he was exiled in Egypt – willingly or not – and wrote there.[14] We may add that the Phoenician idiom, quite close to Classical Hebrew, was still in use.

Moreover, the Egyptian Jews as a whole were reluctant, for at least forty years, to accept the Hasmonean restoration. We read in a twofold letter introduced as a prologue to 2 Maccabees that the Jews of Jerusalem urged, in 124 BCE, the Jews of Egypt to keep the "feast of the pitching of the Temple" (σκηνοπηγία) in Kislev, that is, the Feast of Dedication (חנוכה); the letter is a reminder that quotes a previous one to the same effect, sent in 142 BCE[15] (2 Macc 1:1–10). Their dates are meaningful. In 142 the high priest Simon (144–134) was officially recognized by Rome (1 Macc 15:15–24), which was eager to control the Mediterranean East after the fall of Carthage in 146 BCE. The little state of Judea was a kind of buffer zone preventing any alliance between Egypt and Syria. Apparently, the Egyptian Jews did not feel concerned. The latter date falls under John Hyrcanus (135–104), formally a vassal of Seleucid Syria; but after the death of Antiochus VII Sidetes (139–129) he felt free to conquer Idumaea (*Ant.* 13.249–53). According to Josephus, he destroyed the Gerizim temple sometime after 129 BCE, but according to several coins from various spots, only after a civilian war between Antiochus VIII and Antiochus IX (ca. 113–112), after which the Seleucid dominion over Judea essentially disappeared.[16] Hyrcanus' successors took the title of king.

The background of this refusal is connected with the prologue of the Maccabean crisis. Before it, the high priest Onias was highly esteemed (2 Macc 3:1). He was the son of "Simon son of Onias," also called "Simon the Righteous," and venerated by Ben Sira (Sir 50:1). When Antiochus IV became king of Syria (175 BCE), he replaced Onias with his brother Jason, who paid a bribe. Then Onias' son (or nephew), also named Onias, moved to Egypt, where King Ptolemy VI (180–145) welcomed him for political reasons: he appointed him high priest of the Jews and granted him permission to build a temple in the district of Heliopolis (*Ant.* 12.237–47). The chronology is not very clear, but during the seven years between the death of the high priest Alcimus (in 159, see 1 Macc 9:54–57) and the appointment of Jonathan, the first Hasmonean high priest (in 152, see 1 Macc 10:1, 18–20), Onias of Heliopolis was the only high priest of the Jews (*Ant.* 20.236–37), and the position of Jerusalem was endangered.

III. Zadok, Egypt, Babylon, the Pharisees

We may now ask why the Egyptian Jews would not accept the Hasmonean state, at least in the second century. A conventional answer is that the Hasmonean dynasty lacked Zadokite legitimacy, supposed to come from a continuous family of high priests since Zadok, who was high priest in the time of David and Solomon. But this character is not outstanding in the Bible, nor in Josephus' accounts either. In fact, this view comes from the theory that the later Sadducees were a legitimist, traditional party that hoped to restore the pre-Hasmonean dynasty. However, this hardly squares with Acts 5:17, which states that the associates of the high priest were of the party (αἵρεσις) of the Sadducees; according to the context, this high priest was either Annas or Caiaphas, but nothing suggests a genuine Zadokite descent.

In fact, it is impossible to retrieve from the Bible a clear high-priestly dynasty at any period.[17] If we focus upon the period from Zadok to the beginning of the Hasmoneans, we see first that according to Ezra 7:1–5 there are only four names between Zadok and Ezra himself, for more than five centuries. The parallel list given in 1 Chr 5:34–41 contains another ten names,[18] but a comparison shows that only the first three seem genuine, the others being added by papponymy, and further that Ezra is a brother of Jehozadak, the high priest who was deported by Nebuchadnezzar (587 BCE), which cannot match a Persian dating. But with this literary device, Ezra has full authority as a reformer, even over Jeshua son of Jehozadak, the first high priest returned from exile. It is true that Josephus gives a much longer list of eighteen different names from Zadok to Jehozadak (*Ant.* 10.152–53), which could make sense for a little more than four centuries, but his sources are unknown.

For the Persian period, we have six names from Cyrus to Alexander, for some two centuries, but the lists given in Neh 10:11–12 are not consistent. After Alexander, the gap is much more obvious, for Josephus gives a succession of Oniases and Simons, with some side complications. There is at least one Onias and one Simon of whom nothing is said, and they can be removed. The names are new, and Onias, in spite of his having a Yahwist name (חוניהו, or חוניו as in *m. Men.* 13.10), has definite connections with Egypt, as well as a possible Spartan background (see 1 Macc 12:20–21; 2 Macc 5:9). According to Exod 1:11, the Israelites in Egypt built storage cities, Pithom and Raamses; the LXX adds another place, transcribed Ὤν[19], then translated Ἡλίου πόλις, "City of the Sun." A prophecy announces that five cities of Egypt will speak the language of Canaan and one of them will be called the "City of the Sun",[20] and sacrifices will be performed (Isa 19:18, 21). This alludes to the Onias temple and to other places where Hebrew was spoken. To sum up, there cannot be a legitimate Zadokite descent. As for Onias' pedigree, nothing can be said beyond that Egyptian connection.

This has obvious implications for the Sadducees, who cannot have been a legitimist party, and for the Essenes, who are often said to be "sons of Zadok" (1QS 5:2, 9). One of their founding books is the sectarian Cairo Document (CD), whose purpose is the restore a new covenant in line with the views of the Teacher of Righteousness; it cites a *Book of the Time divisions* also known as the *Book of the Jubilees* and follows its special non-lunar calendar. CD 4:21 quotes Ezek 44:15 as "The priests, the Levites, and the sons of Zadok who kept the charge of my sanctuary when the children of Israel strayed" and explains that they are three grades of "Covenanters" or Essenes. In CD 14:3–4, the grades are spelled out: "The priests first, the Levites second, the children of Israel third, the proselyte (גר) fourth." Thus, "son of Zadok" is the quality of the newcomer who has just become a member; the implication is that "Levites" and "priests" also hold seniority. In Exod 19:6 God has announced that the whole people is to be held as a "kingdom of priests."

Similarly, Josephus mentions four grades of Essenes according to seniority (*War* 2.150), but does not venture to name them, because for him genealogy is of utmost importance. However, he is not very consistent, for he does not hide that the Essenes "disdain marriage, but adopt other people's children" (*War* 2.120), which stresses that they are not interested in genealogy.

There was another family of Egyptian high priests, the Boethusians, apparently unconnected to the Onias dynasty. Nothing is said of Boethus himself, who may have been a family ancestor. His name means "helper" (βοηθός), and a Hebrew equivalent could be עזרא "Ezra," or אליעזר-אלעזר "Eliezer, Eleazar"[21] (cf. Exod 18:4). Under Herod there was one Simon son of Boethus (24–25 BCE, *Ant.* 15.320–22), then Joazar son of Boethus for a short time (4 BCE, *Ant.* 17.165); under Archelaus (4 BCE–6 CE), his brother Eleazar was appointed twice (*Ant.* 17.339 and 18.3); under King Agrippa I (41–44), we hear of Simon Cantheras son of Boethus (*Ant.* 19.297). This Boethusian family was important for at least two generations,[22] and even Josephus admits that starting from Herod's time the high priesthood was given to people lacking significant pedigrees (*Ant.* 20.249).

Rabbinic tradition knows the Boethusians as an influential party or school, and reports some of their views on calendar issues. After a description of Passover (in the middle of the first month), Lev 23:11–16 states that a sheaf of the first-fruits of barley has to be waved before Yhwh on the day after the Sabbath, and from that day seven full Sabbaths are counted, that is, fifty days to the day after the seventh Sabbath. This refers to the period between Passover and Pentecost, but the wording is ambiguous: the mainstream traditions (Philo, Josephus, *b. Pes.* 5a) understand the first "Sabbath" as the day of Passover itself, according to the ancient meaning of שבת as the middle of the Babylonian lunar month (full moon), then the two other "Sabbaths" as periods of seven days, and not exact weeks. This way, Pentecost falls fifty days after Passover. Now, according to *m. Men.* 10.3, the Boethusians say that the rite of waving the sheaf must not be performed on the day following a festival day (יום טוב); so it has to be delayed till after the seven days of Unleavened Bread. Since it has to be done "on the day after the Sabbath," the right date is the Sunday following the first Sabbath after the seven festival days, so that the counting of seven week starts on that day, and Pentecost, the day after the seventh exact week, necessarily falls on a Sunday (*b. Men.* 65b); this arguably is a more literal meaning of the Law. Another tractate reports the story of Boethusians paying false witnesses of a new moon as an attempt to obtain a Pentecost falling on a Sunday (*t. Rosh ha-Shana* 1.15). This calendar matter must have been serious, for *m. Hag.* 2.4 states that if Pentecost happens to fall on a Sunday, it is not a festival day and the high priest does not worship, so that nobody may think that he observes the rules of the Boethusians and Sadducees.

These two names frequently appear together, and according to *Abot de-Rabbi Nathan* § 10 both Boethus (ביתוס) and Zadok, somewhere in the second century BCE, left mainstream Judaism on theological grounds and became apostate. This was not the view of Qirqisani, a Karaite of the tenth century CE, who was able to summarize their opinions and to see their biblical background.[23] He said that Zadok had written a book, now identified as the *Damascus Document.* The Karaite movement was a kind of new brand of Sadduceism focusing on Scripture, born in the ninth century CE. It had been somewhat prompted by the recent discovery of documents (then) in caves around Qumran.

As for the Pharisees, they cling to ancestral customs, often at variance with Scripture. They can be traced back to the Hasmonean dynasty, which was faithful to the Babylonian lunar calendar, an obvious feature of 1–2 Maccabees. Judas Maccabeus was an heir of Nehemiah (2 Macc 2:13–14), who imported from Babylonia specific laws, such as the expulsion of foreign wives or special ways of keeping Sabbath within walled cities. Typically, Neh 13:1–3 puts such customs under Scriptural authority. Later, Hillel the Elder, a founding father of Rabbinic tradition, arrived from Babylonia to Bathyra on the Golan heights, where King Herod had created a peaceful Jewish settlement of Babylonian Jews (*Ant.* 17.23–25; *y. Pes.* 6.1, p. 33a). The *Mishnah*, a collection of the main Rabbinic teachings, was published in Galilee at the beginning of the third century; it was immediately accepted in Babylonia, hence two parallel *Talmuds* corresponding to these two places; but it was not sent to the Greek-speaking world. Its reliance on oral Torah, which is very close to the Pharisean view, was given a motto (*m. Sanh.* 11.3): "It is more serious to teach contrary to the precepts of the scribes than contrary to the written Law."

So we see significant differences between the Egyptian and Babylonian connections. The teachings of the Boethusians invite us to examine some calendar problems, all the more since they seem to be close to the Sadducees.

IV. Sadducees, Calendars, Boethusians, Essenes

The aim of this section is to discuss the historical appearance of the Sadducees under King Alexander Jannaeus (103–76 BCE) and to show that they used the *Jubilees* calendar like the Essenes.

In *War* 1.68, Josephus summarizes the end of the high priest John Hyrcanus (135–104 BCE): "He was the only one to be granted three of the highest privileges, the command of the nation, the high priesthood, and the gift of prophecy." In *Ant.* 13.288–98, before praising Hyrcanus' privileges, Josephus adds that he was first greatly loved by the Pharisees. But there was a banquet, during which some Pharisees urged him to "give up the high-priesthood and be content with governing the people," for he was suspected to be the son of a captive woman. At the close of this episode, Hyrcanus parted from the Pharisees, abrogated the rules they had established for the nation, and associated henceforward with the Sadducees. But two details look awkward: first, ruling the people and being high priest were the same thing for him, for it was Hyrcanus' son Aristobulus who transformed the government into a monarchy and assumed the diadem. Second, if Simon, Hyrcanus' father, had married a captive, he could never have been high priest (cf. Neh 13:28; *Ant.* 11.309).

Another feature is strange: in this story, Josephus for the first time speaks of the Pharisees and Sadducees as extant schools, and refers to a short notice about them that he has given previously, by the time of the high priest Jonathan (*Ant.* 13.171–73). So we may infer that they were extant during the Maccabean crisis. However, they play no role as such, although broadly speaking the crisis was mainly an outcome of rivalries between different Jewish parties. According to 1 Macc 2:41–42, during the persecution of Antiochus IV (167 BCE), Mattathias permitted defensive fighting on the Sabbath, and the *Assideans* (חסידים), totally devoted to the Law, joined him. Josephus, in paraphrasing a Hebrew version of the book,[24] simply says that Mattathias instructed his followers to fight even on that day, in order to prevent any defenseless attack. He adds that the permission has been enforced "to this day," which means that a new feature for a Jewish or Israelite state was enforced. Later, when the Syrian general Bacchides comes with peace proposals, the high priest Alcimus agrees, as well as "some of the citizens" (*Ant.* 12.395), without further clarification, while in 1 Macc 7:13 they are called *Assideans*. According to 2 Macc 14:6, Judas Maccabaeus was the head of the *Assideans*, but Josephus did not know this book.

Moreover, in *Ant.* 15.371, when he mentions the exemptions from taxation which Herod had granted to the Pharisees and the Essenes, Josephus says that he will speak later about these schools without referring to his notices under Jonathan. He does present the schools in *Ant.* 18.11–22, in the time of Judas the Galilean, and refers in this context to the parallel exposé in "the second Book of the War of the Jews." So he misses two opportunities to allude to the notice under Jonathan, which is clearly connected with Hyrcanus' banquet. In other words, there was a significant revision by the author, who introduced both the notice and the banquet after completing *Ant.* 18 or later.[25]

Now we can show that Josephus has put the banquet in the wrong place: it should be related to Alexander Jannaeus.[26] Here are the main reasons: first, Jannaeus may very well have been a bastard, since his father Hyrcanus had always hated him, and "let him be brought up in Galilee from his birth" (*Ant.* 13.322); it is not too far-fetched to surmise that his mother had already been sent there when she was pregnant. Second, in *Ant.* 13.372–73, when Jannaeus was standing beside the altar and was about to sacrifice for the feast of Booths, the people pelted him with citrons (*etrog*), saying he was unfit to hold office for he descended from a captive woman; the king's reaction was violent, but he did not resign. Third, when he was about to die, he told his wife Alexandra, who was to succeed him, to yield some power to the Pharisees, so that the nation would turn favorably towards her. She did that successfully, and restored the Pharisean customs (*Ant.* 13.401, 408). Fourth, Rabbinic tradition (*b. Qid.* 66a) mentions the banquet as Jannaeus', whose birth was deemed suspicious by the Pharisees, so that he decided to abrogate their oral laws and to move to the Sadducees.

As to the reason of Josephus' presentation, it may be a simple mistake, since he is quite often sloppy. But it is possible, too, that he wanted to smooth out a significant gap in the Hasmonean dynasty. The main result of this discussion is that King Jannaeus was the only ruler who chose to rely upon the Sadducees,[27] which eventually proved to be a mistake. Josephus says that whenever the Sadducees assume some office, they have to submit to what the Pharisees say, since otherwise the people would not accept them (*Ant.* 18.17). The *Talmud* reports a saying (*b. Yom.* 19b): "My son, although we are Sadducees, we are afraid of the Pharisees." Incidentally, when Josephus was in Rome, with a view to being a leader of his nation after 70, he wrote his autobiography to display his credentials. He says that after being educated in the three main schools, he chose to govern his life by the rules of the Pharisees (*Life* 12). In his time, they were popular not only in Judea since the time of the Hasmoneans and probably much earlier, but also everywhere in the Roman Empire, with the exception of Egypt.[28]

In his notices on the Sadducees, Josephus makes only few mentions. But prominent Talmudists have shown that an important document from Qumran, called 4QMMT (Miqṣat Ma'aśe ha-Torah), displays minute legal views that Rabbinic tradition definitely relates to the Sadducees;[29] the style is not sectarian or polemical and rather suggests counseling, for a key phrase to the addressee is "we think that..."; the latter must be a high-ranking official of the Temple, for most rules are connected with the purity of worship, but they are sometimes lenient, as if the goal were to be obeyed by the whole people; the background is very biblical, with references to Moses, the Prophets and David. On philological grounds, a smaller piece (4Q448 or 4QPsAp), is thought to belong to the same document;[30] it includes a prayer "on king Jonathan and the whole congregation of your people Israel," with the hope that his wars be brought to an end. All this fits very well the situation of King Jannaeus (a nickname for Jonathan), who may have been at a loss after having cancelled the Pharisean customs;[31] some prominent Sadducees would have endeavored to help him.

One of the most interesting features of 4QMMT is its including a fragment of the non-lunar calendar of the book of *Jubilees*, in which the year contains four thirteen-week trimesters, each one beginning on a Wednesday; the eve of Passover, the fourteenth day of the first month, falls always on a Tuesday evening; Pentecost falls on a Sunday, the counting of the seven full weeks beginning on the Sunday following the days of Unleavened Bread. This is the feast of the first-fruits of wheat, baked into bread. A variant of this calendar has at least another two Pentecosts, corresponding to the first-fruits of the grape (new wine) and the olive (oil): this very feature is to be found in 4QMMT, the Temple Scroll (11QT), as well as the lengthy description of the Essenes by Josephus (*War* 2.147, Slavonic version[32]). This device is hard to reconcile with the Babylonian lunar calendar used by the Pharisees.

Two conclusions are obvious: first, Sadducees and Essenes used the same *Jubilees* calendar; second, we recognize immediately the calendar struggles of the Boethusians, briefly stated in Rabbinic sources, which makes the Egyptian connection much stronger. It has been argued that the very name "Boethusians," sometimes spelled ביתסין or בית סין, refers to the Essenes;[33] as far as calendar issues are concerned, this confusion is quite possible – and not very meaningful. This way we can understand the problem of Jannaeus and later of the Boethusians: changing the calendar has an effect upon everyday life, because of the feasts. For the people as a whole, the problem cannot have been the *minutiae* of the Temple worship, but the removal of the custom of using the Babylonian lunar calendar of old.

Thus, the Sadducees brought in a reform according to Scripture. This may explain their name, for it must depend on one Zadok. Now, we have a short form of a meaningful story about David discovering monogamy. CD 5.2–6 tells us that David did not know the book of the Law, which was hidden in the Ark: it had not been opened in Israel from the day of the death of Eleazar and Joshua, for the people were worshipping the goddess Asherah or Ashtoret (see Judg 2:7–13). But the priest Zadok, who was in charge of the ark (see 2 Sam 15:24), opened it for David. And the Law states that the leader "shall not multiply wives to himself" (Deut 17:17), and from that time on he had only one wife (Bathsheba). As revealers of the written Law, the Sadducees can obviously be termed "sons of Zadok," which has nothing to do with genealogy. As for the Essenes as "sons of Zadok," the same explanation stands: they rely on Scripture.

To sum up, the Sadducees and Essenes sported the same eponym Zadok and the same calendar, against the Pharisees. There was some kinship, seemingly related to Egypt, but Josephus' notices underline major differences in their way of life and in their theological tenets.

V. The Essenes and Rabbinic Traditions

The main component of Rabbinic tradition was Pharisean, with oral laws of Mosaic authority (*m. Abot.* 1.1) and a Babylonian lunar calendar. But besides this it was able to collect a great number of other views, which were adopted or rejected. We have seen above that Sadducean and Boethusian opinions were quoted and disposed of. For the Essenes, there was much more flexibility, and some views have been adopted, as we shall now see. The Qumran discoveries have provided major clarifications.

After the discovery of the first scrolls in 1948, they were quickly related to the Essenes, known by some reports in Greek, authored by Philo, Josephus and Pliny, the latter locating them close to the Dead Sea.[34] In 1952, S. Lieberman drew a comparison between the Community Rule (1QS) and the rules concerning a special brotherhood frequently mentioned in Rabbinic sources, the *Haburah*,[35] a group separated from the "people of the land" (see Est 4:4; 9:1). Its members, or חברים, assumed the obligation of strictly observing the laws of cleanliness. They are venerated as a holy practice of old, but kept at some distance, for their sectarian character introduces a select few within the nation, while the Rabbinic system aims at including the whole people.

The admission of a new member includes some steps, performed with specific oaths in the presence of the *Haburah*, which is sometimes called the *Rabbim* (קהל עליו ברבים, *y. Dem.* 2.2, p. 22d). The initiated were instructed, and after a trial of some twelve months, admitted to dry food, then to liquids and eventually to the ritual garments.[36] The steps involve cleansing immersions (baptisms), and *m. Hag.* 2.6 says: "If someone bathes for a specific level without having been formally admitted, he is as if he did nothing." In this passage, seven steps of holiness are defined. These dispositions are quite close to the admission system of Josephus' Essenes (*War* 2.137–39) and to the one of the Community Rule (1QS 6.13–23): probation time, oaths before the ruling body, represented by the רבים, "many," or *Rabbim*,[37] access by steps to "purity,"[38] which is the community meal; liquid food is harder to keep in a state of fitting purity than dry items[39] (see Lev 11:34–38).

The similarities between the rules of the *Haburah* and those of the Dead Sea Scrolls community are striking, and they use the same terms. According to *m. Hag.* 2.7 the garments of the "people of the land" defile a member as if he had touched a pagan's. In the same way, 1QS 8.23 states that a non-member has the uncleanness of a pagan. Josephus, too, explains that if a senior Essene is touched by a junior, he must take a bath, as after contact with a pagan. This means that circumcision is almost meaningless: the true covenant is the community (cf. CD 1.4; 1QS 1.8, 16, 18 etc.). The main documents insist on the circumcision of the heart (1QS 5.5; 1QpHab 11.13, etc.); traditional circumcision of the foreskin is mentioned in biblical paraphrases only (4Q266 f6ii.6; 4Q367 f1a–b.4).

In connection with this, the Rabbinic "baptism of the proselytes" displays interesting features. It is not biblical; Philo and Josephus never mention it, though many conversions did occur; the most famous event was the forced circumcision of the Idumaeans by John Hyrcanus (*Ant.* 15.255). Obviously, such an important initiation rite cannot have been borrowed from Christianity.[40]

Classical sources about it are scant, but instructive. It is said in *m. Pes.* 8.8 that: "A proselyte who converted (התגייר) on the eve of Passover – the Shammai school says: 'He bathes and eat his Passover in the evening'; but the Hillel school says: 'One who parts from his foreskin is like parting from the tomb'." According to Exod 12:43 circumcision is required to partake of Passover (see Josh 5:3, 10). For the Shammai school, the new convert, after being circumcised, is Jewish in every respect; he is only affected by normal, everyday defilement, and an immersion on the same day is enough to have him cleansed in the evening. A story confirms this traditional view: around the Jerusalem gates, some Roman soldiers got circumcised on the eve of Passover, and after an immersion they could eat of the Passover lamb in the evening; they were only lightly defiled by unavoidable dust (*y. Pes.* 8.8 end).

It is not so for the Hillel school: exiting from a tomb implies a contact with death, a major defilement requiring a cleansing period of seven days (see Lev 15:11–14), so that he cannot join the Passover meal on the same day. In other words, circumcision does not remove the uncleanness of the pagans, but the last cleansing immersion does. The disagreement between the schools appears in another controversy about the minimal requirement for conversion (*b. Yeb.* 46a–b): R. Eliezer says that circumcision is enough, for this is the rule since Abraham's time; R. Yehoshua says that immersion is enough, as with Sarah and the mothers of the nation. These two outstanding Rabbis (end of the first century CE) were good friends. The arguments may seem somewhat inconclusive, but the discussion shows that the importance of the "baptism of proselytes" was growing.

The ritual of conversion is expounded in *y. Yeb.* 46b–47b. It has to be performed before three witnesses known as being competent. In fact, they are judges. Before circumcision, they question the neophyte on some major precepts and some minor ones; they enquire about his reasons to embrace Judaism and exhort him. Later, before baptism, they question and enquire the same way. So there is a twofold gate for getting into the covenant. The first is related to Abraham, but the second cannot be of Pharisean origin, for Ezra and Nehemiah relied upon genealogy. Typically, the Galilean Jews, who were mainly of Babylonian origin, could not accept Herod as king, for he was not of Jewish descent, though his Idumaean forefathers had been circumcised for several generations (*Ant.* 14.403). The second gate definitely suggests a softer form of the admission of the חברים. This can be understood as an extension of the *Haburah* norms for the whole people.[41]

In fact, the three "witnesses" for admission are "Rabbis," an interesting title, already connected above with the חברים. In the New Testament Gospels, Jesus and John the Baptist are called *Rabbi* or *Rabbouni*, with a nuance of teaching authority. The origin of this use has been much discussed. The common Jewish view is that it never appeared before 70, so that there is an anachronism in the Gospels.[42] Others stress that *Rabbi* in the Gospels is always a vocative, with a first-person suffix, a normal use when a disciple addresses his master;[43] this feature even occurs in the *Mishnah* (*m. Pes.* 6.2; *m. Ned.* 9.5). Some look for a compromise by distinguishing between various uses.[44]

It is much easier to seek an Essene connection, as we did in proselyte baptism, for there are some clues beyond the analogies *Rabbim/Haberim*. First, in the list of the Torah transmitters since Moses, the title *Rabbi* appears after Hillel the Elder only (*m. Abot.* 1.1–16), that is, after Herod's time; it refers to a sage with proven competence in *halakhic* matters. Second, it is said that in an early stage Hillel agreed with Menahem, the Essene friend of Herod (*m. Hag.* 2.2; *Ant.* 15.373–75), then the latter left and was replaced by Shammai, for Hillel got closer to the Pharisees. Third, when Hillel arrived from Babylonia he reached Bathyra, a Babylonian settlement set up by Herod on the Golan heights, which attracted many pious Jews (*Ant.* 17.26). There, he was involved in a debate on an unexpected issue (*y. Pes.* 6.1, p. 33a): that year the eve of Passover (14th Nissan) fell on a Sabbath, and the Elders of Bathyra were wondering whether it was permitted to prepare the meal for the evening. With the Babylonian lunar calendar, which is independent of the weekly cycle, such an occurrence happens every seven years on average, and we cannot imagine that the issue was not well known. But with the *Jubilees* calendar, this never happens, for the fourteenth day of the first month is always a Tuesday. Thus, there were at Bathyra some people who had been used to having Passover on a fixed weekday, and for some reason they moved to the Babylonian system. To put it otherwise, tradition places, around Herod's time, a kinship between a branch of the Pharisees and some Essenes.[45]

As a last example, there is an interesting Rabbinic custom that may point to the very origin of the *Jubilees* calendar: the "Blessing of the Sun" (ברכת החמה). It has to be uttered every 28 years, on one Wednesday supposed to be equinoctial, at sunrise, facing East, and its wording refers to Creation. The cyclic duration is related to the *Jubilees* calendar: its year of four 91-day trimesters contains 364 days, while the natural year was known for centuries in Babylonia to have 365.25 days, hence an error of 1.25 day every year; the Rabbis were aware of this, and the natural year was called Shemuel's year. It was enforced in 45 BCE by Caesar (Julian Calendar). Now, in order to adjust the *Jubilees* years to the Julian without breaking the weekly cycle, some additional weeks must be introduced, and a simple calculation shows that the shortest time span for an exact adjustment is 28 years, during which five weeks must have been added. So, if in year X the first day of the first month falls on a Wednesday, the same thing will occur in year X+28 and never before.

The reference is the Creation week: every day runs from morning to morning[46] (Creation work, then evening and morning), and on the fourth day (Wednesday) the two "great luminaries" appear symmetrically, which implies full moon and equinox. Of course, the *Jubilee* calendar is good for Year I, and starting from Year II some correction has to be made because of the discrepancy of the various cycles, but nothing of this kind is hinted at in the Bible, beyond the switch of the new year in Exod 12:1. But it was done in some quarters, as is shown by several Qumran documents.[47]

So, the Blessing of the Sun indicates that the Rabbis inherited some scraps of the Essene calendar; this is all the more interesting in that they bear witness, too, to some struggles to reject it, at least when prompted by the Sadducees or other Boethusians. Besides this, the Blessing leads us to another conclusion, because it is stuck to Shemuel's year (Julian), which is too long; the Gregorian correction gives 365.2468 days. Now, the last occurrence of the Blessing was in 2009, on Wednesday, 8 April, which is more than 16 days after the true astral equinox. A simple calculation allows us to go back to the starting point of the custom: it was on Wednesday, 23 March, 156 BCE, when the astronomical instant of the equinox happened to be very close to the instant of the full moon, as shown by the modern ephemerides. This occurs less than twice a millennium, and can hardly have been unnoticed by the Babylonian astronomers. In conclusion, we cannot imagine that the *Jubilees* calendar was launched before that remarkable date. It may be significant that it falls within the seven years without a high priest in Jerusalem (159–152).

VI. The Essenes and Egypt?

Until now, we have seen the Essenes in a peculiar position: as "sons of Zadok." With the *Jubilees* calendar and biblical sources, they have something in common with the Sadducees, far away from the Pharisees. But the Rabbinic tradition, an heir of the Pharisees, has adopted several rules from them, which implies some relationship, at least in difficult periods. It is well known that after 70 R. Gamaliel, a prominent Pharisee from Jerusalem, was able to organize and unite a network of various Jewish schools in Judea, and some of them may have been Essene-like. This was certainly the origin of the many controversies which are so typical of the Rabbinic sources. For instance, according to a story in *m. Rosh ha-Shanah* 2.8–9, R. Gamaliel successfully urged another Rabbi to forsake his computed calendar on a Day of Atonement, that is, the *Jubilees* calendar, which does not depend on the new moon.

But the ancient descriptions of the Essenes include other features that hardly square with Rabbinic traditions. Josephus says, even in casual allusions, that they are akin to the Pythagoreans (*Ant.* 15.371). It is often thought that this is only a Greek garment for the benefit of pagan readers. But this is not necessarily so, for their way of life is not very biblical:

since the Sinai covenant, the stress is upon the nation, while the Essenes are admitted by co-optation into a "new Covenant"; sharing goods runs against the sabbatical year, when debts are released (cf. Neh 10:31); celibacy and adoption do not match the precept to beget children.[48]

J. Taylor has surveyed the various forms of ancient groups or associations in the Greek world and elsewhere.[49] He concludes that the closest parallel indeed lies in the Pythagorean traditions, although no typical Pythagorean group has been detected during the last two centuries BCE. Here are the common features: co-optation without paying attention to genealogy, with steps for admission; sharing of goods; uncleanness of outsiders; written penalty, including banishment; prohibition of oaths; bathing before meals; white garments; veneration of the sun. There are some differences, too: the Pythagoreans are "philosophers"; they do not eat meat or drink wine, and seem to accept wives or women, but the traditions about celibacy are not very clear. Against them, the Essenes are farmers, they must eat meat, at least for Passover, and they have eschatological views, and not just dualism. But these features are simply biblical; farming in the Promised Land is a major precept, and presenting the first-fruits leads to the recognition that the promises given to Abraham have been fulfilled (Deut 26:1–11). Incidentally, when the Qumran site was identified as an Essene settlement, the excavators faced difficulties with their interpretation, for it lies in the wilderness of Judah, and no real farming of wheat and vine is possible.

Philo provides us with additional material. He neither mentions the Pharisees nor the Sadducees, but he knows of the Essenes: they live in Syria-Palestine, that is, the large Judea of Herod, and their main activity is farming; they are excellent worshippers of God, with the phrase θεραπευταὶ θεοῦ ("servants of God," *Quod omnis probus* § 75). In another place, Philo speaks at length and with admiration of another kind of Jewish group, called θεραπευταί, "Therapeuts": they live in the wilderness, around Alexandria and elsewhere in the world; they are philosophers, avoiding manual work (*De vita contemplativa* § 78). He does not know their origin, and he interprets their name as "physicians of souls and bodies" and "servants of God," which fits the two main meanings of the verb θεραπεύω. It has been recognized that Therapeuts and Essenes are cousins.[50] Moreover, they abstain from meat and wine, so that they are true "philosophers, much closer to the Pythagorean pattern of life. Josephus says that by the time of the Maccabean crisis there were many Jewish temples (ἱερῶν) in Egypt, with much rivalry (*Ant.* 13.66); some communities of Therapeuts, of whom he never speaks, may have been a part of that landscape.

All this leads us to a very simple hypothesis, already voiced in 1835: the Therapeuts were founded first in Egypt as Pythagorean-like communities, then a branch read more closely the Bible and came to Palestine, probably with the idea of restoring a true Israel with the Creation calendar, around the middle of the second century BCE.[51] They were the Essenes, and their name[52] comes from אסיא "healers," which just translates θεραπευταί.[53] They were following in the footsteps of Moses and Joshua ("sons of Zadok"), and then seriously mingled with Hebrew or Eastern traditions, but keeping a kind of Pythagorean way of life, adapted to farming. In other words, there is no reason to reject a Pythagorean influence upon the Essenes,[54] but it was indirect, through the Therapeuts. It is quite possible that Josephus freely embellished his descriptions of the Essenes with additional Pythagorean features taken from his readings in Rome. So we see that the difference between Essenes and Sadducees are meaningful on the background of their analogies and the Egyptian connection.

As for the settlement of Qumran, the best solution is to follow Pliny the Elder's short description of the *esseni* (*HN* 5.15.73): they live among palm-trees, at some distance from the Dead Sea; they have an unusual way of life, without money; they have no wives, but many newcomers have joined them for "thousands of centuries." This picture, with no village mentioned, indicates a temporary dwelling, that is, a kind of pilgrimage of several days. Indeed, the presence of newcomers suggests Pentecost as the admission feast of the candidates, and some specific findings seem to point to the leftovers of Passover meals.[55] Now the formal entrance of Joshua with the Israelites into Canaan was sealed by the Passover celebrated at Gilgal (Josh 5:10–12): the *manna* ceased and they began to eat of the produce of the land; in fact, this produce is not permitted before the feast of the first-fruits, that is, Pentecost again. Thus, the Qumran site would look like a new Gilgal, the shore of the Dead Sea being a prolongation of the Jordan bank. There would have been a compound pilgrimage extending from Passover through Pentecost, to commemorate a renewal of Joshua's arrival. A well-designed cemetery with secondary burials hints at the same conclusion: symbolically, the gate to Heaven is the gate to the Promised land, and vice-versa.

Again, the reader is reminded that this set of hypotheses is neither true nor false: we just hope that it is interesting, or useful.

Notes

1. G. Garbini, *Dio della terra, dio del cielo: dalle religioni semitiche al giudaismo e al cristianesimo* (Biblioteca di cultura religiosa 70; Brescia: Paideia, 2011).

2. G. Garbini, *Il ritorno dall'esilio babilonese* (Studi biblici 129; Brescia: Paideia, 2001).

3. See E. Schürer, *Geschichte des jüdischen Volkes im Zeitalter Jesu Christi* (Helsingfors: Hinrichs, 4th edn, 1907), II, pp. 651–80.

4. Their relationship with the city of Samaria and its Yahwism, which extended far away in the South, is not clear; see Z. Meshel, *Kuntillet 'Ajrud: A Religious Centre from the Time of the Judaean Monarchy on the Border of Sinai* (Jerusalem: Israel Museum, 1978); A. Lemaire, "Who or What Was Yahweh's Asherah? Startling New Inscriptions from Two Different Sites Reopen the Debate About the Meaning of Asherah," *BAR* 10/6 (1984), pp. 2–51; P. K. McCarter, "Aspects of the Religion of the Israelite Monarchy: Biblical and Epigraphic Data," in P. D. Miller et al., *Ancient Israelite Religion* (Philadelphia: Fortress, 1987), pp. 137–55; E. Blum, "Der historische Mose und die Frühgeschichte Israels," *Hebrew Bible and Ancient Israel* 1, no. 1 (2012), pp. 37–63.

5. See É. Nodet, "Israelites, Samaritans, Temples, Jews," in József Zsengellér (ed.), *Samaria, Samarians, Samaritans: Studies on Bible, History and Linguistics* (Berlin/Boston: de Gruyter, 2011), pp. 121–72.

6. See P. Grelot, "Le papyrus pascal d'Éléphantine: essai de restauration," *VT* 17 (1967), pp. 201–207 and pp. 481–82.

7. See X. Durand, *Des Grecs en Palestine au IIIe siècle avant Jésus-Christ: le dossier syrien des archives de Zénon de Caunos (261–252)* (CRB 38; Paris: Gabalda, 1997).

8. See A. J. Droge, *Homer or Moses?* (Tübingen: Mohr-Siebeck, 1989), pp. 1–11. For Hellenistic (Egyptian) Jews as philosophers, see also E. S. Gruen, "Jews and Greeks as Philosophers: A Challenge to Otherness," in D. C. Harlow et al. (eds.), *The Other in Second Temple Judaism* (Grand Rapids: Eerdmans, 2011), pp. 402–22.

9. Photius, *Library* #244, quotes a lost section of Diodorus Siculus, which includes an excursus on the Jews, attributed to Hecateus of Abdera (or Miletus), who lived by the time of Alexander and the Diadochi. The passage follows the same outline, but adds that Moses founded Jerusalem and divided the Jewish people into twelve tribes. See M. Stern, *Greek and Latin Authors on Jews and Judaism* (Jerusalem: Magnes, 1974–84), III, p. 44.

10. Or later, see A. Yarbro Collins, "Aristobulus," in J. Charlesworth (ed.), *The Old Testament Pseudepigrapha* (New York: Doubleday, 1985), II, pp. 831–42.

11. A growing trend in biblical scholarship follows this line. See the review by L. L. Grabbe (ed.), *Did Moses Speak Attic?* (JSOTSup 317; Sheffield: Sheffield Academic, 2001). See also P. Wajdenbaum, *Argonauts of the Desert: Structural Analysis of the Hebrew Bible* (CIS; Sheffield: Equinox, 2011).

12. Philo never mentions the library of Alexandria or any Hebrew department; it seems that everything was accidentally destroyed by Caesar in 48 BCE, see Pliny, *Life of Caesar* 49.6.

13. See P. W. Skehan and A. A. di Lella, *The Wisdom of Ben Sira* (AB 39; New York: Doubleday, 1987), p. 9; M. Gilbert, "Siracide," *DBS* 12 (1996), col. 1402–1405; idem, *Les cinq livres des Sages* (Paris: Cerf, 2003), pp. 155–56; G. Boccaccini, "Where Does Ben Sira Belong? The Canon, Literary Genre, Intellectual Movement, and Social Group of a Zadokite Document," in G. G. Xeravits and J. Zsengellér (eds.), *Studies in the Book of Ben Sira* (JSJSup 127; Leiden: Brill, 2008), pp. 21–41, and other introductions. The two main reasons for this early dating are: first, there was no Hebrew at Alexandria; second, Ben Sira wrote in Jerusalem before the Maccabean crisis, since he does not know of it; but this is clearly begging the question.

14. Following a proposal by P. Guillaume, "New Light on the *Nebiim* from Alexandria: A Chronography to Replace the Deuteronomistic History," *Journal of Hebrew Scriptures* 5 (2005), pp. 169–215.

15. See E. J. Bickerman, "Ein jüdischer Festbrief vom Jahre 124 v. Chr.," in idem, *Studies in Jewish and Christian History* (AGAJU 9; Leiden: Brill, 1980), II, pp. 136–58.

16. See R. Pummer, *The Samaritans in Flavius Josephus* (TSAJ 129; Tübingen: Mohr-Siebeck, 2009), pp. 281–320.

17. In spite of the labors of Josephus, followed by J. C. VanderKam, *From Jeshua to Caiaphas: High Priests After the Exile* (Minneapolis: Fortress, 2004). On the contrary, A. Hunt, *Missing Priests: The Zadokites in Tradition and History* (New York/London: T&T Clark International, 2006), underlines the discontinuities and concludes that no Zadokite genealogy can be restored.

18. The name Zadok occurs sometimes, but without significant consequences: the wife of king Yotam of Judah was "Yerusha daughter of Zadok" (2 Kgs 15:33); under King Hezekiah there was "Azariah the chief priest of the house of Zadok" (2 Chr 31:10).

19. In Egyptian *iwnw*, "pillars" or "place of pillars," probably pronounced *Awanu*; the first letter is weak, and may become a guttural: in Gen 41:45 Joseph marries the daughter of Potiphera, priest of On (MT אן, LXX Ἡλίου πόλις); in Ezek 30:17 it is vocalized אָוֶן, "Awen."

20. So 1QIsa חרס; MT הרס, "City of Destruction"; LXX ασεδεκ (from הצדק), "City of Justice," a phrase that is normally attached to Jerusalem (see Isa 1:26; 62:1; Jer 33:6); it comes from a party that either left Jerusalem after 70 (see *War* 7.433–36), or has rejected it, possibly the Egyptian Jews who did not accept the Hasmonean reform.

21. Or less likely עזריאל, "Azriel"; a Yahwist name is another possibility, עזריה, "Azariah" (king of Judah as in 2 Kgs 14:21, or high priest as in 1 Chr 5:35), or יועזר, "Yoezer, Yoazar," like his brother.

22. Which agrees with Rabbinic tradition (*t. Men.* 13.21). According to *m. Yeb.* 6.4, Jesus son of Gamaliel I, who was appointed by King Agrippa II (63–64 BCE, *Ant.* 20.213), married Martha, a daughter of Boethus.

23. See A. Paul, *Écrits de Qoumran et sectes juives aux premiers siècles de l'Islam. Recherches sur les origines du Qaraïsme* (Paris: Letouzey, 1969), p. 71.

24. Cf. É. Nodet, *La crise maccabéenne* (Paris: Cerf, 2005), pp. 416–31.

25. As aptly shown by J. Sievers, "Josephus, First Maccabees, Sparta, the Three Haireseis—and Cicero," *JSJ* 32 (2001), pp. 241–51.

26. This is the conclusion cautiously ventured by J. Le Moyne, *Les Sadducéens* (EB; Paris: Gabalda, 1972), p. 59, and clearly stated by E. Main, "Les sadducéens selon Josèphe," *RB* 97 (1990), pp. 161–206, and G. Stemberger, *Pharisäer, Sadduzäer, Essener* (SBS 144; Stuttgart: Katholisches Bibelwerk, 1991), pp. 100–102.

27. We can mention the short tenure of Ananus in 62 CE, the only Sadducean high priest known so far, but King Agrippa II, who appointed him, was not a Sudducee (*Ant.* 20.197).

28. See D. R. Schwartz, "Josephus on the Pharisees as Diaspora Jews," in Ch. Böttrich and J. Herzer (eds.), *Josephus und das Neue Testament* (Tübingen: Mohr Siebeck, 2007), pp. 137–46. S. Mason, "Josephus' Pharisees: The Narratives," in J. Neusner and B. Chilton (eds.), *In Quest of the Historical Pharisees* (Waco: Baylor University Press, 2007), pp. 3–40, wants to distinguish them from a common Judaism extant before the Maccabean crisis, but this should be just the plain Israelite religion, shared with the Samaritans of Shechem.

29. Y. Sussmann, "Preliminary Talmudic Observations on *Miqṣat Ma'aśe ha-Torah*," in E. Qimron and J. Strugnell (eds.), *Qumran Cave 4. V – Miqṣat Ma'aśe ha-Torah* (DJD 10; London: Clarendon, 1994), pp. 179–200; L. H. Schiffman, "The Place of 4QMMT in the Corpus of Qumran Manuscripts," in J. Kampen (ed.), *Reading 4QMMT* (Atlanta: Scholars Press, 1996), pp. 81–98.

30. See A. Steudel, "4Q448 – The Lost Beginning of MMT?," in F. García Martínez et al. (eds.), *From 4QMMT to Resurrection* (STDJ 61; Leiden: Brill, 2006), pp. 247–63. Steudel tries to relate the whole to Jonathan the high priest, because of the common view that 4QMMT would have been issued by the Teacher of Righteousness during Jonathan's tenure, but (1) that Jonathan cannot have been called a king, and (2) it is quite unlikely that the Teacher would address a high priest of Pharisean tradition in such a conciliatory tone, without polemics.

31. Such is the conclusion of I. Knohl, "Re-Considering the Dating and Recipient of *Miqṣat Ma'aśe Ha-Torah*," *Hebrew Studies* 37 (1996), pp. 119–25; he follows Josephus and admits that John Hyrcanus left the Pharisees, but he does focus on Jannaeus as the addressee of 4QMMT.

32. For the reasons to think that this version reflects the preliminary Greek edition of the War by Josephus himself, see É. Nodet, "Pharisees, Sadducees, Essenes, Herodians," in T. Holmén and S. E. Porter (eds.), *Handbook for the Study of the Historical Jesus* (Leiden: Brill, 2010), Appendix II, pp. 1525–43.

33. The suggestion was first aired by A. dei Rossi, מאור עיניים [Meor Enayim] (Mantua, 1573), III:32–33. It is still held, see Y. Sussmann, "The History of the Halakha and the Dead Sea Scrolls: Preliminary Talmudic Observations on *Miqṣat Ma'aśe ha-Torah*," *Tarbiz* 59 (1989), pp. 11–76, who tentatively restores בית אסין or בית עסין, which may be connected to a phrase common in the Dead Sea Scrolls, עושי התורה, "doers of the Torah."

34. See E. Sukenik, מגלות גנוזות (Jerusalem: Bialik, 1948), pp. 16–18; A. Dupont-Sommer, *Aperçus préliminaires sur les manuscrits de la Mer Morte* (Paris: Maisonneuve, 1950).

35. S. Lieberman, "The Discipline in the So-Called Dead Sea Manual of Discipline," *JBL* 71 (1952), pp. 199–206, concludes that the differences between the יחד of 1QS and the חברים are not greater than the usual controversies between

Rabbis, and he wonders why a marginal, sectarian movement is so close to such a quintessential Jewish way of life, supposed to be Pharisean; unfortunately, this piece of scholarship is seldom cited. H. K. Harrington, *The Impurity Systems of Qumran and the Rabbis: Biblical Foundations* (SBLDS 143; Atlanta: Scholars Press, 1993), shows that a deep level of the Rabbinic system, especially for impurity issues (in fact, the חברים), is close to the Qumran rules, but she concludes that they were the common practice of the Pharisees described by Josephus; this begs the question. L. H. Schiffman, *Reclaiming the Dead Sea Scrolls* (Philadelphia/ Jerusalem: The Jewish Publication Society, 1994), pp. 81–86 and 104–10, distinguishes between various groups (Essenes, Qumran community, חברים), but without a clear definition of "Judaism," so that he cannot make sense of the internal controversies or banishments.

36. E. Rivkin, "Defining the Pharisees: The Tannaitic Sources," *HUCA* 40 (1969), pp. 205–49, notes the similarities between the חברים and some early "Pharisees" (more exactly the פרושים, "dissidents," of the sources), and concludes that the latter have build rules for individual pietists חסידים (Assideans) who wanted to become חברים.

37. J. Carmignac, "HRBYM: les 'Nombreux' ou les 'Notables'?," *RQ* 7 (1971), pp. 575–86, prefers the qualitative meaning ("Rabbis, noted people") rather than the quantitative ("the many").

38. J. Licht, *Megilat ha-Serakhim* (Jerusalem: Bialik, 1965), p. 122, concludes that the three stages for admission correspond to the three levels of Rabbinical uncleanness: first אב טומאה (of pagans, see *b. Shab.* 14b), then ראשון, and שני.

39. H. K. Harrington, "Did the Pharisees Eat Ordinary Food in a State of Ritual Purity?," *JSJ* 26 (1995), pp. 42–54, follows J. Neusner, *From Politics to Piety: The Emergence of Pharisaic Judaism* (Hoboken: KTAV, 1979), pp. 47–55; they conclude that in the first century the Pharisees used to eat in a state of priestly purity, but the argument actually deals with the Rabbinic חברים.

40. J. Jeremias, *Infant Baptism in the First Four Centuries* (London: SCM, 1960), pp. 24–37, states that of necessity this baptism must have been extant before John the Baptist.

41. For further arguments, see É. Nodet, "Le baptême des prosélytes, rite d'origine essénienne," *RB* 116 (2009), pp. 82–110.

42. Since H. Graetz, *Geschichte der Juden* (Helsingfors: Leiner, 1867), III.2, p. 759, followed by dictionaries and encyclopaedias.

43. Schürer, *Geschichte des jüdischen Volkes im Zeitalter Jesu Christi*, II, p. 325; H. Shanks, "Origins of the Title of 'Rabbi'," *JQR* 59 (1969), pp. 152–57; Y. Breuer, "Rabbi Is Greater than Rav, Rabban Is Greater than Rabbi, The Simple Name Is Greater than Rabban," *Tarbiz* 66 (1996), pp. 41–59.

44. S. Zeitlin, "A Reply," *JQR* 53 (1963), pp. 345–49.

45. For further details, see É. Nodet, "Rabbi," *RB* 118 (2011), pp. 123–29.

46. As recognized by mediaeval Rabbis (Rashbam on Gen 1:4), while the *halakhic* day, which depends on the lunar calendar, runs from evening to evening (*t. Taan.* 2.5, referring to Est 4:16, "three nights and three days"; cf. Dan 8:14).

47. See J. Ben-Dov, "The Initial Stages of Lunar Theory at Qumran," *JJS* 54 (2003), pp. 125–38; idem, *Head of All Years: Astronomy and Calendars at Qumran in their Ancient Context* (STDJ 78; Leiden: Brill, 2008), pp. 122–34.

48. E. Qimron, "Celibacy in the Dead Sea Scrolls and the Two Kinds of Sectarians," in J. Trebolle Barrera and L. Vegas Montaner (eds.), *The Madrid Qumran Congress (18–21 March 1991)* (Leiden: Brill, 1992), I, pp. 287–94, distinguishes after CD 6.11–7.10 between the ones who live in the cities of Israel ("camps") and wed according to the Law, from the ones who expect the restoration of the Temple and keep a permanent priestly purity, which implies celibacy.

49. J. Taylor, *Pythagoreans and Essenes: Structural Parallels* (Coll. REJ 32; Paris, Louvain: Peeters, 2004). See too J. J. Collins, *Beyond the Qumran Community: The Sectarian Movement of the Dead Sea Scrolls* (Grand Rapids: Eerdmans, 2009).

50. See M. Simon, *Les sectes juives au temps de Jésus* (Mythes et religions 40; Paris: Presses Universitaires de France, 1960), pp. 105–13; F. Daumas and P. Miquel (eds.), *De vita contemplativa* (Œuvres de Philon 20; Paris: Cerf, 1963), p. 57; G. di Laura, "Il deserto dei Tera-peuti a confronto con quello di Esseni e Qumranici," *Adamantius* 14 (2008), pp. 52–66.

51. See A. F. Gfrörer, *Kritische Geschichte des Urchristenthums. – 1. Philo und die jüdisch-alexandrianische Theosophie* (Stuttgart, 1835), pp. 299–356.

52. Most probably given by outsiders. Their self-designation, as true heirs of Abraham and Moses, may have been "the Covenant" (ברית, see CD 2.2; 4.9, etc.; 1QS 1.16; 2.10, etc.).

53. Already suggested by T. Godwyn, *Moses and Aaron, or Civil and Ecclesiastical Rites Used by the Ancient Hebrews* (London, 1625), I, pp. 50–59.

54. Most modern scholars ignore the issue, or reject any Pythagorean root, see R. Bergmeier, *Die Essener-Berichte des Flavius Josephus. Quellenstudien zu den Essenertexten im Werk des jüdischen Historiographen* (Kampen: Kok Pharos, 1993), pp. 81–107.

55. The excavations show that the Essene settlement came several years after their arrival, see J.-B. Humbert, "Qumrân, esséniens et architecture," in H. Stegemann (ed.), *Antikes Judentum und frühes Christentum* (Berlin: de Gruyter, 1999), pp. 183–96; idem, "Some Remarks on the Archaeology of Qumran," in K. Galor (ed.), *Qumran, the Site of the Dead Sea Scrolls* (STDJ 57; Leiden: Brill, 2006), pp. 19–39.

A VIEW FROM THE WEST:
THE RELATIONSHIP BETWEEN PHOENICIA AND "COLONIAL" WORLD IN THE PERSIAN PERIOD

Ida Oggiano

> *The meeting of sea and continent, like the meeting of whites and Indians, creates as well as destroys. Contact was not a battle of primal forces in which only one could survive. Something new could appear.*
> —R. White[1]

In the immense bibliography of Giovanni Garbini, which touches on very varied subjects reflecting the great curiosity of the scholar and the man, a significant part has been played by his studies devoted to the relations between East and West in the Persian period.[2] I therefore present here a reflection on such relations, which underline the role of Phoenicia as a bridge between Iran and the Mediterranean.[3]

By the term "Phoenicia" I mean the main nucleus of what was the land of the Phoinikes, the Levantines of whom the ancient Greek sources speak. The land inhabited by the Phoinikes had vague and uncertain borders, and only the existence of territorial boundaries established by force of arms made it possible to determine whether certain geographical areas belonged to one political side or another.

In the Persian period the territories of Phoenicia, Philistia, Israel and Judah became part of the satrapy called Athura (Assyria) in the Persian texts and Abar-Nahara in Aramaic, meaning "beyond the river."[4] During this time we see the assertion of two tendencies on which I intend to dwell: on the one hand, the "Phoenicianization" of the coastal regions, both Syrian and Palestinian, via the movement of groups of people towards some areas (particularly on the Palestinian coast in the centres of Dor and Jaffa, and to the north at Tell Sukas, re-established in the second quarter of the fourth century BCE by people from Arwad);[5] and on the other hand, the even greater significance in terms of cosmopolitanism of the coastal centres where, beyond the political directives and cultural orientation of the ruling classes, there lived Phoenicians, Aramaeans, Philistines (e.g. Ashkelon, a Philistine city belonging to Tyre) and Jews, and also Greeks, Egyptians and, to a somewhat lesser extent, Persians. This characteristic of the cities helped to ensure that the coast – a place of transit and settlement, and hence a place where diverse peoples met – proved to be fertile ground for the elaboration of the cultural koine that we might call "Persian," which extended well beyond the Levantine area. The internal regions of the Levant remained on the margins of this entirely coastal phenomenon: Syria and Transjordan, though maintaining a level of wealth well attested by the archaeological remains of the urban areas and necropolis, were reduced to transit lands, while Judea, crushed by the confrontation with Mesopotamian power which had devastated its territory, already chronically poor in resources, had to come to terms with the difficult situation created within its ethnic and social fabric following the return of the exiles from Babylonia.

Phoenicia, then, was again a point of arrival and departure for people, products, ideas, drives and stresses, the eastern boundary of a Mediterranean that was both a physical space, made of water and circumscribed by shores of very far-flung lands (from the coast of the Syro-Palestinian area to those of the Iberian Peninsula), and at the same time a shared world within which the *Phoinikes* resumed the role of a veritable adhesive that had characterized their first move from East to West.

The many lands in the West that were protagonists in this story of a renewed sharing of the Mediterranean have here been lumped together under the definition "Phoenician colonial world," which, chosen almost of necessity, is certainly inadequate and, in some cases, inappropriate to describe a highly diverse set of realities, united by the lowest common denominator that they were born of the Phoenician colonial expansion (which itself was characterized by different phases and hence by different chronologies and modalities).[6]

Putting the word "colonial" in inverted commas is intended to underline the ambiguity of using a term coined in the modern era to describe the phenomenon of the first settlement "far from home" of Greeks and Phoenicians.[7] Putting "Phoenician" in inverted commas, on the other hand, points out the conventional character of a grouping which lumps together geographical, political and cultural realities under a single cultural label – realities which, during this period, had created their own historical path, often unchained from that of the distant "motherland" and marked by the phenomena of interaction and fusion with the local

Western regional realities.⁸ There were undoubtedly chains of a cultural character (language and religion, above all), but unfortunately the available documentation does not enable us fully to understand how, between the late sixth and fifth centuries BCE, the descendants of the families that had lived in the colonies for several generations saw a geographically distant Phoenician "motherland," with which relations had been interrupted between the second half of the seventh and the sixth century.⁹

From this viewpoint it is interesting to examine the resumption of the relations between East and West, the intensity of the phenomenon and the effect it had on the various levels of the social scale in the communities involved, by placing it within the wider context of the so-called "Axial Age" which in diverse areas – which are also very distant – saw the rewriting of social relationships and the transition to new religious and cultural conceptions.¹⁰

An understanding of Mediterranean history, then, cannot disregard our knowledge of an Orient which, as a geopolitical and cultural entity, was no longer formed only of the states facing the Mediterranean or indirectly in contact with it (such as the great Mesopotamian empires), but was now expanding to encompass even more distant areas, such as Iran. Indeed, in an almost unforeseeable way Persia came to play a crucial role in the history of the Mediterranean peoples, particularly in comparison with an Aegean world which in this period "acquista una propria centralità che viene a contrapporsi e a scontrarsi con l'immagine e la centralità dell'Oriente."¹¹

The worlds that came into contact in the Persian period were apparently very distant, but had long been interconnected. As in a kaleidoscope, the "Orients" (from the coastal Levant to Assyria, Mesopotamia and Persia, encompassing many other regions within these macroregions) and the "Wests" have different appearances depending on how the observer turns the lens through which he or she looks at them. I will therefore try to examine some of the many aspects that marked the contact between these worlds, from time to time pointing the lens first at Phoenicia and then at the Western colonial world, and using the marks that the inhabitants of these places left behind to represent themselves: writings and artefacts.¹²

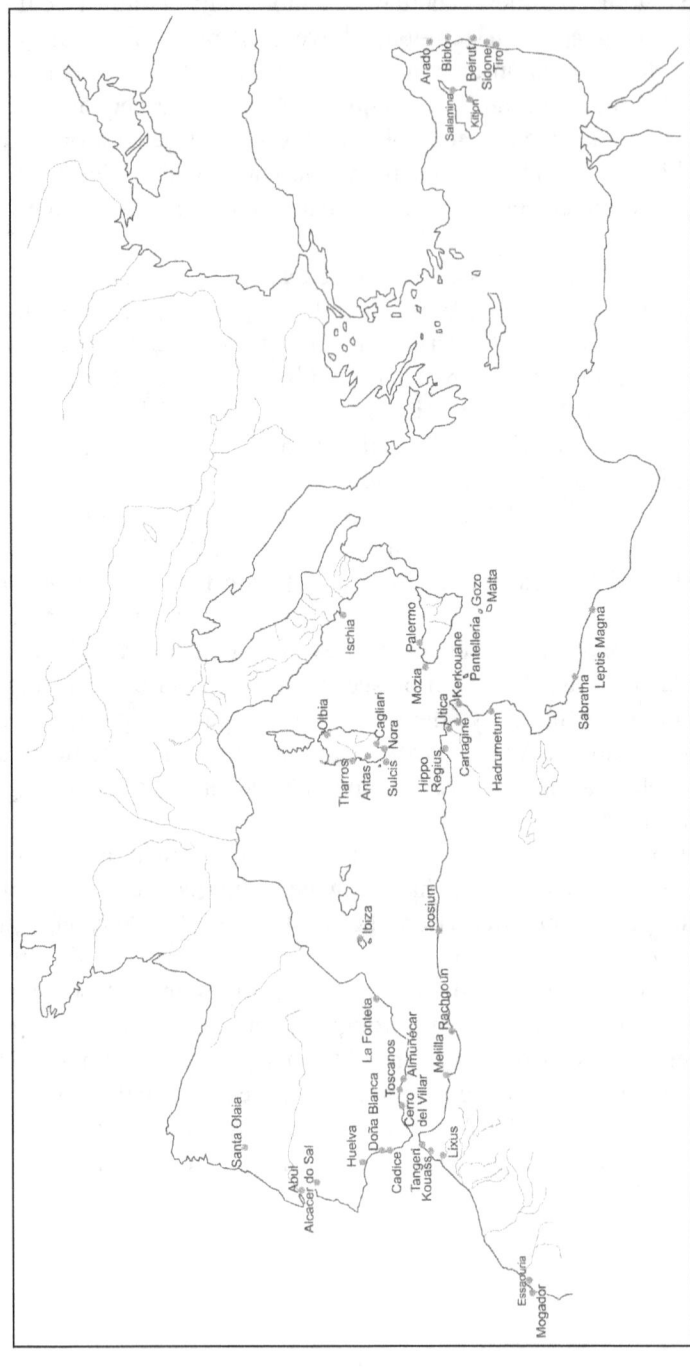

Fig. 1 The main centers of phoenician expansion in the Mediterranean (S.F. Bondì, M. Botto, G. Garbati and I. Oggiano, *Fenici e Cartaginesi. Una civiltà mediterranea* [Rome: Istituto poligrafico e Zecca dello Stato, Libreria dello Stato 2009], p. 95).

"Phoenician Colonial Worlds" Between the Fifth and Fourth Centuries BCE

As we take in consideration the Phoenician colonial world, we are willing to focus our attention to single out those specific elements indicating the renewal of relationships between the central Mediterranean area and the Levant at the end of sixth century BCE (Fig. 1). Contacts between these two areas were interrupted during the second half of the seventh century BCE, when the spur to create new settlements in the West came to an end: this phenomenon led to the interruption of the flow of goods and ideas imported from the Near East towards Etruria and Southern Italy, the areas traditionally touched by commercial activities.[13] From the end of sixth century BCE Sidon and Arwad, together with its hinterland, were the first main cities to reactivate new cultural and commercial exchanges that would connect the Western colonial settlements into the cultural koine of the Persian and Hellenistic worlds. Because of the strong intercultural character throughout these phases, it is very hard to understand properly this complex phenomenon, especially the parallel and contemporaneous relationship between the Phoenician world, understood as the Phoenician Levant, and the Punic Western Mediterranean, and the Greek world, that in this period started to leverage its full influence upon the Mediterranean coasts.

Colonial Areas

By the end of the sixth century BCE and during the whole fifth century BCE, the area we commonly define as the "colonial Phoenician world" is a complex grouping of areas similar in culture but individually distinguishable, all of them sharing a common political hegemony of Carthage.

During the fifth century BCE Carthage went through a process of reorganization of its political structure by strengthening its land control: in Northern Africa, from Libya to Morocco, several settlements were directly controlled by the central power and the area closer to Carthage was subdivided by local districts, such as Maktar (district of Thusca), Ghorfa and Zama (district of Gunzuzi), Dougga and Bulla regia (district of Zeugi).[14] Carthage gradually established a state directly controlling the northern African coast, Sardinia and Sicily, and, in a later moment, the southern coasts of the Iberian Peninsula, becoming one of the great powers in the Mediterranean. All of this process took place within the fifth century BCE, a very important span of time for the city, due to complex relationships, not always peaceful, among the Mediterranean shores.

During the fifth and fourth centuries BCE Sicily was the theatre of the clash between Carthage and the Greek cities, especially Syracuse, to define their own areas of influence. One of the key moments in this dispute was the battle of Himera in 480 BCE, where Carthage was defeated by Syracuse and had to retreat from the island for about seventy years; the period between 410 and 305 BCE was marked by the continuous clash of the African metropolis with the Syracuse tyrants.[15]

Punic control over Sardinia reached its peak between the fourth and third centuries BCE, through the occupation not only of coastal sites but also of inland areas, settling into the island African people. At the same time, aristocratic elites were in power from the beginning of the Punic occupation.[16]

The Iberian Peninsula went through a gradual change of territorial landscape by the mid-sixth century BCE, characterized by the growth of large settlements taking the place of numerous smaller Phoenician centres. Between the sixth and fifth centuries BCE Phoenician settlements such as Malaka, Gadir, Sexi, Abdera and Baria became real cities in shape and structure.[17]

Persia and the West

As we noted above, the beginning of the Persian domination reopened between the end of the sixth century BCE and the early fifth century commercial paths which were interrupted for more than one century. Carthage was at the centre of this renewal process and its culture grew richer in new stimuli coming from the Orient.[18] Of course it is not easy to recognize Near Eastern influxes on the culture of the city. The Levantine coast was the place where in this phase different influxes from various areas came together to be elaborated: Greece, Egypt, Persia and the local Syro-Palestinian traditions all had a role in this play. The aim of our study is to concentrate and stress on the cultural elements directly related to Phoenicia and, indirectly, to Persia; the Greek world is taken into account only when its cultural elements have been elaborated through an Oriental influence and not as an original mainland Greece component. The connection between Punic and Greek components is very well attested by the Carthage *versus* Athens relationship, and the contest all over Sicily between Phoenician colonies and Greek cities; all of these issues sometimes predate the dialogue between the two components on the Levantine coasts.

Carthage and the Persian Empire

In this analysis we have to face the difficult question of the relationship between Carthage and the Persian Empire. We will analyze different kind of sources, epigraphic, numismatic and literary sources, reviewing different positions among those scholars who see elements of political and ideological dependency of Carthage from the Persian Empire,[19] and those who give a more careful, or even opposite, interpretation.[20]

Many Greek and Latin sources mention the kinship that kept Carthage tied to its motherland Tyre. This "filial" relationship is testified by the fact that until Tyre has been conquered by Alexander the Great, Carthage used to ship to the motherland offerings from booties (Curtius Rufus IV 3, 22), and every year the colony used to participate in the festivals dedicated to Melqart (Arrian II 24, 5; Curtius Rufus IV 2, 10). Moreover, the Phoenicians declared the people of Carthage as "their own sons" (Herodotus III 19), when the Persian king Cambyses intended to move west to fight against Carthage after conquering Egypt.

Historical sources have been interpreted in various ways. Some scholars stress the "sentimental" aspect,[21] whereas others have seriously doubted this direct relationship, which seems to have been shaped by a Greek interpretation of the colony/homeland affiliation.[22] Some others interpret Herodotus' text as evidence of the desire of the Persian kings to expand westwards, especially under Cambyses who considered Carthage as an extension of Tyrian power.[23] Actually, these lines could also be interpreted in an opposite way, considering the Punic city as not related, or even as hostile, to the Persian Empire.[24]

A direct relationship between Persia and Carthage is mentioned by Justinus (XIX 1, 10–13). This author recalls that Darius I issued an edict where he requested help in fighting against Greece. At the same time, the king forbade some specific Carthaginian traditions – such as sacrificing humans, eating dogs and cremating the dead – that were in contradiction to Iranian habits.[25] Even in this case interpretations of the text have been very different. For some scholars, Carthage, being a colony of Tyre, belonged to the Persian "coalition" that was supposed to fight against the Greeks,[26] and the prohibitions to the Africanized local traditions are proof of the direct Persian control over the metropolis, regarding religious aspects as well. Others interpret Justinus' text as a proof of the independence of Carthage from the motherland, all the same within strict relationship between East and West.[27]

Within the Persian military strategy against the Greeks, we have to interpret the information reported by Herodotus (VII 165–66) and Diodorus Siculus (XI 1, 4–5) that the Punic defeat in the battle of Himera would be contemporary with the Persian defeat in Salamis in 480 BCE.[28]

The synchrony between these two battles has been read either way, as the indication of the active participation of Carthage in the battles over Greece under the rule of the Persian Empire,[29] or as Greek propaganda to celebrate the victories against the world of the *barbaroi*, stressing the opposition between the two sides of the Mediterranean to be read as "leggenda nazionalistica."[30]

If we skip the written sources, which element can we consider to demonstrate the intermediary role played by Carthage between the Persian Empire and the West?

Between the end of the sixth and fifth centuries BCE, Carthage had to start to deal with its expanding territories, both in terms of political and military administration. At that time, Carthage was the largest state that ever existed on the shores of the central-western Mediterranean. No other similar entity existed back then between Sicily and Etruria, so that the administrative model had to be sought in Phoenicia, organized by this time following the provincial Persian system of Satrapies.[31]

Several scholars indicate some elements as potentially revealing as regards this process.

The territorial organization of the Carthaginian *chora* seems to be derived from a Persian structure in the Near East: the subdivision by districts (the same model being followed in provinces in Sicily, Sardinia and North Africa); the role of Carthaginian citizens with administrative responsibilities in the main centres; Libyans and Libyio-Phoenicians in the colonies; the formation of a local officers class.[32] *Qrthdst* would have been a head administrative centre, connected to the V Satrapy through Tyre and/or capital town of the western territories, enacting in this respect a real "imperial" politics on the Phoenician lands in the west.[33]

Another element would be the carrying out of a "colonial" strategy, moving many ethnic African components in the land overseas. This process is similar to a practice used by Achaemenians, creating colonies with help of loyal local population in areas to be controlled.[34]

Direct connections with Achaemenid institutions can be found in epigraphic and numismatic documents. In the first place the caption *šbʿl sys* in the Phoenician coins from Panormo in Sicily present the "citizens (*optimates*, lords) of sys" as the issuing authority for the city's money, probably resembling administrative structures of the Persian Empire in the fifth century BCE. The word *bʿln*, "citizens, residents," was used from the fifth century BCE in Aramaic texts of Asia Minor to indicate both land owners administering large estates out of town properties that had to pay tribute to the Satrapy, and the "feudi d'armi."[35] Furthermore some Punic institution's offices, especially military ones, as attested by

Neopunic epigraphic evidence in second-century BCE Numidia, seem to point towards an Achaemenid origin and the survival in those areas where sources attest to some Persian presence.[36]

As a final remark, we have to point out that the initial stages of the Punic politics of coinage share some elements of the system adopted in the same period in the Near East. On the one side there is a lack of issues in gold and electrum until the middle of fourth century BCE, probably following the Persian law that allowed golden coinage only to the Great King: Carthage, exactly as Tyre and other Phoenician cities, was not allowed to mint golden coins. On the other hand, money was not currently used in the Near East and in Carthage for commercial transactions and for paying troops until the middle of fourth century BCE.[37]

Scholars have different, and sometimes contrasting, opinions on this matter. Sandro Filippo Bondì[38] thinks that the new administrative system imposed by Carthage to North-African lands after the mid-sixth century is primarily based on the Sidonian system of managing estates, as clearly illustrated by J. Elayi.[39] Bondì does not think that it is demonstrated or even demonstrable that Carthage felt part of the "imperial" political system of the Near East,[40] nor that it could have organized its own structures, and those out of the *chora*, following the complex Achaemenid model. Carthage would have thus a proper Western dimension, or at least a Mediterranean one. Economically and institutionally, Oriental ways had to be elaborated in an autonomous political and ideological system. From the fifth century onwards, Carthage was seen as a protagonist competitor in the politics of the Mediterranean world, but not as a western projection of the great empires of the Levant.

Comparisons and Connections with the Phoenician Area

Once we have defined the limits for analyzing the relationship between the West and the Persian Empire, we can inspect some elements connecting Achaemenid Phoenicia and the central Mediterranean, where Carthage plays its primary role. We will analyze this phenomenon through the same procedure adopted for the East, stressing the reception of new stimuli coming from the eastern area as proof of cultural continuity throughout these years.

The City: Urban Space and Territory

The organization of western cities and their relationship with the territory manifests some traits that are similar to the urban development in the East.

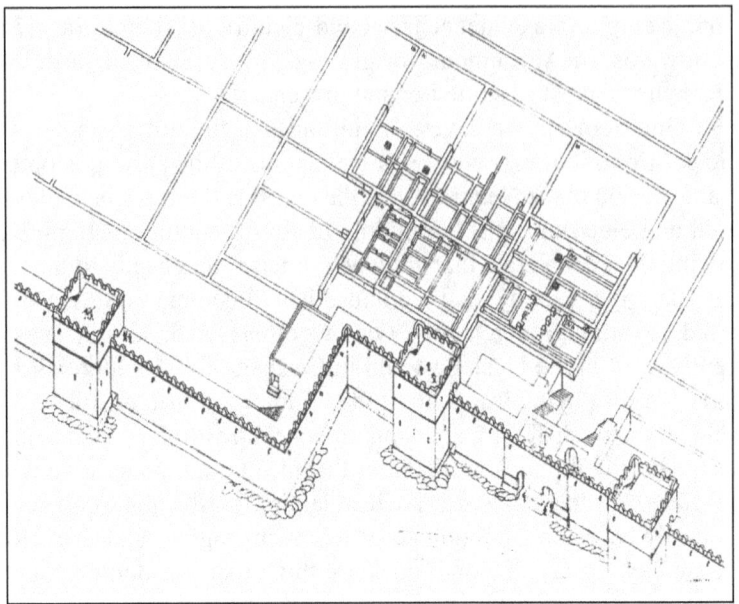

Figure 2: Carthage. Maritime district (proposed reconstruction of the fifth-third century B.C phase). (M. Vegas [ed.], *Cartago fenicio-púnica. Las excavaciones alemanas en Cartago 1975–1997* [Barcelona: Laboratorio de Arqueología, Universidad Pompeu Fabra de Barcelona, 1998).

We have already pointed out how the territorial management of Carthage reflects the administrative organization of Sidon.[41] This organization through administrative districts (ʿrst) is not easily recognizable outside of North Africa, but we can assume that it existed in Sardinia, Sicily and in Iberia in the area of Cádiz. The social structure had to follow this trend, changing its structure and giving birth to a new class of people, the landowners.[42] Concerning the town itself, it is noteworthy that in this phase the urban space was organized by functional and regular areas. This development, comparable to the contemporary solutions developed in the Greek world, shows aspects of originality recalling Oriental models predating Hyppodamus' geometrical town planning.[43]

Between the end of sixth and during fifth centuries BCE Carthage went through a series of renovations and extensions that led it to become a proper metropolis: the town expanded southwards where new districts with public and private buildings were built, and a new large wall close to the beach enclosed the new residential district, the so-called "Magon's district" (Fig. 2). During its first building phase contemporary to the enclosure wall, this area was organized through *insulae* orthogonally displayed, with regular rectangular units following the walls' lay-out.[44]

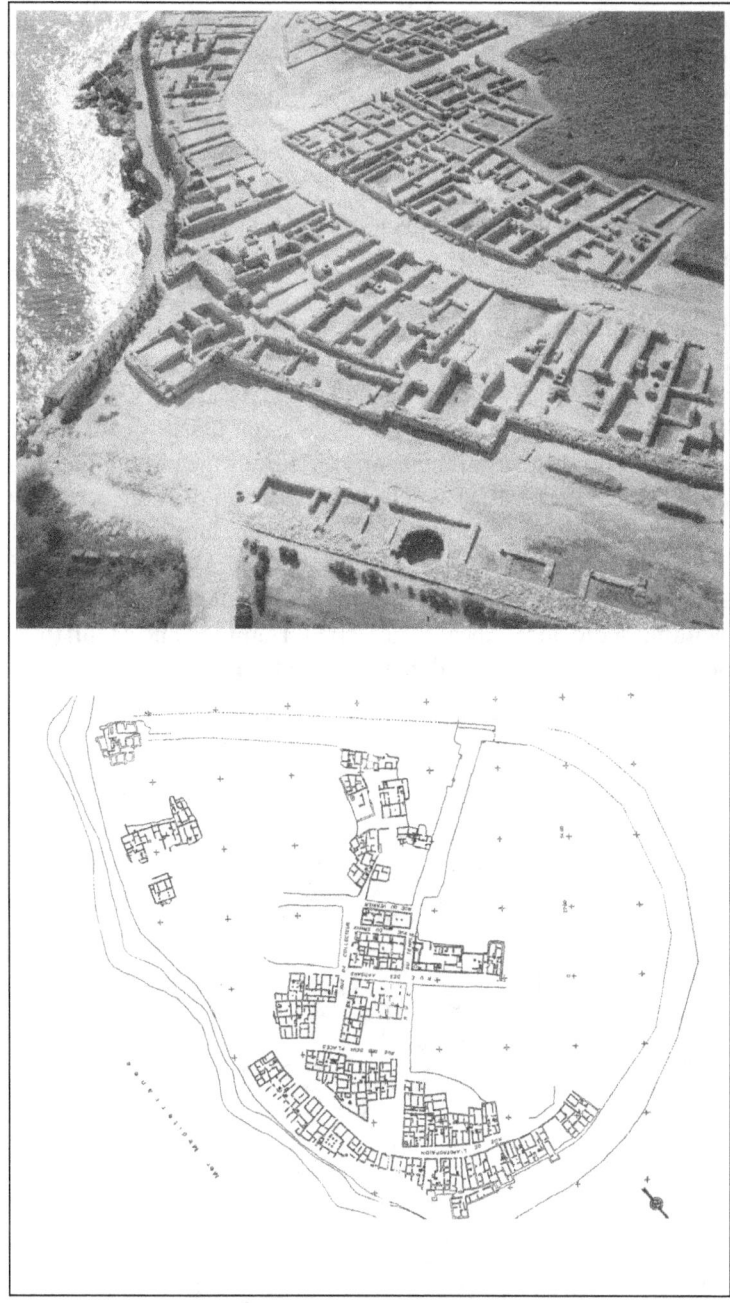

Figure 3: Kerkouane. Aerial view (*I Fenici* [Milan: Bompiani, 1988], p. 177) and plant of the city (M. H. Fantar, *Kerkouane. Città punica nella regione berbera di Tamezrat* [n.p.], p. 114).

Orthogonal urban plans belonging to the same period can be found in North Africa at Kerkouane (Fig. 3) and in Sardinia at Pani Loriga di Santadì and Nora. Probably Olbia, also in Sardinia, could have had a similar orthogonal planning, though documents are too scarce to prove this hypothesis.[45] We can still quote A. Mezzolani's observations regarding Sicily as an example of osmosis of different cultures, stressing more of the Punic role in the urban development of centres like Soluntum and Palermo.[46]

Gods and Cults of the Punic World Between East and West
Which developments of the western religion can be directly linked to the reprise of connections with the East?

We begin this analysis from the cultic area usually considered the most typical and original in the central Mediterranean Phoenician area, the *tofet*.[47] The sacred area, which was created in open air space by the first colonies coming to Carthage and Sardinia in the eighth century BCE, was supposed to collect cremation burials with children and/or animal bones. Urns were sometimes indicated by stones and stele often bearing inscriptions dedicated to the two gods Baal Hammon and Tinnit (this one introduced into Carthage by the end of the fifth century BCE).[48]

Figure 4: Stele from the *tofet* of Mozia (S. Moscati, *L'arte dei Fenici* [Milan: Fabbri, 1990], p. 30).

Figure 5: Stele of Yehawmilk of Byblos (*Liban* l'autre rive. *Exposition présentée à l'Institut du monde arabe du 27 octobre 1998 au 2 mai 1999* [Paris, 1998], p. 111).

Figure 6: Stele from the *tofet* of Carthage (*La Méditerranée de Phéniciens de Tyr à Carthage. Exposition présentée à l'Institut du monde arabe du 6 novembre 2007 au 20 avril 2008* [Paris, 2007], p. 246).

Some elements of cultic activities performed have a clear connection with the East. The first one concerns one of the two gods, Tinnit, who gained a position in the West, especially in Carthage, that she never had in the East, with new peculiar characteristics. It is noteworthy that the first attestations of this goddess in the East belong, on epigraphic grounds, to the sixth century (and in Carthage she appears from the end of the fifth to early fourth centuries BCE),[49] so that we may connect its "migration" to the West as a possible consequence of the renewal of contacts between the two areas of the Mediterranean during the Persian period.

At the end of the sixth century is to be dated the introduction in the *tofet* of stelae in the shape of *aedicule*, corresponding to the *naòs* type in fashion between Phoenicia and Cyprus both in funerary stelae and in temple architecture (Amrit and Ain el-Ayat).[50] A series of Oriental motifs attested on different classes of materials (such as ivory and coroplastic productions, sculpture and glyptic), started to be introduced from the sixth century in the iconographic repertoire of local craftsmanship where *tofet* are documented. In Motya, for instance, new figurines appear: the female figurine holding her breasts (Fig. 4), the one holding a disc and a lotus flower, as elaborated in Achaemenid period,[51] the naked figurine with Egyptian wig, one outstretched arm and the other folded on the chest, the male figurine on one side, with high cap and scepter in hand, and finally the god on a throne. In Carthage, among the many images on stelae, the most represented is the one with man holding a child: he wears a cylindrical cap similar in shape to those well known in Phoenicia (on the stele of Yehawmilk of Byblos and on coinage from Sidon), going back to a Persian tradition continuing in Tyre and Sidon until Hellenistic times (Figs. 5 and 6).[52]

In the Levant in the fifth century is also to be found the origin of the so-called "Tanit symbol," as the most ancient documents show the figurines on the Shavei Zion shipwreck (Fig. 7) and a glass bead from Sarepta show.[53] We have to keep in mind that the analysis of the iconographical motif and the interpretations of religious symbolism[54] are two separate questions, as the different realities in Phoenicia and in the Western Mediterranean show, but it is remarkable that this iconography was discovered and selected by Carthaginian craftsmen only during the second half of the fifth century BCE (Fig. 8).

More data on cultic activities are to be added to the *tofet*'s evidence, showing that new cults are devoted to Phoenician deities such as Shadrafa and Sid only after the sixth century.[55]

Figure 7: Figurine with the "sign of Tanit" from the shipwreck of Shavei Zion (E. Stern, *Material Culture of the Land of the Bible in the Persian Period: 538–332 B.C.* [Warminster: Aris & Phillips, 1982], Fig. 291).

Figure 8: Stele from the *tofet* of Nora with the "sign of Tanit" (S. Moscati, *L'arte dei Fenici* [Milan: Fabbri, 1990], p. 46)

Shadrafa, literally a healer deity, was worshipped all over the Punic world. A public cult was devoted to Shadrafa in Carthage, and he is mentioned in the inscriptions of the "Grotta Regina" in Sicily, of Antas in Sardinia and in one inscription in Leptis Magna in Africa, where he is identified with Liber Pater, presenting itself as a city deity.[56]

Sid was worshipped especially in Sardinia. His cult gained a "new" or "renewed" central role after the occupation of the island by the Carthaginians and the erection of the temple of Antas in the fifth century.[57] He was later identified with the Roman Sardus Pater, representing the Sardus who colonizes Sardinia and becomes the eponymous hero;[58] Sid was therefore a dynastic god, a "divine hero,"[59] an ancestral forefather and connected to the ideological legitimization of the Punic conquest of Sardinia.[60]

The image of god Sid in Sardinia is based on a double meaning: on one side, the Oriental traditions of worshipping people deified after death, such as Eshmun, Shadrafa and Milkashtart; on the other hand, the religious aspects of the substratu culture worshipping deities with a dynastic role – the name B'BY, which follows the name of Sid in Antas' inscriptions, recalls local ancestral traditions reflected in the myth of Sardus, the eponymous hero according to some classical sources.[61]

The search for elements of the Levantine tradition, especially the choice for deities connected to the cult of ancestors and the deification of some of them, fits very well with this moment of great social change in Sardinia, connected to the Punic occupation and the renewal of contacts with Phoenicia and Cyprus. We can probably link this to the trend of the passage in the west of the so-called "*suivant du char royale*" motif, as documented by two seals from Tharros[62] (Fig. 9) and by some *bullae* from Carthage and some votive razors (Fig. 10), present in this period on funerary reliefs and on coins from Sidon and connected by many scholars to the Syro-Palestinian tradition of the deified ancestors.[63]

The last element to be considered in this discussion of the renewal of East–West contacts, is the establishment in the west Mediterranean of healing cults. This phenomenon, attested also in Greece and Italy,[64] saw Eshmun becoming an important deity in the Punic world. In Carthage, as was the case in Sidon, Eshmun was the god protector of the city and the cult was worshipped in the temple of the Byrsa acropolis; it must have had a civic role for a long time, since in this temple the senate of the town continued to meet during the night and it became the final stronghold of the city when Scipio began the final assault on Carthage.[65] Medical properties of the god are preserved in Sardinia until the second century BCE, as testified by two inscriptions: the trilingual from San Nicolò Gerrei and the short epigraph on the clay hand from Cagliari.[66]

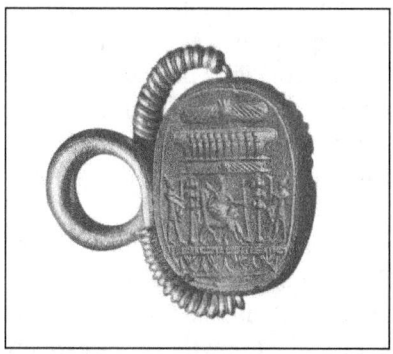

Figure 9: Seal from Tharros (*I Fenici* [Milan: Bompiani, 1988], p. 516).

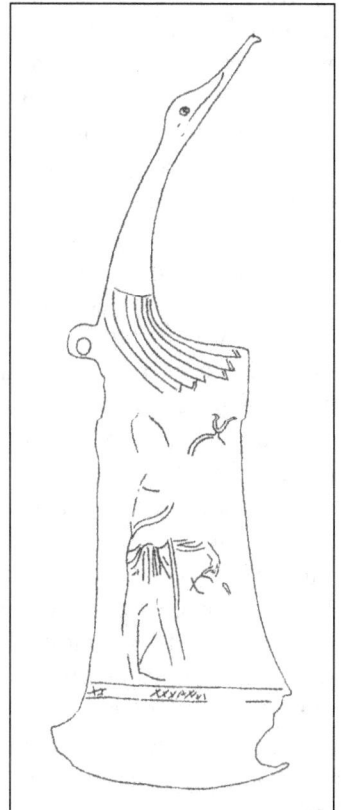

Figure 10: Votive razor from Carthage (E. Acquaro, *I rasoi punici* [Rome: Consiglio nazionale delle ricerche, 1977], Pl. XII, Ca 61).

Eshmun is not the only god related to therapeutic cults, since two inscriptions from Antas quote as well Horon and Shadrafa.[67]

During the Punic and Neo-Punic periods in Sardinia we can hypothesize the establishment of sanctuaries connected to water and to *sanatio*, with sacred areas built around the springs (Mitza Salamu, "health's spring") and the reuse in many cases of sacred wells belonging to Nuragic times.[68]

An indication on the island of the developments of sacred architecture that took place in Oriental areas during the Persian period comes from Nora.[69] From the area Sa Punta 'e Su Coloru comes an *aedicula* in Egyptianizing style (Fig. 11), known as *ma'abed*, preserved only for the crown with *uraei* and the winged sun,[70] to be compared with Oriental specimens like the *naoi* in Amrit (to be dated in its monumental phase, to the fifth-mid fourth centuries) and Ain el-Hayat (Fig. 12).[71]

Knowledge and reception of cultic activities and the related craftsmanship between Cyprus and Phoenicia throughout these phases is evident as well in Sicily and Malta with the presence of anthropomorphic sculpture in Egyptianizing style: two exemplars of male statues come from the Stagnone in Marsala and from Tas Silg (Fig. 13).[72]

Finally, an important role for the contributions from the Levant had definitely to be played by Egypt. The Egyptian world has always been part of the Phoenician religious system, and during the Persian period the relationship between the two was strengthened, also due to the fact that groups of Phoenician people were living and working in Egypt at the same time. New Egyptian influences on the Levant were reflected in the colonial world, as the widespread transmission of the *naos* motif, elaborated in Phoenicia, shows. Also, direct influence between the land of the Nile and Carthage, and probably Spain, can be documented by direct imports in these two western Mediterranean areas.[73]

The importing to Carthage of two tiny bronze figurines representing Arpocrates is likely due to travels of Carthaginians in Egypt; these statuettes had to be placed in some cultic place in Carthage, since this god had great prestige in Punic cultic activities.[74] A series of Egyptian bronzes reached the shores of Spain: the mummy-shaped Osiris from Punta de la Vaca, the Osiris from Villaricos, the seated Imhotep from Minorca. The bronzes came together with many vitreous amulets,[75] probably following the commercial and raw materials routes of bronze between Egypt and Iberia.[76]

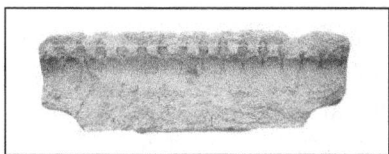

Figure 11: Crowning element from Nora (*I Fenici* [Milan: Bompiani, 1988], p. 275).

Figure 12: *Naòs* of Ayn el-Hayat (E. Renan, *Mission de Phénicie* [Paris, 1864], tav, IX).

Figure 13: Statue from the Stagnone di Marsala (T. Pedrazzi, "Arte fenicia," in S. Giuntoli and T. Pedrazzi, *L'arte fenicia e l'arte etrusca* [La Grande Storia dell'Arte 13; Florence: E-ducation.it, 2006], pp. 17–180 [p. 156, Fig. 11]).

Funerary Practices

The development of funerary practices in the West is to be considered independently. Notably, it is only in cases from the highest social groups of the western colonial population that we observe influence from contemporary funerary practices of Phoenicia.

The first element is to be seen in the habit of the North-African aristocracy to imitate Phoenician examples, especially from Arwad, such as building from the fourth century BCE original funerary monuments in elevated parts of the country from where the fertile land could be controlled,[77] as a visual indicator of the boundaries of large estates.[78]

The second element is the decision of a few important citizens, maybe merchants from the East, to import from Phoenicia some anthropomorphic sarcophagi to be used in burials. This use is proved by the sarcophagi found in Cádiz (Fig. 14).

A peculiar representation is the one known in the area of Sulky (Sardinia), with a funerary relief reproducing an Egyptianized male figure, attested in one tomb in Monte Sirai and two in Sulky (Figs. 15 and 16).[79] Tomb 7 in Sulky is particularly interesting.[80] This grave belongs to the second half of the fifth century and has a large chamber with central pillar: on the front wall of the pillar a sculpture represents a standing man dressed with a short skirt, the left arm folded on the breast and with an object tied to the wrist, the right arm stretched along the body with a scroll in the hand. The arms each have three arm-rings painted in red; red and black painting is used as well for anatomic details and the garments. At the bottom of the chamber were the remains of a wooden coffin, which should have borne the same image, or one very similar to the one represented on the pillar.

The inspiration for the burial has been sought by scholars in Egypt, both for the iconography of the relief, and for the use of a wooden coffin and the *cartonnage*, but also for some elements in the funerary ritual, especially the deposition of the remains of two birds and of some bird eggs.[81] Even if the Egyptian inspiration of this burial is very clear, we cannot avoid noting that the Egyptian style man with a scroll in his hand is well known in Phoenicia and Cyprus, even though not in a funerary context;[82] moreover, the use of multiple moldings as used in the entrance door of this grave resembles examples attested in Cyprus at the end of the sixth century.[83]

The reception of Oriental motifs does not appear to have been passive: the motif of the Egyptianizing figure appears as an original elaboration from works created in the Levant, employed for new religious and funerary customs.

Figure 14: Anthropoid sarcophagus from Cadiz (*I Fenici* [Milan: Bompiani, 1988], p. 298).

Figure 15: Altorilievo funerario da Sulky (*I Fenici* [Milan: Bompiani, 1988], p. 302).

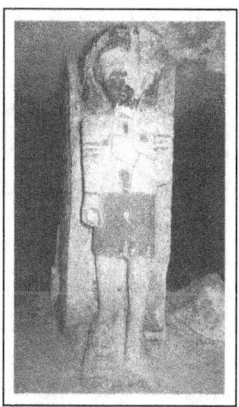

Figure 16: Funerary relief from Sulky (P. Bernardini, "Recenti scoperte nella necropoli punica di Sulcis," *Rivista di Studi Fenici* 33 [2005], pp. 63–80, Fig. 10).

If we interpret, as has been proposed, the iconography in the Sulky reliefs as the image of the dead (following the fact that the image on the wooden coffin recalls the one on the pillar),[84] we are led to think that the Sulky funerary sculptures could express a kind of worship of the dead seen as a hero. This process is probably happening at the same time when in Sardinia cults of a deity like Sid (with strong dynastic connections and linked to the underworld) became popular. The representations on the Sulky reliefs could thus be "probably the most sensible indication of the 'heroic' celebration of high rank people, not so attested in previous periods, at least in the figurative arts."[85] Still displaying great social, political and cultural differences from the Levantine world, the high-ranking people of colonial Sardinian society had probably gained from the Oriental traditions the idea of getting a special rank in the afterlife, with a deep continuity with Syro-Palestinian traditions.

The Craftsmanship Productions and the Protagonists of Exchanges
Until now we have stressed analogies between East and West, but we have to point out that the analysis has been conducted through objects connected with the highest strata of society.

The wonderful jewellery found in Tharros must have been produced in some Near Eastern workshop and imported to Sardinia to satisfy the needs of the rich inhabitants of one of the most prosperous Punic town in the western Mediterranean. The connection with the east would remain the same even if we hypothesize that the jewels were of a local production, showing even more how Tharros, together with Carthage, had been instrumental in opening again routes and connections with the Levant throughout these phases. Both production techniques and iconographic motifs clearly show how these objects come from the Near Eastern tradition.[86]

The Punic glyptic developed independently from Egyptian productions, from the sixth century, and came into contact with contemporary Etruscan productions. Iconographic motifs came from Phoenicia and Persian-period Egypt, reinterpreted through the language of Punic art. Among these we may recall the winged female goddess protecting the birth of Horus on the lotus flower or symmetrically reflected aside the sacred tree; the male deity on a throne in a gesture of benediction; the god on the papyrus boat; the falcon with sacred Egyptian attributes; *Isis lactans*.[87] A peculiar element is the presence on Carthage's *bullae* of the holder of a *ram-headed staff*, testifying once again to the official connection between Carthage and Phoenicia in the Persian period.[88]

These objects, rather than coming from an archaic heritage transmitted to the West through precious items such as ivories or bowls, seem to belong to "Persian period Orientalizing" art that circulated through sketches and models, and probably even craftsmen, providing the new ruling classes in the Western Punic world with iconographic models related to their Oriental origins.

The trading of information was probably not in one direction only. The glyptic from Tharros offers some elements worthy of analysis here. Green jasper scaraboids have been found in Tharros. These were most likely locally produced since mines of the same stone have been identified not far from the city. In Byblos similar items have been recognized, items that were so similar to Sardinian and Carthaginian artefacts that E. Gubel suggested that they might have belonged to the same workshop[89] (Figs. 17 and 18). If we think that these items could have reached Byblos from the central Mediterranean, we can suppose a West-to-East itinerary previously considered impossible.

Figure 17: Seals from Byblos and Cagliari, S. Avendrace (E. Gubel, "Byblos: L'art de la métropole phénicienne," in E. Acquaro et al., *Biblo. Una città e la sua cultura* [Rome: Consiglio Nazionale delle Ricerche, 1994], tav. V, 11-1).

Figure 18: Seals from Byblos and Tharros (E. Gubel, *Byblos: L'art de la métropole phénicienne*, in Acquaro *et alii.*, *Biblo. Una città e la sua cultura* [Rome: Consiglio Nazionale delle Ricerche, 1994], tav. V, 16, and *I Fenici* [Milan: Bompiani, 1988], p. 398).

Figure 19: Funerary stele of Yaamas of Tyre (*La Méditerranée des Phéniciens de Tyr à Carthage. Exposition présentée à l'Institut du monde arabe du 6 novembre 2007 au 20 avril 2008* [Paris: Somogy, Institut de monde arabe, 2007, p. 240, cat. 18).

The presence of high-ranking Carthaginians in Phoenicia in these times is well proven by the stelae found in the area of Tyre[90] (Fig. 19). Some western elaborations in the cultic milieu can be hypothesized for a coinage of Roman-era Ashkelon, quoting Φανηβαλος, "face of Ba'al," the name of goddess Tinnit in the *tofet*'s stelae. We finally recall Arrianus' words (II 21, 9), who, describing Tyre's fleet, mentions *quinquereme* and *quadrireme* as boats adopted by the Sidonians around 340 BCE, and thought to be of Carthaginian invention (Plinius, *Nat. His.* VII 207; Aristoteles, fr. 600; see also Clement of Alexandria, *Strom.* I 45,10).[91]

Among the protagonists of these relationships we definitely lack the lower classes. Proof for this statement is offered by the coroplastic productions.[92] This is strongly locally connoted and does not show any Oriental influence: it lacks most of the iconographies and typologies attested in the Phoenician repertoire of these phases, and is much more connected with contemporary developments in Greek craftsmanship.

Conclusions

The analysis of the relationships between the western "colonial" Phoenician world and Achaemenid Persia helped us in pointing out the primary role that the Levant played in this context. The Phoenician region, with its enlarged boundaries from the North (Syria) to the South (Palestine), was crucial in connecting the core of the Achaemenid empire with the Punic West and at the same time was central in elaborating new ideas, stimuli and motifs that people arriving here, and from here departing, were creating and disseminating all over the Mediterranean.

Between the sixth century and the first half of the fifth, a series of deep and continuous exchanges were established among Phoenicia, Cyprus, Egypt and the Phoenician "colonies." These contacts were in both directions along the Mediterranean, which reappeared to be the vivid area of movements. It was a period of renewed circulation of people and products, and with them ideas, words (which we know only in part) and images, following the same model on the ground as the formation of the Phoenician culture and its foundations in the West. Different parts of societies took part in this process in very different ways. The highest hierarchical ranks of society were the protagonists in this movement: this is connected to the official renewal of contacts between Carthage and the Phoenician cities, with a clear intention of the North-African city in presenting itself ethnically, politically and culturally as the offspring of the Phoenician motherland. Belonging to the highest ranks of society is often expressed through Oriental reminiscences, such as the use of luxury items (seals and jewels) or the adoption of some funerary customs (sarcophagi).

Contacts between East and West are visible in the official aspects of colonial life, from the political and administrative organization (as derived from the Persian administration or from the organization of Phoenician centers like Sidon), to the urban planning and religious practices (sharing some specific deities, some cultic structures, or some cultic objects or images).

The development of local costumes and of local material culture shows instead local or regional traits, and testify to an ethnic and social structure of the colonial population, especially its lower class, subdivided on regional bases and distant from the Eastern world.

The Levantine contributions, different from the Persian, fit into the western world as into a distant, faraway reality, which properly reinterprets the Oriental world rather than feeling part of it.

By the middle of fifth century, things changed again. On a political level, the relationship with the East grew weaker. This was due, in part, to the rise of Carthage to full political maturity, as well as the increased difficulty faced by the Phoenician cities in controlling commercial routes after the Peace of Callias in 448 BCE.[93] The parting of the two is well perceived by Herodotus, who missed the elements of unity which, during the first half of the fifth century, were really renewed and fully vital.

We here mention a final consideration on the relationships between East and West throughout this period. Among the different forms of relationships and exchanges in the Mediterranean in this phase, a primary role is played by the clash between Greece and Persia, upon which ancient and modern historians have constructed the idea of Hellenic (and, later, European) cultural identity. This assumption is based on the contrast of the ideals of democracy and freedom expressed by the Greek world with the despotic and culturally weaker Oriental world represented by the Persians. We have so far seen how the Eastern worlds (from Persia to the Levant, from Cyprus to Egypt) and the Western worlds (from the Aegean to the central Mediterranean, where many spheres were already shared by Greeks and Phoenicians), had deep and close contacts not only on battlefields but, probably most of all, in harbors, boats, markets, craftsmen's workshops, palaces and sacred places. In these melting pots different fluxes of communication were born, in many directions, caused not only from need, but also from curiosity and fascination for distant worlds. Diversity encouraged communication rather than conflict and led to a Mediterranean cultural "identity," which we can (or maybe we should!) still recognize in ourselves.

Notes

1. R. White, *The Middle Ground: Indians, Empires and Republics in the Great Lakes Regions, 1650–1815* (Cambridge: Cambridge University Press, 1991), p. XXV.

2. On the subject of the relations between Carthage and the Persian Empire: E. Acquaro, *Studi di archeologia punica* (Pisa-Rome: Ist. Editoriali e Poligrafici 1997); A. C. Fariselli, "The Impact of Military Preparations on the Economy of the Carthaginian State," in G. Pisano (ed.), *Phoenicians and Carthaginians in the Western Mediterranean* (Rome: Università degli Studi di Roma "Tor Vergata," 1999), pp. 59–67; L. I. Manfredi, *La politica amministrativa di Cartagine in Africa* (Rome: Accademia Nazionale dei Lincei, 2003); C. Peri, "Il nome semitico di Byrsa," *Byrsa* I (2003), pp. 73–84; G. Garbini, "Fenici d'Oriente e Fenici d'Occidente," in A. Spanò Giammellaro (ed.), *Atti del V Congresso Internazionale di Studi Fenici e Punici, I-III, Palermo, 5-8* (Palermo: Università degli Studi di Palermo, 2005), pp. 5–8; S. F. Bondì, "I Fenici in Erodoto," in W. Burkert et al., *Hérodote et les peuples non grecs* (Geneva: Vandoeuvres-Genève: Fondation Hardt, 1990), pp. 255–86; idem, "Aspetti delle relazioni tra la Fenicia e le colonie d'Occidente in età persiana," *Transeuphratène* 12 (1996), pp. 73–83; idem, "La société phénicienne à l'époque perse: un modèle pour le monde punique?," *Transeuphratène* 28 (2004), pp. 67–75; idem, "Frontières culturelles et frontières administratives dans e monde phénicien d'Occident," *Transeuphratène* 35 (2008), pp. 71–81; M. B. Cocco, A. Gavini and A. Ibba (eds.), "Paesaggi del potere tra Oriente e Occidente dagli Assiri a Cartagine," in *L'Africa romana. Trasformazione*

dei paesaggi del potere nell'Africa settentrionale fino alla fine del mondo antico. Atti del XIX Convegno di studio. Sassari, 16–19 dicembre 2010, I (Rome: Carocci, 2012), pp. 161–74.

3. I. Oggiano and T. Pedrazzi, *La Fenicia in età persiana. Un ponte tra il mondo iranico e il Mediterraneo* (*Rivista di Studi Fenici*, XXXIX [2011], Supplemento; Rome: Fabrizio Serra, 2013).

4. For historical and archaeological overviews of the Palestinian area in these periods in E. Stern, *Archaeology of the Land of the Bible*. II. *The Assyrian, Babylonian and Persian (Periods 732–332 B.C.E.)* (New York: Yale University Press 2001); M. Liverani, *Oltre la Bibbia. Storia antica di Israele* (Rome-Bari: Laterza 2003); O. Lipschits and M. Oeming (eds.), *Judah and the Judeans in the Persian Period* (Winona Lake, IN: Eisenbrauns, 2006). For the Syrian area: M. Rossi, "La Vème satrapie de l'empire achéménide: les étapes du développement culturel de la region syrienne entre le long passage de la reorganization territorial provoquée par l'écroulement des empires de l'âge du Fer et la formation d'un vaste empire profondément œcuménique," in F. Baffi, R. Dolce, S. Mazzoni, and F. Pinnock (eds.), *"Ina Kibrāt Erbetti – Le quattro parti del mondo." Studi di archeologia orientale dedicati a Paolo Matthiae* (Rome: Casa Editrice Universitaria La Sapienza, 2006), pp. 565–87; for Phoenicia, see V. S. Jigoulov, *The Social History of Achemenid Phoenicia* (London/Oakville: Equinox, 2010), J. Élayi, *Histoire de la Phénicie* (Paris: Perrin, 2013).

5. E. Stern, *Material Culture of the Land of the Bible in the Persian Period: 538–332 B.C.* (Warminster: Aris & Philipps; Jerusalem: Israel Exploration Society, 1982). A. Nunn, *Der figürliche Motivschatz Phöniziens, Syrien und Transjordaniens vom 6. bis zum 4. Jahrhundert v. Chr.* (OBO 18; Freiburg- Göttingen: Universitätsverlag Vandenhoeck & Ruprecht, 2000), sets the boundary between diverse cultural regions – Syrian and Phoenician – between Lattakia and the Homs corridor, between Tell Sukas and Arwad.

6. On the foundations, see the recent work of S. F. Bondì, "La colonizzazione: modi, tempi, obiettivi," in S. F. Bondì, M. Botto, G. Garbati and I. Oggiano (eds.), *Fenici e Cartaginesi. Una civiltà mediterranea* (Rome: Istituto Poligrafico e Zecca dello Stato, 2009), pp. 92–102.

7. Among others, P. Van Dommelen, "Ambiguous Matters: Colonialism and Local Identities in Punic Sardinia," in E. Lyons and S. V. P. Papadopoulos (eds.), *The Archaeology of Colonialism* (Los Angeles: Getty Publication, 2002), pp. 121–47 (121): "colonialism in (early) modern times is commonly associated with violence, political domination and economic exploitation of indigenous peoples, but the ancient terms primarily referred to absence from home and being in a foreign country." On the subject of the archaeology of colonialism, see the various essays in Lyons and Papadopoulos (eds.), *The Archaeology of Colonialism*.

8. D. Asheri, *Fra Ellenismo e Iranismo: il caso di Xanthos fra il V e il IV sec. a.C. In Forme di contatto e processi di trasformazione nelle società antiche* (Pisa-Rome: Scuola Normale Superiore, École Francaise de Roma, 1983), pp. 485–522.

9. On these phenomena, see the interesting observations in Van Dommelen, "Ambiguous Matters," p. 124

10. On the Axial Age, cf. finally J. P. Arnason, S. N. Eisenstadt, and B. Wittrock (eds.), *Axial Civilizations and World History* (Leiden/Boston: Brill, 2005).

11. M. Liverani, *Antico Oriente. Storia economa società* (Rome-Bari: Laterza, 1991), p. 937.

12. On Persia, see T. Pedrazzi's contribution in Oggiano and Pedrazzi, *La Fenicia in età persiana*, pp. 15–52. On the subject of East–West relations one must refer to a very extensive bibliography which it is not possible to cite here, while on the need to examine the Orient from a multifocal perspective, the observations in E. W. Said, *Orientalism* (New York: Pantheon, 1978), are still fundamental.

13. Bondì, "Aspetti delle relazioni tra la Fenicia e le colonie," p. 75.

14. Manfredi, *La politica amministrativa di Cartagine*; S. Crouzet, "Les statuts civiques dans l'Afrique punique. De l'historiographie moderne à l'historiographie antique," in *Melanges de l'École française de Roma* 115 (2003), pp. 655–703. The district subdivision is actually testified by later sources, but we are led to believe that the process might have happened in this period.

15. G. Garbati, "L'Impero di Cartagine: formazione e dinamiche del mondo punico," in M. Giangiulio (ed.), *Storia d'Europa e del Mediterraneo*, III. *Grecia e Mediterraneo dall'VIII sec. a.C. all'Età delle guerre persiane* (Rome: Salerno, 2007), pp. 465–91.

16. P. Bartoloni, S. F. Bondì, and S. Moscati, *La penetrazione fenicia e punica in Sardegna. Trent'anni dopo* (Rome: Accademia Nazionale dei Lincei, 1997), pp. 63–97.

17. M. Botto, *La Penisola Iberica*, in Bondì et al. (eds.), *Fenici e Cartaginesi*, pp. 239–43.

18. H. Ferjaoui, *Recherches sur les relations entre l'Orient phénicien et Carthage* (Carthage: Fondation nationale, 1992).

19. E. Acquaro, *Studi di archeologia punica* (Pisa-Rome: Istituti editoriali e poligrafici, 1997), pp. 16–17; Fariselli, "The Impact of Military Preparations," pp. 64–65; Garbini, "Fenici d'Oriente e Fenici d'Occidente," pp. 7–8; Manfredi, *La politica amministrativa di Cartagine*, pp. 367–69.

20. Bondì, "La société phénicienne à l'époque perse"; idem, "Aspetti istituzionali, politici e amministrativi nel mondo fenicio e punico: aggiornamenti e nuove prospettive," in A. M. Arruda (ed.), *Fenicíos e púnicos, por terra e mar, Actas do VI Congresso Internacional de Estudos Fenicios e Púnicos. Lisboa, 26 de setembro – 1 de Outubro 2005* (Lisbon: Centro de Arquelogia da Universidade de Lisboa, 2013), pp. 149–56.

21. J. Elayi, "The Relations Between Tyre and Carthage During the Persian Period," *Journal of Ancient Near Eastern Studies* 13 (1981), pp. 15–29.

22. L. M. Günther, "Legende und Identität: die 'Verwandtshaft' zwischen Karthago und Tyros," in M. E. Aubet and M. Barthélemy (eds.), *Actas del IV Congreso Internacional de Estudios Fenicios y Púnicos* (Cádiz: servicio de Publicaciones Universidad de Cádiz, 2000), pp. 161–65.

23. On this topic, see Manfredi, *La politica amministrativa di Cartagine*, p. 367 (with bibliography).

24. Bondì, "I Fenici in Erodoto," pp. 285–86.

25. H. W. Ritter, "Iranische Tradition in Numidien," *Chiron* 8 (1978), pp. 313–17; L. Braccesi, *L'enigma di Dorieo* (Rome: L'Erma di Bretschneider, 1999), p. 62. See also the discussion in Oggiano and Pedrazzi, *La Fenicia in età persiana*.

26. Garbini, "Fenici d'Oriente e Fenici d'Occidente," p. 7, notes that "Dario manda un *edictum* nel quale i Cartaginesi *prohibebantur* e *iubebantur*, con ambasciatori *petentes* ai quali essi temevano di apparire *contumaces*; il re persiano parlava come sovrano di Cartagine anche se poi i suoi ordini venivano eseguiti solo in parte." See Braccesi, *L'enigma di Dorieo*, p. 62.

27. Bondì, "Aspetti istituzionali, politici e amministrativi."

28. The intervention of Carthage followed the occupation of Himera, a confederate of Punic peoples, by Theron, tyrant of Agrigentum. After the defeat of the Punic army, Carthage abandoned Sicily for 70 years.

29. P. Gauthier, "Le parallèle Himère-Salamine au Ve et au IVe siècle av.J.-C.," *Revue des Études Ancienne* LXVIII (1966), pp. 5–32; Garbini, "Fenici d'Oriente e Fenici d'Occidente."

30. Bondì, "Aspetti istituzionali, politici e amministrativi."

31. On the institutions and the administration policy of Carthage, see Manfredi, *La politica amministrativa di Cartagine*; Crouzet, *Les statuts civiques dans l'Afrique punique*, Bondì, "Aspetti istituzionali, politici e amministrativi."

32. Manfredi, *La politica amministrativa di Cartagine*, p. 369; see also E. Acquaro, "Carthage et ses provinces: administration et organisation sociale," in A. Tavares (ed.), *Os Púnicos no extremo ocidente* (Lisbon: Lisboa Universidade Aberta, 2011), pp. 47–56; Peri, "Il nome semitico di Byrsa."

33. Anyway these remarks have to take in account the fact that at the basis of the Carthaginian state organization there is a strong cultural copenetration between Phoenicians and Lybians; this process of copenetration originated from the "africanization" ongoing in the Carthaginian society long since; see Manfredi, *La politica amministrativa di Cartagine*, p. 369.

34. Garbini, "Fenici d'Oriente e Fenici d'Occidente"; J. L. López Castro, "Los Libiofenicios: una colonización agrícola cartaginesa en el Sur de la Peninsula Ibérica," *Rivista di Studi Fenici* 20 (1992), pp. 46–65 (54). G. Garbini reminds that during the Persian domination settlers from Byblos, and maybe even from Carthage, were present at Palmyra; and they were still linguistically recognizable in the Roman period; see G. Garbini, "Palmira colonia fenicia," *La Parola del Passato* 51 (1996), pp. 81–94 (81). The Aramaic root of the toponym Byrsa can hypothetically indicate that Carthage could be subjugated to the imperial authority at least for a period, as Aramaic is the language adopted in the imperial chancery (Peri, "Il nome semitico di Byrsa").

35. Manfredi, *La politica amministrativa di Cartagine*, p. 370.

36. Manfredi, *La politica amministrativa di Cartagine*, pp. 373–74.

37. Manfredi, *La politica amministrativa di Cartagine*, pp. 371–72, with bibliography.

38. Bondì, "La société phénicienne à l'époque perse."

39. J. Elayi, *Recherches sur les cités phéniciennes à l'époque perse* (Naples: Istituto universitario orientale, 1987), pp. 12–21.

40. Bondì, "Aspetti istituzionali, politici e amministrativi."

41. Bondì, "La société phénicienne à l'époque perse."

42. Bondì, "La société phénicienne à l'époque perse," p. 72.

43. A. Mezzolani, "Urbanistica regolare nel mondo punico: note introduttive," in L. Quilici and S. Quilici-Gigli (eds.), *Opere di assetto territoriale ed urbano* (Atlante tematico di topografia antica 3; Rome: L'Erma di Bretschneider, 1994), pp. 147–58. On the Phoenician city planning, see S. Helas and D. Marzoli, *Phönizisches und punisches Städtewesen* (Mainz am Rhein: Philipp von Zabern, 2009).

44. F. Rakob, "La Carthage archaïque, in Carthage et soin territoire dans l'antiquité," in *Actes du IVe Colloque international sur l'histoire et l'archéologie de l'Afrique du Nord (113e Congrès national des Sociétés savantes, Strasbourg, 5–9 avril 1988)* (Paris: CTHS, 1990), pp. 31–43; idem, "Cartago. La topografía de la ciudad púnica. Nuevas Investigationes," in M. Vegas (ed.), *Cartago fenicio-púnica. Les investigaciones alemanas en Cartago 1975–1997* (Barcelona: Bellaterra, 1998), pp. 15–46.

45. For Kerkouane, see M. H. Fantar, *Kerkouane. Cité punique du Cap Bon (Tunisie), I–III* (Tunis: Maison tunisienne de l'édition, 1983–86); for Pani Loriga, see M. Botto, F. Candelato, I. Oggiano, and T. Pedrazzi, "Le indagini 2007–2008 all'abitato fenicio-punico di Pani Loriga," at www.fastionline.org/docs/FOLDER-it-2010-175.pdf; for Nora, see J. Bonetto, "L'insediamento di età fenicia, punica e romana repubblicana nell'area del foro," in J. Bonetto (ed.), *Nora. Il foro romano. Storia di un'area urbana dall'età fenicia alla tarda antihità. 1997–2006* (Padua: Quasar, 2009), pp. 39–198 (136–39); for Monte Sirai and Olbia, see C. Perra, "Nuovi elementi per la tipologia degli insediamenti fenici della Sardegna sud-occidentale," in Helas and Marzoli (eds.), *Phönizisches und punisches Städtewesen*, pp. 353–67, as well as R. D'Oriano, "Elementi di urbanistica punica di Olbia fenicia, greca e punica," ibidem, pp. 369–87.

46. Mezzolani, "Urbanistica regolare nel mondo punico," p. 156. For Palermo and Solunto, see now F. Spatafora, "Dagli empori fenici alle città puniche. Elementi di continuità e discontinuità nell'organizzazione urbanistica di Palermo e Solunto," in Helas and Marzoli (eds.), *Phönizisches und punisches Städtewesen*, pp. 219–39.

47. For the *tophet* of Carthage, see H. Bénichou-Safar, *Le tophet de Salammbô à Carthage. Essai de reconstitution* (Rome: École francaise de Roma, 2004).

48. For Baal Hammon, see P. Xella, *Baal Hammon. Recherches sur l'identité et l'histoire d'un dieu phénico-punique* (Rome: Consiglio nazionale delle ricerche, 1991); idem, "Baal Hammon nel panteon punico. Il contributo delle fonti classiche," in M. Molina Martos, J. L. Cunchillos, and A. González Blanco (eds.), *El mundo púnico. Historia, sociedad y cultura* (Murcia: Editora Regional de Murcia, 1994), pp. 177–93; for Tinnit, see F. O. Hvidberg-Hansen, *La Déesse TNT: une étude sur la religion canaanéo-punique* (Copenhagen: G. E. C. Gad's Forlag, 1979); E. Lipiński, *Dieux et déesses de l'univers phénicien et punique* (Leuven: Peeters, 1995), pp. 438–39; M. G. Lancellotti, *Dea Caelestis. Studi e materiali per la storia di una divinità dell'Africa romana* (Pisa-Rome: Fabrizio Serra, 2010), chapter "L'eredità fenicio-punica: da Astarte e Tinnit alla dea africana," with bibliography.

49. For the different epigraphic attestations, see E. Lipiński (ed.), *Dictionnaire de la civilisation phénicienne et punique* (Turnhout: Brepols, 1992), pp. 438–39; for the Sarepta inscription, where the goddess Tinnit is associated with Astarte, see M. G. Amadasi Guzzo, "Two Phoenician Inscriptions Carved in Ivory: Again the Ur-Box and the Sarepta Plaque," *Orientalia* NS 59 (1990), pp. 58–66.

50. A. M. Bisi, "Un naiskos tardo-fenicio del Museo di Beyrout e il problema delle origini dei cippi egittizzante nel mondo punico," *Antiquités Africaines* 5 (1971), pp. 50–55; S. Moscati, *Le stele puniche in Italia* (Rome: Ist. Plogirafico dello Stato, 1992); S. F. Bondì, "Il *tofet* e le stele," in S Bruni, T. Caruso, and M. Massa (eds.), *Archeologia pisana. Scritti per Orlanda Pancrazzi* (Pisa: Giardini, 2004), pp. 22–25. On the *naòs* and the form of representation of the sacred space in the Phoenician and Punic world, see I. Oggiano, "Lo spazio sacro fenicio rappresentato," in X. Dupré Raventós, S. Ribichini, and S. Verger (eds.), *Saturnia Tellus. Definizioni dello spazio consacrato in ambiente etrusco, italico e celtico, Roma, 10–12 novembre 2004* (Rome: CNR, 2008), pp. 283–300.

51. For the figure with lotus flower, see G. Scandone Matthiae, "Fiori d'Oriente," in E. Acquaro (ed.), *Alle soglie della classicità. Il Mediterraneo tra tradizione e innovazione* (Pisa-Rome: Ist. Editoriali e Poligrafici, 1996), pp. 947–53; for the type with woman and lotus flower during the Achaemenid Empire, see J. Bakker, "The Lady and the Lotus: Representation of Woman in the Achaemenid Empire," *Iranica Antiqua* 42 (2007), pp. 207–20.

52. J. Elayi and A. G. Elayi, "La scène du char sur le monnaies de Sidon d'époque perse," *Transeuphratène* 27 (2004), pp. 89–108 (94–95); P. Calmeyer, "Zur Genese altiranischer Motive X. Die elamisch-persische Tracht," *Archäologische Mitteilungen aus Iran* 21 (1988), pp. 27–51 (37–39, Fig. 9).

53. For Shavey Zion, see E. Linder, "A Cargo of Phoenicio-Punic Figurines," *Archaeology* 26 (1973), pp. 182–87, and M. W. Prausnitz, *s.v.* "Shavei-Zion," in *The Oxford Encyclopedia of Archaeology in the Near East* (Oxford: Oxford University Press, 1997); for Sarepta, see J. B. Pritchard, *Recovering Sarepta: A Phoenician City* (Princeton: Princeton University Press, 1978), Fig. 59.2.

54. For the name and the symbol of Tanit, see S. Moscati, "Un bilancio per TNT," *Oriens Antiquus* 20 (1981), pp. 107–17; more generally for the symbol, F. Bertrandy, *s.v.* "signe de Tanit," in Lipiński, *Dictionnaire de la civilisation phénicienne et punique*, pp. 416–18, with bibliography.

55. On this topic, see Ferjaoui, *Recherches sur les relations*, pp. 347, 358–59, 366–67; Bondì, "Aspetti delle relazioni tra la Fenicia e le colonie," p. 82.

56. See G. Garbati and C. Peri, "Tra Oriente e Occidente. Dèi patres e dèi 'guaritori' nella Sardegna punica: qualche riflessione," in *Actas do VI Congresso Internacional de Estudos Fenicios e Púnicos*, pp. 322–30, with bibliography.

57. On the temple, see E. Acquaro et al., *Ricerche puniche ad Antas. Rapporto preliminare della missione archeologica dell'Università di Roma Soprintendenza alle Antichità di Cagliari* (Rome: Istituto di Studi del Vicino Oriente. Università di Roma, 1969), and P. Bernardini et al., "Il santuario di Antas a Fluminimaggiore: nuovi dati," in P. Bernardini, R. D'Oriano, and P. G. Spanu (eds.), *Phoinikes b Shrdn. I Fenici in Sardegna. Nuove acquisizioni* (Oristano: Ed. S'Alvure, 1997), pp. 105–13. About Sid morphology, see P. Bernardini, "Il culto del Sardus Pater ad Antas e i culti a divinità salutari esoterologiche," in P. G. Spanu (ed.), *Insulae Christi. Il Cristianesimo primitivo in Sardegna, Corsica e Baleari* (Oristano: Ed. S'Alvure, 2002), pp. 17–28; Garbati and Peri, "Tra Oriente e Occidente." See C. Grottanelli, "Melqart e Sid fra Egitto, Libia e Sardegna," *Rivista di Studi Fenici* 1 (1973), pp. 153–64; G. Garbati, "Sid e Melqart tra Antas e Olbia," *Rivista di Studi Fenici* 27 (1999), pp. 151–66.

58. For example, see Pausanias, X 17, 2; Solinus, XII 355–58; Silius Italicus, IV 2; see S. F. Bondì, "Osservazioni sulle fonti classiche per la colonizzazione della Sardegna," in G. Benigni et al., *Saggi fenici - I* (Rome: Consiglio Nazionale delle Ricerche 1975), pp. 49–60, and Grottanelli, "Melqart e Sid fra Egitto, Libia e Sardegna."

59. S. Ribichini, *Poenus Advena. Gli dèi fenici e l'interpretatio classica* (Rome: Consiglio Nazionale delle Ricerche, 1985), pp. 43–73.

60. Bartoloni, Bondì, and Moscati, *La penetrazione fenicia e punica in Sardegna*, pp. 63–112. Garbati and Peri, "Tra Oriente e Occidente," where G. Garbati, as a starting point for further research, quotes Diodorus who says, for the god Iolaus, that "those who sacrifice for this god call him Iolaus father, as Persians do for Cyrus" (V 15).

61. G. Garbini, "Le iscrizioni puniche di Antas," *Annali dell'Istituto Universitario Orientale di Napoli* 29 (1969), pp. 317–31; Garbati and Peri, "Tra Oriente e Occidente."

62. W. Culican, "The Iconography of Some Phoenician Seals and Seal Impression," *Australian Journal of Biblical Archaeology*1 (1968), pp. 40–104 (Fig. 4.65). E. Gubel attributes to the seal a date of seventh–sixth century BCE; see E. Gubel, *Phoenician Furniture* (Leuven: Peeters, 1987), cat. 25, pl. VIII.

63. S. Cecchini, "The 'suivant du char royal': A Case of Interaction Between Various Genres of Minor Art," in C. E. Suter and C. Uehlinger (eds.), *Craft and Images in Contact: Studies on Eastern Mediterranean Art of the First Millennium* (Fribourg-Göttingen: Academic Press, 2005), pp. 254–61, for Carthage, see T. Redissi, "Étude des empreintes de sceaux de Carthage," in F. Rakob (ed.), *Karthago III* (Mainz: Zabern, 1999), pp. 4–92 (*bulla* n. 66).

64. We have already commented on Greek areas. For the Italic area, see A. Comella, "Riflessi del culto di Asclepio sulla religiosità popolare etrusco-laziale e campana di epoca medio e tardo repubblicana," *Annali della Facoltà di Lettere e Filosofia dell'Università degli Studi di Perugia* 20 (1982–83), pp. 217–44.

65. S. Ribichini, "Eshmun-Asclepio. Divinità guaritrici in contesti fenici," in E. De Miro, G. Sfameni Gasparro, and V. Calì (eds.), *Il culto di Asclepio in area mediterranea. Atti del Convegno internazionale. Agrigento, 20–22 novembre 2005* (Rome: Gangemi, 2010), pp. 201–17.

66. For S. Nicolò Gerrei (Corpus Inscriptionum Semiticarum I, 143 = M. G. Amadasi, *Le Iscrizioni fenicie e puniche delle colonie di Occidente*, Rome 1967, Sardegna 9, pp. 91–93); for Cagliari (Corpus Inscriptionum Semiticarum I, 141 = M. G. Amadasi, *Le Iscrizioni fenicie e puniche delle colonie di Occidente*, Rome 1967, Sardegna 4, p. 129).

67. About medical gods in Sardinia, see Bernardini, "Il culto del Sardus Pater ad Antas," with bibliography.

68. G. Garbati, "Tra Cartagine e Roma: riflessioni sulla diffusione del votivo anatomico in Sardegna tra il VI e il II sec. a.C.," in S. F. Bondì and M. Vallozza (eds.), *Greci, Fenici, Romani: interazioni culturali nel Mediterraneo* (Viterbo: Università degli Studi della Tuscia, 2005), pp. 139–54 (146 n. 6), where the author stresses the necessity of putting in the insular framework of the Punic period the acceptance of religious features from the motherland, and the necessity of analyzing these features in a framework in which also the important relations with the

Etrusco-Latial area are appreciated. See also G. Garbati and C. Peri, "Considerazione sul 'culto delle acque' nella Sardegna punica e tardo-punica: l'esempio di Mitza Salamu," in Dupré Raventós, Ribichini, Verger (eds.), *Saturnia Tellus*, pp. 385–95.

69. I. Oggiano, "Lo spazio sacro a Nora," in *Atti del V Congresso Internazionale di Studi Fenici e Punici*, pp. 1029–44.

70. G. Pesce, *Nora. Guida agli scavi* (Bologna: "La Zattera," 1957), pp. 86–89, Fig. 63.

71. On the *"maabed"* of Amrit see I. Oggiano, "Architectural Point to Ponder Under the Porch of Amrit," *Rivista di Studi Fenici* XL, 2 (2014), pp. 181–209 (with bibliography).

72. For Tas Silg, see *Missione Archeologica italiana a Malta* (Rome: Centro di Studi Semitici, Istituto di Studi del Vicino Oriente, 1964), pp. 76–78; for Marsala, see G. Falsone, "La statua fenicio-cipriota dello Stagnone di Marsala," *Sicilia Archeologica* 10 (1970), pp. 54–61; G. Falsone, "Da Nimrud a Mozia. Un tipo statuario di stile fenicio e egittizzante," *Ugarit Forschungen* 21 (1989), pp. 154–93.

73. About the relationship between Carthage and the Egypt, see E. Acquaro, "I Fenici, Cartagine e l'Egitto," in F. De Salvia and R. Murgagno (eds.), *Calabria antica ed Egitto. Atti del Convegno (Castel Ducale di Corigliano Calabro, CS, 15–16 dicembre 2004)* (Catanzaro: Studi Bruttium, 2006), pp. 183–89.

74. About this topic, see S. F. Bondì, "La bronzistica figurata egiziana nell'Occidente fenicio," in S. F. Bondì, S. Pernigotti, F. Serra, and A. Vivian (eds.), *Studi in onore di Edda Bresciani* (Pisa: Giardini, 1985), pp. 85–96, who highlights the connection between the importation of Egyptian bronzes towards the West and the depletion of the Phoenician and Cypriot production and export.

75. I. Gamer-Wallert, *Aegyptische und aegyptisierende Funde von der Iberischen Halbinsel* (Wiesbaden: Reichert, 1978).

76. J. Padró, "Le rôle de l'Égypte dans les relations commerciales d'Orient et d'Occident au premier Millénaire," *Annales du Service des Antiquités de l' Égypte* LXXI (1987), p. 222, points out that the Persian expansion will end the relationship between Spain and Egypt for the supply of bronze.

77. See F. Padros Martínez, *Arquitectura Púnica. Los monumentos funerarios* (Madrid: CSIC - CSIC Press, 2008), *contra* Di Vita and F. Rakob, who understand the tower-shaped monuments, whether funerary or commemorative, to be a Greek creation.

78. About this topic, see N. Ferichou, "Le paysage pré-romain en Tunisie antique à l'ouest de Carthage," in M. H. Fantar and M. Ghaki (eds.), *Actes di III Congrès International des Études Phéniciennes et Puniques* (Tunis: Institut National du Patrimoine, 1995), pp. 435–45.

79. For more on Sulky, see S. Moscati, *Il mondo punico* (Turin: Utet, 1980), pp. 175–76; S. Moscati, *L'arte della Sardegna punica* (Milan: Jaca, 1986), pp. 71–76 n. 25; P. Mattazzi, "Sull' altorilievo funerario di Sulcis," in Acquaro (ed.), *Alle soglie della classicità*, pp. 863–79. On Monte Sirai, see S. Moscati, *Italia punica* (Milan: Bompiani, 1986), p. 272.

80. P. Bernardini, "A Occidente del Grande Verde: memorie d'Egitto nell'artigianato della Sardegna fenicia e punica," in M. C. Guidotti and F. Tiradritti (eds.), *L'uomo egizio. L'antica civiltà faraonica nel racconto dei suoi protagonisti* (Milan: Anthelios Edizioni, 2004), pp. 163–219, and P. Bernardini, "Recenti scoperte nella necropoli punica di Sulcis," *Rivista di Studi Fenici* 33 (2005), pp. 63–80.

81. Bernardini, "Recenti scoperte nella necropoli punica di Sulcis," p. 79.

82. Bondì, "Aspetti delle relazioni tra la Fenicia e le colonie," pp. 80–82. For more on the Egyptianizing figurines, see F. Faegersten, *The Egyptianizing Male Limestone Statuary from Cyprus* (Lund: Lund University, Department of Archaeology and Ancient History, 2003).

83. On the multiple-frame motif, see S. F. Bondì, "Un tipo di inquadramento architettonico fenicio," in *Atti del I Convegno Italiano sul Vicino Oriente Antico (Roma, 22–24 aprile 1976)* (Rome: Centro per le antichità e la storia dell'arte del vicino Oriente, 1978), pp. 147–55.

84. Especially, the analysis is related to the relief in the tomb 7 at Sulky: Bernardini, "Recenti scoperte nella necropoli punica di Sulcis," p. 76.

85. G. Garbati, "Antenati e 'defunti illustri' in Sardegna: qualche considerazione sulle ideologie funerarie di età punica," *Bollettino di Archeologia on line* 1 (2010; vol. spec.), pp. 37–47 (www.archeologia.beniculturali.it/pages/pubblicazioni.html); even if we do not necessarily see in the Sulcis sculpture the representation of one of the Rephaim, with traits identical to those in the Levantine area. In fact, we have to take into account the simple but deep differences of the chronological and historical contexts.

86. On Tharros jewellery, see G. Pisano, *I gioielli fenici di Tharros nel Museo Nazionale di Cagliari* (Rome: Consiglio Nazionale delle Ricerche, 1974), S. Moscati, *I gioielli di Tharros. Origini, caratteri, confronti* (Rome: Consiglio Nazionale delle Ricerche, 1988).

87. D. Ciafaloni, "L'art glyptique," in V. Krings, *La civilisation phénicienne et punique: Manuel de recherche* (Leiden: Brill 1995), pp. 501–508 (504); G. Hölbl, "Iconografie egiziane e documenti archeologici dell'Italia punica," in E. Acquaro and G. Savio (eds.), *Studi iconografici nel Mediterraneo antico* (Sarzana: Agorà, 2004), pp. 65–82 who talks about the "Punic egyptianizing."

88. Redissi, "Étude des empreintes de sceaux de Carthage," *Bullae* 66 and 172; Cecchini, "The "suivant du char royal," p. 261.

89. E. Gubel, "Byblos: L'art de la métropole phénicienne," in E. Acquaro et al., *Biblo. Una città e la sua cultura* (Rome: Consiglio Nazionale delle Ricerche, 1994), pp. 73–95, who suggests that the Western products are imported from the East.

90. H. Sader, *Iron Age Funerary Staele from Lebanon* (Barcelona: Bellaterra, 2005). Stela 60 mentions a generation of *sufetes* and *rabs*. In Stela 62 a scriba is mentioned.

91. Peri, "Il nome semitico di Byrsa," pp. 77–78.

92. A. Ciasca, "L'art céramique et coroplastie," in Krings (ed.), *La civilisation phénicienne et punique*, p. 446.

93. Bondì, "Aspetti delle relazioni tra la Fenicia e le colonie."

A COUPLE OF STONE DISKS OR SIMPLY A PAIR OF DISKS? ABOUT THE HEBREW WORD *OBNAYIM* (EXODUS 1:16; JEREMIAH 18:3)

Fabrizio A. Pennacchietti

> *Amicorum communia omnia,*
> *inter quae autem maxime*
> *amici praeceptoris*
> *doctrina lucet*

The Hebrew lexica of the Old Testament contain, besides *hapax legomena*, words which, although occurring two or three times, present, as do hapaxes, a meaning recoverable only through context. To this group of words belongs *oben,[1] a word which, in the dual form *obnayim*, occurs only twice, namely in Exod 1:16 and in Jer 18:3. While in Jer 18:3 the meaning of *obnayim* is easily recognizable, in Exod 2:16 its meaning has not yet been satisfactorily explained.

Let us first examine Jer 18:3 in Hebrew:

> wā-ʾered bêt hay-yôṣer w-hinnehû ʿōśe mlāʾkā ʿal hā-ʾobnāyim
>
> I went down to the potter's house, and behold, he was doing work upon the wheel. (RSV)

From the context it is not hard to infer that *obnayim* hints at a potter's wheel, namely to the round and rotating wooden stand on which a mass of clay is transformed into a pot.

Let us now see how Exod 1:16 reads:

> b-yalledken et ha-ʿibriyyôt u-rʾîten ʿal hā-ʾobnāyim im ben hûʾ wa-hamitten ōtô w-ʾim bat hîʾ wā-ḥāyā
>
> When you serve as midwives to the Hebrew women, and see them upon the birth stool, if it is a son you shall kill him; but if it is a daughter, she shall live. (RSV)

The translations of this verse in Greek (Septuagint) and in Syriac (Peshitta) sound differently. The Septuagint interprets the prepositional phrase ʿal hā-ʾobnayim, headed by the preposition ʿal which governs the definite article hā- and the substantive obnayim, as "(when they are) on bearing," namely "when they are bearing [i.e. giving birth],"[2] whereas Peshitta interprets it as "when they kneel down [in order to bear]."[3]

It may be objected that the Hebrew preposition ʿal, meaning approximately "on," which governs hā-ʾobnayim, points neither to a place (e.g. a delivery room) nor to an event (childbirth), but rather focuses attention on a particular object. The question is now what this object might be.

The lexica of the Hebrew Old Testament list several possibilities for interpreting obnayim. Because of its dual grammatical form, obnayim has been explained by some exegetes as "testicles" or as "the male and the female genital organs,"[4] namely the recognizable sex of the newborn children. The interpretation "testicles" derives from the fact that the word *oben is similar to the word eben which, moreover, is written <ʾBN> exactly like *oben. The meaning of eben is "stone, cobblestone, rock"; furthermore, it also metaphorically indicates a unit of weight.[5] The dual obnayim, if interpreted as "two cobblestones," could by extension mean "testicles." In contrast the second aforementioned meaning, "both sexes," seems to find no justification.

Other exegetes have tried to find some possible relation between the occurrence of obnayim in Jer 18:3 ("potter's wheel") and that in Exod 1:16. I list here the proposals with which I am acquainted.

1. In 2003 Scott Morschauser supposed that obnayim translates the ancient Egyptian word nḥp/nḥb, which usually means "potter's wheel," but which, in this particular case, would relate to the mythological potter's wheel of the ram-headed Egyptian god Khnum, by means of which this god is believed to mold the fertile mud of the Nile and create every kind of being, human babies included. Therefore Morschauser maintains that the Hebrew sentence u-rʾîten ʿal ha-ʾobnayim of Exod 1:16 means "when you look/determine upon the potter's wheel [i.e. when you undertake a prenatal examination]."[6] According to the Egyptian belief, as long as the unborn child lies in the mother's womb, they are in the hands of the potter god Khnum. This way of explaining the word obnayim nevertheless raises a not negligible question: how could the Egyptian midwives foretell the sex of the babies before their birth? The author gets round this by referring to ancient Egyptian medical texts containing prognostic prescriptions to determine the sex of unborn children

as well as prescriptions to interrupt a pregnancy by means of special potions. At any rate, Morschauser's proposal seems to me rather questionable and somewhat farfetched.
2. In 2006 Kevin McGeugh, on the basis of ancient Egyptian archaeological finds depicting scenes of childbirth, interpreted *obnayim* as two "birth bricks," namely a pair of adobes on which, in the olden days, Egyptian women in labor supposedly kneeled during the delivery or on which the midwives ritually laid down the newborn children. According to this hypothesis there was a "conceptual link between childbirth and ceramic manufacture in the ancient Near East."[7] Did not the Lord God form the man of dust from the ground (Gen 2:7)? However, the supposed cognitive connection between ceramic production and human reproduction has no linguistic justification. Actually the root /ᵓBN/ of *obnayim* immediately recalls a stone, not a brick. The way Franz Zorell explains *obnayim* (Jer 18:3: "rota figuli, i.e. duo disci *lapidei* qui volvuntur unus super alium"; Exod 1:16: "sella mulieris parturientis...quae in forma primitiva ex 2 *lateribus* constabat") is a clear proof of the semantic confusion, which reigned in the mind of some exegetes apropos of "stone" (*lapis*) and "brick" (*later*).[8] By contrast, people speaking Semitic languages, who may have been producing bricks since the Late Neolithic era, called and continue to call these handiworks by a name which is in no way related to the concept "stone," unlike, for example, German *Ziegelstein*, *Baustein*, *Backstein*, Icelandic *múrsteinn*, Swedish *tegelsten*, Finnish *tiiliskivi* and other languages of North West Europe, an area where bricks had been introduced no earlier than the late Middle Ages. The root the Semitic languages use to indicate "brick" is /LBN/: see Akkadian *libittu*, Hebrew *lebēnā* [lveyná], Syriac *lebentā* [lvetta] and Arabic *labina* "brick."
3. Since the word *oben shares with the word *eben* ("stone") the root /ᵓBN/, the majority of biblical exegetes obviously explain *obnayim* as a variant of *abnayim*, dual of *eben*. Thus they think they have found a tangible link between the potter's wheel of Jer 18:3 and the object related to childbirth mentioned in Exod 1:16.

In order to follow the thread of such an argument we ought to have in mind what a potter's wheel looks like. It is composed of a vertical cylindrical pivot on whose top a wooden disk is tightly fixed. On this disk one puts the clay to be molded. At the lower part of the cylindrical pivot another wooden disk is fixed so that the potter's feet can rotate it.

As the rotation of the lower disk also involves the cylindrical axis as well as the upper disk, the potter quickly manipulates the clay put on it and gives it the expected shape.

Now, with regard to the Jer 18:3, the compilers of two important Hebrew dictionaries of the Old Testament maintain that in that verse the potter's wheel has been called *obnayim* on account of the assumed similarity of its two disks to a pair of millstones.[9] Both the pair of disks of the potter's wheel and a pair of millstones are actually vertical, but one may ask if such a similarity is sufficient to justify the use of the same word for both. Who has ever seen a potter's wheel whose pair of disks are made of stone?

Otherwise some Hebrew dictionaries of the Old Testament maintain that in Exod 1:16 the word *obnayim*, being a dual form, hints at a birthing stool consisting of two separated stones on which the women in labor sat.[10] I think that, for a woman facing one of the most crucial moments of her life, nothing is more uncomfortable and anxiety-inducing then a rigid and cold birthing stool of stone. But, apart from this, it is worth mentioning that the Hebrew language and other Semitic languages, in this case too, have no need to resort to a word meaning "stone" (namely *eben*/**oben*) in order to denote the grinding wheels of a mill. Probably since Early Neolithic times they had at their disposal a specific word for "millstone," making use of the root /RḤY/; see Hebrew *reḥayim*, Syriac *raḥyā*, plur. *rḥawwātā*, Arabic *raḥan*, du. *raḥawāni/yāni*. In contrast, English (*millstone*), German (*Mühlstein*), Swedish (*kvarnsten*), Polish (*kamień młyński*), Finnish *myllynkivi*, Estonian *veskikivi*, Latvian *dzirnaknens* and other languages of North West Europe have recourse to a compound containing a word meaning "stone."

Beyond the above-mentioned proposals for interpreting *obnayim* there is still space for a further proposal which, in my opinion, can satisfactorily explain the occurrence of this word in both Jer 18:3 and Exod 1:16. Up to now, *obnayim* has been regarded as a word deriving from the root /ʾBN/, the same root as that of the Hebrew word *eben* ("stone"). Jacob Barth, it is true, suggested the hypothesis that *obnayim* might derive from the root /BNY/, "to build,"[11] but, as far as I know, only quite marginally[12] has the possibility been considered that the original root of this word could be /ʾPN/, "to revolve," a root which is probably connected with /PNY/, "to turn."

Linguists dealing with Semitic languages have long known the phenomenon of the exchange of voiceless with voiced consonants and vice versa, especially when they are plosive labials like /p/ and /b/.[13] Consider the following examples:

1. Hebrew *peten*, Jewish Palestinian Aramaic *pitn* and Syriac *patnā* versus Akkadian *bašmu*, Ugaritic *bṯn* and Arabic *baṯan*, "viper."[14]
2. Hebrew, Phoenician Aramaic and Arabic /PʿL/ versus Ugaritic and Amorritic /BʿL/, "to do."[15]
3. Phoenician /NBŠ / and /NPŠ/, "soul."[16]

The possibility that the original root of **oben* and its dual *obnayim* was /ʾPN/ is confirmed by the fact that the Hebrew language preserves two significant words containing this root: **open* [ófen] and *ôpān* [ofán]. The latter means "a wheel of a vehicle,"[17] the former means "a circumstance, condition, manner,"[18] but it may be that its original meaning was "a turning."[19]

The cluster of concepts "something flat, round and revolving," "wheel" and "disk" is fully consonant with the meaning of *obnayim* in Jer 18:3. In point of fact a potter's wheel consists of two revolving wooden disks, certainly not two disks made of stone. It is certainly harder to find congruence between "something flat, round and revolving" and the *obnayim* occurring in Exod 1:16. Nevertheless it may be imagined that the birthing stool of the Hebrew women consisted in ancient Egypt of two wooden disks or of two halves of a wooden disk – one on the right, the other on the left – on which the woman in labor had to sit during delivery. It is doubtful that a specific seat, suited for a woman to be delivered of a child, consisted of stones or bricks.

To conclude, in the light of this hypothesis (**oben* deriving from /ʾPN/), the twofold occurrence in the Hebrew Bible of the dual word *obnayim* may receive an interpretation which is suitable to both Exod 1:16 and Jer 18:3: "two flat, round and revolving things (made of wood)," that is "a couple of disks (made of wood)." In fact, the potter's wheel consists of two wooden disks fixed on a vertical rotating axis; probably in Egypt and the surrounding area two wooden disks or two halves of a wooden disk also formed the particular seat of the birthing stools.

Notes

1. The singular form **oben*, written <ʾBN> and nowadays pronounced [óven], has been reconstructed by analogy with words having the same morphology, e.g. *ōzen* "ear," written <ʾZN> and pronounced [ózen], whose dual/plural is *oznayim*.

2. *Septuaginta. Vetus Testamentum Graecum*, II, 1, *Exodus* (ed. J. W. Wevers; Göttingen: Vandenhoeck & Ruprecht, 1991), p. 69: *pròs tô tíktein*, "on bearing."

3. *Peshitta. Pentateuchus syriace post Samuelem Lee. Recognovit emendavit edidit G. E. Barnes* (London: Apud Societatem Bibliophilorum Britannicam et Externam, 1914), p. 100: *mā d-bārkān*, "when they kneel."

4. Cf. L. Koehler and W. Baumgartner, *Lexicon in Veteris Testamenti Libros* (Leiden: Brill, 1958) p. 7: "genitals"; F. Zorell, *Lexicon Hebraicum et Aramaicum Veteris Testamenti* (Rome: Pontificio Istituto Biblico, 1968), p. 8: "duo sexus," "uteri ostium," "labrum pelvis."

5. Cf. M. E. Artom (ed.), *Vocabolario ebraico–italiano* (Rome: Fondazione per la Gioventù Ebraica, 1965), pp. 3-4.

6. S. Morschauser, "Potters' Wheels and Pregnancies: A Note on Exodus 1:16," *JBL* 122.4 (2003), pp. 731-33 (733).

7. K. McGeough, "Birth Bricks, Potter's Wheels and Exodus 1,16," *Biblica* 87.3 (2006), pp. 305-18 (311 and 318).

8. Cf. Zorell, *Lexicon Hebraicum*, p. 8.

9. BDB, p. 7: "potter's wheel (two discs revolving one above the other; name from likeness to mill-stones)"; Zorell, *Lexicon Hebraicum*, p. 8: "rota figuli, i.e. duo disci lapidei qui volvuntur unus super alium."

10. Koehler and Baumgartner, *Lexicon in Veteris Testamenti Libros*, p. 7: "stones of delivery"; BDB, p. 7: "bearing-stool, midwife's stool (from likeness to potter's wheel)."

11. J. Barth, "Vergleichende Studien. II. Uralte pluralische Analogiebildungen," *Zeitschrift der Deutschen Morgenländischen Gesellschaft* 42 (1888), p. 346 n. 3: "Dessgleichen ist…die Ableitung des Wortes *obnayim* von einem Stamm BNH sehr beachtenswerth, aber angesichts der Dunkelheit namentlich der zweiten Stelle schwerlich zu entscheiden."

12. Zorell, *Lexicon Hebraicum*, p. 8: "opportunum tempus (= *opnayim* Pr. 25,11) [Demutatio vocis *eben*]"; *obnayim* as "the right time (for giving birth)."

13. Cf. G. Garbini, "L'aramaico antico," *Memorie. Accademia Nazionale dei Lincei, Classe Sc. Mor. St. e Filol.*, Ser. VIII, Vol. VII, 5 (1956), p. 258; idem, "Note aramaiche. 1. *p > b* in ya'udico," *Antonianum* 31 (1956), pp. 310-11; idem, "Note aramaiche. 2-4," *Antonianum* 32 (1957), pp. 427-30; idem, "Nuovo materiale per la grammatica dell'aramaico antico," *Rivista di Studi Orientali* 34 (1959), p. 43; idem, Review of M. Dahood, *Proverbs and Northwest Semitic Philology*, Roma 1963, *Rivista degli Studi Orientali* 40 (1965), pp. 327-28; idem, *Il semitico nord-occidentale: Studi di storia linguistica* (Studi semitici, Nuova serie 5; Rome: Dipartimento Studi Orientali, 1988), pp. 136-37; G. Garbini and O. Durand, *Introduzione alle lingue semitiche* (Brescia: Paideia Editrice, 1994), p. 78.

14. Cf. G. Garbini, "Considerazioni sulla parola ebraica *peten*," *Rivista Biblica* 6 (1958), pp. 263-365. In Modern Hebrew *peten* means "cobra," cf. R. Sivan and E. A. Levenston (eds.), *The Megiddo Modern Dictionary Hebrew–English* (Tel Aviv: Megiddo, 1967) p. 577b.

15. Cf. E. Lipiński, *Semitic Languages. Outline of a Comparative Grammar* (Orientalia Lovaniensia Analecta 80; Leuven: Peeters, 1997), §11.4, p. 110.

16. Cf. S. Segert, *A Grammar of Phoenician and Punic* (Munich: Beck, 1976), p. 295; Ch.-F. Jean and J. Hoftijzer (eds.), *Dictionnaire des inscriptions sémitiques de l'Ouest* (Leiden: Brill, 1965), p. 183.

17. Cf. Koehler and Baumgartner, *Lexicon in Veteris Testamenti Libros*, p. 21; BDB, p. 66; Zorell, *Lexicon Hebraicum*, p. 23. From [ofán] Modern Hebrew derived [ofanáyim] "bicycle," [ofanán] "cyclist" and [ofananít] "woman cyclist," [ofanóa] "motorcycle," etc., cf. Artom, *Vocabolario ebraico–italiano*, p. 12.

18. Cf. Koehler and Baumgartner, *Lexicon in Veteris Testamenti Libros*, p. 78; BDB, p. 67; Zorell, *Lexicon Hebraicum*, p. 74. In the Hebrew Bible *open [ófen] occurs only in plural: *opānîm* [ofaním]. From [ófen] Modern Hebrew derives [ofná] "fashion," [ofnút] "formula" and [ifnún] "modulation," etc., cf. Artom, *Vocabolario ebraico–italiano*, p. 42.

19. Cf. BDB, p. 67.

JONAH AND THE TRIFFID:
A SUGGESTION FOR THE *QIQAYON*

Chiara Peri

"A strange, cartoonish little proto-gospel": I have always found this definition of the book of Jonah[1] quite appropriate for a prophetic book, which stands out for its peculiarities. It ends with a question (unanswered). Unlike other prophetic books, it is not a collection of oracles but the story of a disobedient, narrow-minded prophet who is angry at the outcome of the sole message he delivers (3:4). Finally, in the narrative there are many absurd passages, such as the sacrifice of the sailors of their ship (1:16) or the fasting imposed on the cattle (3:7). Nevertheless, this short composition still has an important place in Jewish and Christian liturgical tradition: it is read in its entirety by Jews as part of the afternoon prayer of the Day of Atonement and as scripture for the Easter vigil by Byzantine Christians. In the New Testament Gospels, Jonah is quoted nine times (five in the Gospel of Matthew and four in the Gospel of Luke).

The translation of the name of the fast-growing plant that provided relief for Jonah when he had withdrawn from Nineveh (קיקיון, a word used only in this biblical book) become a source of contention in early Christianity between Augustine and Jerome. In a heated exchange of letters between the two, starting in 394 and continuing through 406,[2] Augustine complained about the fact that Jerome had translated the name of Jonah's plant as "ivy" (*hedera*). Such a new rendering of the Vulgate, "very different from that with had been of old familiar to the sense and memory of all worshipers" had caused "such a tumult in the congregation, especially against the Greeks, correcting what had been read, and denouncing the translation as false, that the bishop was compelled to ask the testimony of the Jewish residents (it was in the town of Oea)." The answer from Jerome sounds quite resentful:

> I have already given a sufficient answer to this in my commentary on Jonah. At present, I deem it enough to say that in that passage, where the Septuagint has "gourd," and Aquila and the others have rendered the word "ivy" (*kissos*), the Hebrew MS. has "ciceion," which is in the Syriac tongue, as now spoken, "ciceia." It is a kind of shrub having large leaves like a vine, and when planted it quickly springs up to the size of a small tree, standing upright by its own stem, without requiring any support of canes or poles, as both gourds and ivy do. If, therefore, in translating word for word, I had put the word "ciceia," no one would know what it meant; if I had used the word "gourd," I would have said what is not found in the Hebrew. I therefore put down "ivy," that I might not differ from all other translators. But if your Jews said, either through malice or ignorance, as you yourself suggest, that the word is in the Hebrew text which is found in the Greek and Latin versions, it is evident that they were either unacquainted with Hebrew, or have been pleased to say what was not true, in order to make sport of the gourd-planters.[3]

Augustine and the "Greek" of Oea were defending the Septuagint translation, where the Hebrew קיקיון was translated as *kolokynthi*, a version reflected also by the ancient Latin translation (*cucurbita*, gourd). And a gourd is definitely the plant of Jonah in Judeo-Christian iconography, beginning in the third century: for example, in the mosaic of Aquileia, the prophet is usually depicted as sleeping, nude, under a trellis from which hang elongated fruits.[4]

A third line of interpretation, derived from Jerome's description of the plant, identifies the קיקיון with the *ricinus communis*, otherwise known as the Castor-oil plant or the Palma Christi:

> *Est autem genus virgulti, vel arbusculae, lata habens folia in modum pampini, et umbram densissimam, suo trunco se sustinens, quae in Palestina creberrime nascitur, et maxime in arenosis locis* (in Jon., ad loc.).

For many scholars the strongest evidence for the identification of Jonah's plant with the ricinus derives from the similarity of the Hebrew word קיקיון to the names for the ricinus in Egyptian and Greek. Herodotus 2.94 speaks of the Egyptians who live in the region of the marshes anointing themselves with κίκι oil (presumably Egyptian $k_3 \ k_3$). There seems no doubt that the Egyptians called the ricinus by the name *kiki* and that the name was borrowed by the Greeks.

The most comprehensive article on the history of the translation of the word קיקיון was written by Bernard P. Robinson in 1985:[5] after examining carefully all the different interpretations, ancient and modern, of the plant name, the author makes an interesting remark:

> Could it be the case that the author did not intend by the word *qiqayon* to designate a specific plant or tree at all? There are Assyrian texts speaking of a plant called the *kukkānītu(m)*, found in a royal garden. Modern lexicographers are unable to identify the plant, and perhaps our author was in the same boat: he had heard of this Assyrian plant and without knowing its Hebrew equivalent thought it appropriate to the Assyrian setting of his story... I am not certain that the author had a specific type of plant or tree in mind at all. My conclusion, therefore, like that of Rasselas, must be one in which nothing is concluded.[6]

In this short essay, I will suggest a possible explanation for the use of the mysterious word קיקיון in the book of Jonah. My idea is based on the suggestion I made, in a previous study,[7] on the structure and the general message of this peculiar biblical book. I will therefore briefly summarize my own views on Jonah.

Jonah as a Recycling of Scripts

The book of Jonah, as noted already in 1947 by André Feuillet,[8] far from being a naive short story, is a complex architecture of quotes from other biblical books. Yvonne Sherwood[9] describes this narrative style, pointing out the similarity between the composition of Jonah and of the New Testament Gospel narratives, but she does not seem to appreciate particularly the author's ability:

> Read in the broader context of the Hebrew Bible, the book of Jonah looks rather like a performance put on by a low-budget "rep" company, scouring the attic of the canon for existing props, to be dusted down and re-used, and looking in the backstage storehouse for fragments of existing scripts: it takes "old" texts and makes them "new," like the Passion account in the Gospel of Matthew.

I have the impression that the construction of this short book was more sophisticated than depicted by Sherwood. It is true that, at least in some passages, the result appears to the reader weird if not completely absurd (this is the case, for example, with the sailors who "offered a sacrifice" on their ship, in the middle of the sea – 1:16). But the use of specific words and quotes form in fact a rather coherent web of cross-references, which lies under the surface of the silly and even comic story of the stubborn prophet who tries to run away from his mission. I will give here just a couple of examples.

One of the key words in the book is the verb ירד, "descend," especially in the first chapter. It is used three times in the first five verses of the book. In 1:3, the expression "went down" into the ship is definitely unusual: in Hebrew the verb ירד is used for people descending from a ship (Ezek 27:29: "All who handle the oars will abandon their ships"), not the opposite. I do not think that the use of this verb was a mistake, or the will of the author of anticipating the descent of Jonah "into the innermost parts of the ship": this is only one element used by the author to create the space where all the actions of Jonah take place. As was remarked also by Philip J. Nel,[10] the prophet is constantly out of the borders of the Land of Israel and, somehow, out of the borders of the world: in the sea, in a foreign land, in the desert. Since the very beginning of the book, Jonah's travel has the flavor of a *katabasis* and the prophet starts to "go down," far from the presence of God and from his normal sphere of action: "Tarshish, ship, fish, Nineveh, shelter outside the city – become station on the road to death."[11]

The ship, in the first chapter, is usually called אניה and, not casually, is heading toward Tarshish: it looks as a sort of paraphrase of the well-known biblical expression "ships of Tarshish" struck by the anger of God in Isa 2:16 and "shattered by an east wind" (the same wind sent to harass Jonah in the last chapter) in Ps 48:8. But in the passage which describes the strange attitude of Jonah who, in the middle of the storm, goes down (again) into the innermost parts of the ship, the term used to indicate the vessel is ספינה, a *hapax legomenon* of clear Aramaic origin. It is highly probable that the intention of the author was evoking through assonance the expression ירכתי צפון, "the remote parts of Zaphon," a well-known mythical expression found, for example, in Isa 14:13, Ezek 38:6, 15 and Ps 48:3.

Another incoherency in the first chapter of Jonah is the alternation between דג and דגה in the narrative, which has generated several rabbinic speculations on the sex of the fish who swallows the prophet. Again, the unexpected use of the feminine word may be a way of creating a link with Deut 4:18, where it is forbidden to make an idol of "any fish (דגה) in the waters beneath the earth." The specific habitat of the "female" fish makes clear that the intended creature should be more viewed as more similar to a dragon than to a tuna. The Greek Bible in fact translated the word with χῆτος, "sea monster."[12]

The whole situation of the sailors on the high sea seems inspired by a passage of Ps 107, sacrifice included (22–30): as in the Gospels, a biblical quote is turned into a new story, conserving the distinctive elements which allow the one who is familiar with the whole biblical text to decode the message.[13]

The Message of the Book of Jonah: An Hypothesis

It is another apparently inappropriate use of a word, in Jon 1, which draws the reader's attention to another inter-textual connection, which appears to me particularly relevant to the understanding of the message of the book. When the sailors try desperately to avoid the storm, in Jon. 1:12, the author uses the verb חתר. Translated as "row hard," the literal meaning is in fact "dig." This peculiar use of the verb reminds the reader of a passage of the book of Amos (9:2–4):

> If they dig into Sheol,
> from there shall my hand take them;
> if they climb up to heaven,
> from there I will bring them down.
> If they hide themselves on the top of Carmel,
> from there I will search them out and take them;
> and if they hide from my sight at the bottom of the sea,
> there I will command the serpent, and it shall bite them.
> And if they go into captivity before their enemies,
> there I will command the sword, and it shall kill them;
> and I will fix my eyes upon them
> for evil and not for good.

This text presents a sort of catalog of places out of the borders of the world, where men may think that the hand of God cannot reach. But sinners have no possibility of escape: the Lord will search them and catch them, directly or through his intermediaries.

The whole story of Jonah can be read in the light of this passage. Jonah tries hard to escape, out of the borders, at the bottom of the sea, in a waste place outside of the foreign town of Nineveh. But Yahweh constantly looks for him and finds him. The same is true for all the sinners in Nineveh: they are not even sons of Israel, yet Yahweh puts his eyes on them and sends to them his prophet. The attitude of the Lord towards Jonah and towards all men is just the opposite of the one described in the passage of Amos: he fixes his eyes upon them for good and not for evil. But what is similar is the will and the possibility of reaching men even in the most remote places, even in the kingdom of Death, which is evoked constantly through all the repertoire of well-known images: the sea, the desert, the "city."[14]

Yahweh in the book of Jonah is certainly very active: every step of the story is in fact caused by a direct divine intervention. He sends the strong wind to cause the storm (1:4), he orders the big fish to swallow the prophet (2:1) and then to vomit him on the dry land (2:11). He makes the plant grow (4:6) and then he sends the worm to chew it (4:7). Finally, he sends the hot wind to exasperate Jonah (4:8) and creates the opportunity for the final lesson. It is interesting to notice that, according to Giovanni Garbini,[15] a completely different view of the direct action of Yahweh in the world would be the one of the author of the book of Job, who – according to the Italian scholar – would have shared epicurean positions. In this case, one could ponder the possibility that the book of Jonah, at least in this aspect, is a sort of polemical answer to Job.

Jonah and Amos

In the last chapter of the book, where the story of the fast-growing plant is related, the book of Amos is referred to at least twice. When the hot sun beats down on his head, Jonah faints: the verb used is יתעלף, a Hitqattel form used with this meaning only in Amos 8:13: "In that day shall the fair virgins and the young men faint for thirst."

Another important reference is the construction of the "booth" by Jonah (4:5). The term used here is סוכה, a word that is used in an important passage from the book of Amos (9:11–12), which reverberates deeply in Christian tradition:[16]

> In that day I will raise up
> the booth of David that is fallen
> and repair its breaches,
> and raise up its ruins
> and rebuild it as in the days of old,
> that they may possess the remnant of Edom
> and all the nations who are called by my name

The universality of the message connected to the messianic booth is very pertinent to the final answer of Yahweh to Jonah, where he makes clear that all men created by God will be included in his love and compassion.

But there is still something unclear in the story of the booth of Jonah. The prophet builds it, the קיקיון quickly grows and then the plant dies and the booth seems to have disappeared too, since poor Jonah finds himself under the sun. The סוכה and the קיקיון quite strangely become one, as two members of one of the *parallelismi membrorum*, so common in biblical poetry. This observation brought me to another passage of the book of Amos, a very difficult and obscure one:[17] Amos 5:26. The verse, in MT, reads: *ūnᵉśāʾtem ʾēt sikkût malkᵉkem wᵉʾēt kiyyûn ṣalmēkem kôkab ʾĕlōhēkem ʾăšer ʾăśîtem lākem*. I will not here attempt a critical analysis of the text, which presents important variants in all ancient versions: I will only consider how in this passage of the MT the word סוכה is used in parallelism with a second object, the כיון *kiyyûn*, which most commentaries and some of the monographs on this specific text consider the name of a Babylonian god (Kewan?), in a vocalization attributable to a "dysphemism" (opposite of euphemism) in which the vowel of *šiqqûṣ* ("abomination") is used.[18]

The author of the book of Jonah shows a deep knowledge of biblical texts and a remarkable freedom in tailoring them to his needs, using also assonance (as in the case of ירכתי צפון sounding like ירכתי ספינה in ch. 1). My suggestion here is that the author, having in mind Amos 5:26, has played with the parallelism there and invented a new name for a fictional fast-growing plant which "sounded like" the quite mysterious כיון *kiyyûn* and was closely related to a סוכה. And, to the joy of future biblical scholars, the קיקיון was born. Considering the Mesopotamian setting the existence of an Assyrian *kukkānītu(m)* plant could have inspired the author.

It is not so surprising that the translation was not an easy one: even if the translator was able to understand the reference, in Greek and Latin texts of the Bible the pun would not work. It is only one of the many nuances of this short biblical book which is completely lost in other languages. The translated book of Jonah becomes a half-funny fairy-tale, the story of a stubborn prophet in amazing situations. The Hebrew book of Jonah is, instead, a fine web of textual references, where the apparent naivety of the narrative hides a deeper theological message (which is, by the way, not so different from the one we find in the Gospels): God cares for all human beings and he is ready to overcome any boundary – including that of the kingdom of Death – to rescue those beloved ones.

Notes

1. Y. Sherwood, *A Biblical Text and Its Afterlives: The Survival of Jonah in Western Culture* (Cambridge: Cambridge University Press, 2000), p. 14.

2. The English translations of the letters are excerpted from the *Letters of Augustine* (No. 28, 71, 82) and the *Letters of Jerome* (No. 112), in *A Select Library of Nicene and Post-Nicene Fathers of the Christian Church, Translated into English with Prolegomena and Explanatory Notes Under the Editorial Supervision of Henry Wace and Philip Schaff* (Oxford/New York: The Christian Literature Co., 1890–1900).

3. *Letters of Jerome* (No. 112), in *A Select Library of Nicene and Post-Nicene Fathers of the Christian Church*.

4. The plant depicted in early iconography is the long fruited *Lagenaria siceraria* (bottle or calabash gourd), a fast-growing climber; see J. Janick and H. S. Paris, "Jonah and the 'Gourd' at Nineveh: Consequences of a Classic Mistranslation," in G. J. Holmes (ed.), *Proceedings of Cucurbitaceae 2006* (Raleigh, NC: Universal Press, 2006), pp. 349–57.

5. B. P. Robinson, "Jonah's Qiqayon Plant," *ZAW* 97 (1985), pp. 390–403.
6. Robinson, "Jonah's Qiqayon Plant," pp. 401–402
7. C. Peri, "Tra mare e deserto: il viaggio di Giona," *Materia Giudaica* VII/1 (2002), pp. 14–23.
8. A. Feuillet, "Les sources du livre de Jonas," *RB* 54 (1947), pp. 161–86.
9. Sherwood, *A Biblical Text and Its Afterlives*, p. 231.
10. P. J. Nel, "The Symbolism and Function of Epic Space in Jonah," *Journal of North West Semitic Languages and Literatures* 25 (1999), pp. 215–24.
11. Nel, "The Symbolism and Function of Epic Space in Jonah," p. 222.
12. A quite vivid memory of Perseus' fight with a κῆτος is largely documented in Roman times in Joppa: it was possible to visit the skeleton of the monster and, according to Plinius, even to purchase bones as souvenirs. On this point, see P. B. Harvey Jr., "The Death of Mythology: The Case of Joppa," *Journal of Early Christian Studies* 2 (1994), pp. 1–14. Harvey suggests that the identification of Joppa as the place of Perseus' deeds was influenced by the biblical book. I would rather suggest the opposite: Joppa was mentioned by the author of the book also because the well-known presence of a sea monster there. Apart from the quite obvious late date for the composition of the book, the tradition concerning Jonah is emerging after the Greek one and gradually replace it completely. On this point, see F.-M. Abel, "Le culte de Jonas en Palestine," *Journal of Palestine Oriental Society* 2 (1922), pp. 175–88.
13. Other examples may be found in Peri, "Tra mare e deserto."
14. On all these images, I still consider useful the study by N. J. Tromp, *Primitive Conceptions of Death and the Nether World in the Old Testament* (Rome: Pontifical Biblical Institute, 1969). See also C. Peri, *Il regno del nemico. La morte nella religione di Canaan* (Brescia: Paideia, 2003).
15. G. Garbini, "La metereologia di Giobbe," *Rivista Biblica* 43 (1995), pp. 85–91.
16. On the use of this passage in Christian tradition, see G. Garbini, "La capanna del re," in G. Sfameni Gasparro (ed.), Ἀγαθὴ ἐλπίς. *Studi storico-religioso in onore di Ugo Bianchi* (Rome: L'Erma di Bretschneider, 1994), pp. 173–76.
17. On this passage, see G. L. Prato, "Idolatry Compelled to Search for Its Gods: A Peculiar Agreement Between Textual Tradition and Exegesis (Amos 5:25–26 and Acts 7:42–43)," in G. O'Collins (ed.), *Luke and Acts* (New York/Mahwah: Paulist, 1991), pp. 181–96.
18. For a different interpretation, see Prato, "Idolatry," pp. 190–96.

ON FINDING MYTH AND HISTORY IN THE BIBLE: EPISTEMOLOGICAL AND METHODOLOGICAL OBSERVATIONS*

Emanuel Pfoh

Introduction

Giovanni Garbini is one of the forerunners of recent critical biblical historiography – if not one of the very first "minimalists" of the late-twentieth century.[1] In the mid-1980s, with the publication of his *Storia e ideologia nell'Israele antico*, he challenged the existence of the United Monarchy of David and Solomon as depicted by the biblical narrative and he proposed to date *the whole* of the Old Testament to the third century BCE, two questions that would later be defended as an essential position of "minimalism."[2] In effect, and despite some reservations regarding his proposals,[3] his provocative views in this book on several topics set forward a number of key issues for Old Testament studies that would fully develop during the 1990s through the so-called "minimalism–maximalism" controversy, although with a much wider scope.

The extensive work of the French school of *les Annales* during a large part of the twentieth century established that creating problems in historiography is to advance our historical knowledge, fostering our historical methodologies and our ways of doing history.[4] In this sense (and without claiming that our author is an *annaliste*!), with *Storia e ideologia* Garbini intervened not that much as a biblical scholar but rather as *a real historian*, in the professional sense of the term: not as someone who simply evokes diachronically the past or narrates it, but as someone who problematizes the knowledge of the past in order to write history.

In what follows, and inspired by the critical spirit of Garbini's *Storia e ideologia*, I will address questions related to how we may interpret biblical stories, or better the intellectual world assumed by biblical stories; how to understand these sources from a critical epistemological and methodological outlook; and finally how to proceed in order to produce a sound historiography of the world of biblical literature and the past of ancient Palestine. My interest in the present contribution is not to sift history from ideology – as Garbini originally intended in his opus – but rather to investigate whether history can be found behind (or inside) mythical evocations in the Bible or not. From the outset, I make my view on the question explicit: reading the Bible primarily as history is highly problematic since it excludes not only the possibility of grasping the mythic character of ancient Near Eastern stories, but also creates virtual pasts, rationalistic paraphrases of ancient worldviews expressed in those stories. The present contribution, therefore, attempts to establish an epistemological awareness and as such it proposes only critical observations for doing history and interpreting ancient texts.

A terminological caveat before proceeding: the present writer is aware that there is no "Bible" as a single textual artefact. Nonetheless, the term is used in this essay to refer to the biblical corpus in general, for the sake of the epistemological argument advanced, and since it is proposed in the pages which follow that both Old and New Testaments, together with the rest of the biblical writings, are embedded in a mythic discourse that functions as a charter of theology and myth, thus creating many problems for writing history directly out of them.

How to Read the Bible Historically?

In one of his volumes of collected essays, *Mito e storia nella Bibbia*, Garbini addresses a number of biblical stories, looking at their literary nature and the ways they may be read or interpreted.[5] The key concept in this interpretation is "myth" and how we can decode biblical stories, attempting to understand them and the message they convey. Garbini's way of dealing with these stories resembles, and seems to be influenced in some way by, the reading that Thomas L. Thompson has offered in his provocative *The Bible in History*,[6] in which it is proposed to interpret the Bible not as merely reflecting history, but instead as expressing a particular theology and understanding of the divine and human worlds, without distinguishing history from myth in its stories. Even if we concede – as Garbini does – that such mythic interpretation of events have some anchor in real historical situations,[7] what is relevant for the historian from this interpretative perspective is the biblical discourse as a cultural element that must be seriously considered in order to grasp the nature of the biblical sources when attempting to draw data from them.

In effect, the interpretative path proposed by Thompson and Garbini allows indeed for acknowledging a series of considerations related to historical interpretation that transcend the simple use of biblical images as reflecting real historical events from the past.

The first one has to do with the epistemological contexts of interpretation: to assume that the Bible was read or understood throughout the last two millennia in some loose and general way as primarily dealing with a real, historical past (especially from Gen 12 on), that is, as we may read it in modern days, is nothing but an ethnocentric assertion that otherwise needs to be proven. Our first methodological duty as historians should be to recognize that, given that the society that produced the biblical stories differs in so many ways from our modern or contemporary society (from a socio-anthropological perspective), the Bible cannot be used as a direct source, a direct testimony of the past, but it must first be culturally decoded. The intellectual revolution brought upon Western society by the Enlightenment since the eighteenth century onwards changed radically ways to understand and explain the universe, natural and human history and the ultimate reality of things; and with that, of course, the Bible. The so-called "triumph of Reason" meant that the biblical narrative was historicized, its contents inscribed in History, and the primeval manner of understanding the biblical stories, as a (theological) myth, was therefore gradually erased and replaced by modern theology and modern biblical scholarship, with German historical-critical methodologies as the key instruments for dissecting the Bible.[8]

This leads us to the second consideration about terminology and conceptual terms. Throughout scholarly literature the dichotomy between "history" and "fiction" is usually found, deeming a negative meaning to the term "fiction." Also the wording of the creation of tradition as "invention" connotes the notion of elaborating something from scratch and perhaps with the intention of deceiving a targeted audience. Of course, when such a deception contains a considerable degree of "historical truth" the notion of propaganda comes immediately to mind.[9] I think instead that the concept of *myth*, as it is used by ethnographical and anthropological research, offers much better analytical outcomes that the perspective created by the dichotomy history/myth, once it is detached from the Western modern and popular connotation of "lie," or something relating precisely to some sort of invention.[10] Actually, the concept of myth has an important heuristic value when it is understood as an explanatory worldview employed by "natives" to process and represent reality, past, present and future. In this context, the notion of myths as having essentially to do with divine beings and their interaction with humans is secondary. It also should be noted that rationalistic understandings of mythic compositions miss the point when attempting an interpretation without considering the mythic mindset behind those compositions.

Accordingly, to read the Hebrew Bible from Genesis to Ezra–Nehemiah–Chronicles, or the Christian Bible from Genesis to Revelation, *as a myth*, without sifting historical reality from religious imagination or deliberate authorial fiction, means essentially to attempt an understanding of these ancient stories as an ancient Near Eastern audience or readership would, by using ethnographic analogies and through sound scholarly interpretations.[11] This is a key epistemological instance in order to use biblical narrative as a historical source: knowing precisely the characteristics of the source and the historical and intellectual contexts of its production. Unlike the archaeological and the epigraphic records of the South Levant, the Old Testament writings are secondary (or even tertiary) sources for Iron Age Palestine; however, their status is upgraded when we are dealing with the second half of the first millennium BCE to the second century CE, as they certainly represent a primary source for the intellectual history of Jewish communities and their understanding of an ancient past that informs them about their origins and identity,[12] an identity created or invented, with a mythopoetic nature that is at home in the Eastern Mediterranean and ancient Near Eastern cultural world – but that is another question.[13]

A Key Matter: Historical Kernels in Mythic Wrappings?

One particular aspect of Garbini's historical scholarship is his ability to find hidden traces of "history" in the biblical texts. Of course, this ability depends greatly on his philological skills, more than in proper historical criticism.[14] In some ways, this procedure is likened to the "archaeology of the text," widespread in biblical studies for more than a century (i.e. historical-critical studies).[15] In spite of some valuable and progressive results of this method during the last century, an alternative approach can also be pursued. A rather different approach, in fact.

The question is not, indeed, whether the Old Testament may contain historical information, that is, information that can be found in extra-biblical Near Eastern sources,[16] but whether it is possible to retrieve such information from biblical stories beyond a mere historicist "corroboration" and use it directly to write history. This matter, in effect, takes us back some two hundred years, to the foundational work of W. M. L. de Wette (1780–1849), who regarded the Old Testament as a collection of myths and traditions with no historical information in them.[17] Of course, de Wette wrote in a time when the archaeological research in the "land of the Bible" had not yet occurred. The development of "biblical archaeology" would switch opinions towards a positive attitude regarding biblical historicity in general.[18] In the present, the idea that there is some correspondence between the history of ancient Palestine and the biblical narrative has been dominant and widespread at least since de Wette's death, or better said, since the proper development of "biblical archaeology" and historical-critical studies throughout the nineteenth century. But this conception is not the sole patrimony of traditional European biblical scholarship or American conservative evangelical scholars. Critical scholars such as Garbini (especially in his *Scrivere la storia d'Israele*), Knauf, Liverani and many others who stand at the centre of the historiographical path, between "skeptical minimalism" and "credulist maximalism" – should these representations of scholarly positions be valid – think that it is indeed methodologically possible to write history from the biblical texts after a proper sifting of the textual data.[19]

Yet the quarrel at this stage of the argument in the present study is not with methodology but with epistemology: How can we unwrap a mythic story in order to get to the historical kernel? Is such a cross-epistemological procedure not only possible but valid at all? Distancing myself from the always-complicated procedures of German historical-critical studies,[20] I would argue, on one hand, that we should attempt to interpret biblical narrative as a myth *in toto*, without distinguishing myth from history, and, on the other hand, to produce a history (or histories) of the contexts of creation of such narratives but without crossing lines or mixing information, that is, in a parallel arrangement of the data (see further below).

It is necessary to understand the intellectual development of the last two centuries in order to explain the epistemological matrix of contemporary biblical studies, especially its handling of historical questions. As noted above, the notion of reading history or historical events into biblical stories is a modern Western activity, a cultural setting of the mind after the European Enlightenment that cast anything not inscribed in History to the realm of fantasy, imagination or "myth" (as synonymous with something unreal or even untrue). However, such a rationalistic distinction between "history" and "myth" when evoking reality was non-existent in the ancient Near Eastern *Umwelt* of the biblical stories. The key distinction between what we, from an Enlightened perspective, would call "history" and "myth" was intertwined into one single conception and representation; what we would call "historical events" was understood according to the mythic archetypes that arranged the cosmos and reality for ancient Near Eastern peoples.²¹ It is thus highly doubtful that we can peel away layers of mythic stories in order to find a core of historical truth. Also in this way, unless we have external evidence of a biblical event, it is very difficult to know what is truly "historical" and what is not. Of course, this does not mean the Hebrew Bible/Old Testament should be left aside when writing a history of Iron Age Palestine; it means, instead, that the biblical narrative is not the first or main source for commencing the production of a critical historical reconstruction.

I leave now this brief epistemological discussion and will propose, then, a methodological procedure for dealing with the writing of ancient Palestine's past and the use of biblical narrative as a historical source.

Myth and History Apart

It is no novelty, especially after some 40 years of criticism within Old Testament historical studies, to claim that the biblical narrative and the archaeological should be kept separated, not comingled. Thompson argued already in his *The Historicity of the Patriarchal Narratives* from 1974 that "[a]rchaeological materials should not be dated or evaluated on the basis of written texts which are independent of these materials; so also written documents should not be interpreted on the basis of archaeological hypotheses."²² Nonetheless, since pleas or attempts to establish or foster a "dialogue" between both sets of data have been proposed rather frequently in biblical studies and archaeology, evolving from a different epistemological basis and aiming at producing some sort of "corroboration,"²³ the matter has to be addressed once again.

To speak of "corroboration" implies the possibility of relating two sets of different data that refer to *one single past*, in an ontological sense. Yet, since the mythical discourse of the Bible evokes events for theological purposes from a mythic epistemology and the modern historiographical discourse shapes the historical past of ancient Palestine according to rationalistic principles, it is possible to affirm that such dialogue, when offered *on the same epistemological terms*, is utterly erroneous. The Bible and modern history-writing cannot corroborate each other as if both discourses belong to the same epistemological matrix, referring to the same historical past. A more correct insight seems to be that modern historiographical techniques explain why the Bible evokes some events that can be confirmed as historical by archaeological reconstructions and epigraphic finds. The Bible is not a direct witness to the past of Iron Age Palestine, but a much later reflection on that past. The biblical past is not the same past we, in modern times, seek to reconstruct – even if key events and places appear to be coincident. In the Bible we find a theological myth that uses what we would call "historical events" for conveying a certain message. That does not qualify the Bible as the primary blueprint to write historically about ancient Palestine. *In sum, modern historical research can explain the Bible in its various complexities, but the Bible cannot explain the history of ancient Palestine for us in scientific or realistic terms.*

We can indeed have a biblical and theological myth, going through the stories of the Old Testament, and we can have a history and archaeology of Palestine (or the South Levant, if a less politicized term is preferred); but we cannot have them both as a blend anymore – we cannot inhabit both worlds *at the same time*. The "myth of Israel" that we find in the Bible is food for theology, which is its main matter of concern. In other words, a mythic interpretation of biblical stories is perhaps the most valid path for the relevance of theology as a contemporary intellectual reflection and discourse.[24] But this should not be confused with ancient history. The historical episodes, bits and notices in biblical narrative would better be explained by secular, non-confessional and apart-from-theology histories of the ancient South Levant. The paradigm of "the Bible as history," in the modern sense of the term *history*, has come fully to an end as to its analytical value. This paradigm should then not be perpetuated by attempts to find historical kernels inside the mythic wrappings of ancient stories, for it is not a matter of quantity – how much historical data it is possible to extract from myth, which is at times, and under certain circumstances, actually feasible – but of quality, of different epistemologies setting up different intellectual discourses to refer to the universe and everything inside it (including the notion of past times!) that – again – should not be mixed.

In the end, however, the question also depends on the discursive realms we all inhabit: conservative evangelical scholarship regards this methodology as destructive, leaving little to work with, preferring instead to use the Old Testament as a key source for understanding and reconstructing the past of ancient Israel – which is conceptualized as the same thing as biblical and/or historical Israel.[25] But the problem with this choice is that conservative evangelical scholarship's attempts to write history does not live up to the standards of the professional historical discipline. It is rather dictated by the confessional need of having the Bible as a *historical* narrative – meaning an evocation of events that actually happened more than two millennia ago – in order to support and legitimate the relevance of a particular theological discourse in the present. Once this strategy is dismantled, it is easy to realize that the importance of writing modern "biblical histories of Israel" resides not in what may be discovered, in a truly scientific spirit, but actually in what can be confirmed (*ergo historia ancilla theologiae!*). Conservative evangelical scholarship builds on a confessional transference of textual (biblical) realities into the archaeological and historical records, creating a rationalized yet bogus image of ancient Palestine's past. It is thus not only misleading but essentially wrong in historical terms to speak, for instance, of a "biblical period" in the history of the South Levant, or of a time of a United Monarchy, or even of David and Solomon – as it would equally be to refer to an "Odyssey period" or the time of Ulysses and Achilles when addressing the history of ancient Greece. Such references have no historical support and appear to be valid only within the boundaries of a conservative evangelical approach to ancient Palestine's past, or a "biblical archaeology" discourse, blending myth and history into one final outcome, or a nationalist (Zionist) retelling of ancient foundational events and scenarios.[26]

A Final Comment

Hyper-critical or extremely radical as it may seem, my stand in this essay is concerned not with having eventually a minimal history of ancient Palestine written, but rather with securing a sound basis for writing history and understanding biblical narrative in its ancient intellectual context, without retrojecting theological (or political) readings of the present into the past. Concerning the historian's task, the challenge for the future is to write histories of the South Levant without the biblical narrative or "ancient Israel" as the leading sketch for such historiography, which seems to be the proper outcome of some four decades of challenging thinking in biblical historical studies.[27] This is precisely the general disposition defended in the preceding: that biblical narrative should not dictate how the history of ancient Palestine is to be understood and written anymore. Dealing historically with ancient Palestine should not start with the Bible, but – as already suggested – the Bible should be explained and understood after an evaluation, among other aspects, of the political, economic, social, religious, demographic, ecological situation of Palestine in its own right. If the Old Testament's stories can indeed shed some light on Iron Age Palestine, it will be only after sketching such a past historically, basing our reconstructions on primary sources, and only then proceeding with secondary sources.

Notes

* It is a pleasure to dedicate this paper to Professor Garbini, whose work and scholarly attitude have been so inspiring to me.

1. The other candidate would be Bernd Jørg Diebner from the University of Heidelberg (see, for instance, his essay "'Es lässt sich nicht beweisen, Tatsache aber ist...': Sprachfigur statt Methode in der kritischen Erforschung des AT," *DBAT* 18 [1984], pp. 138-46), but he kept himself within the confines of German-speaking biblical scholarship, resulting in an almost complete lack of awareness of this scholar's writings among English-speaking members of the scholarly guild. For sure, Garbini would have met the same fate, were his works not translated into English.

2. G. Garbini, *Storia e ideologia nell'Israele antico* (Biblioteca di storia e storiografia dei tempi biblici 3; Brescia: Paideia, 1986). Of course, these theses became more widely known in the scholarly world after the English translation of this work: *History and Ideology in Ancient Israel* (London: SCM, 1988).

3. See, to name but a couple of examples of constructive criticism, M. Liverani's review in *Oriens Antiquus* 27 (1988), pp. 303–309; T. L. Thompson, *Early History of the Israelite Peoples: From the Written and Archaeological Sources* (SHANE 4; Leiden: E. J. Brill, 1992), pp. 117–26.

4. See the now-classic works of the first generation of *les Annales*: M. Bloch, *Apologie pour l'histoire, ou Métier d'historien* (Paris: Armand Colin, 1949); and L. Febvre, *Combats pour l'histoire* (Paris: Armand Colin, 2nd edn, 1965), where the concept *histoire-problème* ("problem-oriented history") was coined. F. Braudel, a second-generation historian of this school, presented his views in *Écrits sur l'histoire* (Paris: Flammarion, 1969). A representative collection of the third generation's historiographical concerns is J. Le Goff and P. Nora (eds.), *Faire de l'histoire* (3 vols.; Bibliothèque des Histoires; Paris: Gallimard, 1974). Cf. also the evaluation in P. Burke, *The French Historical Revolution: The* Annales *School, 1929–89* (Cambridge: Polity, 1990).

5. G. Garbini, *Mito e storia nella Bibbia* (Studi Biblici 137; Brescia: Paideia, 2003); ET: *Myth and History in the Bible* (JSOTSup 362; London: Sheffield Academic, 2003). Another notable anthology of studies by Garbini is *Letteratura e politica nell'Israele antico* (Studi Biblici 162; Brescia: Paideia, 2010).

6. T. L. Thompson, *The Bible in History: How Writers Create the Past* (London: Jonathan Cape, 1999).

7. Garbini, *Mito e storia*, p. 9.

8. The whole question can in fact be traced back to the appearance of Humanism during the Renaissance and also to the Reformation; cf. P. Gibert, *L'invention critique de la Bible, XVe–XVIIIe siècle* (Bibliothèque des Histoires; Paris: Éditions Gallimard, 2010); and M. Legaspi, *The Death of Scripture and the Rise of Biblical Studies* (Oxford: Oxford University Press, 2010); H. Spieckermann, "From Biblical Exegesis to Reception History," *Hebrew Bible and Ancient Israel* 1 (2012), pp. 327–50. See also N. P. Lemche, *The Old Testament Between Theology and History: A Critical Survey* (LAI; Louisville, KY: Westminster John Knox, 2008), pp. 31–98.

9. Cf. the critical address of this concept in M. Liverani, "Propaganda," in *ABD*, V, pp. 474–77.

10. Many authors and works could be referred to in this regard; see, among others: B. Malinowski, *Magic, Science and Religion* (Glencoe, IL: The Free Press, 1948), especially pp. 72–124; C. Lévi-Strauss, "The Structural Study of Myth," *Journal of American Folklore* 78 (1955), pp. 428–44; idem, *La pensée sauvage* (Paris: Plon, 1962); M. Eliade, *Myth and Reality* (New York: Harper & Row, 1963); C. Geertz (ed.), *Myth, Symbol, and Culture* (New York: W. W. Norton, 1974). In Old Testament studies, N. Wyatt has produced some important works related to this perspective: see his "The Mythic Mind," *SJOT* 15 (2001), pp. 3–56, and further his important anthology *The Mythic Mind: Essays on Cosmology and Religion in Ugaritic and Old Testament Literature* (BibleWorld; London: Equinox, 2005).

11. A point already made by N. P. Lemche in "Are We Europeans Really Good Readers of Biblical Texts and Interpreters of Biblical History?," *JNSL* 25 (1999), pp. 185–99; and also addressed, although from a different (more historiographical) perspective, by E. Ben Zvi, "General Observations on Ancient Israelite Histories in Their Ancient Contexts," in L. L. Grabbe (ed.), *Enquire of the Former Age: Ancient Historiography and Writing the History of Israel* (ESHM 9; LHBOTS 554; London: T&T Clark International, 2011), pp. 21–39, especially pp. 23–24.

12. Primary sources are not necessarily more "historical" than secondary ones; both categories are meaningful only within an interpretative framework or hypothesis that relates their relevance; cf. R. G. Kratz, *Historisches und biblisches Israel: Drei Überblicke zum Alten Testament* (Tübingen: Mohr Siebeck, 2013), pp. 5–9. The question is one of method, not of epistemology in this regard.

13. Garbini, *Mito e storia*, pp. 21–22. On the question of history and ancient historiography, a recent collective treatment is K.-P. Adam (ed.), *Historiographie in der Antike* (BZAW 373; Berlin: de Gruyter, 2008); a useful survey focussed on the Hebrew Bible is T. M. Bolin, "History, Historiography, and the Use of the Past in the Hebrew Bible," in C. Shuttleworth Kraus (ed.), *The Limits of Historiography: Genre and Narrative in Ancient Historical Texts* (Mnemosyne Supplement 191; Leiden: Brill, 1999), pp. 113–40; but cf. also E. Pfoh, "Ancient Historiography, Biblical Stories and Hellenism," in T. L. Thompson and P. Wajdenbaum (eds.), *The Bible and Hellenism: Greek Influence on Jewish and Early Christian Literature* (CIS; Durham: Acumen, 2014), pp. 19–35.

14. G. Garbini, "Biblical Philology and North-West Semitic Epigraphy: How Do They Contribute to Israelite History Writing?," in M. Liverani (ed.), *Recenti Tendenze nella Ricostruzione della Storia Antica d'Israele* (Rome: Accademia Nazionale dei Lincei, 2005), pp. 121–35; idem, *Scrivere la storia d'Israele: Vicende e memorie ebraiche* (Biblioteca di storia e storiografia dei tempi biblici 15; Brescia: Paideia, 2008); cf. my review of Garbini's history of Israel in *Palamedes: A Journal of Ancient History* 4 (2009), pp. 191–95.

15. The most sound example of this methodology, especially as related to historical questions, is probably illustrated by E. A. Knauf's many contributions; see, for instance, E. A. Knauf, "Towards an Archaeology of the Hexateuch," in J. C. Gertz, K. Schmid and M. Witte (eds.), *Abschied vom Jahwisten: Die Komposition des Hexateuch in der jüngsten Diskussion* (BZAW 315; Berlin: de Gruyter, 2002), pp. 275–94. One should not disregard, however, the criticism to this general analytical procedure in B. J. Diebner, "Wider die 'Offenbarungs-Archäologie' in der Wissenschaft vom Alten Testament. Grundsätzliches zum Sinn alttestamentlicher

Forschung im Rahmen der Theologie," *DBAT* 18 (1984), pp. 30–53. Elsewhere, and earlier, Knauf pointed out: "The Old Testament narratives may actually contain as much historical information as the naïve, or fundamentalist, reader expects them to contain, or even more. *But this history is not so much recoverable from the narratives, as it is from the knowledge at the narrators' disposal, and from the linguistic, economic, social and political structures which shaped the narratives*" (E. A. Knauf, "Eglon and Ophrah: Two Toponymic Notes on the Book of Judges," *JSOT* 51 [1991], pp. 25–44 [39, my emphasis]), and one can very much agree with this statement. The matter is how to achieve this goal: how can we know what the knowledge at the narrator's disposal was?

16. See, for instance, the anthology of contributions in L. L. Grabbe (ed.), *"Like a Bird in a Cage": The Invasion of Sennacherib in 701 BCE* (JSOTSup 363; ESHM 4; Sheffield: Sheffield Academic, 2003).

17. In his *Auffoderung zum Studium der hebraischen Sprache und Litteratur* (1805), de Wette wrote: "a complete and thoroughgoing criticism will show that not one of the historical books of the Old Testament has any historical value, and that they all more or less contain myths and traditions; and that we do not have from among any of the books of the Old Testament any real historical witnesses, except for several prophetic books, which, however, yield little historical information." (I reproduce here the translation in J. Rogerson, *W. M. L. de Wette: Founder of Modern Biblical Criticism: An Intellectual Biography* [JSOTSup 126; Sheffield: JSOT, 1992], p. 47.) This understanding is also found in his renowned work *Beiträge zur Einleitung in das Alte Testament* (1806–1807).

18. On the development of "biblical archaeology," see N. A. Silberman, *Digging for God and Country: Exploration, Archaeology, and the Secret Struggle for the Holy Land, 1799–1917* (New York: A. A. Knopf, 1982); and T. W. Davis, *Shifting Sands: The Rise and Fall of Biblical Archaeology* (Oxford: Oxford University Press, 2004).

19. To the references in nn. 14–15, one may add: M. Liverani, *Oltre la Bibbia: Storia antica di Israele* (Rome-Bari: Laterza, 2003), ET: *Israel's History and the History of Israel* (BibleWorld; London: Equinox, 2005); and cf. the review in P. R. Davies, "Way Beyond the Bible – But Far Enough?," in Grabbe (ed.), *Enquire of the Former Age*, pp. 186–93.

20. Cf. further the criticism in T. L. Thompson, "Das Alte Testament als theologische Disziplin," in B. Janowski and N. Lohfink (eds.), *Religionsgeschichte Israels oder Theologie des Alten Testaments?* (JBTh 10; Neukirchen–Vluyn: Neukirchener, 1995), pp. 157–73.

21. A now somewhat dated but still fundamental synthesis of ancient Near Eastern thought is M. Liverani, "La concezione dell'universo," in S. Moscati (ed.), *L'alba della civiltà. Società, economia e pensiero nel Vicino Oriente antico* (Torino: UTET, 1976), III, pp. 437–521. See also B. Albrektson, *History and the Gods: An Essay on the Idea of Historical Events as Divine Manifestations in the Ancient Near East and in Israel* (CBOT 1; Lund: Gleerup, 1967); and H. H. Schmid, *Gerechtigkeit als Weltordnung: Hintergrund und Geschichte der alttestamentischen Gerechtigkeitsbegriffes* (BHT 40; Tübingen: J. C. B. Mohr [Paul Siebeck], 1968). From anthropology we can get many useful insights in this regard, attending for instance to the debate between Marshall Sahlins and Gananath Obeyesekere regarding how

natives (Hawaiians) interpret events, in this case, the arrival of Captain Cook to Hawaii in 1779; see M. Sahlins, *Historical Metaphors and Mythical Realities* (Ann Arbor: The University of Michigan Press, 1981); idem, *Islands of History* (Chicago: University of Chicago Press, 1985); G. Obeyesekere, *The Apotheosis of Captain Cook: European Mythmaking in the Pacific* (Princeton: Princeton University Press, 1992); and Sahlins' response to the criticism in his *How "Natives" Think: About Captain Cook, for Example* (Chicago: University of Chicago Press, 1995).

22. T. L. Thompson, *The Historicity of the Patriarchal Narratives: The Quest for the Historical Abraham* (BZAW 134; Berlin: de Gruyter, 1974), pp. 3–4.

23. B. Halpern, "Text and Artifact: Two Monologues?," in N. A. Silberman and D. B. Small (eds.), *The Archaeology of Israel: Constructing the Past, Interpreting the Present* (JSOTSup 237; Sheffield: Sheffield Academic, 1997), pp. 311–40; as for the finding of corroborations between archaeology (and epigraphy) and texts, see W. G. Dever, *What Did the Biblical Writers Know & When Did They Know It? What Archaeology Can Tell Us About the Reality of Ancient Israel* (Grand Rapids: Eerdmans, 2001), pp. 124–31; L. L. Grabbe, *Ancient Israel: What Do We Know and How Do We Know It?* (London: T&T Clark International, 2007), pp. 164–66, 212–15.

24. Cf. the critical considerations in P. R. Davies, "The Intellectual, the Archaeologist and the Bible," in J. A. Dearman and M. P. Graham (eds.), *The Land That I Will Show You: Essays on the History and Archaeology of the Ancient Near East in Honour of J. Maxwell Miller* (JSOTSup 343; Sheffield: Sheffield Academic, 2001), pp. 239–54.

25. See V. P. Long, D. W. Baker, and G. J. Wenham (eds.), *Windows into Old Testament History: Evidence, Argument and the Crisis of "Biblical Israel"* (Grand Rapids: Eerdmans, 2002); and I. W. Provan, V. P. Long, and T. Longman, III, *A Biblical History of Israel* (LAI; Louisville, KY: Westminster John Knox, 2003), a book most problematic on methodological grounds (if not ideologically as well), from the perspective of professional history-writing. Cf. the reviews in N. P. Lemche "Conservative Scholarship on the Move," *SJOT* 19 (2005), pp. 203–52; and L. L. Grabbe, "The Big Max: Review of *A Biblical History of Israel* by Iain Provan, V. Philips Long and Tremper Longman, III," in Grabbe (ed.), *Enquire of the Former Age*, pp. 215–33; K. W. Whitelam, "The Death of Biblical History," in D. Burns and J. W. Rogerson (eds.), *Far from Minimal: Celebrating the Work and Influence of Philip R. Davies* (LHBOTS 484; London: T&T Clark International, 2012), pp. 485–504.

26. I am aware that the "biblical archaeology" movement, which was triumphant between the 1920s and the 1970s, entered into difficulties in its later stages (Davis, *Shifting Sands*, pp. 123–44), but it has recently been resuscitated under the name of "new (or historical) biblical archaeology"; see now, for instance, T. E. Levy (ed.), *Historical Biblical Archaeology and the Future: The New Pragmatism* (London: Equinox, 2010). This reappearance expresses, in my view, a change or update in terminology but not in historical epistemology. On "biblical archaeology" as an incompetent reading of the Bible, see Davies, "The Intellectual." On Zionist interpretations of ancient Palestine's past, see now N. Masalha, *The Zionist Bible: Biblical Precedent, Colonialism and the Erasure of Memory* (BibleWorld; Durham: Acumen, 2013).

27. For a sample of more secular, or less Bible-based histories of Palestine, cf. the various proposals in Thompson, *Early History*, passim; K. W. Whitelam, "Sociology or History: Towards a (Human) History of Ancient Palestine," in J. Davis, G. Harvey, and W. G. E. Watson (eds.), *Words Remembered, Texts Renewed: Essays in Honour of John F. A. Sawyer* (JSOTSup 195; Sheffield: Sheffield Academic, 1995), pp. 149–66; idem, *Rhythms of Time: Reconnecting Palestine's Past* (Sheffield: BenBlackBooks, 2013); Lemche, *The Old Testament Between Theology and History*, pp. 393–453.

"HISTORICAL" ISRAEL AND "BIBLICAL" ISRAEL, OR ETHNICITY AS A SYMBOL

Gian Luigi Prato

In introducing his volume on the history of Israel and outlining the assumptions that would guide his methodological principles, Giovanni Garbini wrote among other things that the Bible is "a book that ignores a 'Jewish people'" and "that it was written for the 'children of Israel'."[1] The work succeeded then in adequately explaining the meaning of these two statements. In fact, what is called Israel would not be a monolithic reality, but the result of a merging of various historical nations. The formation of biblical literature should be seen as dependent on a memory that will define a collective identity. A social and literary pluralism would then merge together to form that image of the "children of Israel" that we know well from the biblical writings. Consequently, the history of Israel which is commonly known and described is an attempt to retrospectively insert that image in the context of the history of the ancient Near East. As I pointed out in my critical review of the volume,[2] these conclusions raise the complex issue of ethnic repercussion of such an image of Israel, resulting from a literary processing aimed at creating an identity. If this image helps to clarify an already existing reality, one must wonder where it comes from and how it was formed, if originally there were different peoples. If instead this image creates an identity on the literary level, how then to understand its relationship with a people who, at least in the later stages of the history, refer to it as their foundation?

In outlining his history of Israel, Garbini certainly takes into account the biblical text. One can agree or disagree with him on how he uses this text to reconstruct individual points on the course of history. However, all in all, in this case the text serves as a basis for comprehensively comparing the history that is outlined in it with the alternative or antithetical history that emerges as a result of its reconstruction by the historian. But it is interesting to note how the results which Garbini arrives at largely coincide with those achieved through purely exegetical analysis of the text, practiced with the intent of defining what the meaning of "biblical Israel" is. Actually this is the work carried out some years ago by Philip R. Davies,[3] who concludes in fact that "biblical Israel" is a collective and identity-making reality. For him, in fact, this would be the result of a memory of Judah, which tried to endorse a previous memory of Benjamin by erasing it as much as possible and even usurping the features of superiority that distinguished Benjamin. Here too, it is not important to find the questionable concrete ways in which the route taken by that memory is outlined, up to its crystallization in the present biblical text; what is relevant is the general idea that the Israel the text is talking about is a literary reconstruction that somehow stands at the foundation of an identity, with considerable repercussions on subsequent eras and traditions in which that text plays an authoritative function.

In the following pages I would like to revisit this problem, which increasingly emerges in some areas of current research (and not only in exegetical and historiographical venues); first, I want to substantiate it more fully with regard to its constituent elements, and then deal with some inevitable reflections that stand out – even with some urgency – as a result of deductions that one should draw. To integrate the literary image derived both from a comparison with the history of Israel and the configuration of "biblical Israel," I would like to adduce some texts in which one notes more clearly the explicit intent to build or to present an identity for Israel, in order to observe how this image concretely takes shape. This image is tied to a particular people and stands in a dialectical relationship with a universal vision both of the nations and the history. Therefore, it is necessary to pause both on the ethnic value of particularism, if this is to be understood only as a literary construct, and on the characteristics with which this self-image claims its legitimacy (and also its particular distinction) in relation to the characteristics of other peoples.

It should be noted, however, that the issue should not be simplistically formulated as an immediate comparison between the "historical" and "biblical" Israel, with the consequent apologetic stances which can condition it. Rather, it involves the more complex idea of "nationalism" and the ways in which a definition and consciousness within a collective reality that tries to present itself as a "people" have been elaborated. In fact, it is in these terms that the problem is also being studied for ancient Israel, albeit with due caution because of the easy danger of anachronistically allowing oneself to be guided by the configurations of modern nationalisms.[4] More specifically, then, this "national" self-conception is confined inside the historical world of that time (the environment is, of course, Greco-Roman).[5] It is seen emerging from a comparison between the images of self and other.[6] As is natural, studies focused on particular texts, such as the books of Ezra and Nehemiah,[7] Ruth[8] and *3 Maccabees*[9] are not lacking. Besides, from the methodological side it should be noted that ethnicity is not an objective reality, available for example through archaeological research, but a mental construct connected to self-consciousness and the way we relate with others.[10]

Israel Among the Nations: The Ideal Image Elaborated in the Context of Prayer

Let us consider four texts, relatively recent and not included within the Jewish biblical canon, although regarded as deuterocanonical books of the Old Testament in the Christian Bible (though not in all its confessional denominations) in their Greek linguistic formulation. This fact indicates that they are quite late texts, coming from a time when the yearning for self-definition is more acute, especially in relation to the external environment. Moreover, here it is about prayers by which one turns to God to actualize that image of the nation that is described to him and requested of him. For this reason, these prayers are particularly significant. Seen from a distance, this definitional process that hides itself in the genre of prayer (and more particularly petitionary prayer) is an unrealistic and yet ideal framework for the self; it is then projected onto God as in a mirror, so that in its reflected ray that falls down on the earth it might take on the traits of a concrete reality.

The first is the so-called "prayer for Israel" of Sir 36:1–22,[11] a composition rich in exegetical insights, which – as usual in Ben Sira – arise mainly from a comparative analysis of the different linguistic versions (especially Hebrew, Greek, Syriac and Latin).[12] It is enclosed between two invocations to God whose universal characteristics are expressly underlined (v. 1: "Lord, God of all things" or "God of the universe"; v. 22: "God of the ages" for the Greek, "Eternal God" in the Hebrew). Soon after the view extends to other peoples (thus, in the plural for the Greek, while the Hebrew thinks of only one, perhaps the Greeks: v. 3), over whom the divine power is about to be poured; a chiastic relationship is established with them, which has as its purpose the simultaneous exaltation of Israel and God, as is clear from v. 4: "As, in their sight, you have proved yourself holy to us, so now, in our sight, prove yourself great to them."[13] The God who thus manifests himself thereby becomes "unique" (v. 5); not so much in the metaphysical sense, but because once again he reveals himself as the powerful deity who did not hesitate to cast down the enemies with disdain and anger in favour of his people: in vv. 6–12 the powerful enterprises of the past – especially and implicitly including those of the exodus – are evoked summarily and with paradigmatic value. If indeed one wishes to speak here of an exodus model raised to a cosmic and creative plan, it should be noted, however, that "the belonging of the people in relation to their deity is not the point of arrival or the result of the salvific intervention and thus elective of the deity itself, but it is rather a prerequisite":[14] in other words, the model is inverted not so much in chronological terms as in its more profound constitutive value. After this placement among the nations from which these people stand out in the vertical dimension, the attention is focused on themselves, who invoke reunion after dispersion and mercy for Israel defined as "firstborn"[15] (vv. 13a + 16b, 17). The image is finally completed or intrinsically linked with two realities that are considered essential for Israel's self-definition: the first is the city of Jerusalem understood as centre of the cultic apparatus and thus also as institutional centre, because it is the seat of the temple and of the cult (vv. 18–19);[16] the second is prophecy, here recalled and transformed into a prediction in the sense that its implementation in the present would ensure that the prophets of old are found "worthy of belief" (vv. 20–21). Once again, then, a component of religious history serves the function of dialectic exaltation.[17]

In this prayer Israel becomes as a symbol that draws its demonstrative effectiveness from history, since events of the past are summarized in the manner of prodigies and as such must be repeated in the present. At the same time, a centrality that is geographically represented in Jerusalem is extolled: from the people thus defined and from their centre radiates a universality that qualifies and legitimates their own God on the cosmic level.

Though not in a fixed combination, these components of the image of Israel reappear elsewhere, and together they become almost an obligatory *topos* in the context of a prayerful attitude.[18] In this way we come to the second text, taken from the book of Tobit. After the events that led to his healing through the journey of his son Tobias in a distant land, the aged Tobit raises a hymn to God in Jerusalem, which at the end of the book sounds like a song of personal thanksgiving (Tob 13:1–18). It begins with an invocation to God who "lives forever" (v. 2) but who is also the "God of Israel" (v. 18, according to Codex Sinaiticus). It continues with a comment on the dispersion and a reunification which here takes on the tones of a "conversion," both collective and personal (vv. 5–6).

Expressed in classical terms, this return journey is both physical and spiritual (v. 8). However, it leads to a centre: here it is, almost as a necessary deduction, the praise to Jerusalem (vv. 9–18) where the "king of heaven" (v. 9, Codices Alexandrinus and Vaticanus) will welcome many nations that will flow from the ends of the earth (v. 13, more explicitly in Sinaiticus and with clear reference to Isa 60). In this case, the religious model (we might say almost analogous to the prophecy in Sir 36) is recalled to Israel, but is at the same time proposed to the nations: although it may seem that the spiritual sublimation ennobles the path of conversion or return, in fact the others are forced to go through the ways of Israel, because the centre remains the same for everyone. That is, the universalization does not consist in a centrifugal expansion but in a centripetal concentration.

In the book that bears her name, Judith prepares for the decisive undertaking that will bring her victory over the dreaded Holofernes by way of a gesture of feminine astuteness, invoking her God for help (Jdt 9:1–14). It is an action that has a vindictive flavour and so begins from an "historic" *exemplum*, the justified punishment for the outrage done to Dinah at the time of the patriarchs (Gen 34). But the most profound motivation for this re-vindication that is about to be fulfilled is found in a God who is Creator and Lord of the universe. The elements of the world are at his disposal as members of a military army, thus commemorating a known cosmogonic motif. Therefore he must intervene not so much and not only against war enemies, but against those who oppress the weak (vv. 8–11, with a clear symbiosis between physical struggle and universalizing religious transposition). In this sense, God is almost morally obligated to intervene, because he is at the same time "God of my father, God of the heritage of Israel, Lord of heaven and earth, Creator of the waters, King of all your creation" (v. 12). De facto, one reads here a short (biblical) history of Israel, and even the way modern scholars reconstruct it in its evolution from a religious viewpoint: the God of the fathers, then the Yahwistic phase with its election of Israel, and finally the late expansion to creation. There is even a hint here of Jerusalem's centrality (v. 13), and especially the recognition of God as "the only One" at the same time he protects the progeny of Israel (v. 14). The contingent event of the fight against Holofernes also becomes an opportunity to elevate the present to the dignity of sacred history, assimilating it to a past that is considered as such. Particularly relevant here is the triangular structure of the passage: from concrete history one passes to the God of Israel, who manifests himself as the universal God. Appeal is made to this latter prerogative to require further intervention, that is revealing and saving, which defeats the enemy and exalts the weak. In fact, it is through the reflection of this composite image of God that one presents oneself before others.

Finally, there is one last text, or rather two passages similar to each other, which we read in the Greek expansion of the book of Esther. The prayer of Mordecai (EstGr 4:17a–h) immediately begins with the invocation of God who has power over the cosmos and history (v. 17b–c), and therefore also knows the present situation of the petitioner, that is, his innocence (v. 17d–e). Therefore the intervention of re-vindication required for the present is justified on the basis of historical antecedents represented by Abraham and the exodus event (v. 17f–g), and ends with a recognition that is by nature universal (v. 17h). Mordecai is like an intercessor who prays for the salvation of self and hence of his people, by appealing to the fact that no one can oppose his God when he decides to save Israel. In the analogous prayer of Esther, which follows immediately after (4:17k–z), it is interesting to note that from the very beginning the oneness of God is interwoven with the loneliness of Esther, as if there were founded the certainty of a hoped-for liberation (v. 17l). One then moves to the "historical creed," which Esther repeats here because she heard it from the tradition, within her own family (v. 17m). The need for divine intervention, which sounds almost compulsory, combines an invocation of salvation for one's people, who recognize themselves to be sinful, and the fact that their enemies are idol-worshipers (read: of other gods). The struggle is thus elevated to a divine plane and so it is clear that one's God is urged to commit himself to succeed as superior: he should not give up his scepter to those which "do not even exist," which should not "laugh at our fall" (v. 17o–q). It is clear that these statements have no ontological value, because they would become nonsensical. Rather, they intend to disqualify realities that cannot stand in the face of that God who is postulated as the victor. Just as our oppressive enemies identify themselves with their gods which are idols (which are vain), so we, though sinners, must succeed as victors because we are assimilated to you, "the only God," who is necessarily a victor. Note that the purely religious relationship with a God who induces his people to recognize their sin is here bypassed or resolved with a theodicy in which God himself is ensnared. Translated into more human terms, this means that the hope of the sinner finds its foundation not in a divine mercy understood as one attribute among many, but in a divine nature which is the result of a winning comparison; or at least it is such because it reflects the way the faithful think. The rest of Esther's prayer (v. 17r–z) is the application to the specific case of this "theology." Therefore, the "servant" can rejoice in the "Lord, God of Abraham," who however, is the one who exercises his strength over all and listens to the voice of the desperate (v. 17y–z). To the extent that the model is expressed on a religious level, it tends to become valid for everyone, but the concrete way it is applied is that of the historical creed of Israel: if others adopt it, they cannot fail to identify a universal God with the God of Israel. In other words, to get to know Israel one must (re)cognize its God, who acts as exclusive intermediary: the encounter between Israel and the others cannot leave aside this "supernatural" dimension.

The Transposition of the Image on the Cultural Level

Being a matter of prayer, it is obvious that the definition of self, which is evident in these texts, is expressed predominantly on a theological level. Nevertheless, we can find another equivalent that is elaborated with comparative categories on an historical-cultural plane. That is, we can briefly expand the view on the literature that does not fall into some biblical canon, but is equally relevant for a comprehension of the identity that Israel was about shaping. I refer to those fragmentary pieces of Judeo-Hellenistic works of authors who, especially in the field of historiography, have attempted a comparison between their own tradition and those of the civilizations that were close to them, and in particular the Greek one of the Hellenistic period (preeminent among whom are Demetrius, Eupolemus – including the text attributed by moderns to one Pseudo-Eupolemus – and Artapanus[19]). The fact that these people, when they revisit their past or refer to people like Abraham, Moses and Joseph, commemorate names and episodes that we know from the biblical text, does not mean that they knew this text in the form in which we possess it, nor that they attributed to it that authoritative weight that it has taken on through its "canonical" codification.

It is true that it can sometimes be difficult for us to track down an organic conception or a complete view of the "national" heritage that these authors may have outlined in their works, since we only possess fragments that we have received through other ancient authors who have incorporated them into their own works, mostly historiographical (among these especially Alexander Polyhistor, Flavius Josephus, Eusebius of Caesarea). Nevertheless, in some cases even the consistency and the breadth of the treatise that we read in the work of the mediator can give us an idea of the general intent of the ancient author that is quoted. Such is the case, for example, with the long celebratory exhibition of Moses found in the *Stromata* of Clement of Alexandria (I, 101–82 = chs. XXI–XXIX).[20] In general, the points on which the comparison is established, illustrating the priority and superiority of one's tradition or civilization, are basically two: the invention of goods of civilization, that are taught to the others by personages of one's history, and the Law of Moses, on which other ancient legislators draw.[21] But the comparison also regards other aspects of cultural heritage, one's own and that of the others, such as mythology. In this respect also a genealogy of one's past is exploited to absorb mythological units concerning foreign territories, almost to ascribe to oneself their intellectual and geographic conquest: consider the example of "Africa" in the short fragment of Cleodemus Malchas.[22] Overall, however, these writings are part of a literary movement that on the historiographical level dedicates itself to ethnographic reconstruction of one's own tradition which becomes conscious of itself, and especially of the distinctive features with which it legitimizes itself in a pluralistic environment. The most famous representatives of this literary genre remain Manetho for Egypt and Berossus for Babylon.[23] On the Jewish side there is an attempt to bring out the image that we have outlined above, where the formulation and theological priorities translate into a cultural celebration that extols the values related to one's Torah.[24] On the other hand it would be too reductive to consider these witnesses only in the light of an anti-Jewish polemic – which is certainly not absent, especially when one takes into account the exodus from Egypt,[25] or when the apologetic attitude is explicit (as in *Against Apion* by Flavius Josephus). We, however, are not so much interested here in following all aspects of Jewish historiography of antiquity, as to note how the self-image is formed in a broader literary context area compared to the biblical texts, to stay in tune with that comparison between biblical Israel and the Israel reconstructed by the (modern) historiography with which we began.

Implications

If we were now to draw some conclusions from this process that leads to define one's own identity by reconstructing a history and involving in it one's own God, we would have to emphasize once again that three factors play a role here: God, the people, and the others. However, it is difficult to identify from which one of the three to start, or which is the one on whom the other two rely: it is not necessarily the divine element, which enjoys primacy only in principle, but which in this correlation interacts with the other two on the same level. The same difficulty would arise even if we were to translate the correlation in terms of ethnicity and culture, or if we were to specify in what concrete relationship one wants to place oneself in relation to others. In concluding his analysis of the four biblical texts that we have examined, Zappella states: "The ethnic priority of Israel at this point becomes also a cultural priority."[26] This is true if we suppose an ethnic coherence to be already defined by one of the three elements at issue, which of course one does not deny but which here is still involved in a process that aims at defining it. If we carefully think about the correlation which we are speaking of, we can also assert the converse, namely that it is cultural priority which at least contributes to pinpoint ethnic priority.

If the terms within which identity is constructed are correctly understood, we should say that the ethnic aspect with which it is expressed, turns out to be of symbolic rank. This, regardless of the actual ethnic coherence that one might suppose and which is the task of historical research to trace. For this reason, it is malleable and can be transferred to other areas. The religious component, which is involved in an essential way, can become the instrument through which both the translation and the interpretation are implemented. To be more explicit, otherwise one would not understand the disputes over *verus Israel* that have arisen in the context of those communities of whom the writings of the New Testament are a witness: it is about defining an Israel that must retain the same exclusivist prerogatives of the starting one, that is, "biblical" (and after all it too aims at becoming "biblical"). It is clear that this symbolic value contains a potential political (even military) conflict, wherever the ethnic aspect tends to recur in real historical terms. This, however, does not happen only in this case, but rather each time the tradition or the biblical message are interpreted with an uncritical and fundamentalist approach, or are retranslated into concrete practice. Instead, the very nature of this identity thus defined means that it can be reformulated and applied to different historical contexts, by just resorting to the Bible. One can speak actually of a Bible under construction, as Alan T. Levenson tried to show for three modern environments in which Jewish identity has expressed or expresses itself in different ways.[27] It is this kind of identity that justifies a sort of re-appropriation of the Bible in a field of research that is explored mainly in a Christian environment, that is, in biblical theology: beyond the disputes arising in the past on this subject, and in particular on the nature and the coherence of a "Jewish" biblical theology, one can recognize that in this setting each of the two religious traditions projects, by a similar procedure, its own identity onto a biblical text which in turn is understood and exploited as a basis for it. The circularity of the process joins and legitimates self-consciousness by resorting to the image of a "biblical" Israel in which each tradition finds itself.[28]

However, there remains an unsolved problem. The universalism that the "biblical" identity thus obtained tries to reach, remains tied to a centre, which according to what has been said, may be formed by a God or by a people, and of which the reference to Jerusalem is only an idealized "geographical" expression. We noticed that in its "biblical" formulation, properly understood, universalism is malleable and translatable. Now, normally it is believed that its Christian version is proposed as truly universal, eliminating any barrier, even and especially "ethnic" (albeit in the symbolic terms which we are talking about). In the theoretical dispute over the existence of possibly universal religions, this qualification has certainly been recognized in Christianity. Yet at this stage of our reflection we are not interested in a similar fact; it is necessary, instead, to point out that in the alleged universalism recognized in Christianity is simply seen a universalization of European culture, as the American scholar Tomoko Masuzawa has stated a few years ago.[29] This kind of reproach is certainly a common finding, but also somewhat trivial. However, one cannot help but observe that one reproposes in different terms the problem of cultural priority that we have hinted at above. Then the doubt that the reference model, which is de facto and ultimately the "biblical" Israel, could actually dissolve itself from this bond might arise. In relation to the work of Masuzawa, there has recently been an attempt to connect this issue with the universalistic perspective of which both Abraham Kuenen and Julius Wellhausen spoke in their time. This situation was seen as a "persistence" of the Wellhausenian model.[30] As one recalls, Wellhausen saw in the biblical prophets a universalistic opening, suffocated by the particularism of the Torah, which prevailed. Therefore – as it was for Kuenen – Judaism remains linked to particularism while Christianity imposes itself as universal. In reality, the issue goes beyond the Wellhausenian terms and certainly beyond the Hegelian ideological background that inspires them. It may be noted that Wellhausen did not take into account "biblical" Israel in its entirety. However, the main issue of the problem does not reside in this point; rather, it is in the easy solution which consists of an escape towards a universalism that in the end remains hypothetical and artificial. Returning to our problems and the triad God, people, and the others, since these elements are closely linked, even if one starts from God one cannot escape the dilemma. When it comes to dialogue between religions or "inculturation," one should first of all reflect on the possibilities but also on the limits within which "biblical" Israel can be interpreted, inasmuch as it is an "identity expression" of the "historical" Israel.

Notes

1. Giovanni Garbini, *Scrivere la storia d'Israele* (Bibliografia di storia e storiografia dei tempi biblici 15; Brescia: Paideia, 2008), p. 11.
2. Gian Luigi Prato, "L'antico Israele tra storia e memoria: una storia d'Israele 'scritta' da Giovanni Garbini," *Rivista Biblica* 47 (2009), pp. 93–100.
3. Philip R. Davies, *The Origins of Biblical Israel* (LHBOTS 485; New York/London: T&T Clark International, 2007). See also my review of this volume in *Rivista Biblica* 68 (2010), pp. 501–506.
4. As an introduction to the problem, see Kenton L. Sparks, *Ethnicity and Identity in Ancient Israel: Prolegomena to the Study of Ethnic Sentiments and Their Expression in the Hebrew Bible* (Winona Lake, IN: Eisenbrauns, 1998), and then in particular Doron Mendels, *The Rise and Fall of Jewish Nationalism* (ABRL; New York: Doubleday, 1992); Stuart D. E. Weeks, "Biblical Literature and the Emergence of Ancient Jewish Nationalism," *BibInt* 12 (2002), pp. 144–57; David Goodblatt, *Elements of Ancient Jewish Nationalism* (Cambridge: Cambridge University Press, 2006); also useful are the collected essays of Steven Elliott Grosby, *Biblical Ideas of Nationality: Ancient and Modern* (Winona Lake, IN: Eisenbrauns, 2002).
5. Erich S. Gruen, *Heritage and Hellenism: The Reinvention of Jewish Tradition* (Hellenistic Culture and Society 30; Berkeley: University of California Press, 1998); Siân Jones and Sarah Pearce (eds.), *Jewish Local Patriotism and Self-Identification in the Graeco-Roman Period* (JSPSup 31; Sheffield: Sheffield Academic Press, 1998); Meir Sternberg, *Hebrews between Cultures: Group Portraits and National Literature* (Indiana Studies in Biblical Literature; Bloomington: Indiana University Press, 1998); Matthias Konradt and Ulrike Steinert (eds.), *Ethos und Identität: Einheit und Vielfalt des Judentums in hellenistisch-römischer Zeit* (Studien zu Judentum und Christentum; Paderborn: Ferdinand Schöning, 2002); Lee I. Levine and Daniel R. Schwartz (eds.), *Jewish Identities in Antiquity: Studies in Memory of Menahem Stern* (Texte und Studien zum Antiken Judentum 130; Tübingen: Mohr Siebeck, 2009).
6. Jacob Neusner and Ernest S. Frerichs (eds.), *"To See Ourselves as Others See Us": Christians, Jews, "Others" in Late Antiquity* (Scholars Press Studies in the Humanities Series; Chico, CA: Scholars Press, 1985); Robert Goldenberg, *The Nations that Know Thee Not: Ancient Jewish Attitudes towards Other Religions* (The Biblical Seminar 52; Sheffield: Sheffield Academic Press, 1997).
7. Jacob L. Wright, *Rebuilding Identity: The Nehemiah-Memoir and Its Earliest Readers* (BZAW 348; Berlin: de Gruyter, 2004); cf., in connection with this volume, Gary N. Knoppers (ed.), "Revisiting the Composition of Ezra–Nehemiah: In Conversation with Jacob Wright's *Rebuilding Identity: The Nehemiah-Memoir and Its Earliest Readers*," *Journal of Hebrew Scriptures* 7, Article 12 (online: https://ejournals.library.ualberta.ca/index.php/jhs/article/view/5646/0). Along with Knoppers, Deirdre N. Fulton, David M. Carr and Ralph W. Klein took part in the panel discussion.
8. Peter Hon Wan Lau, *Identity and Ethics in the Book of Ruth: A Social Identity Approach* (BZAW 416; Berlin: de Gruyter, 2010).

9. Sara Raup Johnson, *Historical Fictions and Hellenistic Jewish Identity: Third Maccabees in Its Cultural Context* (Hellenistic Culture and Society 43; Berkeley: University of California Press, 2004).

10. Dermot Anthony Nestor, *Cognitive Perspectives on Israelite Identity* (LHBOTS 519; New York: T&T Clark International, 2010).

11. The numbering of the verses of this passage is rather complex. For the sake of simplicity, I follow here that of the critical edition of the Greek text edited by Joseph Ziegler (*Sapientia Jesu Filii Sirach* [Septuaginta – Vetus Testamentum Graecum XII/2; Göttingen: Vandenhoeck & Ruprecht, 2nd edn, 1980], pp. 290–92). As is known, we also possess this text in Hebrew (= 36:1–17), preserved in manuscript B (with its precious marginal notes), among those discovered in the Cairo *genizah* at the end of the nineteenth century. For an edition of this text, cf. Pancratius C. Beentjes, *The Book of Ben Sira in Hebrew: A Text Edition of All Extant Hebrew Manuscripts and a Synopsis of All Parallel Hebrew Ben Sira Texts* (VTSup 58; Leiden: Brill, 1997), pp. 62–63.

12. As testified by the meticulous work of Maria Carmela Palmisano, *"Salvaci, Dio dell'universo!": Studio dell'eucologia di Sir 36H, 1–17* (Analecta Biblica 163; Rome: Editrice Pontificio Istituto Biblico, 2006).

13. The Hebrew text concludes the verse with the expression "to us," which is corrected in the marginal note of the manuscript B with "to them." This way it agrees with Greek and carefully balances the two statements of the verse.

14. So Marco Zappella, "L'immagine dell'elezione come strumento dell'esaltazione apologetica di Israele secondo quattro testi ebraici in lingua greca (Tobia, Ben Sira, Giuditta, Ester)," in Cristina Termini (ed.), *L'elezione di Israele: origini bibliche, funzione e ambiguità di una categoria teologica*. Atti del XIII Convegno di Studi Veterotestamentari (Foligno, 8–10 Settembre 2003), *Ricerche storico bibliche* 17/1 (2005), pp. 167–201 (174); the essay tackles with a detailed analysis of the four texts we are dealing with and recommends itself for its acute observations on the issue within which we consider them.

15. In v. 17 we note an interesting divergence between the Hebrew "whom you called firstborn" (with etymological allusion to the episode of Gen 32:23–33, esp. 29, but in connection with Hos 12:4–5) and the Greek "whom you made like a firstborn" (with attenuation of one's own qualification in front of other people; however, some minuscule codices have a verb which is equivalent to the Hebrew one; cf. the critical apparatus of Ziegler, p. 291). Regardless, even in this case the birthright is not so much the result of an election in the course of time but a prerogative fixed at creation; cf. again Zappella, "L'immagine dell'elezione," pp. 176–79.

16. While in the Hebrew text in v. 19b God is invoked to fill the temple with his glory, in the Greek text he is prayed to fill the people with his "aretalogy." This particular interpretation should be safeguarded, reading in Greek *laon* ("people") rather than emending it to *naon* ("temple") on the basis of the Hebrew *hekal* (as unfortunately one reads in Ziegler, p. 209, against all the evidence of the codices and ancient versions): just as in aretalogies or in aretalogical genre a deity exalts itself or is magnified for the miracles it works, so here the people must itself become an aretalogical celebration of its own divinity. If Hebrew is understandable within the boundaries of Israel itself, here the horizon considerably widens and adapts to the cultural parameters of the Greek world. For an ample treatment of v. 19 in the

context of the entire passage, see Marco Zappella, "L'immagine di Israele in Sir 33(36),1–19 secondo il ms. ebraico B e la tradizione manoscritta greca. Analisi letteraria e lessicale," *Rivista Biblica* 42 (1994), pp. 409–46, esp. 427–35; cf. also briefly *idem*, "L'immagine dell'elezione," pp. 196–97.

17. Cf. also Palmisano, *"Salvaci, Dio dell'universo!,"* pp. 229–71.

18. See, for example, the short prayer voiced by Jonathan, accompanied by Nehemiah and the choir of those present, in 2 Macc 1:24–29.

19. Their Greek texts are collected in Felix Jacoby, *Die Fragmente der griechischen Historiker*, IIIC/2 (Leiden: E. J. Brill, 1958), pp. 667–83 (= nr. 722–24 and 726); cf. also Carl R. Holladay, *Fragments from Hellenistic Jewish Authors*. I. *Historians* (Society of Biblical Literature – Texts and Translations 20/Pseudepigrapha 10; Chico, CA: Scholars Press, 1983), pp. 51–91, 93–156, 170–77, 204–22.

20. Cf. Clément d'Alexandrie, *Les Stromates – Stromate I. Introduction de Claude Mondésert - Traduction et notes de Marcel Caster* (Sources chrétiennes 30, Paris: du Cerf, 1951), pp. 126–77.

21. I treated it in more detail in my "Cosmopolitismo culturale e autoidentificazione etnica nella prima storiografia giudaica," *Rivista Biblica* 34 (1986), pp. 143–82, esp. 151–60 (now also in Gian Luigi Prato, *Identità e memoria nell'Israele antico: Storiografia e confronto culturale negli scritti biblici e giudaici* [Biblioteca di storia e storiografia dei tempi biblici 16; Brescia: Paideia, 2010], pp. 232–65, esp. 239–46).

22. Starting from the offspring of Abraham and Keturah (Gen 25:1–4), and speculating on the names of Efa and Efer of the biblical text, one arrives at the name "Africa." This offspring is combined with the undertakings of Heracles against Libya and the giant Antaeus. These statements attributed to Cleodemus Malchas are reported by Flavius Josephus (*Ant*. 1.238–41), who says to have drawn on Polyhistor (but see also Eusebius, *Praep. ev*. 9.20.2–4). For the Greek text, cf. Jacoby, *Fragmente*, pp. 686–87 (= nr. 727).

23. Cf. Gregory E. Sterling, *Historiography and Self-Definition: Josephos, Luke–Acts and Apologetic Historiography* (VTSup 64; Leiden: Brill, 1992), pp. 103–225 (and my critical review of the work in *Gregorianum* 74 [1993], pp. 751–59).

24. It is precisely under this aspect that the cited authors, together with other Jewish-Hellenistic writings, are treated in Reinhard Weber, *Das Gesetz im hellenistischen Judentum: Studien zum Verständnis und zur Funktion der Thora von Demetrios bis Pseudo-Phokylides* (Arbeiten zur Religion und Geschichte des Urchristentums 10; Frankfurt am Main: Peter Lang, 2000).

25. On the entire issue, we simply refer to Peter Schäfer, *Judeophobia: Attitudes toward the Jews in the Ancient World* (Cambridge, MA: Harvard University Press, 1997). For the Italian translation, by Eleonora Tagliaferro and Marcello Lupi, see *Giudeofobia: L'antisemitismo nel mondo antico* (Rome: Carocci, 1999 [repr.: Quality Paperbacks, 135, 2004]).

26. Zappella, "L'immagine dell'elezione," p. 186.

27. Alan T. Levenson, *The Making of the Modern Jewish Bible: How Scholars in Germany, Israel, and America Transformed an Ancient Text* (Lanham, MD: Rowman & Littlefield, 2011). As enunciated in the title itself and then exposed in the book, in Germany the Bible was read in order to define a religious identity, while

in Israel it served to strengthen national identity (one recalls, e.g., David Ben-Gurion), and in America it gave a clearer configuration to the Jewish component of that pluralist society.

28. An approach from a Jewish point of view is outlined in Marvin A. Sweeney, *Tanak: A Theological and Critical Introduction to the Jewish Bible* (Minneapolis, MN: Fortress Press, 2011).

29. See Tomoko Masuzawa, *The Invention of World Religions: Or, How European Universalism Was Preserved in the Language of Pluralism* (Chicago: University of Chicago Press, 2005). The work has been criticized not so much for this concept of European culture as for the idea itself of the universal religion and its possible historical manifestations; cf., e.g., Finbarr Curtis in *Epoché: The University of California Journal for the Study of Religion* 23 (2005), pp. 265–69.

30. See Walter Brueggemann and Davies Hankins, "The Invention and Persistence of Wellhausen's World," *CBQ* 75 (2013), pp. 15–31.

ETHNICITY AND THE BIBLE: MULTIPLE JUDAISMS

Thomas L. Thompson

Palestine and Ethnicity

In this study I wish to address one of the central ideological roles that the Bible has played in our understanding of both ancient Israel and early Judaism: that role assumed to be reflected in the implicit voice of that tradition, in terms of which what has been narrated has been judged.[1] Palestine, or the Southern Levant, has – economically or geographically – neither integrity nor any implicit unity of its own. This southern fringe of Syria's "Mediterranean economy" with its regionally determined cash crops based in specializations of grain agriculture, herding and terraced-based horticulture and viniculture, fostered a fragmentation of the population into many small units spread over some 30 ecologically distinct regions, which distinguished themselves, both politically and in terms of sedentarization, since at least the Early Bronze Age.[2] The geographical fragmentation of the Bronze Age, moreover, supported a local patronage system, organized in small, but regionally dominant towns and associated clusters of villages and encampments. This regional character, since very early times, supported a patronage form of society, which was centred around small burghs under the control of each region's patron, providing Palestine's many small enclaves with both markets and defence. Political domination over the whole area of Palestine – to the extent it existed at all in the ancient South Levant – has ever been imperial and external. This is important not only for our own historical strategies – for we have not one, but many more than a dozen histories to write – but also for understanding the ideology of ethnicity in our biblical texts.

The typical structure of Palestinian politics in antiquity becomes particularly clear in the more than three-century-long transition between the Late Bronze II and Iron II periods. Already in the Late Bronze Age, the entire western Levant suffers economic stress, periodically intensified by drought, collapse of trade and changes in imperial and political support systems. The Palestinian coast was host to immigration – especially from the Aegean and coastal Anatolia as a result of the Great Mycenean drought – and was witness to a long process of assimilation. Other regions – most notably the highlands, where the border of aridity moved north of Jerusalem – suffer a process of desedentarization, including a shift in their economy towards pastoralism. In yet other regions, depopulation is so sudden and destructive that they are threatened with demographic collapse. While the drought-induced collapse of trade left no region unchanged, each followed its own timetable and specific variation of stress, collapse and recovery. Just as it is a mistake to speak singularly of the effects of drought in the Late Bronze period throughout the whole of Palestine, it is also a mistake to think of recovery as a coherent and singular return to prosperity. Of the thirty or so geographic sub-regions of Western Palestine, it can be said that no two or three of them witnessed a common history of the transition from the beginning of the drought at the onset of the Late Bronze Period to the great expansion of the population in Iron Age II. The relations of sub-regions to one another affected primarily the periphery of the neighbour. Such conditions readily require a small regional orientation of the historian in his presentation of the onset of the Assyrian period. Palestine's system of local patrons – as, for example, witnessed as early as the "Execration Texts" and the Amarna tablets – undermined the development of power, embracing multiple regions, except in the formation of coalitions among at least nominally equal patrons to meet specific crises or threats. The petty chiefdoms and small kingdoms based in a considerable number of small, heavily fortified towns, which dominated Palestine in the Early and Middle Bronze Age continued to define the political landscape of the Iron Age.[3]

The re-introduction of imperial politics in the region in the mid-ninth century, however, brought Assyrian influence to bear on Palestine's patrons in such regional centers as Gaza, Ashkelon, Ekron, Tantura, Akka, Lakisi, Gazri, Urusalim, Samaria, Megiddo, Hasura and Dan. While this hardly encouraged coherent, ethnic autonomies, it supported and strengthened indigenous political patronage and the traditional market economy. At the same time the mixed patterns of settlement and economy in the many, small regions of Palestine, effectively prevented any single region from accumulating power sufficient to maintain an indigenous opposition to the Assyrians. Although Shalmanezer III, for example, met an initially effective resistance from a Syro-Palestinian coalition mustered by Hadadezer of Damascus at the Battle of Qarqar in 853 BCE, he had brought Syria and the whole of northern Palestine under Assyrian tribute by 841 and hardly a decade later had brought Tyre, Megiddo and Damascus, along with their client regions, directly into the Assyrian empire, as far South as the southern edge of the Jezreel and Beisan valleys and, in the Transjordan, the northern border of Bit Ammani. The regional fragmentation of Palestinian politics gave no resistance to the Assyrian takeover. Indeed, the Assyrian provincial system rather stabilized the local, indigenous orientation of its population. When resistance to Assyrian policies threatened stability in any substantive way, imperial policies of deportation and re-settlement[4] not only effectively eliminated such resistance and provided Assyria's armies and growing cities with fresh troops and workers, but also created foreign colonies under its patronage, which were wholly dependent on Assyrian patronage for their legitimacy. Such policies continued to be used with effect by the Persians, Macedonians and Romans, in their turn, effectively eliminating any sense of Palestine as a whole.

Geography and Ethnic Cohesion

I have dealt with the geographic and ethnic fragmentation of Palestine elsewhere.[5] Awareness of this fragmentation and of the indigenous structural divisions of Palestine's economy, which was strengthened under imperial domination, make it paramount for historians to present both evidence and argument before asserting the existence of a people or any coherence in the population within the borders of the Southern Levant. Without such evidence, we cannot speak of ancient Palestine in any "national," ethnic or analogous way. Although the legend of Jacob becoming Israel offers a remarkable reiteration of the Merneptah stele's mythic song of Pharaoh – where Pharaoh has brought fertility to his bride Khurru, a female figure personifying the land of Palestine, who is now the widow of the former patron of Palestine, Yisr'r, "whose seed is no more"[6] – this song's mythic quality, like that of Israel, the biblical patriarch and his 12 sons becoming 12 tribes and inheriting the whole of the land of Palestine, cannot be read as if it rendered history. Neither Otto Eissfeldt's understanding of the patriarchal narratives as tribal saga[7] or Kathleen Kenyon's and G. Buccellati's view of them as reflecting a migration of Amorites[8] ever provided grounds for their initial assumptions about the Bible's ancient tropes of ethnicity, which centre around the theme of the Benei Yisra'el as the "people of God," Yahweh's "firstborn" and "inheritance."

Yahweh and His People

Genesis's motifs hardly reflect historical past, but they rather cluster around themes of promise and hope as in Ezra's referents to Jer 29:10 and in its allegorical reiterations of Isa 44–45. Ezra's "Yahweh, the god of Israel" has been transformed from 2 Chr 36:23's "Yahweh, the God of Heaven, whose home is to be in Jerusalem of Judah," in the introduction to Ezra's ironic critique of the theme of "holy-war." In Ezra's version of Cyrus' decree, Yahweh's people are to go up to Jerusalem, which is in Judah, and "build the house of Yahweh, the god of Israel" [sic] – He is the god who (shall be) in Jerusalem." The critical question is the supersessionist transfer of the god from Israel to Judah. The geographical rhetoric, I think, is pertinent. What is the implicit identification of Yahweh in the reference that a temple to Yahweh of Israel be built in Judah's Jerusalem? Is Yahweh so identified because of the temple on Gerizim? And does this variation on the decree refer to the Chronicler's ideologically supersessionist centralization of Yahweh's cult in Jerusalem – an ideology, whose legitimacy Ezra 10's ironic polemic questions deeply? [9]

The Chronicler's *Yahweh hashamayim* is already very clear to us from the Neo-Assyrian period's *Baʾal shamem*, the expansive cults of the Harran's lunar cult of *Sin* and from the many references in the Persian period to the "god of heaven," as well as from the Hellenistic references to the solar deity *Helios*, especially in the role of representing cosmic order, which is often identified with Yahweh. In the Bible, however, we often find Yahweh playing a role within the perspective of inclusive monotheism. Yahweh plays the role of the divine name; he is *Yahweh, ʾeloha yisraʾel*, the "messenger" of *El Elyon*. He is not himself *ʾelohé Shamayim*, but the past's representation of god.[10] In Exod 3:12, Yahweh is *Elohim* in that he is *ʾehyeh ʿimak*; that is, Emanu'el, as in Isa 8:8, 10.[11] In the biblical discourse on the presence of the divine, the multiplicity of divine names, epithets, art and symbol, familiar to us – but not to the Bible – from archaeology and inscriptions from the Iron Age through the Hellenistic period, become transformed in the biblical tradition through the systematic interpretation and reflection on the divine, as a coherent reality of the heavens, as well as on its diverse, but also false and distorting, characteristics as they are understood from human traditions; that is, those traditions about god of old and lost Israel.

The question of the biblical Yahweh's historicity can be clarified quickly with reference to the theme of divine inspiration in the narrative of Exod 31–34. The story opens with reference to the divinely inspired Hephaestus-like figure of the craftsman Bezalel, to create all of the furniture for the Tent of Meeting (Exod 31:1–11). Reiterating such inspiration, he then gives to Moses the tables of stone, with the law and the commandments (from Exod 24:12–18), "written with the finger of God" (Exod 31:18)! Here, however, such inspiration and revelation is fatally undermined by Aaron's golden calf, which opens the comic scene of divine wrath, whose reiteration structures the Pentateuch's narrative of Exodus–Numbers (cf. Exod 32; Num 11 and Num 13–14). Yahweh will destroy them and make a new people with Moses. Moses, however, calms Yahweh, "who repents of the evil he intended against his people" (Exod 32:14). When Moses, however, then descends the mountain with the two tables of the testimony in his hands: "the work of God and the writing was the writing of God, cut into the tables" (Exod 32:16), it is his turn to throw a tantrum in imitation of the divine wrath: "He threw the tablets down and broke them at the foot of the mountain" (Exod 32:19). In the final closure of this narrative, Yahweh – rather than writing, himself, the words that were on the broken tables (Exod 34:1) – makes a new covenant with a repentant Israel and orders Moses to write the "words of this covenant" on his new tables of stone, as the divine remains ever at a distance (Exod 34:27–35), traceable only in the transformation of Moses' face. It is in such restructuring of the tradition that the implied voices of the Bible become clear.

The question of Yahweh's historicity is clarified by the Pentateuch with a Mosaic *torah*, as the biblical authors hold the Yahweh of history ever at a distance, even as the extra-biblical Yahweh[12] may not be entirely unknown to the Bible's story world. The earliest known references to Yahweh comes first in the Middle Bronze Mari letters and in the form of a toponym in fourteenth-/thirteenth-century Egyptian texts, which is associated with the land of Shasu Bedouin and possibly with the region of Se'ir in Edom. We also have considerable evidence for a plurality of Yahwehs from the Iron Age. We know a Yahu/Jau of Nebo (captured by Mesha for Ashtar-Chemosh) and Yahweh of Teman and Samaria with his Asherah – including possible pictures – from Kuntillet ʿAjrud. Such references could well imply the existence of cult places or temples dedicated to the deity. We also have a considerable number of personal names with a Yah, Yau or Yahu theophoric element over a considerable geographic spread. Such theophoric names may include the royal names, Azriyau and Yau-/Ilu-bidi in Syrian Hamat. A number of societies are reflected, which variously identified this divine name with such central divine functions as fertility and weather. Baʾal and Hadad are better-known names for a deity of this type.

Jews and Judaea

We also find Yahweh in later periods: from Elephantine's Yahw to Philo of Byblos's Jao. Nor is the god Ieuw of northern Syria, mentioned by Eusebius, to be ignored. We find Persian-period coins with Yahweh's image and symbols.[13] In the Persian and Hellenistic periods, we find Yahweh temples or references to them at Gerizim, Jerusalem, Leontopolis, Araq al-Amir, Sereinica and possibly Beersheva. Such an extra-biblical Yahweh is hardly unknown to the biblical narrative. Deuteronomy 33:2, Judg 5:4 and Hab 3:3, for example, associate Yahweh's origins with Sinai, Edom, Midian, Seir, Teman and Paran. Yet, the literary Yahweh, which we meet in the Bible, is deeply anachronistic and only marginally confirmed by the Yahwehs of history. Our problem of historicity, is not entirely resolved by the Bible's theological reinterpretation of Yahweh. It is also a problem of the Bible's implied voice over against its historical context, which we typically assume to be Jewish, understood variously and uncertainly to describe either an ethnic or religious quality.

Judaea is first of all a geographic name, which, in biblical and archaeological scholarship is often used to refer variously to include several regions, such as the southern Jordan Valley, the western shores of the Dead Sea basin, the northern Negev, the Judean desert, the Judean highlands, the Jerusalem saddle, the southern Shephelah and the southern coastal plain. In contrast, the name the region or district of *Jaudáa/Jaudí* and the province of *Yehud* are political names of, respectively, a patronage kingdom in southern Palestine (*Pilishté*) during the Assyrian-Babylonian periods and an imperial province of the Persian–Early Hellenistic periods.[14] *Jaudáa* was bordered by *ʾAduma* and *Maʾab* to the East, Gaza and Ashkelon to the West and *Bit Humri* to the North, while *Yehud* was bordered by *Idumea*, centred in Lachish, to the Southeast, South and West and the province of *Samerina* to the North. The name Judah is primarily fictive and eponymic and is used to refer to the patriarch Judah, son of Jacob, as well as to the region and kingdom of Judah as heritage of the descendants of Judah, while *Yehudim* referred variously to both the religious cult of Jerusalem and to contemporary or former residents of *Yehud*.[15] However, the geographic spread of people referred to as *Yehudim* in antiquity is so great that it would be rash to assume that this name refers to their actual place of origin.

Judaism and Ethnicity

Even less can we understand the term "Jew" as an ethnic designation. By the Rabbinic period, *yehudim* is clearly religiously descriptive and it is such religious association which seems most constant in the spread of the name in the Roman Empire. Both Philip Davies and Jacob Neusner have independently clarified much in this discussion, insisting that we understand the term religiously rather than ethnically, as well as to suggest that we speak of "many Judaisms" in antiquity.[16] This is a significant discussion already in regard to the Persian Period, where the ambiguity of the term "Jew" becomes apparent.

Jedoniah, priest of the military colony of Elephantine, sent a letter in 407 BCE, on behalf of his fellow priests and Jews: the citizens of Elephantine, to the governor of *Yehud* to ask support in rebuilding their temple, dedicated to *Yaho*, which had been destroyed by the Egyptians. He claims that the temple and military colony had been in Elephantine since pre-Persian times. Whether the Jews of Jerusalem recognize such religious ties is uncertain and their identity as "Jews" makes no explicit claim of origins in *Yehud* or *Judáa*. They use the designation "Aramaean" in contrast with "Egyptian." They use the self-identifying designation "Aramean," which contrasts with "Egyptian." They also may have originally come from the South Levant, given the dominance of West-Semitic and, especially, Yahwistic theophoric personal names, together with numerous Hebraisms in their Aramaic. The deities supported by this "Jewish" garrison – *Yaho*, *Ishumbethel* and *Anathbethel* – probably reflect South-Syrian origins. Other deities, of more international origins, are honoured by Elephantine's "Jews": an oath is sworn to the goddess *Sati* and greetings are given to *Bel* and *Nabu*, *Shamash* and *Nergal*, *Jaho* and *Knub*. The traditional nexus of religion and family makes it difficult to conclude the "Jewish" religious associations, suggested by their proper names and their deity *Jaho*, are to be understood as ethnic. Far as they are from the relative homogeneity of a provincial homeland, immigrants are, ethnically speaking, notoriously promiscuous. Mibtahiah, daughter of Mahseiah, son of Yedoniah (Yahwist names all) offers a wonderful example for understanding Jewish associations in the *diaspora*. Her grandfather, Yedoniah, is described as an "Aramaean of Syene,"[17] while her father, Mahsehiah, in another text, is described as a "Jew." Obviously, this is a term that does not exclude one also being an "Aramaean" as by Mibtahiah's third marriage, her father is described, like his father before him, as an Aramaean from Syene. Mibtahiah's first husband had a Yahwist name, Yezanaiah, as well as a Yahwist patronym, ben Uriah. Her second husband, however, bears the Egyptian name Piʾ,

with the Egyptian patronym Phi. He was a builder at the fortress of Syene. Her third husband, also a builder, bears the Egyptian name Ashor, with the Egyptian patronym Seho. However, he later adopts the Hebrew name Nathan. Whether this is for family or religious reasons is a moot point.

Josephus' Ubiquitous Jews

In Book 12 of *Antiquities*, Josephus recounts an etiology of the Jews of Egypt as the result of deportations under Ptolemy: "from the mountains of Judea and from the places about Jerusalem, Samaria and near Mount Gerizim" (*Ant.* 12.1.1). These he describes as two groups – nevertheless, Jews all – who dispute whether they should send their tribute to Jerusalem or to Samaria. The interesting issue is that Josephus presents the diaspora as both of disparate origins and loyalties and as functioning as a single community. In this, he echoes 2 Macc 6:1–2's understanding of the Samaritans and their temple as "Jewish"! The term bears neither an ethnic nor a geographic referent, but, rather, describes a religious association or identity. Josephus' attempt to refute the Samaritan claim in *Ant.* 12.5.5 that their Sabbath observance and the propriety of their sacrifices had derived from their "forefathers" by claiming that they, in fact, were not Jews, but Sidonians, is supported by the claim that they had changed the name of their temple to "the temple of Jupiter Hellenius." He goes on to accuse them of claiming to be Jews only when it suits them and seeking a remission of taxes by claiming to be descendants of Joseph, Ephraim and Manasseh and by observing the Jubilee year: claiming to be true Hebrews, but only Sidonians in name (*Ant.* 11.8.6)! Josephus, of course, here ignores his own explanation (*Ant.* 12.2.4–5) that Yahweh was, indeed, to be identified with Jupiter Hellenius and that the renaming of the Samaritan temple hardly implied apostasy! Implicitly, Josephus witnesses to the fact that the Samaritans upheld the traditions as their own (esp. *Ant.* 11.8.7).

We find that Egyptians are Jews, Syrians are Jews, Samaritans are Jews. Josephus refers to Jews throughout the inhabitable earth and of "those that worshipped God" through Asia and Europe. He speaks of knowing of Jews carried captive beyond the Euphrates. Citing Strabo, he fills much of Alexandria with Jews and Jews live in many of Egypt's cities, in Cyrene and Cyprus. They control Cleopatra's army. "It is hard to find a place...that has not admitted this tribe of men and is not possessed by them" (*Ant.* 13.10.4 and 14.7.2). He speaks of the Jews of the diaspora much as did Philo: they are model citizens of the empire.

Indeed, nations imitate the Jews and, learning from them, become prosperous by following their laws. Josephus' Jews of the Diaspora are also matched by his description of the "Jewish cities" of Palestine, including the cities of the Transjordan, Idumea, Phoenicia and the great cities of Syria, among which he mentions Apollonia, Joppa, Jamnia, Ashdod, Gaza, Ashqelon, Raphia, Rhinocolura, Aora, Marissa, Scythopolis, Gadara, Seleucia, Gabala, Heshbon, Madaba, Lemba, Oronas, Gelithon, Zara and Pella (*Ant.* 13.15.3–4). Josephus seems to identify as Jews all who believe in the Almighty God. Even followers of Jesus – both Jews and Gentiles – form part of his comprehension of Judaism (*Ant.* 18.3.3).

The Theology of the Way

While Josephus tended to include all among the growing adherents of monotheism as Jews, Philo made sharp and uncompromising distinctions. For this Jew of Alexandria, it was "we Greeks" who stood in the path of truth: against the Barbarians; we Jews, descendants of the *Hebraioi*, against the Egyptians, the godless and the *ethnoi*!

Notes

1. As understood by G. Garbini, *History and Ideology in Ancient Israel* (London: Crossroads, 1988). The central theme of this study has been taken up earlier in T. L. Thompson, "Hidden Histories and the Problem of Ethnicity in Palestine," in M. Pryor (ed.), *Western Scholarship and the History of Palestine* (London: Melisende, 1998), pp. 23–40.

2. T. L. Thompson, *The Settlements of Palestine in the Bronze Age* (BTAVO 34; Wiesbaden: Dr. Reichert Verlag, 1979); for the following, see Thompson, *Early History of the Israelite People from the Written and Archaeological Sources* (Leiden: Brill, 1992), pp. 205–300.

3. Contra G. Buccellati, *Cities and Nations of Ancient Syria: An Essay on Political Institutions with Special Reference to the Israelite Kingdom* (Rome: Istituto di Studi Del Vicino Oriente, Università di Roma, 1967).

4. B. Oded, *Mass Deportation and Deportees in the Neo-Assyrian Empire* (Wiesbaden: Harrassowitz, 1979).

5. Thompson, *The Settlement of Palestine*, pp. 5–68; idem, *Early History*, pp. 301–10, 334–39; idem, "Ethnicity and a Regional History of Palestine," in Ingrid Hjelm and Thomas L. Thompson (eds.), *History, Archaeology and the Bible Forty Years After "Historicity": Changing Perspectives 6* (CIS; Abingdon: Routledge, 2016), pp. 159–73.

6. I. Hjelm and T. L. Thompson, "The Victory Song of Merneptah: Israel and the People of Palestine," *JSOT* 27 (2002), pp. 3–18.

7. O. Eissfeldt, "Stammessage und Novelle in den Geschichten von Jakob und vom seinen Söhnen," *Eucharisterion* (1923), pp. 56–77.

8. K. Kenyon, *Amorites and Canaanites* (London: Oxford University Press, 1966); G. Buccellati, *The Amorites of the Ur III Period* (Naples: Istituto Orientale di Napoli, 1966); T. L. Thompson, *The Historicity of the Patriarchal Narratives: The Quest for the Historical Abraham* (Berlin: de Gruyter, 1974), pp. 67–143.

9. See, on this reading of Ezra: T. L. Thompson, "Holy War at the Center of Biblical Theology: *Shalom* and Cleansing of Jerusalem," in T. L. Thompson (ed.), *Jerusalem in Ancient History and Tradition* (JSOTSup 381; London: T&T Clark International, 2003), pp. 223–57.

10. H. Röllig, "Baal-Shamem," *DDD*, pp. 283–88; H. Nier, *Der Höchste Gott*, (BZAW 190; Berlin: de Gruyter, 1990); idem, "The Rise of YHWH in Judahite and Israelite Religion: Methodological and Religio-Historical Aspects," in D. Edelman (ed.), *The Triumph of Elohim* (Kampen: Pharos, 1995), pp. 45–74.

11. T. L. Thompson, "How Yahweh Became God: Exodus 3 and 6 and the Heart of the Pentateuch," *JSOT* 68(1995), pp. 57–74.

12. For an excellent discussion of the name Yahweh in extra-biblical texts, see K. van der Toorn, "Yahweh," *DDD*, pp. 1711–30.

13. D. Edelman, "Tracking Observance of the Aniconic Tradition Through Numismatics," in eadem (ed.), *The Triumph of Elohim*, pp. 185–225.

14. Hezekiah is referred to by Sennacherib as *amel Jaudáa* ("man of Jaudáa"). See J. B. Pritchard, *Ancient Near Eastern Texts Related to the Old Testament* (Princeton: Princeton University Press, 1969), pp. 287–88.

15. For this and the following, see also T. L. Thompson, "Memories of Esau and Narrative Reiteration: Themes of Conflict and Reconciliation," *SJOT* 25.2 (2011), pp. 174–200; idem, "Palestine's Pre-Islamic Heritage: A Proposal for Palestinian High-School Curriculum Revision," *HLS* 12 (2013), pp. 1–21.

16. P. R. Davies, "Scenes from the Early History of Jerusalem," in Edelman (ed.), *The Triumph of Elohim*, pp. 145–82; J. Neusner, "Was Rabbinic Judaism Really Ethnic?," *CBQ* 57 (1995), pp. 281–305; see also, more recently, S. Sand, *The Invention of the Jewish People* (London: Verso, 2009); Thompson, "Palestine's Pre-Islamic Heritage," pp. 9–11.

17. For this and the following, see Pritchard, "Aramaic Papyri from Elephantine," *ANET*, pp. 222–23 and "Letters of the Jews in Elephantine," *ANET*, pp. 491–92.

CORRESPONDENCE*

Jim West

In late 1989 Giovanni Garbini's *History and Ideology in Ancient Israel*[1] landed on my desk as an early Christmas present to myself whilst I was in the final stages of completing a Th.M. at Southeastern Baptist Theological Seminary. It was stunning and shattering and brilliant and enthralling and I was so amazed by it that I decided I simply had to read more by this provocateur. Unfortunately there was not much more in English at that time (or, for that matter, even now) published.

After a couple of years of thinking about Professor Garbini's work, and finishing in addition to the Th.M., a Th.D., I decided that it was high time I contacted this gifted scholar. And so a more-than-decade-long friendly correspondence commenced.

In what follows, with as little intrusion by me as possible aside from setting the stage historically, will be found selected excerpts of Professor Garbini's correspondence to me.[2] I hope that this token of my immense esteem for him and my gratitude for his friendship over the years brings him the wide appreciation he deserves.

Our correspondence began in late 1999, but due to the vagaries of life, those earliest notes and cards have not survived. This is very regrettable. The first piece which still survives, and with which we begin, is a Christmas card, sent in December (n.d.), 2003.[3]

> The best wishes to you and your family – and the warmest thanks for your kind letter and your appreciation – *Giovanni Garbini*

From 16 June, 2005

> Dear Jim,
> I am very grateful to you for your kind letter and the information you give.[4] Your age is just an intermediate between those of my children Paolo, born in 1959, and Enrica, born in 1962; you have seen their names in the dedication of one of my books.

I congratulate you for the brilliant career you have got and also for the spirit with which you live your life of faith, together with your family, so dear to you.

Since I see from your bibliography that you can read Italian I send you two old articles of mine that have perhaps escaped your attention.[5]

Thanks again for your kindness, and many wishes for you and your work. Warm greetings also to Doris and the little Rachel (who probably would say she is not "little"). Thank you also for the wishes for my birthday (October 8th 1931).

Sincerely Yours,
Giovanni Garbini

From 25 October, 2005

Dear Jim,

Since more than one month I am spending all my time in the correction of the proofs and indexes of my new book "Introduzione all'epigrafia semitica" (from Protosinaitic to consonantal Ethiopic inscriptions). This is the reason why I delayed until now to answer both your kind letter and the card with your wishes for my 74th birthday: tantissime grazie! A few days later I also received the beautiful *Festschrift* Lemche[6] (I see that you have helped in its realization), and now I have just begun to read it, but not the Danish articles: this has been a wonderful gift from you. I have much to be grateful to you.

I acknowledge I am an outsider in the field of Biblical studies; my approach to the history of ancient Israel and to Biblical texts is the same I follow studying the Phoenicians or the South Arabians and their inscriptions; the main difference is that the inscriptions are contemporary with what they say, while the Bible is not; the latter has a tremendous ideological weight, increased by more than two millennia of history, which other documents do not have. Try to think in a rational, not religious way: what is the difference between the promise of Yahweh to Israel and that of Venus to the Romans? Both are fictions created by human writers with strong nationalistic ideologies; the difference is that the Romans *did have* the empire promised to them and the Jews (i.e. the Judeans) did not possess neither Philistia nor Samaria. What would you think if modern Italy claim Spain, France, England and Wales (not Scotland!) because in the past they belonged to the Roman empire?

I have always avoided the theoretical, "Philosophical" discussions that, according to the right opinion of Popper, cannot be proved to be false: they are, in my mind, simply unuseful. When I draw a conclusion from the study of the Bible I feel like the well known child saying "the king is naked!"; it seems to me impossible that great scholars, over several centuries, have not seen what is evident to my eyes. As an example I send you the still unpublished text of a relation presented last May in a meeting on the Septuagint. I have seen your good knowledge of Italian![7]

The best wishes and greetings to you and your family,
Giovanni Garbini.

From 2 July, 2006

Dear Jim,
Many thanks for your letters and the useful printing from *Science Now*,[8] that has been enlightening for me. [...][9]

I do not know if you have seen my book on the Canticles I published in 1992.[10] I think that this book is the most important of mine, because I believe to have understood the true meaning of *Shir ha-shirim*, without allegory but with philological research. If you don't have it, I'll have the pleasure to send you a copy.

In next days I shall leave Rome for my holidays, now in my country house in central Italy and then, in the second half of August, in Greece with all my family (enlarged to children and grandchildren), to celebrate the 50 years of my marriage. But sometimes I'll be in Rome for few days.

I wish you a good summertime with your family and send you my best greetings.

Yours sincerely
Giovanni Garbini

From 1 September, 2006

Dear Jim,
This is the first letter I write after my coming back home from quite long holidays. I arrived to Rome just yesterday from a trip in Greece, where I was together with all my family for celebrating the 50th year of our wedding (we call this "nozze d'oro," i.e. "golden wedding").

Well, now I have the pleasure to thank you for the beautiful "Babylonian" mug[11] (you are very kind) and your booklet about your church: a very nice story written with evident sympathy (but are you sure to have taken up residence at Petros on September 31? – p. 51).[12]

Compliments for your translation of Zwingli's book:[13] I'm fearing that the Christian community of Petros will become the most learned in the States!

Thanks again, dear Jim, and many greetings to you and to Doris (surely a patient wife) and many wishes to Rachel.

Yours, *Giovanni*

From 12 April, 2007

Many thanks for your letter and the note from the *Jerusalem Post*.[14] Nothing new under the sun, said Qohelet.

Jerusalem was a small fortified town since XIV cent. B.C. at least; later it was occupied by the Philistines, according to the Bible, who surely did not live in tents. The Bible says also that in Jerusalem there was a ʿ*ir dawid*, i.e., "the fortress of the *dawid*," where the governor from Samaria lived (cfr. the *dawid* [*dwd*] of Moab, Ariel [the same name as in the Bible], in the Mesha inscription). The last *dawid* of Jerusalem was probably Saul, who after the battle of Qarqar (853 B.C.) gained his independence from Ahaz of Israel. Such is the history of Israel according to me.

In Rome we still have the "Servian" walls, but we know that they were built in the IV cen. B.C.

The "Biblical Archaeology," helas!

The best greetings from
   Giovanni Garbini

From 1 July, 2007

Dear Jim,

Many thanks for the book on Zwingli;[15] it is a pleasant editorial achievement and I congratulate warmly with you for it.

Maybe I can explain the "fable" of Granny.[16] I think it is based on the fact that in European country-houses, where in the past lived many children, it was usual that two boys slept in one bed (I also had this experience in my childhood, when I was with my grandparents). The position of children in the bed is shown in this drawing:

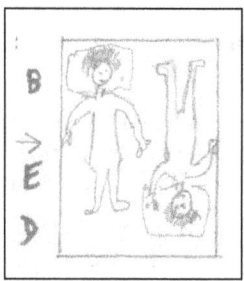

Figure 1

In Italian we say "dormire da capo" (to sleep on the part of the head) and "dormire da piedi" (to sleep on the part of the feet);[17] the latter sentence is used in popular speech to mean "not to know something happened." Since Jesus slept "da piedi," his feet were near the face of St. Peter, so that when the lady of the house woke up St. Peter by plucking his hair Jesus was woken too, probably because the movements of the Apostle tickled Jesus' feet.

Best wishes to you and to Doris and Rachel.

Sincerely *Giovanni Garbini*

From 1 February, 2008

Dear Jim,

I have delayed my answer to your letter until I receive your two books;[18] this happened just yesterday, precisely 51 days after the sending; the books have been stopped more than one month in a customs office: this is Italy. I am very grateful to you for your kind gift: many, many thanks! I enjoy to see that Philip Davies has discovered that in the Hebrew Bible there is a "Second History" and that the tribe of Benjamin was more important than what the Bible says. [...] I do not think that archaeology and *longue duree* (Hebrew history is so short!) can help historical research on ancient Israel; [...]

As for me, I have just ended to write a book on the history of Israel which will appear the next autumn. The title is "Writing the History of Israel. Hebrew Deeds and Records."[19] I have accomplished in a systematic manner what I had begun in previous years, with specific studies on single items (you know what I wrote in 2003 for the meeting held in Rome and organized by Liverani). My history begins in the II mill. B.C. and reaches 135 A.D. It is not only a reconstruction of historical facts but also a parallel discussion of the "growth of the OT," as H.H. Rowley wrote. The story of the monarchical period is *very* interesting, *pace* Liverani; the post-exilic centuries are essential for understanding what was actually the "Judaism" which created the "Law and Prophets," the first "Bible"; this *corpus* was written between 158 and 152 B.C., during the "priestly vacance"; the birth of Christianism and Gnosticism was the consequence of a reaction against the "Law." In his book Grabbe speaks about "ethnicity"; I have studied onomastics and have discovered that the last "Israelite" name was "Azariah"; the typical Hebrew names (Isaiah, Ezechia etc.) were all of North-Arabian origin (see the work by L. Harding).

I consider myself a "maximalist of the pre-Masoretic Bible," because the most important source for my researches has been the Bible itself; external sources have helped, but the core of the information was in the Bible; one must learn to read it.

I do thank you for your letter and your greetings and wishes; you do receive mine, together with your family. Best 2008!

Hearty greetings from
Giovanni Garbini

From 3 September, 2008

Dear Jim,

At the end of my vacation time I can answer the kind letter you sent me the last July. All is well for me and my family, and I hope the same is for you and yours.

The "Messiah Tablet"[20] is amusing and represents the newest "Annual Summer Fake" which the Holy Land produces yearly for imbeciles' sake. It is a pity that ideological *gihad* among monotheistic religions does not seem to be appeasing.

At the beginning of October my book on the history of Israel will appear (and you will receive a copy);[21] I hope that an English translation will follow in a short time, but I am not sure about it. I should like to know your opinion, especially with regard to the few pages where the origins of Christianity are sketched.

Best wishes!
Giovanni Garbini

From 13 September, 2009

Dear Jim,

I am glad to tell you that all is well for me – until now; I am sorry that my laziness in epistolography has caused you some preoccupation regarding me.[22]

In summer I made a trip to Austria with my wife; Austria is dear to us because it was the first foreign country we have visited in our youth and have passed there some weeks.

In July I corrected the proofs of a new book of mine; it is a collection of a dozen of my previous articles about the literature of ancient Israel, especially in relation with politics (title: "Letteratura e politica nell'Israele antico").[23]

My work on ancient Semitic religions goes on.

I thank you for sending informations about new discoveries and some odd ideas, like that of Rachel Elior: according to her methodological approach Christians never existed![24]

It is truly a damage that archaeologists always speak of their work as a big discovery. The temple of Tell Tayinat is known since the Thirties of the last century; already in 1956 W.F. Albright expressed his doubts about the existence of a "dark age" in northern Syria during the X cent. B.C. What T. Harrison calls "the land of Palastin" is probably the "land of Patina": Patina (a form derived from Khattina) is the name of the region whose capital was Tell Tayinat; it is mentioned by the Assyrian king Assurnasirpal II.

Well now you know of my recent past; the several mistakes in typewriting reveal that I have become old.

I am grateful to you for your kind friendship; with many greetings and wishes for you and your Family I remain

Sincerely yours
Giovanni Garbini

From 19 December, 2011

Dear Jim,

I have been very glad to hear from you again; I am well and work compatibly with my years.

Your book on Zwingli[25] is truly interesting and helps to understand his thought; I am very grateful to you to have got it.

Probably this letter will reach you at the beginning of the New Year; at any rate I send you my best greetings and wish you a Merry Christmas and a Happy New Year.

Sincerely Yours
Giovanni Garbini

From 28 January, 2012

I hope you have received my previous letter mailed on December. I am very glad to hear from you again; your new letter has cleared to me that your two years long silence was due to a black out in the communication channels.[26]

My new book is a general survey on ancient Semitic religions.[27] For the oldest period my research has been based on linguistic analysis; this has revealed that the idea of "god" in the ancient Near East was originally derived from the spirits of the dead and later from the spirits of dead kings; these spirits had their home obviously in the depths of the earth. The Phoenicians were the first among Semitic peoples to transfer El, their most important deity, from the earth to the heavens at the beginning of the first millennium B.C. The religion of Israel did not differ from that of Canaan until late times; in the Persian period polytheism was still alive among Jews (goddess Anat, cult of the Persian king) and in the 3rd cent. B.C. the ceremonies in the temple of Jerusalem were similar to those of Adon and Dionysus.

As for my position with regard to the chronology of the Biblical writings I exposed it already in my previous book on the history of Israel; in the new one I have tried to specify the several aspects of Yahweh according to the different theological ideas of the clergy of Jerusalem. The idea of a god "one and trine" lies behind the story of the creation of man: "let *us* make man in *our* image"; the same words are used for the birth of Seth, born from Adam and Eve; Adam was created by Yahweh together with Hokhmah and Ruah (the Holy Spirit of the Christians); cfr. *Gen.* 18.

Well, I will stop here my letter and send you the best wishes for you and your family. I stay in Rome and wait for a visit when you will pass in this part of the world.

Sincerely yours
Giovanni Garbini

From 23 September, 2012

Dear Jim,

I have been deeply happy in reading your *long* letter[28] when I came back to Rome at the beginning of this month. *Congratulações* for the success of your daughter and especially for the richness and the appreciation of your scholarly work. For my part, my family is well, even if my wife and I begin to suffer the weight of our eighties.

My work is going slowly but regularly. In 2010 I published a collection of my previous articles about "literature and politics in ancient Israel"; in 2011 appeared a book of mine about the ancient Semitic religions, from the beginnings until the birth of Christianity (its title is "Dio della terra, dio del cielo. Dalle religioni semitiche al giudaismo e al cristianesimo"[29]). Just now a new edition of my book on the Philistines has appeared[30] (first edition 1997); the book contains corrections, additions and two new chapters: one on the city of Gat of David (which was actually Jerusalem itself) and a second on the *goren* of Jerusalem and elsewhere: the *goren* was the place in the temple of Jerusalem where the God dead was mourned.[31] About the Philistines, an important discovery was made a year ago in Sardinia (the great Italian island): in a pit dated to the 8th cent. B.C. a jar of Canaanite type was found with fragments of inscriptions; one fragment had Phoenician letters, other ones had several signs of a Philistine writing, one of them equal to a sign painted on the ostrakon from Ashkelon published in 2006: it is just the ostrakon whose picture you sent to me some years ago! Now I am writing the final pages of my translation and commentary of the Ugaritic Poem (not cycle!) of Baal.

Well, now you know my recent enterprises. If you want to receive some of my books (in Italian!) I'll be glad to send you them.

With my best wishes I greet you and your family.
Sincerely yours
Giovanni Garbini

From 19 April, 2013

Dear Jim,
In this letter I send you a copy of the fragmentary inscriptions found on the Canaanite jar is Sardinia; the last line is Phoenician, the others are in Philistine writing (see *I Filistei*,[2] p. 297).

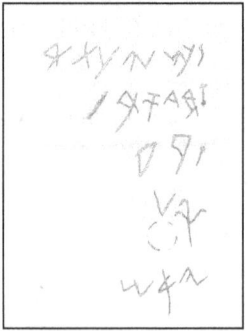

Figure 2

In these weeks I have studied the episode of the Queen of Sheba and I have understood two points of the story; the first one is that the original text of 1 Kings 10,13 spoke of the sexual intercourse between the queen and Solomon (the word *hefes* "pleasure" has been omitted by the ancient translations and *yad* is the known euphemism for the male sex); in the Song of Songs Solomon meets with the woman coming from the desert with her exotic scents (=Sheba) to celebrate a wedding; in Matthew 12,42 and Luke 11,31 a conversion of the queen to Hebrew religion is presupposed. The second point is the Jewish damnatio memoriae of the queen after her mention in the Gospels; for this same reason Jewish Hellenistic tradition compared the queen to the Greek female demon Empousa, called also Ono(s)kelis "donkey-legged woman."

Now, it is enough; thank you, dear Jim, for your interest; many greetings and wishes to you and to your family.

Giovanni

* * *

I am pleased to help my colleagues around the world show our esteem and respect for Professor Garbini with this small token of appreciation. His friendship has meant a lot to me over the years and he has taught me an immeasurable amount. Indeed, he has helped me intellectually in ways he shall never know. With appreciation, I dedicate this to him.

Notes

* With thanks to Professor Giovanni Garbini for years of friendship.

1. Giovanni Garbini, *History and Ideology in Ancient Israel* (New York: Crossroad, 1988).

2. As a note of introduction to those unfamiliar with the present contributor: I am one of those people with a foot in both the world of academia and the church: I serve as pastor of a local Baptist church and also as an Adjunct Professor of Biblical Studies for the Quartz Hill School of Theology, where I teach biblical studies and Greek. My primary project at present is a rather large one – my publisher is publishing a series of commentaries on every book of the Bible (a very long, multi-year effort that continues even now). It's written on a very, very basic level for "people in the pew" who have no background in academic biblical study but who wish to know the contents and meaning of Scripture. I've also authored an introduction to Biblical studies, a book on Zwingli, and a fairly extensive number of journal articles, essays, dictionary entries, and book reviews. I've on several occasions served as a consultant to the BBC for "bible themed" programs they've produced and am sometimes enquired of by the media when some story or other about this or that papyrus fragment or archaeological "discovery" surfaces. I try to keep busy so I'm on the editorial board of the *Copenhagen Seminar Series* (Equinox) and the *Scandinavian Journal of the Old Testament* (Taylor & Francis). I also help moderate the Biblical Studies List and I post an occasional this or that on the blog Zwinglius Redivivus: http://zwingliusredivivus.wordpress.com. And, finally (and already this is too long) I'm a member of the American Schools of Oriental Research, the Society of Biblical Literature, the European Association of Biblical Studies, the Society for Old Testament Studies, the Catholic Biblical Association, and of course the Zwingliverein. I hope that is sufficient information about myself and that it serves to set the stage for what follows.

3. None of the grammar or spelling in Professor Garbini's letters has been changed. They are as they were received, letter for letter and word for word, including his own emphases as he indicates through underlining various words.

4. Professor Garbini had asked me in a previous card to send a copy of my CV.

5. These were "Qualche riflessione sui pronomi personali semitici," *OA* 27 (1988), pp. 105–13, and "La luce di Zaccaria 14,6," *Henoch* 8 (1986), pp. 311–19.

6. Niels Peter Lemche, Professor of Old Testament at the University of Copenhagen, is meant, and the Festschrift is M. Muller and Th. L. Thompson (eds.), *Historie og konstruktion* (Copenhagen: Museum Tusculanums Forlag, 2005).

7. The title of the paper here referenced is G. Garbini, "Problemi di storiografia nei Libri di Samuele-Re tra TM e LXX: la conquista di Gerusalemme."

8. *Iraq Antiquities Find Sparks Controversy*, by Sue Lawler, http://news.sciencemag.org/sciencenow/2006/04/10-01.html?ref=hp, accessed May 1, 2006.

9. Bracketed material is of a personal nature and so, since of little interest to "outsiders" to our conversations, left aside.

10. Giovanni Garbini, *Cantico dei cantici* (Rome: Paideia, 1992). The volume arrived as promised and was inscribed "a Jim con amicizia, Giovanni."

11. He's referring to a mug produced by Eisenbrauns, which was sent to him which featured various artwork from the Babylonian period.

12. Jim West, *Petros Baptist Church: A History* (Quartz Hill, CA: Quartz Hill Publishing, 2006).

13. Jim West, *The Humor of Huldrych Zwingli: The Lighter Side of the Protestant Reformation* (New York: Edwin Mellen, 2007). Though not published till 2007, I had informed Professor Garbini of its impending appearance.

14. I had sent Professor Garbini a clipping from the Jerusalem Post on the purported discovery of "Nehemiah's wall," http://www.jpost.com/Israel/Article.aspx?id=83627, accessed 6 November 2012. (Note, though the date of the essay is November 2007, the story had run previously in the year and, oddly, was re-run later. The older, original edition is un-locatable.)

15. See n. 12.

16. Professor Garbini is referring to this passage from the book – "My Grandmother," he said (Z II, 777.7) "often told me the fable of how Peter and our Lord God went on an overnight trip together. Peter always had to lie in the front of the bed and the Lord behind. When the lady of the house came up in the mornings, she plucked only the front one by the hair and thus woke up the Lord," op. cit., p. 35.

17. The expression isn't exactly clear in English; however, it simply means to rest one's head at the head of the bed and at the foot of the bed.

18. The two books sent to Professor Garbini were Philip Davies, *The Origins of Biblical Israel* (London: T&T Clark International, 2007); and L. L. Grabbe, *Ancient Israel: What Do We Know and How Do We Know It?* (London: T&T Clark International, 2007).

19. Giovanni Garbini, *Scrivere la Storia D'Israele: Vicende e memorie ebraiche* (Brescia: Paideia, 2008).

20. See the story as reported in the New York Times: http://www.nytimes.com/2008/07/06/world/middleeast/06stone.html?pagewanted=all&_r=0 (accessed on 9 January, 2013).

21. See n. 18 above.

22. I had written a month previously enquiring into Professor Garbini's health, since I had not heard from him for nearly (at that time) a year.

23. This volume was published in 2010 by Paideia in Brescia.

24. He is referring to Elior's views as described in this essay in *Ha'aretz*, http://www.haaretz.com/print-edition/news/scholar-the-essenes-dead-sea-scroll-authors-never-existed-1.272034 (Accessed 11 January, 2013).

25. Jim West, *Christ Our Captain: An Introduction to Huldrych Zwingli* (Quartz Hill, CA: Quartz Hill Publishing, 2011).

26. It should be noted that Professor Garbini does not use email and is not connected to the internet. Hence, all correspondence requires the postal services, which, as all will recognize, are not either swift nor always reliable.

27. The book, which Professor Garbini sent along with the present letter, is *Dio Della Terra, Dio Del Cielo* (Brescia: Paideia, 2011). It is inscribed "al Dr. Jim West, con amicizia, Giovanni Garbini."

28. My letters to Professor Garbini tend to be very brief. In September 2012 I had written a fairly long one and it is to the unusual length of the missal which he is reacting to.

29. See n. 26 above.

30. *I Filistei* (Brescia: Paideia, 2012).

31. Garbini means "the dead God."

INDEX OF REFERENCES

HEBREW BIBLE/
OLD TESTAMENT
Genesis
1–3	109
1	62
1:2	112
1:4	145
1:26–29	103
1:26	103, 108, 109, 112
1:27	104, 105, 107
1:28	104
2–3	113, 115
2	106, 111
2:5	113
2:7	183
2:10	8
2:14	106
2:21	107
2:23	113
3:8	112
3:16	7, 8
5:2	107, 110
14:17–24	76
14:18	62
15:13	75
18	239
18:27	22
22:14	74
22:17	54
25:1–4	221
32:23–33	220
32:29	220
34	213
41:45	143
41:49	54
47:11	125

Exodus
1:16	181–85
2:10	125
3:12	226
4:3–4	66
4:14	63
6:7	63
11:8–12:2	50
12:1	139
12:6	125
12:18	125
12:23	119
12:27	119, 120
12:43	136
15:13	74
16:33	66
18:4	130
18:14	66
19:4	11
19:6	129
24:12–18	227
24:12	66
26:21	107
31–34	226
31:1–11	227
31:18	66, 227
32	227
32:14	227
32:16	66, 227
32:19	227
32:20	65
34:1	227
34:27–35	227

Leviticus
10:16	126
11:34–38	136
15:11–14	137
19:26	65
21:18–20	116, 121
23:11–16	130

Numbers
11	227
13–14	227
17:10	66
19:1	124
21	66
21:9	66

Deuteronomy
1:3	75
4:18	191
9:21	65
10:5	66
12	75
17:14–20	104
17:17	135
18:10	65
26:1–11	140
32:11	119
33:2	228
33:5	63
34	66

Joshua
5	62
5:3	136
5:10–12	141
5:10	136
24:25–26	126

Judges
1:16	66
2:7–13	135
4:11	66
5:4	228
9:37	74

Index of References

1 Samuel		22:8	124	*Job*	
8:11–18	104	22:39	91	2:8	22
12:9–11	68	23	104	3–31	21, 25
13:5	54	23:4	112	3:7	10
22:1–2	78	23:22	68, 124	5:17	21
25:37	6			7:16	21
		1 Chronicles		8:6	119
2 Samuel		4:12	120	8:20	21
5	77, 116	5:34–41	128	9:21	21
5:6–10	116, 117	5:35	143	10:3	21
5:6–8	118–21	11:6	117	12:12	8
5:6	117	11:11	118	19:18	21
5:8	48, 116, 117, 121			29:15	116
		2 Chronicles		30:1	21
5:11–12	124	5:10	66	31:13	21
15:24	135	31:10	143	32–42	23
17:11	54	32	40	33:31	24
23:8	122	32:3–4	48	34:33	21
23:18	118	32:30	48	36:5	21
		34:1	77	38–42	23
1 Kings		35:18	124	38–41	25
4:20	54	36:23	226	38:2	24
5:9	54			40–41	23, 28
5:15 LXX	124	*Ezra*		40:3–5	23, 24, 28
6:37	124	2:49	120	40:5	24
8	104	7–10	1	41:26	28
8:9	66	7:1–5	128	42:1–6	18–20, 23–25, 28
10:13	240	10	226		
12	104			42:2	26
12:16–17	51	*Nehemiah*		42:3–4	21
15:13	112	3:6	120	42:3	26
18:13–16	88	8	1	42:4	24
18:17–19	88	8:17–18	124	42:5	26
18:37	88	9:27–28	68	42:6–7	25
		10:11–12	129	42:6	20–22, 24, 27
2 Kings		10:31	140		
14:21	143	11:1	79	42:7	24, 28
15:33	143	11:18	79		
17:17	65	12	1	*Psalms*	
17:34 LXX	126	13:1–3	131	8:1–10	11
18–19	88	13:28	132	14:1	109
18:4	64, 68			48:2	79
18:13–16	92	*Esther*		48:3	191
21:7	112	4:4	135	48:8	191
21:10–17	89	4:16	145	53:2	109
22:1	77	9:1	135	71:20	11

Job (cont.)		29:10	226	9:2–4	192
73:11	109	31:8	116	9:11–12	193
76:3	62	33:6	143		
84:4	10	44:15–19	112	*Jonah*	
87:1	79	44:25	112	1	192, 194
107	191			1:3	190
107:22–30	191	*Ezekiel*		1:4	192
107:30	8	14	25	1:11–12	8
110:2–4	62	20:27–29	68	1:12	192
118:22	6	21:18	27	1:16	188, 190
		23:14	110	2:1	192
Proverbs		23:15	110	2:11	192
5:10	10	27:29	191	3:3	28
		28	104	3:4	188
Ecclesiastes		28:12	104	3:7	188
3:5	6	30:17	143	4:5	193
		37	59	4:6	192
Song of Songs		37:22	59	4:7	192
5:2–8	14	38:6	191	4:8	193
5:2	13	38:12	74	4:10–11	24
7:11	8	38:15	191		
		40–48	72	*Micah*	
Isaiah		44:15	129	3:12	82
1:26	143				
2:16	191	*Daniel*		*Habakkuk*	
7:3	48	8:14	145	3:3	228
8:8	226	9:9	29		
8:10	226	9:24	79	*Zechariah*	
10:22	54	11:31–35	83	8:13	79
10:26	118			9:13	118
14:13	191	*Hosea*		13:7	118
19:18	129	1:1	54		
19:21	129	1:2–9	53	*Malachi*	
22:8	48	2:1–3	53	2:12	119
31:5	120	2:1	53–55	3:23–24	68
36:2	48	2:2	51, 53, 54,		
44–45	226		59	**NEW TESTAMENT**	
48:2	79	2:3	53	*Matthew*	
49:10	68	3:5	51	11:5	116
52:1	79	8:9	16	12:42	240
60	213	12:4–5	220		
62:1	143	14:10	53	*Luke*	
				11:31	240
Jeremiah		*Amos*		14:31	116
7:16–20	112	5:26	193, 194		
18:3	181–85	7:13	104	*Acts*	
26:18	82	8:13	193	5:17	128

Index of References

1 Corinthians
11:3	112
11:7–9	107
11:11–12	108

SEPTUAGINT
1 Esdras
4:45	76

Tobit
13:1–18	212
13:2	212
13:5–6	212
13:8	213
13:9–18	213
13:9	213
13:13	213
13:18	212
14:5	82

Judith
9:1–14	213
9:8–11	213
9:12	213
9:13	213
9:14	213

Additions to Esther
4:17a–h	214
4:17b–c	214
4:17d–e	214
4:17f–g	214
4:17h	214
4:17k–z	214
4:17l	214
4:17m	214
4:17o–q	214
4:17r–z	214
4:17y–z	215

Ecclesiasticus
7:31	127
10:8	127
12:10	127
17	115
24:7–12	75
24:23	66, 67, 127
25:7	127
34:18–19	127
36	213
36:1–22	211
36:1–17	220
36:1	211
36:3	211
36:4	211
36:5	211
36:6–12	212
36:10–17	127
36:13	212
36:16	212
36:17	212, 220
36:18–19	212
36:19	220
36:20–21	212
36:22	211
39:1–3	67
44–49	67
45:26	67
46:1–49:7	67
46:1–8	67
48:10	68
48:17	48
48:20–23	67
48:22–23	68
49:6–10	67
49:10	52
49:13	123
50:1	128
51:13–14	127

1 Maccabees
1:16–57	66
2:2	76
2:41–42	132
2:42–44	78
2:44–48	83
2:49–68	77
3:10	83
3:15	55, 83
3:37	83
3:41	55
4:30	83
4:35	83
5:6	83
5:38	83
6:6	83
6:41	83
6:63	83
7:5–25	83
7:9	55
7:10	83
7:13	55, 132
7:23	55
7:27	83
9:23–27	83
9:43	83
9:54–57	128
9:60	83
10:1	128
10:18–20	128
10:68	83
10:69	83
10:73	83
11:13	83
11:44	83
11:56	83
11:63	83
12:20–21	129
12:24	83
13:1	83
13:8	78
13:12	83
14:25–46	78
15:15–24	127
16:5	83

2 Maccabees
1:1–10	127
1:10	125
1:24–29	221
2:13–14	131
2:13	61
3:1	128
4:9	83
4:19	83
4:33	83
5:9	129
5:21	55, 57, 83
5:22–23	55

5:22	55	**QUMRAN**		*Nedarim*	
6:1–2	230	*1QS*		9.5	137
8:35	83	1.8	136		
11:36	83	1.16	136, 146	*Parah*	
13:23	83	1.18	136	3.5	124
13:26	83	2.10	146		
14:6	132	5.2	129	*Pesahim*	
14:27	83	5.5	136	6.2	137
		5.9	129	8.8	136, 137
OLD TESTAMENT		6.13–23	136		
PSEUDEPIGRAPHA		8.23	136	*Rosh HaShanah*	
1 Enoch				2.8–9	139
89:67	76	*1QpHab*			
89:73	76	11.13	136	*Sanhedrin*	
90:28	76			11.3	131
90:29	76	*4Q266*			
		f6ii.6.6	136	*Yebamot*	
Jubilees				6.4	143
2:14	106	*4Q367*			
3:8	107	f1a–b.4	136	**BABYLONIAN TALMUD**	
8:19	74			*Menahot*	
18:13	74	*CD*		65b	130
23:21	82	1.4	136		
32:16–24	74	2.2	146	*Pesahim*	
32:18	75	4.9	146	5a	130
32:23	74	4.21	129		
32:24	75	5.2–6	135	*Qiddushin*	
44:1	75	6.11–7.10	146	30a	126
49:18	75	14.3–4	129	66a	133
49:21	75				
		MISHNAH		*Shabbat*	
Letter of Aristeas		*'Abot*		14b	145
§30	67	1.1–16	138		
		1.1	135	*Sanhedrin*	
Life of Adam and Eve				38b	114
33:4–5	113	*Baba Batra*			
		14b	58	*Yebamot*	
Sibylline Oracles				46a–b	137
1:22–37	113	*Hagigah*			
		2.2	138	*Yoma*	
Testament of Levi		2.4	131	19b	133
14:7–16:5	82	2.6	136		
		2.7	136	*Zebahim*	
Testament of Moses				118b	75
4:8	82	*Menahot*			
5:3–4	82	13.10	129		

Index of References

JERUSALEM TALMUD
Demai
2.2   136

Pesahim
6.1   131, 138

Yebamot
46b–47b   137

TOSEFTA
Menahot
13.21   143

Rosh HaShanah
1.15   131

Ta'anit
2.5   145

OTHER RABBINIC WORKS
'Abot de Rabbi Nathan
A 5   115
§10   131

Bereshit Rabbah
8.1   107
8.9   108

PHILO
De cherubim
59–60   114

Quod omnis probus liber sit
§75   140

De opificio mundi
152   114

Quaestiones et solutiones in Genesin
1.25   114

De vita contemplativa
§78   140

JOSEPHUS
Jewish Antiquities
1.32–36   113
1.238–41   221
7.68   76
10.152–53   129
11.309   132
11.8.6   230
11.8.7   230
12.1.1   230
12.2.4–5   230
12.5.5   230
12.132–53   73
12.133–46   73
12.138–144   55
12.141   73
12.156   73
12.237–47   128
12.395   132
13.10.4   230
13.15.3–4   231
13.66   140
13.171–73   132
13.217   75
13.249–53   128
13.288–98   132
13.299   77
13.301   77
13.322   133
13.372–73   133
13.401   133
13.408   133
14.7.2   230
14.403   137
15.255   136
15.320–22   130
15.371   133, 139
15.373–75   138
17.23–25   131
17.26   138
17.165   130
17.339   130
18   133
18.3   130
18.3.3   231
18.11–22   133
18.17   133
19.297   130
20.213   143
20.236–37   128
20.249   130

Life
2   115
12   133

Jewish War
1.36   82
1.68   132
2.120   130
2.137–39   136
2.147   134
2.150   130
2.165   108
6.438   76
7.433–36   143

CLASSICAL AND ANCIENT CHRISTIAN WRITINGS
Aristoteles
fr. 600   170

Arrian
II 24, 5   153

Arrianus
II 21, 9   170

Clement of Alexandria
Stromata
1.15.1–3   125
1.153.4   81
I 45, 10   170
I,101–82   215

Curtius Rufus
IV 2.10   153
IV 3, 22   153

Diodorus Siculus
XI 1, 4–5   153
XL.3   66

Eupolemus	*Justinus*	*Solinus*
Frag 2.1–2 68	XIX 1, 10–13 153	XII 355–58 178
Eusebius	*Pausanius*	**PAPYRI**
Praeparatio evangelica	X 17, 2 178	*TADAE*
9.20.2–4 221		I, A4.1 125
9.30.5 75	Photius	
9.34.10 75	*Library*	**ANCIENT NEAR**
9.34.11 76	#244 142	**EASTERN TEXTS AND**
12. 126		**INSCRIPTIONS**
13.12.1–12 126	Plato	*ARE*
	Symposium	II 9 97
Herodotus	189E–190A 107	
I 203 99		*El Amarna Letters*
2.94 189	Pliny the Elder	292 ll. 29–40 100
III 19 153	*Naturalis historia*	
IV 181–85 98	II 207 170	*RS*
VII 165–66 153	5.15.73 141	15.86: 4 97
		16.277: 2 97
Homer	Pliny	
Odyssey	*Life of Caesar*	*Urk.*
XI 568–71 101	49.6 142	IV, 3, 10 97
Horace	*Silius Italicus*	
Satires	IV 2 178	
1.69–70 26		

INDEX OF AUTHORS

Abel, F.-M. 195
Abraham-Eitan, Ch. 15
Acquaro, E. 172, 174, 175, 177, 179
Adam, K.-P. 205
Adamthwaite, M. R. 94
Albrektson, B. 206
Albright, W. F. 93, 101
Alt, A. 95
Altmann, R. I. 46, 49
Amadasi, M. G. 176, 178
Amichai, O. 17
Arnason, J. P. 173
Artom, M. E. 186, 187
Asheri, D. 173
Avigad, N. 48

Back, R. T. 15–17
Baker, D. W. 207
Bakker, J. 177
Balzer, K. 71
Baneth, E. 115
Barnes, G. E. 185
Barnett, R. D. 70
Barr, J. 94
Barstad, H. M. 79, 80
Barth, J. 186
Bartolini, P. 174, 178
Baumgartner, W. 186, 187
Becking, B. 70
Beckwith, R. T. 115
Beentjes, P. C. 220
Ben-Dov, J. 145
Ben Zvi, E. 58, 70, 205
Bénichou-Safar, H. 176
Berg, E. van den 70
Bergmeier, R. 146
Bernardini, P. 177, 178, 180
Beyerle, S. 70
Bialik, H. N. 16
Bianchi, F. 14
Bickel, S. 114

Bickerman, E. 81, 83, 143
Billerbeck, P. 114
Bird, P. A. 111
Bisi, A. M. 177
Bloch, M. 204
Blum, E. 142
Boccaccini, G. 143
Bolin, T. M. 28, 29, 83, 205
Bondì, S. F. 172–75, 177–80
Bonetto, J. 176
Botto, M. 174, 176
Børresen, K. E. 111
Boucher, M. 114
Braccesi, L. 174, 175
Braudel, F. 204
Brenner, R. F. 17
Breuer, Y. 145
Briant, P. 80
Bright, J. 93
Brueggemann, W. 222
Bruneau, P. 59, 60, 84
Buccellati, G. 231, 232
Büchler, A. 81
Budde, K. 29
Burchardt, M. 101
Burke, P. 204
Burnshaw, S. 17

Calmeyer, P. 177
Candelato, F. 176
Carmignac, J. 145
Carr, D. 28, 29
Carter, C. E. 59, 79
Cecchini, S. 178, 180
Charlesworth, J. H. 71
Chavalas, M. W. 94
Ciafoloni, D. 180
Ciasca, A. 180
Clines, D. J. A. 26–28, 110, 111, 114
Cocco, M. B. 172, 173
Cohn, E. W. 47

Collins, J. J. 115, 146
Comella, A. 178
Contini, R. 26
Corriente, F. 113
Crenshaw, J. 15
Crouzet, S. 174
Culican, W. 178
Curtis, F. 222
Curtis, J. B. 26, 27

D'Angelo, M. R. 114
D'Oriano, R. 176
Dalley, S. 84, 113
Dante 26
Daumas, F. 146
Davies, P. R. 46, 47, 71, 110, 206, 207, 219, 232, 242
Davis, T. W. 206, 207
Day, J. 58
De Groot, A. 47
Dever, W. G. 94, 112, 207
Dexinger, F. 81
Dhorme, E. 27, 28
Diebner, B. J. 204–206
di Lella, A. A. 143
Dothan, T. 95
Driver, S. R. 122
Droge, A. J. 142
Duhm, B. 29
Dupont-Sommer, A. 144
Durand, O. 186
Durand, X. 142
Dušek, J. 59, 60

Edelman, D. 70, 232
Egger, R. 81
Eisenstadt, S. N. 173
Eissfeldt, O. 232
Elayi, A. G. 177
Elayi, J. 173–75, 177
Eliade, M. 205
Epstein, I. 58
Erman, A. 101
Erslev, K. 94

Fadida, A. 47
Faegersten, F. 180
Fallon, F. 81
Falsone, G. 179
Fantalkin, A. 69

Fantar, M. H. 176
Fariselli, A. C. 172, 174
Faulkner, R. O. 101
Faust, A. 95
Febvre, L. 204
Ferichou, N. 179
Ferjaoui, H. 174, 177
Fernández Marcos, N. 113
Feuillet, A. 195
Finkelstein, I. 48, 59, 81, 94, 95
Fohrer, G. 29
Freedman, H. 113
Frerichs, E. S. 219
Fried, L. 80
Friend, R. 15
Frumkin, A. 48, 49
Fuller, R. E. 58
Fullerton, K. 26, 28, 29

Gamer-Wallert, I. 179
Garbati, G. 174, 177–80
Garbini, G. 4, 14–17, 26, 28, 69–71, 82, 92, 93, 95, 109, 110, 112, 114, 115, 122, 142, 172, 174, 175, 178, 186, 195, 204, 205, 219, 231, 241–43
Gardiner, A. H. 110
Garr, W. R. 110
Garton, R. E. 58
Gauthier, H. 101
Gauthier, P. 175
Gavini, A. 172, 173
Geva, H. 48
Gfrörer, A. F. 146
Gibert, P. 204
Gilbert, M. 143
Gill, D. 48
Gimbutas, M. 15
Gitin, S. 95
Glasson, T. F. 122
Godwyn, T. 146
Gold, N. S. 15
Goldberg, A. 114
Goldberg, L. 14
Goldenberg, R. 219
Goldstein, J. A. 82, 83
Good, E. M. 27, 28
Goodblatt, D. 219
Goody, J. 95
Gordis, R. 27, 28
Görg, M. 102

Goshen-Gottstein, A. 71, 110
Grabbe, L. L. 57, 83, 142, 206, 207, 242
Graetz, H. 145
Grapow, H. 101
Grayson, A. K. 94
Grelot, P. 142
Griffiths, J. G. 102
Grimm, G. 95
Gröndahl, F. 101
Grosby, S. E. 219
Gross, W. 111
Grottanelli, C. 177, 178
Gruen, E. S. 142, 219
Gubel, E. 178, 180
Guil, Sh. 48, 50
Guillaume, P. 26, 69, 71, 143
Günther, L. M. 174
Guthe, H. 49

Habachi, L. 101
Habel, N. 27
Hadari, A. 16
Hadley, J. M. 112
Halpern, B. 122, 207
Hankins, D. 222
Hanson, R. S. 49
Harl, M. 114
Harrington, H. K. 145
Harvey Jr., P. B. 195
Hayes, J. H. 4
Helas, S. 176
Hemmer Gudme, A. K. de 60
Hendel, R. S. 46
Herzog, Z. 94
Hirschfeld, A. 15, 17
Hjelm, I. 4, 70, 80–84, 231
Ho, E. 26, 27
Hoftijzer, J. 186
Hölbl, G. 180
Holladay, C. R. 221
Hornung, E. 110–12
House, P. R. 57
Humbert, J.-B. 146
Hunt, A. 143
Hvidberg-Hansen, F. O. 176

Ibba, A. 172, 173
Irwin, W. H. 122

Jacoby, F. 221
Janick, J. 194
Jean, Ch.-F. 186
Jeremias, J. 57, 145
Jervell, J. 114
Jigoulov, V. S. 173
Johnson, S. R. 220
Joines, K. R. 70
Jones, S. 219

Kartveit, M. 84
Kenyon, K. 232
Kiperwasser, R. 114
Kitchen, K. A. 94
Knauf, E. A. 205, 206
Knohl, I. 144
Knoppers, G. N. 80, 219
Knudtzon, J. A. 101, 102
Koehler, L. 186, 187
Konradt, M. 219
Kratz, R. G. 83, 205
Krauss, S. 14
Krüger, T. 26, 27
Kuhrt, A. 80
Kuyper, L. J. 26, 27

Lamarche, P. 15
Lancellotti, M. G. 176
Lau, P. H. W. 219
Laura, G. di 146
Lauterbach, J. 115
Lawler, S. 242
Le Goff, J. 204
Le Moyne, J. 115, 144
Legaspi, M. 204
Lemaire, A. 83, 142
Lemche, N. P. 57, 95, 204, 205, 207, 208
Leuchter, M. 58
Levenson, A. T. 221
Levenston, E. A. 186
Lévi-Strauss, C. 205
Levin, Ch. 59
Levine, L. I. 219
Levy, T. E. 207
Licht, J. 145
Lieberman, S. 144
Lieblich, A. 15–17
Linder, E. 177
Lipiński, E. 176, 177, 186
Lipschits, O. 59, 79, 173

Liverani, M. 93, 101, 102, 173, 174, 204, 206
Long, V. P. 207
Longman III, T. 207
López Castro, J. L. 175
Luckenbill, D. D. 94, 95
Luisada, P. 15

Macchi, J. D. 58
Macintosh, A. A. 58, 59
Magen, Y. 60, 80, 81
Main, E. 144
Malinowski, B. 205
Manfredi, L. I. 172, 174, 175
Marín, J. A. B. 101
Marshak, A. K. 84
Marzoli, D. 176
Masalha, N. 207
Mason, S. 144
Masuzawa, T. 222
Mattazzi, P. 179
Mazar, A. 93, 94
Mazar, E. 94
McCarter, P. K. 122, 142
McGeough, K. 186
McLean, D. M. 49
Meeks, W. A. 114
Mendels, D. 81, 219
Mendenhall, G. E. 93
Merlo, P. 112
Meshel, Z. 142
Mezzolani, A. 176
Milik, J. T. 113
Miller, J. M. 4
Miller II, R. D. 95
Milman, Y. 16
Miquel, P. 146
Miron, D. 16, 17
Misgav, H. 80
Moran, W. L. 101, 102
Moro, C. 109, 111, 112
Morrow, W. 26, 27
Morschauser, S. 186
Moscati, S. 174, 177–80
Muenchow, C. L. 26–28

Na'aman, N. 70
Naveh, J. 95
Nel, P. J. 195
Nestor, D. A. 220

Neusner, J. 145, 219, 232
Newell, B. L. 26, 27
Newsome, C. A. 28
Ngwa, K. 29
Niccacci, A. 111
Nickelsburg, G. W. E. 82
Niebuhr, B. G. 94
Niehr, H. 83
Niesiołowski-Spanò, Ł. 95, 122
Nodet, E. 80–82, 142–45
Nogalski, J. 57, 58
Nora, P. 204
Norin, S. 47
Noth, M. 93
Nunn, A. 173

Obeyesekere, G. 207
Oded, B. 231
Oeming, M. 173
Oesch, J. M. 111
Oggiano, I. 173, 176, 177, 179
Olyan, S. 122
Ong, W. J. 95

Padrò, J. 179
Padros Martínez, F. 179
Palmisano, M. C. 220, 221
Paris, H. S. 194
Parpola, S. 110
Patrick, D. 26, 27
Paul, A. 143
Pearce, S. 219
Pedrazzi, T. 173, 174, 176
Peri, C. 172, 175, 177–80, 195
Perra, C. 176
Person Jr., R. F. 95
Pesce, G. 179
Pfoh, E. 205
Pilcher, E. J. 49
Piñero, A. 113
Pisano, G. 180
Ploeg, J. P. M. van der 27
Pope, M. 27
Pope, M. H. 17, 27
Porten, B. 60
Prasse, K.-G. 102
Prato, G. L. 195, 219, 221
Prausnitz, M. W. 177
Prinzivalli, E. 111
Pritchard, J. B. 177, 232

Propp, W. C. 122
Provan, I. W. 207
Pummer, R. 60, 80, 143

Qimron, E. 146

Rakob, F. 176
Redissi, T. 178, 180
Reich, R. 47, 49
Renz, J. 50
Ribichini, S. 178
Ritter, H. W. 174
Rivkin, E. 145
Roberts, J. J. M. 70
Roberts, K. L. 70
Robinson, B. P. 195
Robinson, E. 47
Rogerson, J. W. 46, 206
Röllig, H. 232
Römer, T. 58, 110, 111
Rosenbaum, J. 48
Rossi, A. dei 144
Rossi, M. 173
Ruiten, J. A. T. G. M. van 113

Sacchi, P. 110
Sader, H. 180
Sahlins, M. 207
Said, W. 174
Salustri, C. A. 26
Sand, S. 84, 232
Sasson, J. 93
Sayce, A. H. 49
Scagliarini, F. 110
Scandone Matthiae, G. 177
Schäfer, P. 221
Scheindlin, R. P. 15
Schenkel, W. 102
Schiffman, L. H. 144, 145
Schmid, H. H. 206
Schmid, K. 115
Schmidt, B. B. 93
Schroer, S. 70
Schunck, M. 26
Schürer, E. 142, 145
Schwartz, D. R. 144, 219
Segert, S. 186
Shalev, E. 49
Shanks, H. 47, 70, 145
Shepherd, D. 27

Sherwood, Y. 194, 195
Shiloh, Y. 48
Shimron, A. 48, 49
Shukron, E. 47, 49
Sievers, J. 83, 143
Silberman, N. A. 206
Simon, M. 146
Simon, R. 29
Singer-Avitz, L. 94
Sivan, R. 186
Ska, J.-L. 113, 115
Skehan, P. W. 143
Smelik, K. D. 49
Smith, M. S. 83
Sneh, A. 49
Soggin, J. A. 4, 110
Sparks, K. L. 219
Spatafora, F. 176
Spicehandler, E. 16
Spieckermann, H. 204
Stahl, N. 17
Steinert, U. 219
Stemberger, G. 115, 144
Stenhouse, P. 81
Sterling, G. E. 221
Stern, E. 79, 173
Stern, M. 142
Sternberg, M. 219
Steudel, A. 144
Strack, H. L. 114
Stuart, D. 59
Sukenik, E. 144
Sussmann, Y. 144
Swanson, K. A. 70
Sweeney, M. A. 222

Tal, O. 69
Taylor, J. 146
Tcherikover, V. 83
Thompson, T. L. 4, 84, 204, 206, 207, 231, 232
Tigay, J. H. 84
Tiller, P. A. 82
Tilley, T. 26
Toorn, K. van der 83, 84, 232
Tromp, N. J. 195
Troy, L. 112, 113
Tsedaka, B. 82
Tsefania, L. 80
Tyson, C. W. 122

Ussishkin, D. 46, 94
Van Dommelen, P. 173
Van Seters, J. 111, 113
VanderKam, J. C. 113, 143
Vaux, R. de 93
Veltri, G. 114
Vicchio, S. J. 26, 28
Vilmar, E. 81
Vincent, A. 83

Wacholder, B. Z. 71, 81, 82
Wajdenbaum, P. 142
Weber, R. 221
Weeks, D. E. 219
Weill, R. 47
Weinberger, R. 49
Weinfeld, M. 83
Weiss, Y. 14
Wenham, G. J. 207
West, J. 242, 243
Westermann, C. 28, 110
Wevers, J. W. 185
White, M. 59, 60
White, R. 172
Whitelam, K. W. 207, 208

Wiseman, D. J. 94
Wittrock, B. 173
Wöhrle, J. 58
Wolde, E. van 26–28
Wolfe, R. E. 57
Wolff, H. W. 57
Wolters, A. 26, 27
Woude, S. van der 27
Wright, J. L. 219
Wyatt, N. 205

Xella, P. 112, 176

Yadin, Y. 70, 93, 122
Yarbro Collins, A. 142
Yardeni, A. 60
Young, R. A. 70

Zamagni, C. 71
Zappella, M. 220, 221
Zeitlin, S. 145
Ziegler, J. 220
Zorell, F. 186